Visual Reference

Microsoft® Excel 97 At a Glance

Microsoft® Press

Microsoft Excel 97 At a Glance

Published by **Microsoft Press**
A Division of Microsoft Corporation
One Microsoft Way
Redmond, Washington 98052-6399

Library of Congress Cataloging-in-Publication Data
Microsoft Excel 97 at a glance / Perspection, Inc.
p. cm.
Includes index.
ISBN 1-57231-367-6
1. Microsoft Excel for Windows. 2. Business--Computer programs.
3. Electronic spreadsheets. I. Perspection, Inc.
HF5548.4.M523M5157 1996
005.369--dc20 96-36632
CIP

Printed and bound in the United States of America.

1 2 3 4 5 6 7 8 9 QEQE 1 0 9 8 7 6

Distributed to the book trade in Canada by Macmillan of Canada, a division of Canada Publishing Corporation.

A CIP catalogue record for this book is available from the British Library.

Microsoft Press books are available through booksellers and distributors worldwide. For further information about international editions, contact your local Microsoft Corporation office. Or contact Microsoft Press International directly at fax (206) 936-7329.

For Perspection, Inc.
Managing Editor: **Steven M. Johnson**
Writer: **Elizabeth Eisner Reding**
Production Editor: **David W. Beskeen**
Developmental Editor: **Mary-Terese Cozzola**
Copy Editor: **Jane Pedicini**
Technical Editor: **Christine Spillett**

For Microsoft Press
Acquisitions Editors: **Lucinda Rowley, Kim Fryer**
Project Editor: **Lucinda Rowley**

Contents

"How can I get started quickly in Excel?"

see page 6

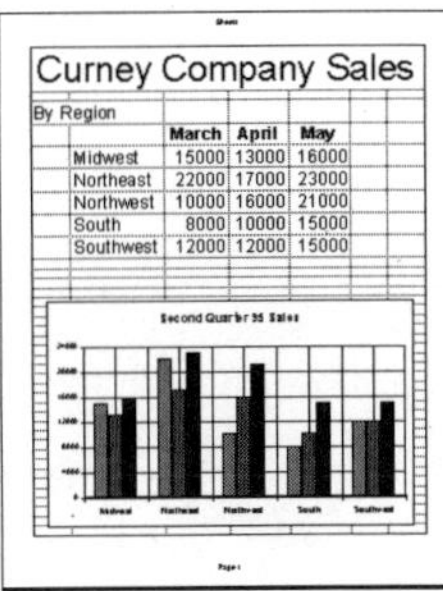

Print a Worksheet

see page 22

1 About At a Glance 1

No Computerese! 1
Useful Tasks 2
And the Easiest Way To Do Them 2
A Quick Overview 2
A Final Word (or Two) 3

2 Getting Started with Excel 5

Starting Microsoft Excel 97 6
Viewing the Excel Window 7
Opening a File 8
Moving Around the Workbook 10
Working with the Excel Window 12
Working with Menus and Toolbars 14
Working with Dialog Boxes and Wizards 16
Getting Help 18
Saving a Workbook 20
Printing a Worksheet 22
Closing a Workbook and Exiting Excel 24

3 Basic Workbook Skills 25

Making Cell Entries in a Worksheet 26
Undoing and Redoing an Action 27
Entering Labels in a Worksheet 28
Entering Values in a Worksheet 30
Editing Cell Contents 32
Selecting Multiple Cells 34
Clearing Cell Contents 36
Understanding How Excel Pastes Data 37
Copying Cell Contents 38
Moving Cell Contents 40
Inserting and Deleting a Cell 42

"I want to create a formula!"

see page 46

"How can I modify my worksheet?"

see page 46

Change a Font Style

see page 78

4 Working with Formulas **45**

- Creating a Simple Formula 46
- Editing a Formula 48
- Understanding Relative Cell Referencing 50
- Using Absolute Cell References 51
- Simplifying a Formula with Ranges 52
- Using AutoCalculate 53
- Performing Calculations Using Functions 54
- Creating Functions 55

5 Modifying Worksheets and Workbooks **57**

- Selecting and Naming a Worksheet 58
- Inserting and Deleting a Worksheet 59
- Moving and Copying a Worksheet 60
- Inserting a Column or Row 62
- Deleting a Column or Row 64
- Hiding a Column or Row 65
- Adjusting Column Width and Row Height 66
- Setting Up the Page 68
- Adding a Header or Footer 69
- Customizing Print Settings 70
- Saving Print Settings 72

6 Formatting a Worksheet **73**

- Formatting Text and Numbers 74
- Designing Conditional Formatting 76
- Copying Cell Formats 77
- Changing Font Styles 78
- Changing Data Alignment 80
- Controlling Text Flow 82
- Changing Data Color 83
- Adding Color and Patterns to Cells 84

Adding Borders to Cells 86
Formatting Data with AutoFormat 88
Modifying an AutoFormat 89
Creating and Applying a Style 90
Modifying a Style 92

7 Inserting Graphics and Related Material **95**
Inserting Pictures 96
Accessing the Office 97 CD-ROM for Extras 98
Stylizing Text with WordArt 100
Editing WordArt Text 102
Applying WordArt Text Effects 104
Inserting an Organization Chart 106
Modifying an Organization Chart 108
Correcting Text with AutoCorrect 110
Creating and Reading a Cell Comment 112
Editing and Deleting a Cell Comment 113
Looking Up Reference Material 114

8 Drawing and Modifying Objects **115**
Drawing Lines and Arrows 116
Drawing AutoShapes 118
Drawing a Freeform Object 120
Editing a Freeform Object 122
Moving and Resizing an Object 124
Rotating and Flipping an Object 126
Choosing Object Colors 128
Adding Object Shadows 130
Creating a 3-D Object 132
Aligning and Distributing Objects 134
Arranging and Grouping Objects 136

Stylize Text with WordArt
see page 100

Add a Shadow to an Object
see page 130

9 Creating Charts and Maps 139

Understanding Chart Terminology 140
Choosing the Right Type of Chart 141
Creating a Chart 142
Editing a Chart 144
Selecting a Chart 145
Changing a Chart Type 146
Moving and Resizing a Chart 147
Pulling Out a Pie Slice 148
Adding and Deleting a Data Series 150
Enhancing a Data Series 152
Enhancing a Chart 154
Drawing on a Chart 156
Changing Chart Fonts 158
Creating a Map 159
Modifying a Map 160

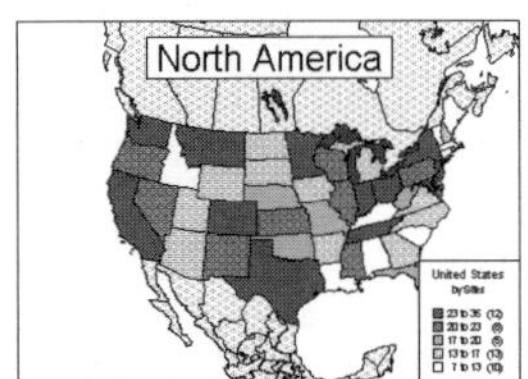

Create a Map
see page 160

10 Analyzing Worksheet Data 161

Understanding List Terminology 162
Creating a List 163
Understanding a Data Form 164
Adding Records Using a Data Form 165
Managing Records Using a Data Form 166
Sorting Data in a List 168
Displaying Parts of a List with AutoFilter 170
Creating Complex Searches 171
Entering Data in a List Quickly 172
Analyzing Data Using a PivotTable 173
Updating a PivotTable 174
Charting a PivotTable 175

"What is a PivotTable?"

see page 173

11 Tools for Working More Efficiently 177

Viewing Multiple Workbooks 178
Changing Your Worksheet View 179
Customizing Your Excel Environment 180
Freezing Columns and Rows 182
Creating a Toolbar 183
Customizing a Toolbar 184
Adding a Macro to a Toolbar 186
Saving Time with Templates 188
Creating a Template 189
Working with Templates 190
Tracking Changes in a Worksheet 192
Protecting Your Data 194

"How can I save time with templates?"

see page 188

12 Building More Powerful Worksheets 195

Creating Links Between Worksheets and Workbooks 196
Consolidating Data 198
Understanding How Macros Automate Your Work 200
Recording a Macro 201
Running a Macro 202
Understanding Macro Code 203
Debugging a Macro Using the Step Mode 204
Editing a Macro 205
Adding Comments to a Macro 206
Understanding Excel Program Add-Ins 207

"How can I record and run a macro?"

see pages 200-202

13 Tools for Working Together 209

Sharing Workbooks 210
Merging Workbooks 212
Sharing Information Among Documents 214
Exporting Data 215
Linking and Embedding Files 216

Link and Embed a File

see page 216

Get Clip Art from the Web
see page 228

Creating Scenarios 218
Generating Multiple Page Reports 220
Getting Data from Another Program 222
Converting Excel Data into Access Data 224
Inserting an Internet Link 225
Creating HTML Internet Output 226
Getting Data from the Web 228

Index **231**

Acknowledgments

The task of creating any book requires the talents of many hard-working people pulling together to meet impossible deadlines and untold stresses. We'd like to thank the outstanding team responsible for making this book possible: the writer, Liz Reding, the editor, MT Cozzola, the copy editor, Jane Pedicini, and the production team, Steven Payne, Patrica Young, and Gary Bedard.

At Microsoft Press, we'd like to thank Lucinda Rowley for the opportunity to undertake this project and Kim Eggleston for production expertise with the At a Glance series.

Perspection

Perspection

Perspection, Inc. is a technology training company committed to providing information to help people communicate, make decisions, and solve problems. Perspection writes and produces software training books, and develops interactive multimedia applications for Windows-based and Macintosh personal computers.

Microsoft Excel 97 At a Glance incorporates Perspection's training expertise to ensure that you'll receive the maximum return on your time. With this staightforward, easy-to-read reference tool you'll get the information you need when you need it. You'll focus on the skills that increase productivity while working at your own pace and convenience.

We invite you to visit the Perspection World Wide Web site. You can visit us at:

http://www.perspection.com

You'll find a description for all of our books, additional content for our books, information about Perspection, and much more.

1

About *At a Glance*

IN THIS SECTION

No Computerese!

Useful Tasks...

...And the Easiest Way To Do Them

A Quick Overview

A Final Word (or Two)

Microsoft Excel 97 At a Glance is for anyone who wants to get the most from their computer and their software with the least amount of time and effort. You'll find this book to be a straightforward, easy-to-read reference tool. With the premise that your computer should work for you, not you for it, this book's purpose is to help you get your work done quickly and efficiently so that you can get away from the computer and live your life.

No Computerese!

Let's face it—when there's a task you don't know how to do but you need to get it done in a hurry, or when you're stuck in the middle of a task and can't figure out what to do next, there's nothing more frustrating than having to read page after page of technical background material. You want the information you need—nothing more, nothing less—and you want it now! And it should be easy to find and understand.

That's what this book is all about. It's written in plain English—no technical jargon and no computerese. There's no single task in the book that takes more than two pages. Just look up the task in the index or the table of contents, turn to the page, and there's the information, laid out step by step and accompanied by a graphic that adds visual clarity. You don't get bogged down by the whys and wherefores; just follow the steps, look at the illustrations, and get your work done with a minimum of hassle.

Occasionally you might want to turn to another page if the procedure you're working on has a "See Also" in the left column. That's because there's a lot of overlap among tasks, and we didn't want to keep repeating ourselves. We've also scattered some useful tips here and there, and thrown in a "Try This" once in a while, but by and large we've tried to remain true to the heart and soul of the book, which is that information you need should be available to you at a glance.

Useful Tasks...

Whether you use Excel 97 for work, play, or some of each, we've tried to pack this book with procedures for everything we could think of that you might want to do, from the simplest tasks to some of the more esoteric ones.

...And the Easiest Way To Do Them

Another thing we've tried to do in *Excel 97 At a Glance* is to find and document the easiest way to accomplish a task. Excel often provides many ways to accomplish a single end result, which can be daunting or delightful, depending on the way you like to work. If you tend to stick with one favorite and familiar approach, we think the methods described in this book are the way to go. If you like trying out alternative techniques, go ahead! The intuitiveness of Excel invites exploration, and you're likely to discover ways of doing things that you think are easier or that you like better. If you do, that's great! It's exactly what the creators of Excel 97 had in mind when they provided so many alternatives.

A Quick Overview

This book isn't meant to be read in any particular order. It's designed so that you can jump in, get the information you need, and then close the book and keep it near your computer until the next time you need it. But that doesn't mean we scattered the information about with wild abandon. If you were to read the book from front to back, you'd find a logical progression from the simple tasks to the more complex ones. Here's a quick overview.

First, we assume that Excel 97 is already installed on your machine. If it's not, the Setup Wizard makes installation so simple that you won't need our help anyway. So, unlike most computer books, this one doesn't start out with installation instructions and a list of system requirements. You've already got that under control.

Sections 2 through 5 of the book cover the basics: starting Microsoft Excel 97; working with menus, toolbars, and dialog boxes; entering text labels and numbers; creating simple formulas; modifying worksheets and workbooks; and printing and saving workbooks.

Sections 6 through 8 describe tasks that are useful for enhancing the look of a worksheet: formatting worksheets; adding and modifying pictures; drawing shapes; inserting comments; and creating charts and geographic maps.

Section 9 describes tasks that are a little more technical but really useful: analyzing worksheet data.

Sections 10 through 12 cover information that isn't vital to using Excel, but will help you work more efficiently, such as customizing your environment, creating complex worksheets, and working with the Internet.

A Final Word (or Two)

We had three goals in writing this book, and here they are:

- Whatever you want to do, we want the book to help you get it done.
- We want the book to help you discover how to do things you *didn't* know you wanted to do.
- And, finally, if we've achieved the first two goals, we'll be well on the way to the third, which is for our book to help you enjoy doing your work with Excel 97. We think that would be the best gift we could give you as a "thank you" for buying our book.

We hope you'll have as much fun using *Excel 97 At a Glance* as we've had writing it. The best way to learn is by doing, and that's what we hope you'll get from this book.

Jump right in!

2

Getting Started with Excel

IN THIS SECTION

Starting Microsoft Excel 97

Viewing the Excel Window

Opening a File

Moving Around the Workbook

Working with the Excel Window

Working with Menus and Toolbars

Working with Dialog Boxes and Wizards

Getting Help

Saving a Workbook

Printing a Workbook

Closing a Workbook and Exiting Excel

If you're spending too much time number-crunching, rewriting financial reports, drawing charts, and searching for your calculator, you're probably eager to start using Microsoft Excel 97. This book teaches you to use Excel's most popular features so you can become productive immediately.

Microsoft Excel is a *spreadsheet program,* which is designed to help you record, analyze, and present quantitative information. Excel makes it easy to track and analyze sales, organize finances, create budgets, and accomplish a variety of business tasks in a fraction of the time it would take using pen and paper.

The file you create and save in Excel is called a *workbook*. It contains a collection of worksheets which look similar to an accountant's ledger sheets, but you can use Excel to perform calculations and other tasks automatically.

Using Excel, you can create a variety of documents that can be used for analysis and record keeping, such as:

- Monthly sales and expense reports
- Charts displaying annual sales data
- An inventory of products
- A payment schedule for an equipment purchase

Starting Microsoft Excel 97

Before you can begin using Excel, you need to start Excel. The easiest way to start Excel is to use the Start button on the taskbar. If you have installed Excel as part of the Microsoft Office 97 suite of programs, you can start Excel from the Office Shortcut Bar located at the top of your screen. When Excel starts, it displays a new workbook so that you can begin working immediately.

TIP

Use the Office Shortcut Bar to start Excel. *If the Office Shortcut Bar is installed on your computer, you can click the Start A New Document button on the Office Shortcut Bar. If the Office Shortcut Bar is not installed, run Office setup and add the functionality.*

Start Excel from the Start Menu

1. Click the Start button on the taskbar.
2. Point to Programs.

   If you see the Microsoft Office folder on the Programs menu, point to it and then proceed to Step 3.
3. Click Microsoft Excel.

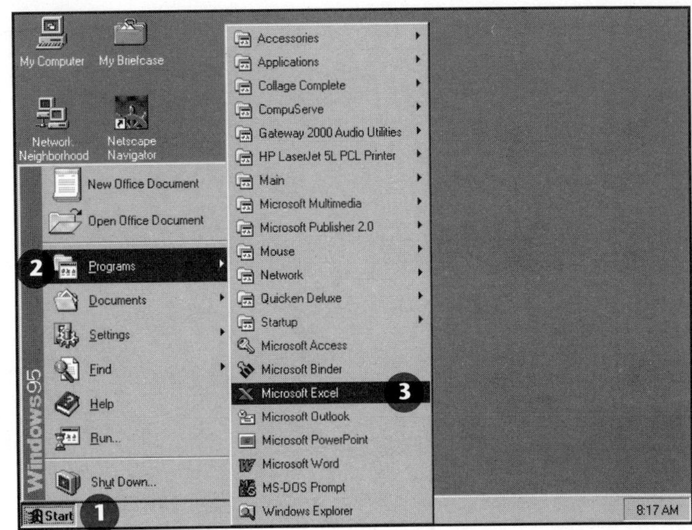

Start Excel from Microsoft Office

1. Click the Start menu on the taskbar, and then click New Office Document.
2. Click the General tab in the New Office Document dialog box.
3. Click Blank Workbook.
4. Click OK.

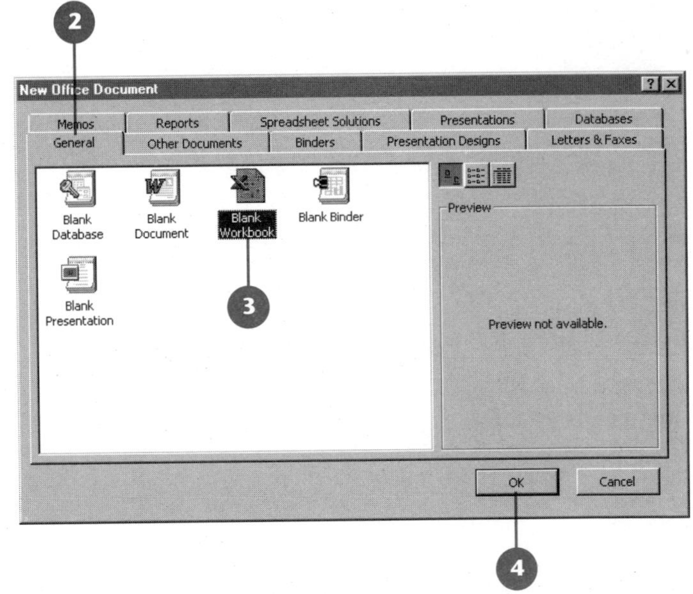

Viewing the Excel Window

When you start Excel, the Excel program windows opens with a blank workbook—ready for you to use. The Excel window contains everything you need to work with your Excel workbook.

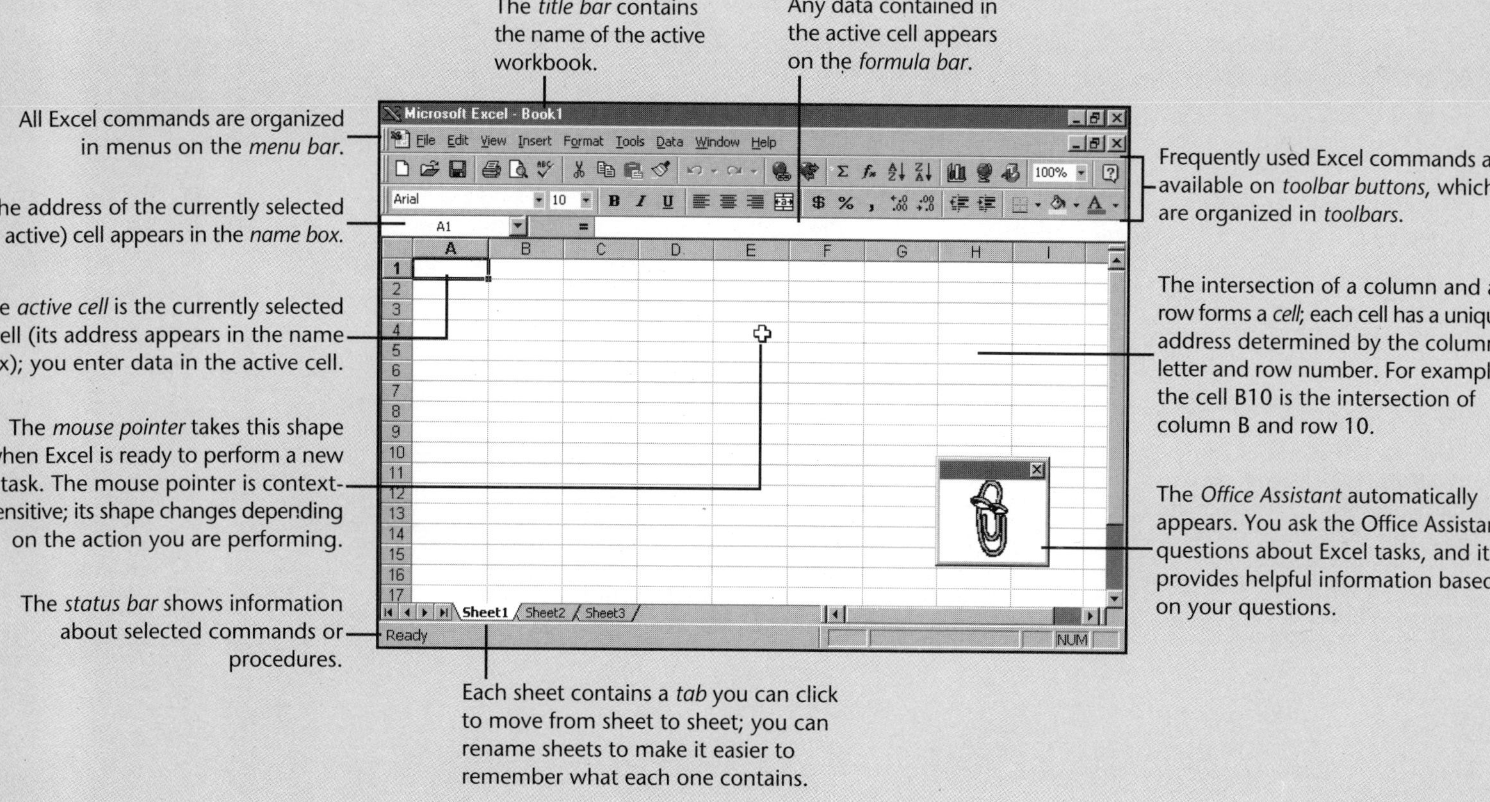

Opening a File

When you want to use a workbook you have previously created, you must first open it. You can open a file and start Excel at the same time from the Documents menu, if the file is one you opened recently, or using the Open Office Document command. Or, after you start Excel, you can open any Excel workbook files or files created in other spreadsheet programs using the Open dialog box. If you can't remember the workbook's name or location, Excel even helps you find files.

TIP

Use the File menu to open a file quickly. *Recently opened files appear on the File menu. If you have recently opened and closed a file, you can click the File menu and then click the file you want to quickly open the file again.*

Open a File from the Excel Window

1. Click the Open button on the Standard toolbar in the Excel window.
2. If you know the location of the file, click the Look In drop-down arrow, and select the folder where the file is located. If you don't know the exact folder, it's better to search your entire drive, since you could overlook the file by specifying the wrong folder.
3. If necessary, click the Files Of Type drop-down arrow, and then click the type of file you want to open (click Microsoft Excel Files to see workbook files).
4. Click the name of the workbook file.
5. Click Open.

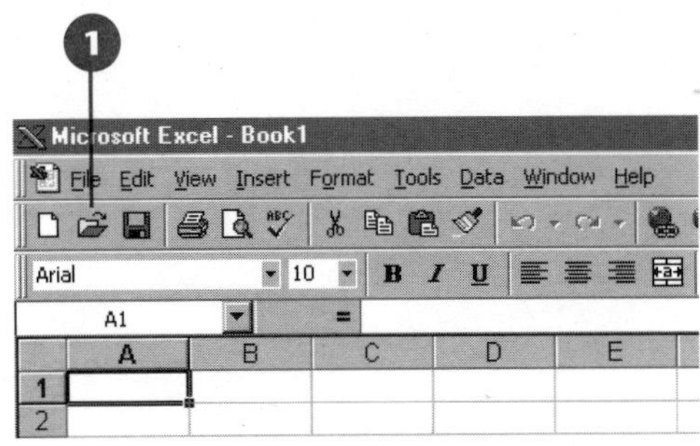

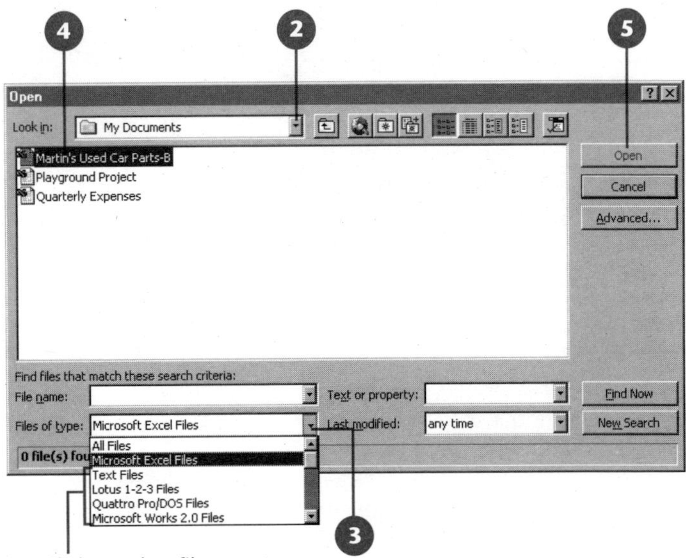

Click another file type to open files created in other programs.

TRY THIS

Find a file in the Open dialog box. *You can open a file even if you're not sure of the filename or file location. In the Open dialog box, click the Look In drop-down arrow and select the drive where the file might be located. If you know any characters contained in the file name, type them in the File Name text box. If you know any text or other property in the file, click the Text Or Property drop-down arrow and enter it. If you know when you last worked on the file, click the Last Modified drop-down arrow and click one of the choices. When you've supplied as much information as you know, click Find Now. Excel lists all files that match the data you supplied.*

TIP

Open files created in other spreadsheet programs. *If the name of the spreadsheet program you want to open doesn't appear in the Files Of Type list, use the Excel setup program to install the necessary filters.*

Open a Recently Opened File from the Start Menu

1. Click the Start button on the taskbar.
2. Point to Documents. The Documents menu displays a list of recently opened files.
3. Click the Excel file you want to open.

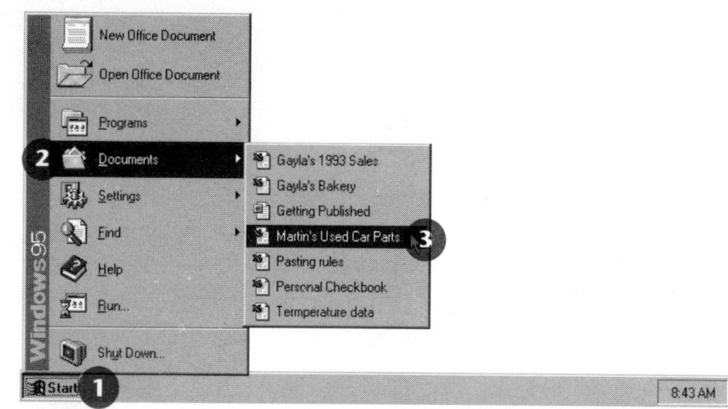

Open an Office File from the Start Menu

1. Click the Start button on the taskbar, and then click Open Office Document.
2. If necessary, click the Files Of Type drop-down arrow, and then click the type of file you want to open (click Microsoft Excel Files to see workbook files).
3. Click the Look In drop-down arrow, if necessary, and select the drive and folder containing the workbook file you want to open.
4. Click the name of the file.
5. Click Open.

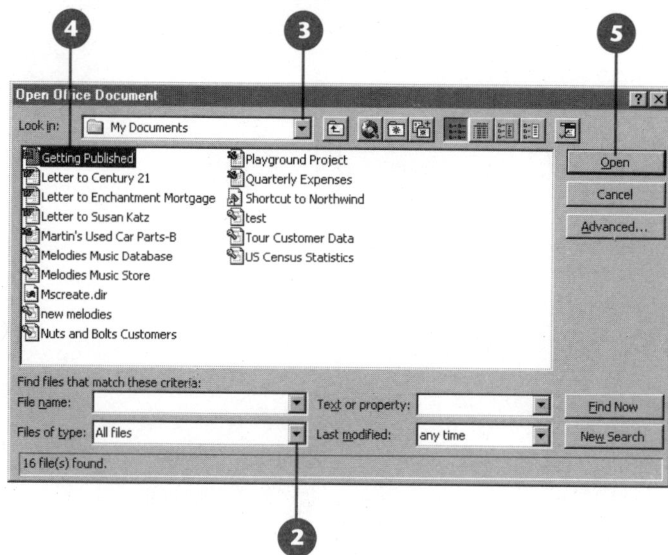

2

Moving Around the Workbook

You can move around a worksheet or workbook using your mouse or the keyboard. You might find that using your mouse to move from cell to cell is most convenient, while using various keyboard combinations is easier for covering large areas of a worksheet quickly. However, there is no one right way; whichever method feels the most comfortable is the one you should use. If you have the new Microsoft Mouse—with the wheel button in between the left and right buttons—you can click the wheel button and move the mouse in any direction to move quickly through the worksheet.

Use the Mouse to Navigate

Using the mouse, you can navigate to:

- Another cell
- Another part of a worksheet
- Another worksheet

To move from one cell to another, point to the cell you want to move to, and then click.

The wheel button looks like this when clicked. Drag the pointer in any direction to move to a new location quickly.

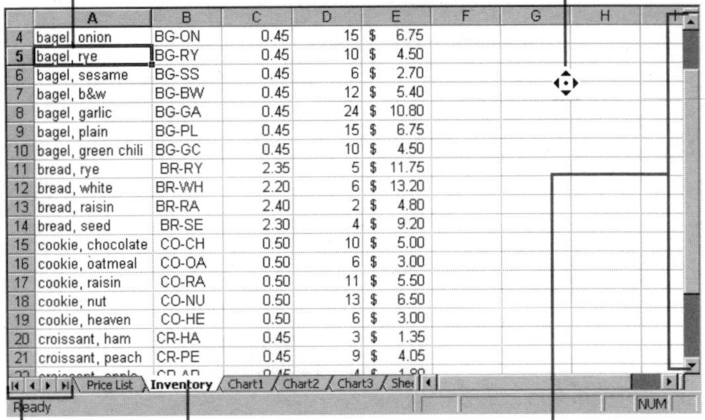

	A	B	C	D	E
4	bagel, onion	BG-ON	0.45	15	$ 6.75
5	bagel, rye	BG-RY	0.45	10	$ 4.50
6	bagel, sesame	BG-SS	0.45	6	$ 2.70
7	bagel, b&w	BG-BW	0.45	12	$ 5.40
8	bagel, garlic	BG-GA	0.45	24	$ 10.80
9	bagel, plain	BG-PL	0.45	15	$ 6.75
10	bagel, green chili	BG-GC	0.45	10	$ 4.50
11	bread, rye	BR-RY	2.35	5	$ 11.75
12	bread, white	BR-WH	2.20	6	$ 13.20
13	bread, raisin	BR-RA	2.40	2	$ 4.80
14	bread, seed	BR-SE	2.30	4	$ 9.20
15	cookie, chocolate	CO-CH	0.50	10	$ 5.00
16	cookie, oatmeal	CO-OA	0.50	6	$ 3.00
17	cookie, raisin	CO-RA	0.50	11	$ 5.50
18	cookie, nut	CO-NU	0.50	13	$ 6.50
19	cookie, heaven	CO-HE	0.50	6	$ 3.00
20	croissant, ham	CR-HA	0.45	3	$ 1.35
21	croissant, peach	CR-PE	0.45	9	$ 4.05

Price List | Inventory | Chart1 | Chart2 | Chart3 | She

Ready NUM

To see more sheet tabs *without* changing the active sheet, click a sheet scroll button.

To move from one worksheet to another, click the tab of the sheet you want to see.

To see other parts of the worksheet *without* changing the location of the active cell, click the horizontal and vertical scroll bars, or drag the scroll buttons.

SEE ALSO

See "Moving and Copying a Worksheet" on page 60 for more information on changing the order of worksheets within a workbook.

SEE ALSO

See "Viewing the Excel Window" on page 7 for more information on the Excel worksheet.

Use the Keyboard to Navigate

Using the keyboard, you can navigate to:

- Another cell
- Another part of a worksheet

Refer to the table for keyboard shortcuts for navigating around a worksheet.

KEYS FOR NAVIGATING IN A WORKSHEET

Press These Keys	To Get This Result
[Left arrow]	Moves one cell to the left
[Right arrow]	Moves one cell to the right
[Up arrow]	Moves one cell up
[Down arrow]	Moves one cell down
[Tab]	Moves one cell to the right
[Shift]+[Tab]	Moves one cell to the left
[PgUp]	Moves one screen up
[PgDn]	Moves one screen down
[End]+ arrow key	Moves in the direction of the arrow key to the next cell
[Home]	Moves to column A in the current row
[Ctrl] [Home]	Moves to cell A1
[Enter]	Moves one cell down

2

Working with the Excel Window

You can open more than one workbook window at a time. To switch from workbook window to workbook window, you can use the Window menu. You can arrange the open windows so they are displayed on the screen at one time, and then click the window you want to work in. You can also move and resize each window to suit your needs.

SEE ALSO

See "Viewing the Excel Window" on page 7 for more information on the Excel worksheet.

Switch Between Worksheet Windows

1. Click the Window menu to display the list of open workbook windows.
2. Click the name of the workbook you want to switch to.

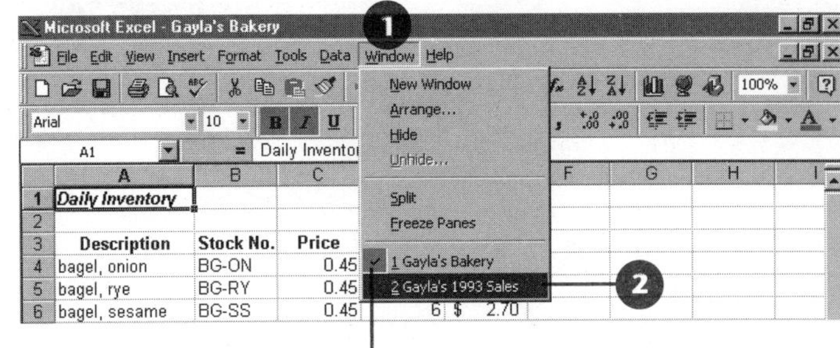

Checkmark indicates active workbook window.

Resize and Move Windows

- Minimize a window

  To reduce a window to a button on the task bar, click the Minimize button.
- Restore a window

  To return a window to its previous size, click the Restore button.
- Resize a window

  When the mouse pointer is positioned over an edge of the window, it turns into a double-sided arrow. Drag this arrow to change the size of the window.
- Move a window

  To change the window's location, drag the title bar of the worksheet window to a new location.

Title bar

Minimize button

Restore button

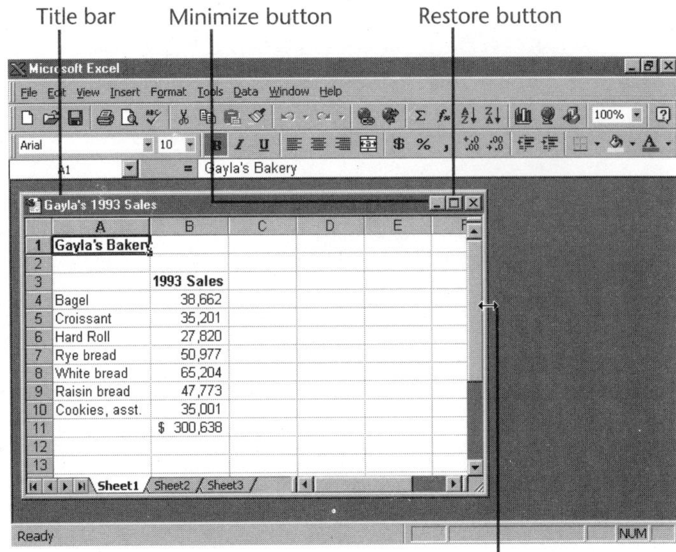

Double-sided arrow

TIP

Use the mouse button to activate a window. *When you have multiple windows open, click the cell you want to work in to make that worksheet window and cell active. If you can't see that particular cell that you want to work in, you can click any part of the worksheet window that's showing.*

Arranging Multiple Windows

1. Click the Window menu, and then Click Arrange.
2. Click an Arrange option button.
   - Tiled. Even numbers of windows are arranged starting in the upper left corner of the screen; odd numbers of windows are arranged with the active window appearing on the left.
   - Horizontal. All windows display in horizontal panes with the active window on top (as shown).
   - Vertical. All windows display in vertical panes with the active window on the left.
   - Cascade. All windows are displayed in a stack with the active window on top and all title bars visible.
3. Click OK.

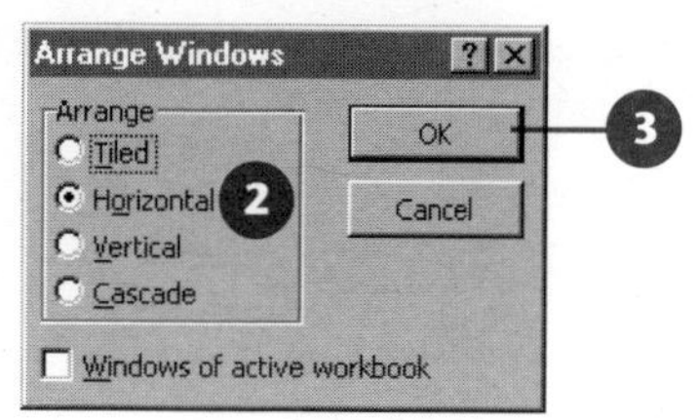

This indicates the window number.

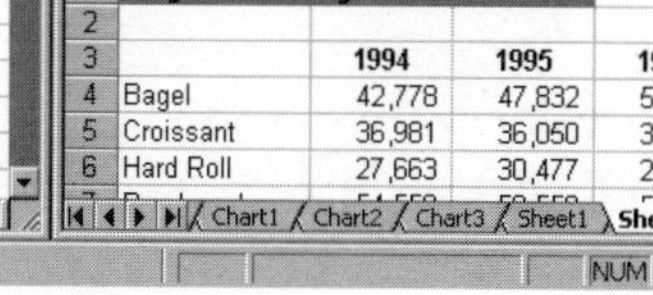

Working with Menus and Toolbars

All Excel commands are organized in menus on the menu bar, and each menu contains a list of related commands. If the command is followed by an ellipsis (...), a dialog box opens so you can provide additional information. If the command is followed by an arrow, a submenu opens displaying related commands. If there is an icon to the left of the command, there is a toolbar button available for that command. If a keyboard combination appears to the right of the command, there is a *shortcut key* that you can use instead of the menu command. A toolbar contains buttons you can click to carry out commands you use frequently. When you position the mouse pointer over a toolbar button, the name of the button appears in a small box called a *ScreenTip*.

Choose a Command Using a Menu

1. Click a menu name on the menu bar to display a list of commands
2. Click the command you want, or point to the arrow to the right of the menu command to display a submenu of related commands, and then click the command.

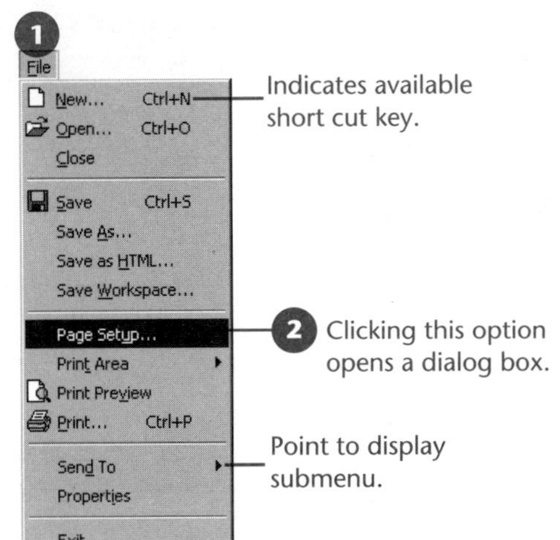

Indicates available short cut key.

Clicking this option opens a dialog box.

Point to display submenu.

Choose a Command Using a Toolbar Button and Display a ScreenTip

1. Click a button on the toolbar to choose a command. For example, to save a file, click the Save button on the Standard toolbar.
2. Position the pointer on the toolbar button to display a ScreenTip.

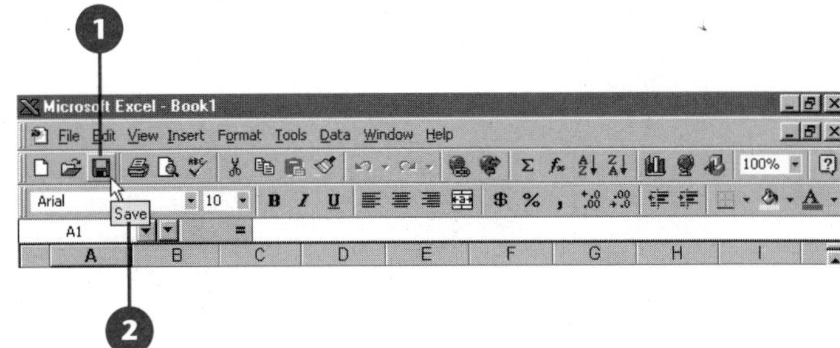

TRY THIS

Move and reshape a toolbar. *A toolbar that appears at the top or on the edge of a window is* docked*; if it appears somewhere else on the screen, it is* floating*. To move a toolbar to another location, click in a blank area of the toolbar (not on a button), and then drag the toolbar to a new location. To change the shape of a floating toolbar, position the mouse pointer over the edge of the toolbar, and then drag to reshape it.*

Choose a Command Using a Shortcut Key

1. To choose a command using a shortcut key, press and hold the first key, and then press the other key. For example, press and hold the Ctrl key, and then press S to issue the Save command.

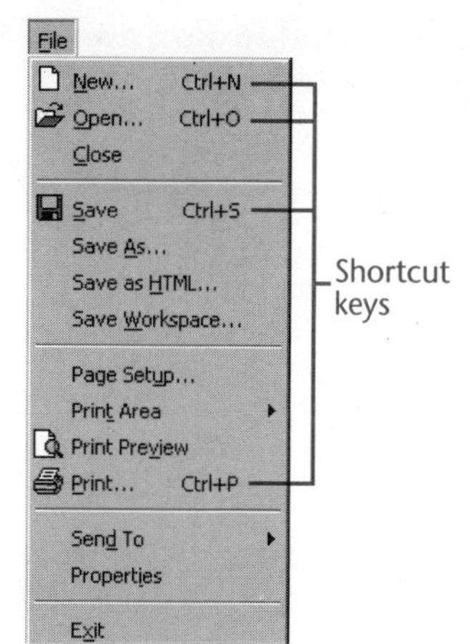

Display or Hide a Toolbar

1. Click the View menu, and then point to Toolbars.
2. Click theunchecked toolbar you want to display, or the checked toolbar you want to hide. (A check mark next to the toolbar name indicates that it is currently displayed on the screen.)

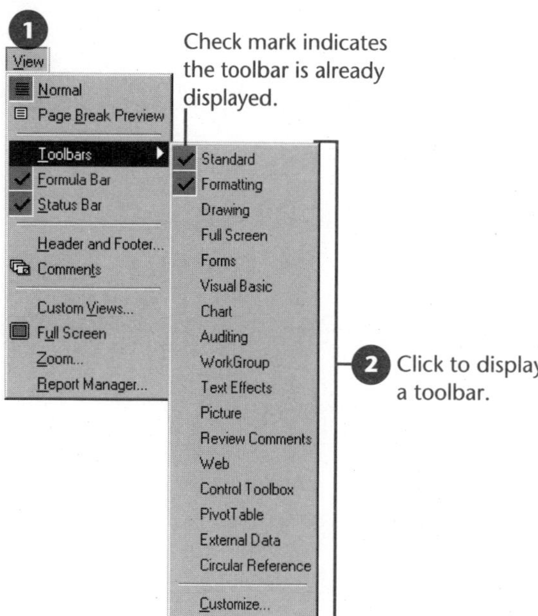

Working with Dialog Boxes and Wizards

A *dialog box* is a special window that opens when Excel needs additional information from you in order to complete a task. You indicate your choices by selecting a variety of option buttons and check boxes; in some cases, you type the necessary information in the boxes provided. Some dialog text boxes consist of a single window, while others contain *tabs* that you click to display more sets of options. *Wizards* are special dialog boxes that guide you through a task; they are powerful tools that make complicated tasks, such as creating a chart or analyzing data, easy.

Select Dialog Box and Wizard Options

- A dialog box may contain one or more of these features.
- After you select or enter the information you want, click OK to complete the command; click Cancel or press the Esc key to cancel the command and close the dialog box.

Click tabs to choose options for Excel features.

Click the drop-down arrow of a list box to open a list of available choices, and then click the item that you want.

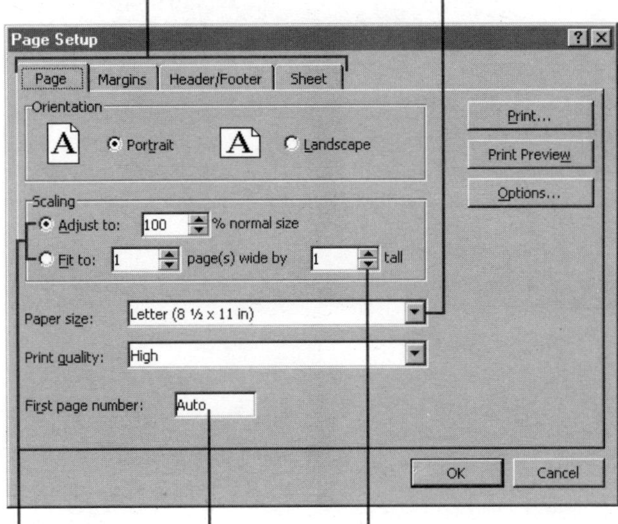

Click one option button to activate the feature you want. You can only choose one option button at a time.

Type necessary information directly into a text box.

Click the up arrow or down arrow of a spin box to change a quantity or measurement, or type the value in the corresponding text box.

SEE ALSO

See "Creating a Chart" on page 142 for more information on using the Chart Wizard.

Chart Wizard button

Make Choices in a Wizard Dialog Box

Make your Wizard dialog box selections as you would in any dialog box. Because a Wizard guides you through a series of dialog boxes, there are additional options that allow you to move backward and forward through the dialog boxes. As you make selections within a Wizard, you can change your mind—and your selections—and view your results.

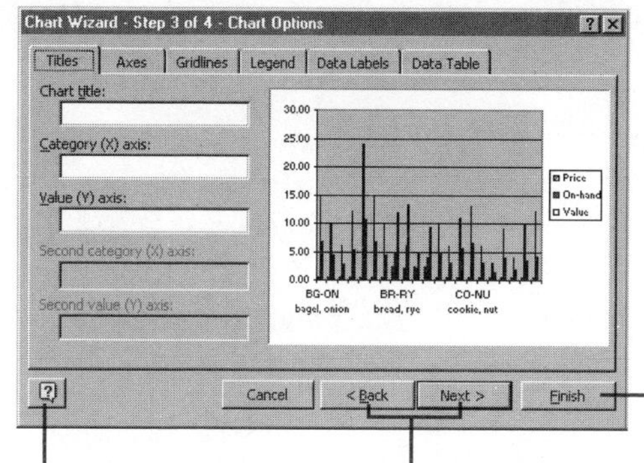

Click the Finish button to let Excel complete the Wizard.

Click the Hide/Display Assistant button to get additional information.

Click the Back button or click the Next button to move to the previous or next Wizard dialog box.

A single wizard dialog box uses tabs to offer opportunities to make changes.

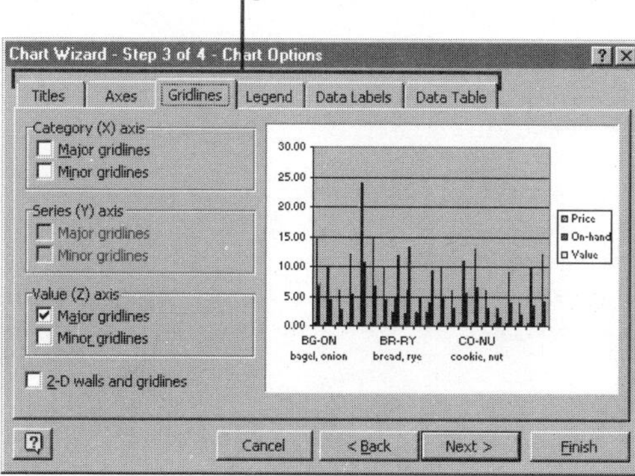

2

Getting Help

Excel provides an extensive online Help system to guide you in completing tasks. You can get help any time in Excel by clicking the Help button on the title bar of a dialog box, by using the commands on the Help menu, or by clicking the Office Assistant button on the Standard toolbar.

Help button

TIP

Use keyboard shortcuts to access help. *To access the Help button using the keyboard, hold down the Shift key and press the [F1] key. To access Office Assistant button using the keyboard, press the [F1] key.*

Get Help Using the Help Button

1. Click the Help button on the title bar of a dialog box or click the Help menu, and then click What's This.
2. Click the Help pointer on any area of the worksheet or an item in a dialog box to display a Help definition box.
3. Click the mouse button or press Esc to close the definition box.

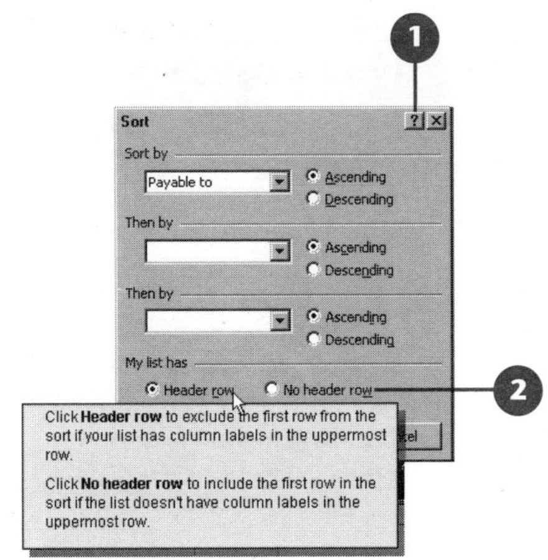

Search for Help Topics

1. Click the Help menu, and then click Contents And Index.
2. Click the Index tab.
3. Type the first few characters of the topic you want help with. As you type the first few characters, the list of index entries scrolls.
4. Click a topic. (click a subtopic, if necessary.)
5. Click Display.
6. Click Cancel when you finish reading the topic; click Cancel again to close the Help Topics dialog box.

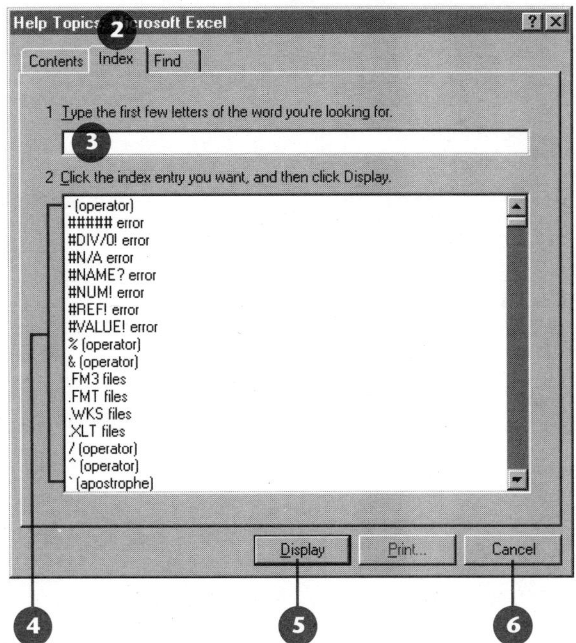

Office Assistant button

TIP

Use the Office Assistant to get a tip. *If a light bulb appears in the Office Assistant, Excel has a tip to help guide you through your current task. Click the light bulb to read it.*

TRY THIS

Turn off the Office Assistant. *Right-click the Office Assistant, and then click Hide Assistant, or click the Close button on the Office Assistant title bar. To turn the Assistant back on, click the Office Assistant button on the Standard toolbar.*

Ask for Help from the Office Assistant

1. Click the Office Assistant or click the Office Assistant button on the Standard toolbar.
2. Type your question—you don't need to select the text in the Help text box.
3. Click Search.
4. Click the button for the topic you're interested in.
5. Click the Close box when you finish reading.

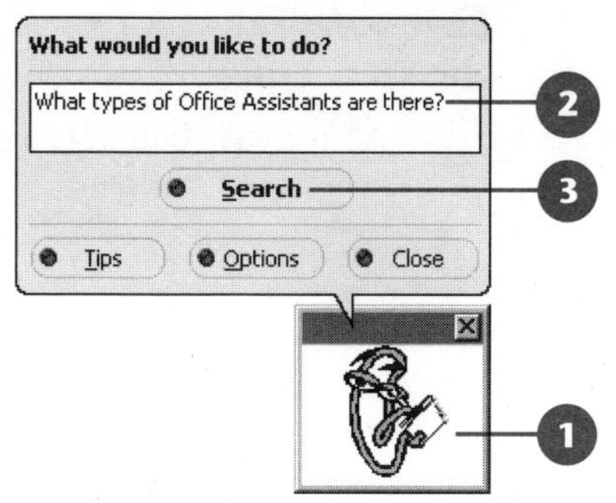

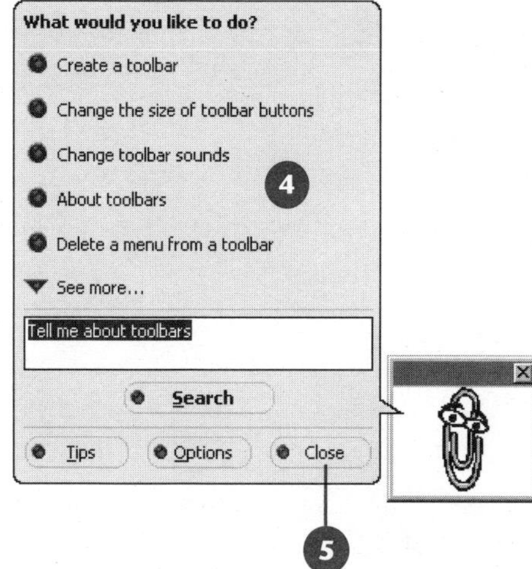

2

Saving a Workbook

When you open a new Excel workbook, the title bar displays a default title such as Book1 or Book2. When you save a workbook for the first time, you need to give it a meaningful name and specify where you want to store it. Filenames can contain up to 256 characters, including uppercase and lowercase letters, spaces, and punctuation. Once you have saved a workbook, you must continue to save the changes you've made before closing the workbook or exiting the Excel program.

Save button

Save a Workbook for the First Time

1. Click the Save button on the Standard toolbar.
2. Click the Save In drop-down arrow, and then select the drive and folder that you want to store the workbook file in.
3. Type the new workbook name in the File Name text box.
4. Click Save. The new name appears in the title bar.

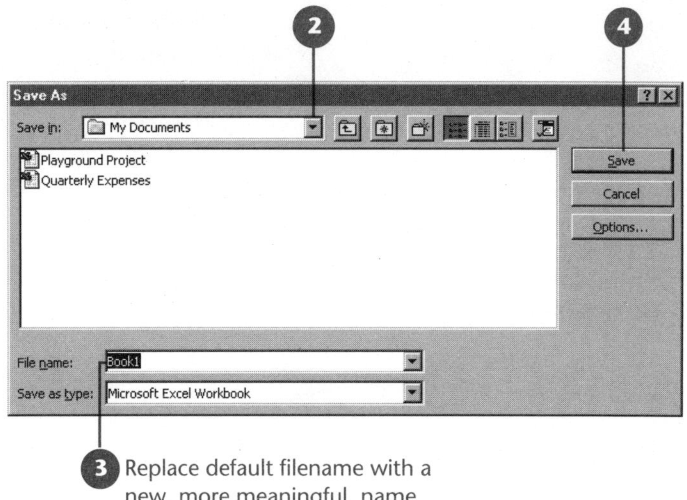

3 Replace default filename with a new, more meaningful, name.

TIP

Use the Save As command to save an Excel file to a previous version of Excel. *In the Save As dialog box, click the Save As Type drop-down arrow and click a previous version of Excel available in the list.*

TIP

Use the Save As command to save a worksheet with a different name. *To save a workbook with a different name, so you have the original workbook and a copy with changes you may or may not want, use the Save As dialog box, replacing the current filename with a new filename. You will then have two files: the original and one with the changes.*

TRY THIS

Create a new folder in the Save As dialog box. *In the Save As dialog box, click New Folder, type the name of the folder in the Name text box, and then click OK.*

Save a Named Workbook in a Different File Format

1. Click the File menu, and then click Save As.
2. Click the Save In drop-down arrow, and then select the drive and folder that you want to save the workbook file in.
3. Type the new filename in the File Name text box.
4. Click the Save As type drop-down arrow.
5. Select the file format you want.
6. Click Save.

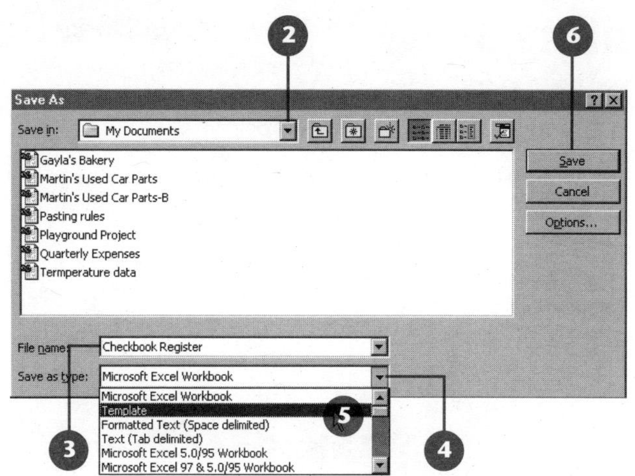

2

Printing a Worksheet

You should always *preview* your work before sending it to the printer. A *print preview* is a miniature view of the entire worksheet that shows you how your worksheet will look when it is printed. You can print a copy of your worksheet quickly to review it, or use the Print dialog box to specify several print options, such as choosing a new printer, selecting the number of pages in the workbook your want printed, and specifying the number of copies.

Print Preview button

Print button

SEE ALSO

See "Saving a Workbook" on page 20 for more information above saving a workbook.

Preview a Worksheet

1. Click the Print Preview button on the Standard toolbar.
2. Click the Zoom button or click the Zoom pointer anywhere on the worksheet to enlarge a specific area of the page.
3. Click the Print button on the Print Preview toolbar to print your worksheet.
4. Click the Close button to close Print Preview.

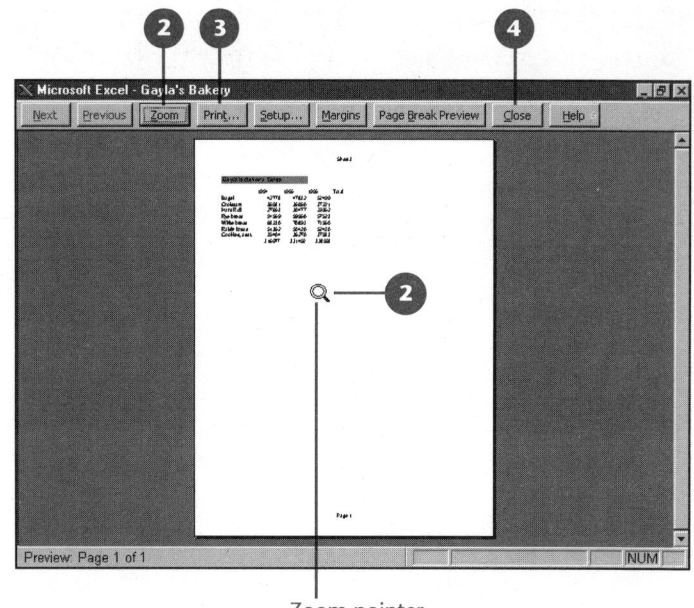

Print a Copy of a Worksheet Quickly

1. Click the Print button on the Standard toolbar.

   Excel prints the selected worksheet with the current Print dialog box settings.

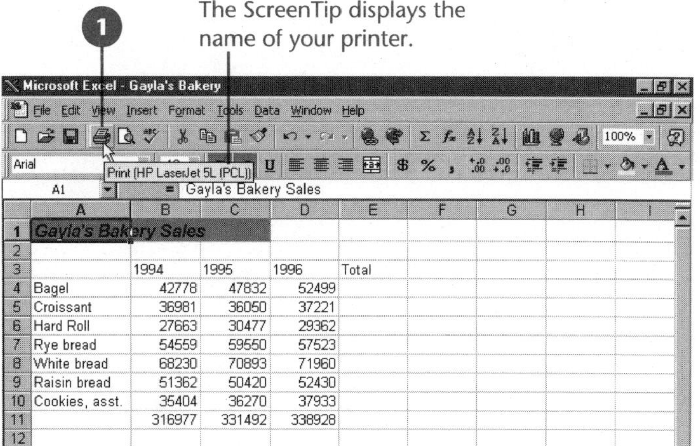

TIP

You can change printer properties. *Click the Properties button to change general printer properties for paper size and orientation, graphics, and fonts.*

TIP

You can preview your workbook. *Click the Preview button to preview your workbook with the specified options.*

Specify Print Options Using the Print Dialog Box

1. Click the File menu, and then click Print.

    - To choose another (installed) printer, click the Printer drop-down arrow, and then select the printer you want to use.
    - To print selected pages (rather than all pages), click the Page(s) option button, and then click the From and To spin arrows in until the number of pages is defined.
    - To print more than one copy of the print range, click the Number Of Copies spin arrows until the number of copies is defined.
    - To change the worksheet print area, click one of the Print What option buttons that correctly identifies the area to be printed.

2. Click OK.

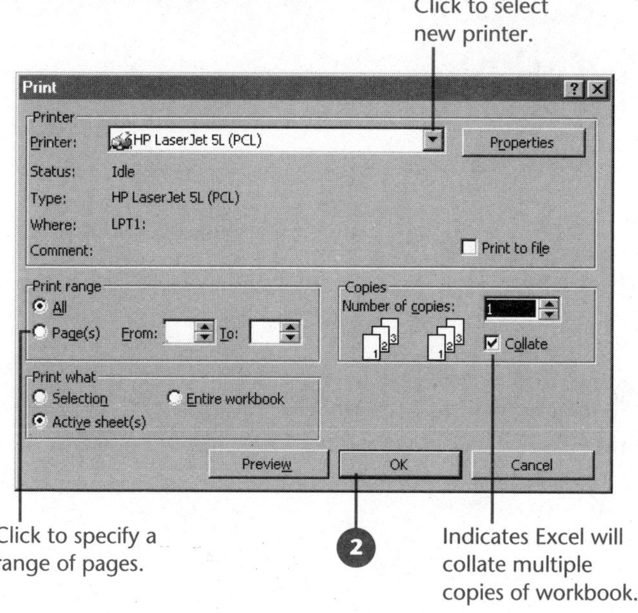

Click to select new printer.

Click to specify a range of pages.

2

Indicates Excel will collate multiple copies of workbook.

2

Closing a Workbook and Exiting Excel

After you finish working on a workbook, you can close it. Closing a file makes more computer memory available for other processes. Closing a workbook is different from exiting Excel: after you close a workbook, Excel is still running. When you're finished using Excel, you can exit the program. To protect your files, always exit from Excel before turning off the computer.

Close button

Close a Workbook

1. Click the File menu, and then click Close or click the Close button on the worksheet window title bar.
2. If you have made any changes to the workbook since last saving it, a dialog box opens asking if you want to save changes. Click Yes to save any changes you made to your workbook, or click No to ignore any changes you might have made.

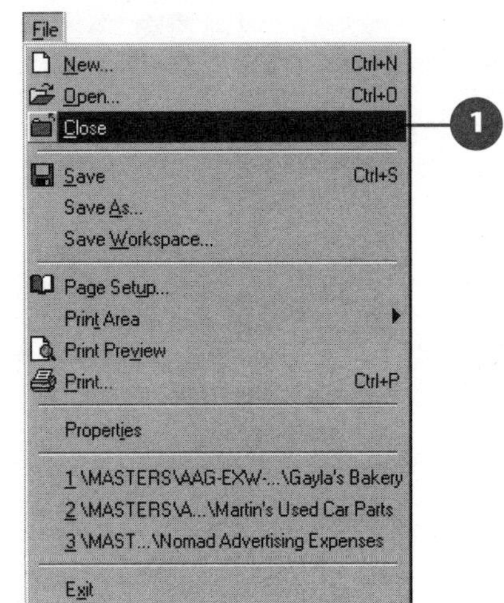

Exit Excel

1. Click the Close button on the Excel program window title bar, or click the File menu, and then click Exit.
2. If any files are open and you have made any changes since last saving, a dialog box opens asking if you want to save changes. Click Yes to save any changes you made to your workbook, or click No to ignore any changes you might have made. If no files are open or have been changed, the program closes automatically.

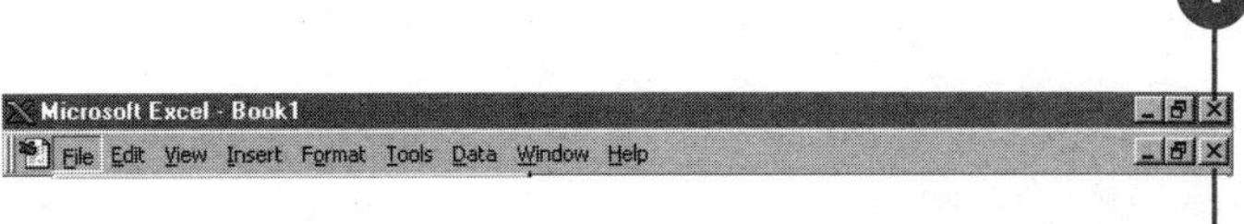

Clicking this button closes the worksheet window only.

3

Basic Workbook Skills

IN THIS SECTION

- **Making Cell Entries in a Worksheet**
- **Undoing and Redoing an Action**
- **Entering Labels in a Worksheet**
- **Entering Values in a Worksheet**
- **Editing Cell Contents**
- **Selecting Multiple Cells**
- **Clearing Cell Contents**
- **Understanding How Excel Pastes Data**
- **Copying Cell Contents**
- **Moving Cell Contents**
- **Inserting and Deleting a Cell**

Creating an Excel workbook is as simple as entering data in the cells of an Excel worksheet. Cells contain either labels or values (or a combination of label and values) and any entries can be modified using a combination of a function key and the keyboard. In addition to making entries with the keyboard, Excel includes several tools that make data entry easier. Once entries are made, their contents can be moved or copied into other cells: this ability increases your efficiency and decreases the amount of time you spend typing.

When working with manual spreadsheets, the only way to increase the size and depth of your work is to write down all the data you want. With Excel, you can automate many data entry tasks and copy and paste large amounts of repetitive information. Regardless of how careful you plan your worksheet, the need will arise to add cells within a worksheet. When adding or deleting a cell, Excel lets you choose how existing cells are moved.

Making Cell Entries in a Worksheet

There are three basic types of cell entries: labels, values, and formulas. A *label* is text that you enter in a cell that identifies the data in the worksheet so readers understand the purpose of the worksheet. Excel does not use labels in its calculations. For example, the label "Description" identifies the kinds of daily inventory listed in this worksheet.

A *value* is a number you enter in a cell. Excel knows to include values in its calculations. To perform a calculation in a worksheet, you enter a *formula* in a cell. A formula is a calculation that contains cell references, values, and arithmetic operators. The result of a formula appears in the worksheet cell where you entered the formula. For example, cell E4 in the figure displays "6.75"; however, the cell actually contains the formula "=C4*D4" (or Value=Price x On-hand)—which appears in the formula bar. The advantage of a cell containing a formula is that when you change the data in the worksheet or copy the formula to other cells Excel automatically adjusts the cell references in the formula and returns the correct results.

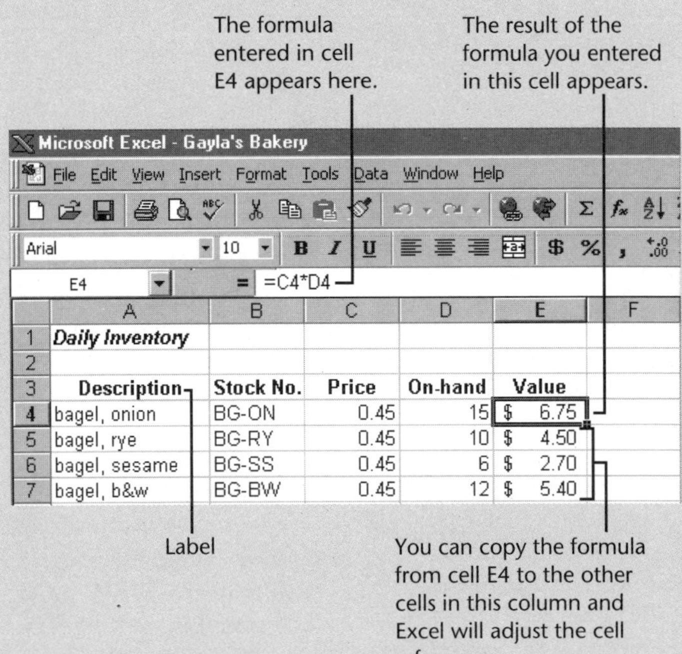

Undoing and Redoing an Action

As you create your worksheet, you may realize you've made a mistake shortly after completing an action or a task. The Undo feature allows you to "take back" the results of previously entered data, menu commands, or toolbar buttons. For example, if you were to enter a number in a cell and then decide the number was incorrect, you could undo the entry by clicking the Undo button on the Standard toolbar. Maybe the number you deleted was correct after all; the Redo feature would restore it to the cell. If you were to find you needed to repeat or restore a recent action, you could use the Redo button on the Standard toolbar.

Undo an Action

- Click the Undo button on the Standard toolbar to undo the last action you completed.
- Click the Undo drop-down arrow on the Standard toolbar to see a list of recently completed actions that can be undone. As you point to an action on the list you want to undo, Excel highlights that action and all actions above it (those that occurred since the action you want to undo).
- Click an action. Excel reverses the selected action and all the subsequent actions.

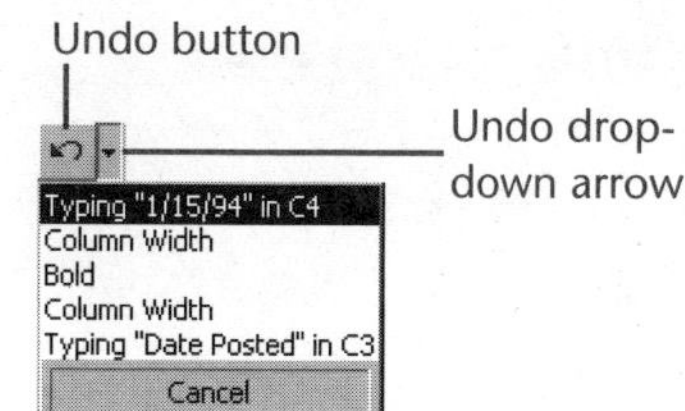

Redo an Action

- Click the Redo button on the Standard toolbar to repeat your last action.
- Click the Redo drop-down arrow to see a list of recently completed actions that can be repeated. As you point to an action on the list you want to repeat, Excel highlights that action and all actions above it (those that occurred since the action you want to repeat).

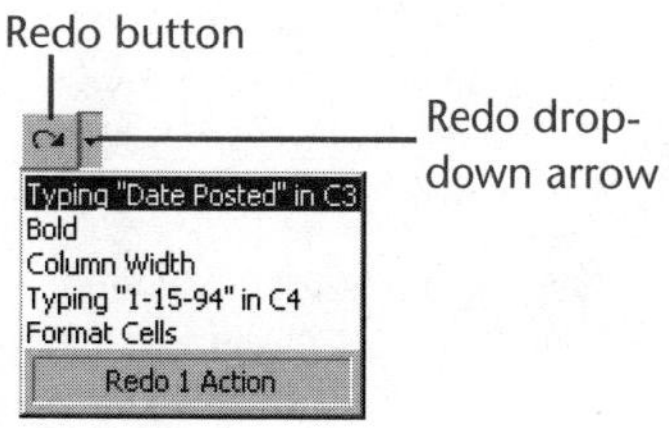

3

Entering Labels in a Worksheet

Labels turn a worksheet full of numbers into a meaningful report by clarifying the relationship between the numbers. You use labels to identify the data in the worksheet columns and rows. To help keep your labels consistent, Excel's AutoComplete and PickList features automatically complete your entries based on labels you have entered previously. To enter a number as a label, for example, the year 1997, you type an apostrophe (') before the number. Then Excel does not use the number in its calculations.

TIP

Different ways to enter a label. *Clicking the Enter button on the formula bar leaves the insertion point in the same cell, and pressing Enter moves the insertion point down one cell.*

Enter a Text Label

1. Click the cell where you want to enter a label.
2. Type a label. A label can include uppercase and lowercase letters, spaces, punctuation, and numbers.
3. Click the Enter button on the formula bar or press Enter.

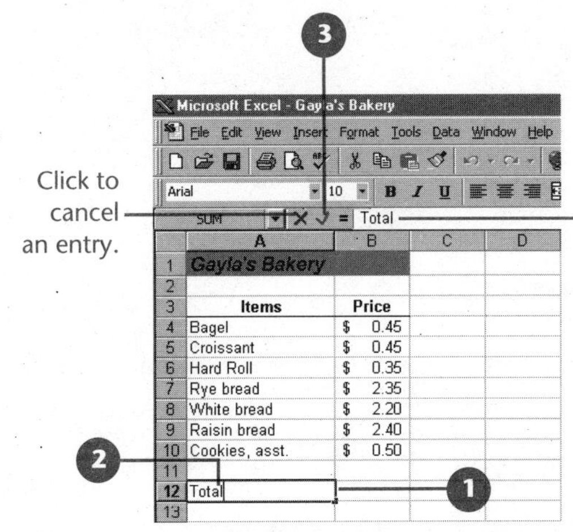

Enter a Number as a Label

1. Click the cell where you want to enter a number as a label.
2. Type ' (an apostrophe). The apostrophe is a *label prefix* and does not appear in the worksheet.
3. Type a number value. Examples of numbers that you might use as labels include a year, a social security number, or a telephone number.
4. Click the Enter button on the formula bar, or press Enter.

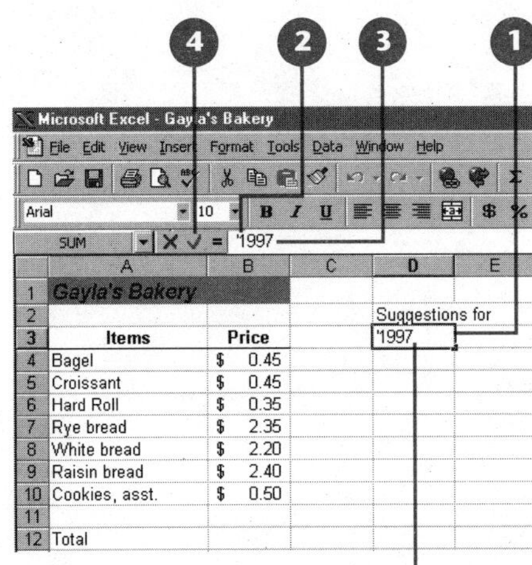

TIP

Long labels might appear truncated. *When you enter a label that is wider than the cell it occupies, the excess text appears to spill into the next cell to the right—unless there is data in the adjacent cell. If the adjacent cell contains data, the label will appear truncated—you'll only see the portion of the label that fits in the cell's current width.*

SEE ALSO

See "Adjusting Column Width and Row Height" on page 66 for information on changing the width of a column.

Enter a Label Using AutoComplete

1. Type the first few characters of a label.
2. If Excel recognizes the entry, AutoComplete completes it, and then you press Enter or click the Enter button on the formula bar. If Excel does not recognize the entry, AutoComplete is not activated so you can continue typing the entry, and then press Enter or the click Enter button on the formula bar.

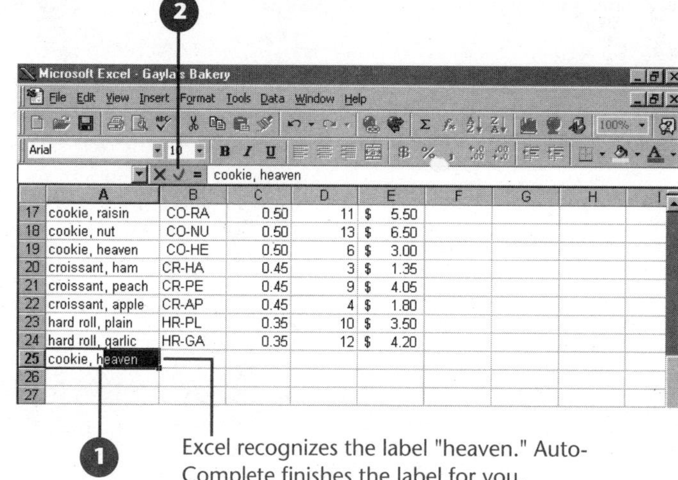

Excel recognizes the label "heaven." AutoComplete finishes the label for you.

Enter a Label Using the PickList

1. Right-click the cell where you want to enter a label, and then click Pick From List.
2. Click an entry from the drop-down list.

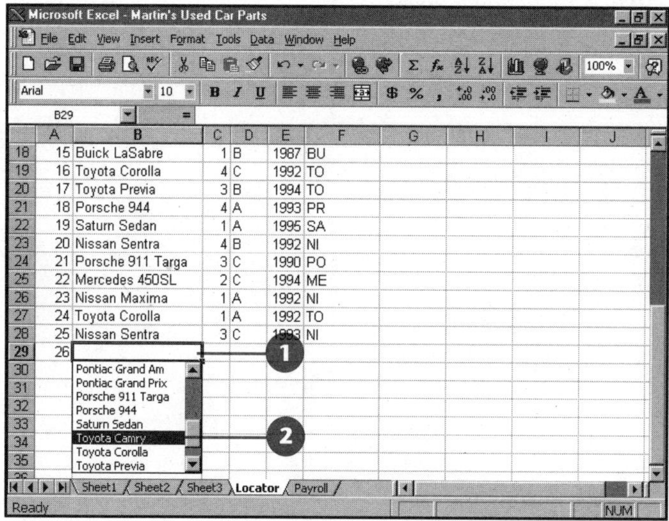

Entering Values in a Worksheet

You can enter values as whole numbers, decimals, percentages, or dates. You can enter values using the numbers on the top row of your keyboard, or the numeric keypad on the right. When you enter a date or the time of day, Excel automatically recognizes these entries (if entered correctly) as numeric values and changes the cell's format to a default date or time format.

> **TIP**
>
> **Use Format Cells to help you enter data.** *Enter values as simply as possible to make data entry quicker. For example, to enter the value "10.00" just type "10". You can then format your cell entries with the number of decimal places, commas, and dollar signs.*

Enter a Value

1. Click the cell where you want to enter a value.
2. Type a value. To simplify your data entry, type the values without commas and dollar signs and apply a numeric format to them later.
3. Press Enter, or click the Enter button on the formula bar.

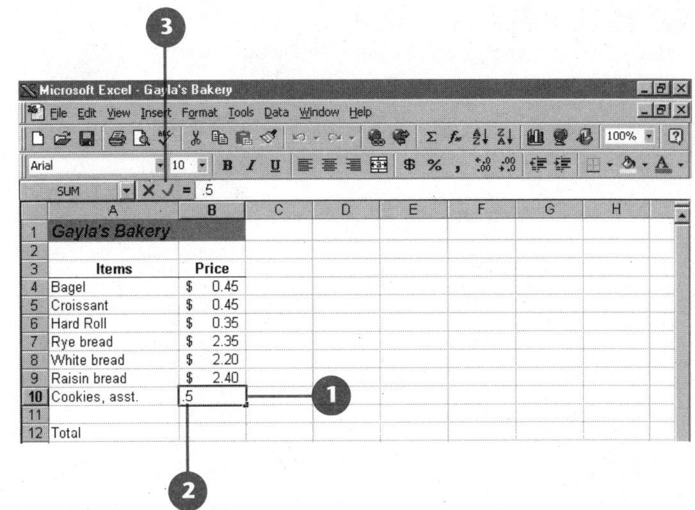

Enter a Date or Time

1. To enter a date, type the date using a slash (/) or a hyphen(-) between the month, day, and year in a cell or the formula bar.
2. To enter a time, type the time based on a 12-hour clock using a colon (:) between the hour and the minutes, followed by a space, and then an "a" or a "p" to denote morning or evening.
3. Press Enter, or click the Enter button on the formula bar.

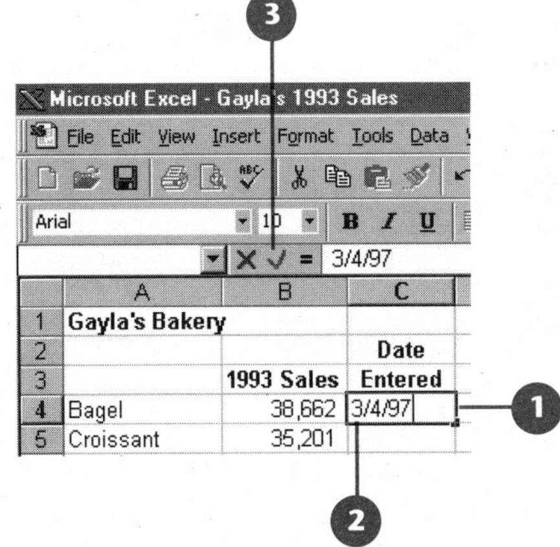

SEE ALSO

See "Formatting Text and Numbers" on page 74 for more information on changing the way numbers appear in a worksheet.

TIP

Use the numeric keypad to enter numbers. *Before using the numeric keypad, make sure NUM appears in the lower right corner of the status bar. If NUM is not displayed, you can turn this feature on by pressing the Num Lock key on the numeric keypad. You can then use the numeric keypad like a calculator to enter numbers in your worksheet.*

4. If necessary, change the date format by right-clicking the cell containing the date, and then click Format Cells. The Format Cells dialog box opens with the Date or Time category selected, and the available format types displayed in the Type box.
5. Select the date or time format from the list.
6. Click OK.

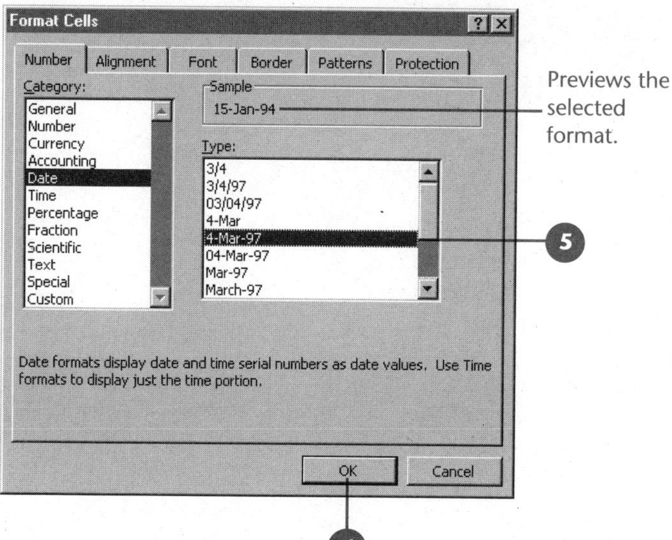

Editing Cell Contents

No matter how much you plan, you can count on having to make changes in a worksheet. Sometimes it's because you want to correct an error; other times you might want to incorporate new information, or see how your worksheet results would be affected by different conditions, such as higher sales, fewer units produced, or other variables. You edit data just as easily as you enter it, using the formula bar or directly editing the active cell.

Edit Cell Content Using the Formula Bar

1. Click the cell you want to edit.
2. Press F2 to change to the Edit mode. (The status bar now displays Edit instead of Ready in the lower left corner.)
3. If necessary, use the mouse pointer or the Home, End, and arrow keys to position the insertion point in the cell.
4. If necessary, use any combination of the Backspace and Delete keys to erase unwanted characters.
5. If necessary, type new characters.
6. Press Enter to accept the edit, or press Esc to cancel it.

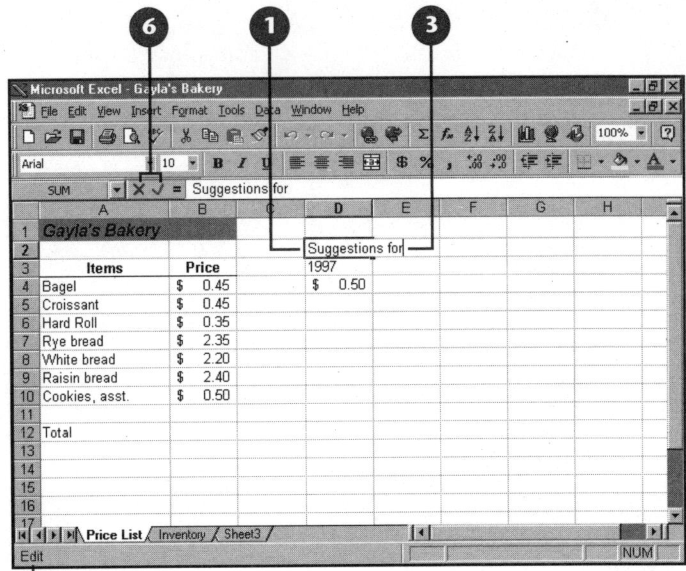

2 The mode indicator changes to edit.

SEE ALSO

See "Entering Labels in a Worksheet" on page 28 for more information on entering data quickly.

Edit Cell Content In-Cell

1. Double-click the cell you want to edit. The insertion point appears within the cell.
2. If necessary, use the mouse pointer or the Home, End, and arrow keys to position the insertion point where you want it.
3. If necessary, use any combination of the Backspace and Delete keys to erase unwanted characters.
4. If necessary, type new characters.
5. Press Enter to accept the edit, or press Esc to cancel it.

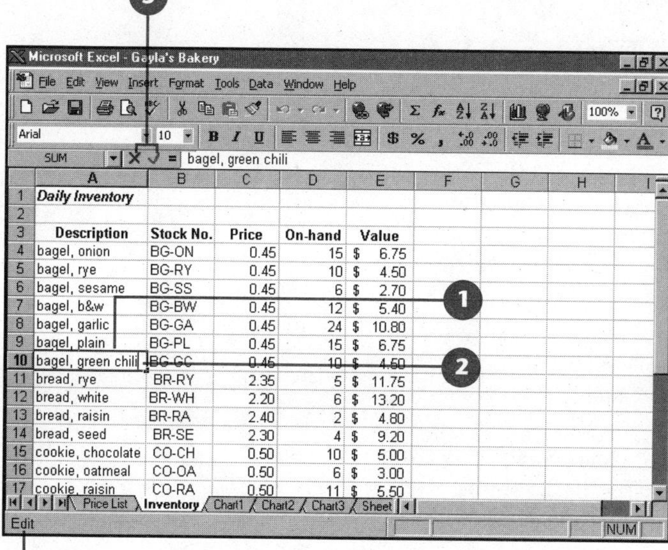

The mode indicator changes to Edit.

3

Selecting Multiple Cells

A *range* is one or more selected cells that you can edit, delete, format, print, or use as an argument in a formula just as you would a single cell. A range can consist of *contiguous* cells (where all the selected cells are adjacent to each other) or *noncontiguous* cells (where all the cells are not adjacent to each other). A range reference begins with the top leftmost cell in the range, followed by a colon (:), and ends with the cell address of the bottom rightmost cell in the range. To make working with ranges easier, Excel allows you to name them. The name "Sales," for example, is easier to remember than the coordinates B4:D10.

Select a Range

1. Click the first cell you want to include in the range.
2. Drag the mouse diagonally to the last cell you want to include the range. When a range is selected, the top, leftmost cell is surrounded by the cell pointer while the additional cells are highlighted in black.

Select a Non-contiguous Range

1. Click the first cell you want to include in the range.
2. Drag the mouse diagonally to the last contiguous cell.
3. Press and hold the Ctrl key and drag the mouse over the next group of cells you want in the range.
4. Repeat steps 3 and 4 until all the cells are selected.

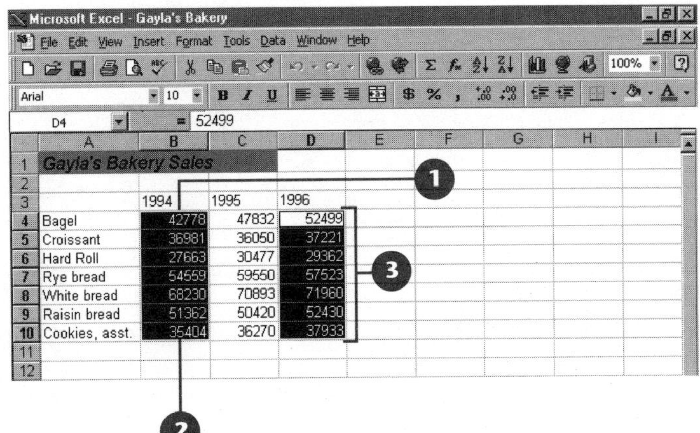

Name a Range

1. Select a range you want to name.
2. Click the Name box on the formula bar.
3. Type a name for the range. A range name can include uppercase or lowercase letters, numbers, and punctuation. Try to use a simple name that reflects the type of information in the range, such as "Sales94."
4. Press Enter. The range name will appear in the Name box whenever you select the range.

	A	B	C	D
1	Gayla's Bakery Sales			
2				
3		1994	1995	1996
4	Bagel	42778	47832	52499
5	Croissant	36981	36050	37221
6	Hard Roll	27663	30477	29362
7	Rye bread	54559	59650	57623
8	White bread	68230	70893	71960
9	Raisin bread	51362	50420	52430
10	Cookies, asst.	35404	36270	37933

Select a Named Range

1. Click the Name box drop-down arrow on the formula bar.
2. Click the name of the range you want to select. The range name appears in the Name box, and all cells included in the range are highlighted in the worksheet.

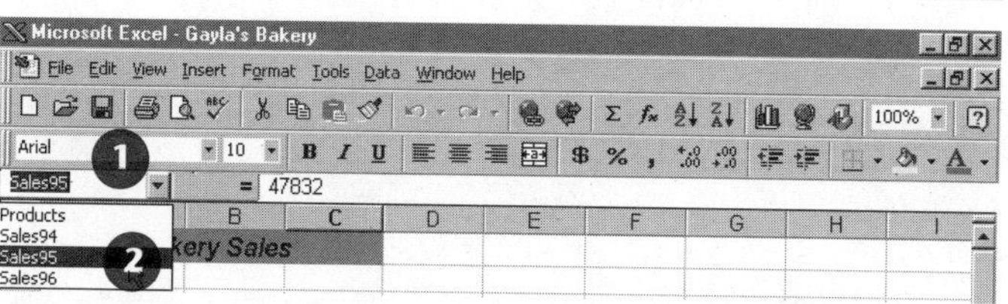

SEE ALSO

See "Using AutoCalculate" on page 53 for more information on this feature.

TRY THIS

Go to a named range in a worksheet. *Press the F5 key to see a list of named ranges. Click the name of the range you want to go to, and then click OK.*

Clearing Cell Contents

You can remove everything in a cell instead of just editing it. Clearing a cell does not remove the physical cell from the worksheet; it just removes the contents of the cell of whatever elements you specify. Cells can contain data, comments (also called cell notes), and formatting instructions, and you can choose to clear just the data, just the comments, just the formatting, or all of these.

TIP

Deleting a cell removes the physical cell from the worksheet. *When you choose Delete from the Edit menu or the shortcut menu, you must choose to move the remaining cells left or up or remove the entire row or column.*

TRY THIS

Clear just the formatting within a cell. *Select a cell or range, click the Edit menu, point to Clear, and then click Formats. The data remains but the formatting is removed.*

Clear the Contents of a Cell

1. Click a cell or range you want to clear.
2. Click the right mouse button, and then click Clear Contents or press the Delete key.

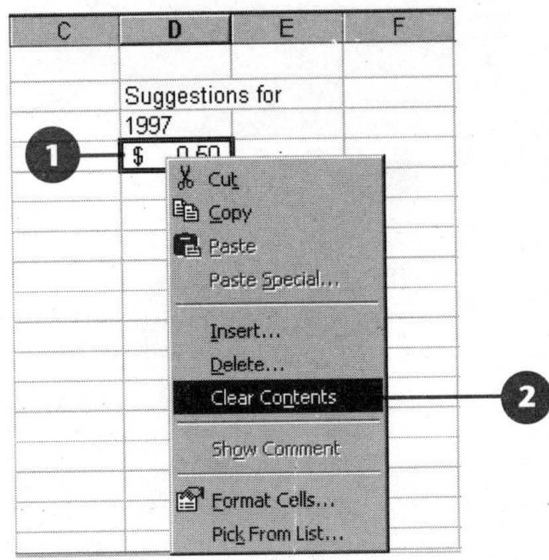

Clear All Parts of a Cell

1. Click a cell or range you want to clear.
2. Click the Edit menu, and then point to Clear.
3. Click All.

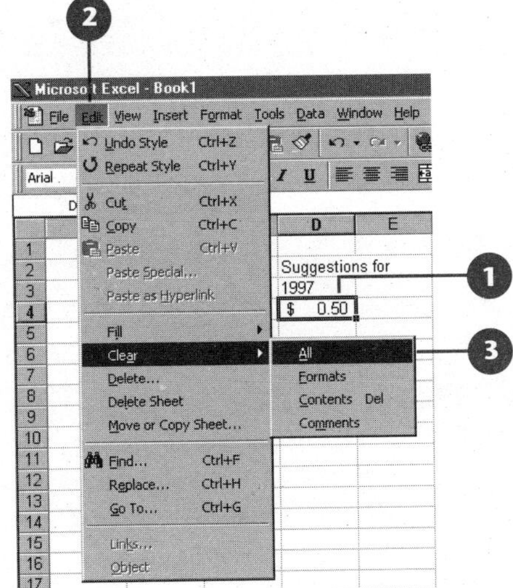

Understanding How Excel Pastes Data

When pasting a range of cells from the Clipboard, you only need to specify the first cell in the new location. After you select the first cell in the new location and then click the Paste button, Excel automatically places all the selected cells in the correct order. Depending on the number of cells you select before you cut or copy, Excel pastes data in one of the following ways:

- **One to one**

  A single cell in the Clipboard is pasted in one cell.

- **One to many**

  A single cell in the Clipboard is pasted into a selected range of cells.

- **Many to one**

  Many cells pasted into a range of cells, but only the first cell is identified. The entire contents of the Clipboard will be pasted starting with the selected cell. Make sure there is enough room for the selection; if not, the selection will copy over any previously occupied cells.

- **Many to many**

  Many cells pasted into a range of cells. The entire contents of the Clipboard will be pasted into the selected cells. If the selected range is larger than the selection, the data will be repeated in the extra cells.

Select a cell as the destination.

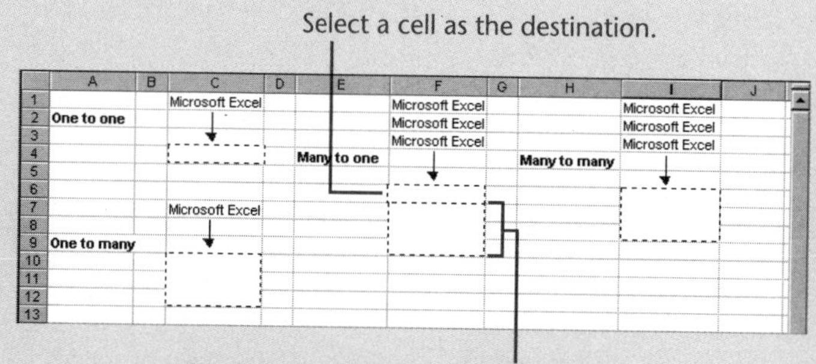

The plus sign indicates you are copying data to a new location.

To turn off the selection marquee and cancel your action, press Esc.

3

Copying Cell Contents

You can copy and move data in a worksheet from one cell or range to another location in any worksheet in your workbook. When you *copy* data, Excel places a duplicate of the selected cells in the *Clipboard*, which is a temporary holding area in your computer's memory. When you *move* data, you must first cut the data. When you *cut* data, Excel removes the selected cell or range content from the worksheet and places it in the Clipboard. To complete the copy or move, you must then *paste* the data that is in the Clipboard in another location on the worksheet (or workbook). To copy or move data without using the Clipboard, you can use a technique called *drag-and-drop*. For copying information a short distance on a worksheet, use drag-and-drop. For copying between worksheets, use the copy and paste commands.

Copy Data Using the Clipboard

1. Select the cell or range that contains the data you want to copy.
2. Click the Copy button on the Standard toolbar. The data in the cells remains in its original location and an outline of the selected cells, called a *marquee*, shows the size of the selection. If you don't want to paste this selection, press Esc to remove the marquee.
3. Click the first cell where you want to paste the data.
4. Click the Paste button on the Standard toolbar. The marquee disappears. The data is still in the Clipboard and still available for further pasting, until you replace it with another selection.
5. If you don't want to paste this selection anywhere else, press Esc to remove the marquee.

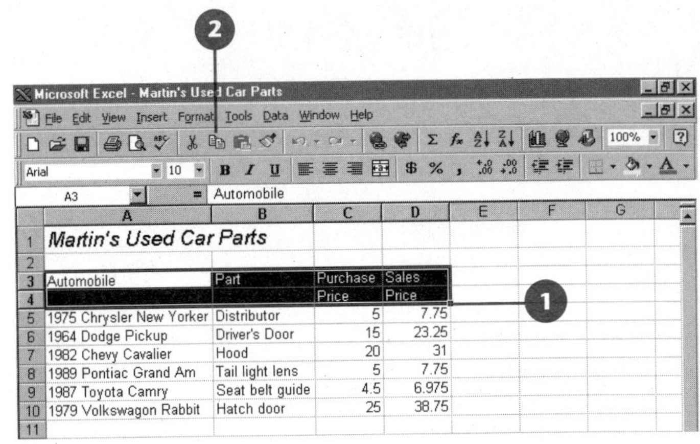

When you copy cells, the data remains in its original location.

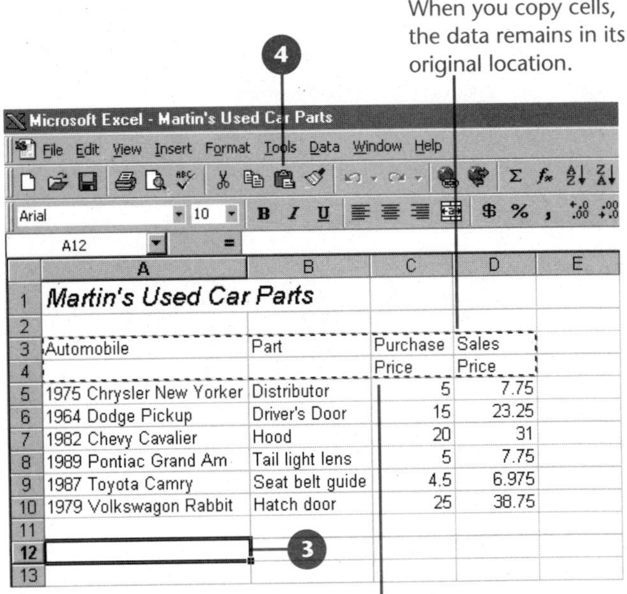

The marquee disappears after you paste the selection.

TIP

Use drag-and-drop to save time and create consistent labels. *Using drag-and-drop to copy information gives your worksheet consistent labels. You'll also be less likely to have words spelled differently throughout your worksheet.*

Copy Data Using Drag-and-Drop

1. Select the cell or range that contains the data you want to copy.
2. Move the mouse pointer to an edge of the selected cell or range until the pointer changes to an arrowhead.
3. Press and hold the mouse button and the Ctrl key. The pointer now appears with a small plus sign to the right (+).
4. Drag the selection to its new location, and then release the mouse button and the Ctrl key.

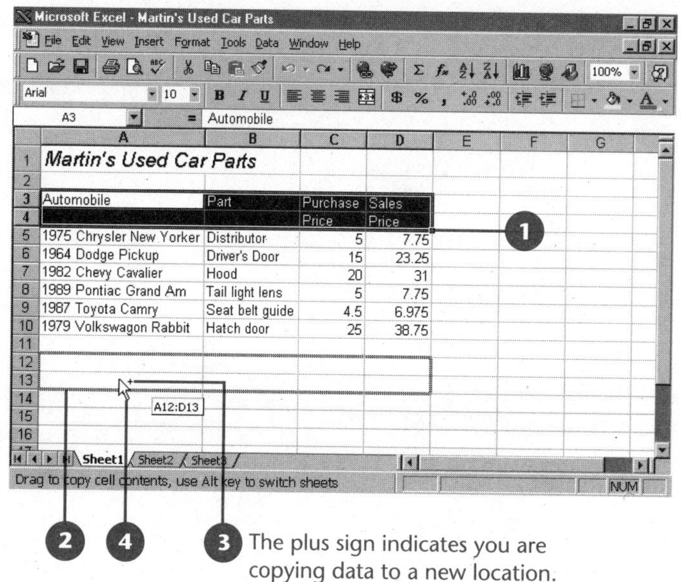

The plus sign indicates you are copying data to a new location.

3

Moving Cell Contents

Unlike copied data, information that has been moved is no longer in its original location. Perhaps you typed data in a range of cells and decided that you want it to be in another location. Moving data lets you change its location without having to retype it.

> **TIP**
>
> **The Clipboard changes when you copy or cut information.** *The contents of the Clipboard changes each time you copy or cut data. The most recent selection is available until you copy or cut another selection.*

> **SEE ALSO**
>
> *See "Copying Cell Contents" on page 38 for information on copying cell contents.*

Move Data Using the Clipboard

1. Select the cell or range that contains the data you want to move.
2. Click the Cut button on the Standard toolbar. An outline of the selected cells, called a *marquee*, shows the size of the selection. If you don't want to paste this selection, press Esc to remove the marquee.
3. Click the top leftmost cell of the range where you want to paste the data.
4. Click the Paste button on the Standard toolbar. The marquee disappears. The data is still in the Clipboard and still available for further pasting until you replace it with another selection.

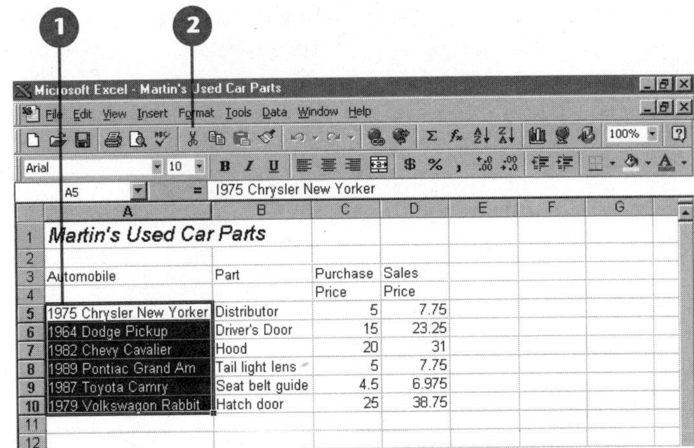

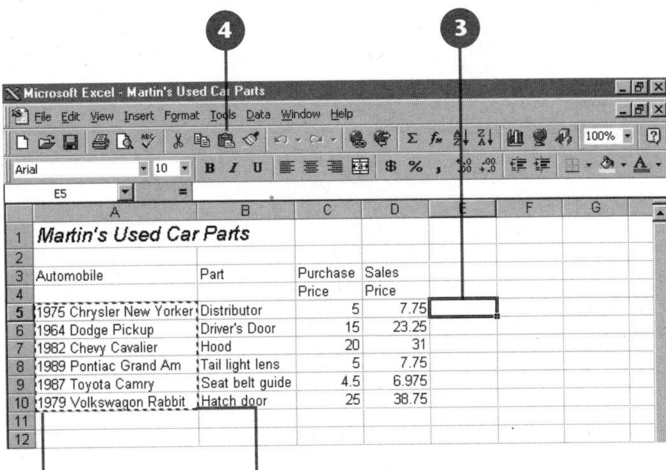

The marquee indicates the size of the selection.

The data will disappear from these cells after you paste the selection in its new location.

TIP

Reposition the mouse pointer to use drag-and-drop. *If the mouse pointer changes to a thick plus sign, reposition the pointer on the edge of the selected range until the pointer changes to an arrowhead.*

TIP

Different mouse pointer for moving data using drag-and-drop. *The mouse pointer for moving data using drag-and-drop looks identical to the pointer for copying, except that it does not have a plus to its right.*

Move Data Using Drag-and-Drop

1. Select the cell or range that contains the data you want to move.
2. Move the mouse pointer to an edge of the cell until the pointer changes to an arrowhead.
3. Press and hold the mouse button while dragging the selection to its new location, then release the mouse button.

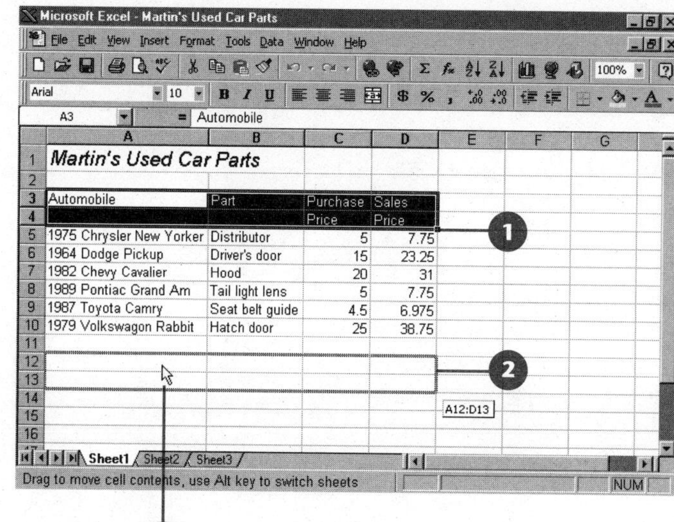

3

Inserting and Deleting a Cell

You can insert new, blank cells anywhere in the worksheet, so you can enter new data, or data you forgot to enter earlier, exactly where you want it. Inserting cells moves the remaining cells in the column or row in the direction of your choice and adjusts any formulas so they refer to the correct cells. You can also delete cells if you find you don't need them; deleting cells shifts the remaining cells to the left or up—just the opposite of inserting cells. When you delete a cell, Excel removes the actual cell from the worksheet.

SEE ALSO

See "Inserting a Column or Row" on page 62 or see "Deleting a Column or Row" on page 64 for more information about inserting and deleting in Excel.

Insert a Cell

1. Select the cell or cells where you want to insert the new cell(s). For example, to insert two blank cells at the position of C10 and C11, select cells C10 and C11.
2. Click the Insert menu, and then click Cells.
3. Click the option you want. If you want the contents of cells C10 and C11 to move to cells D10 and D11, click the Shift Cells Right option button, or if you want the contents of cells C10 and C11 to move to cells C12 and C13, click the Shift Cells Down option button. Either way, two blank cells are now at the position of C10 and C11.
4. Click OK.

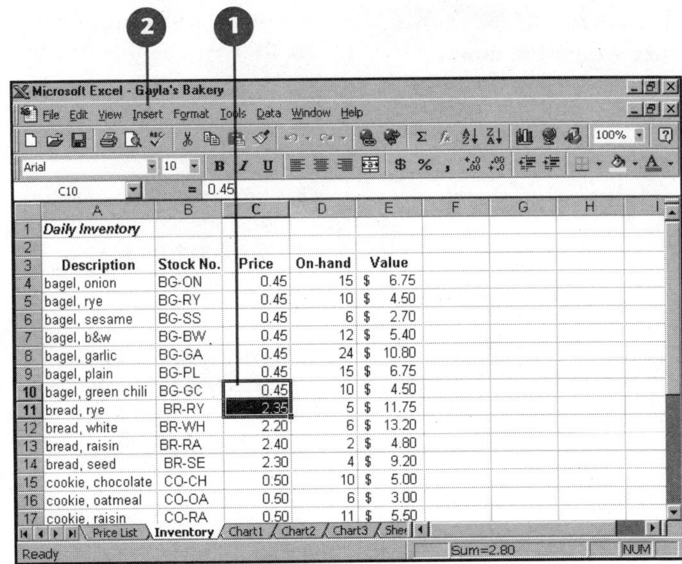

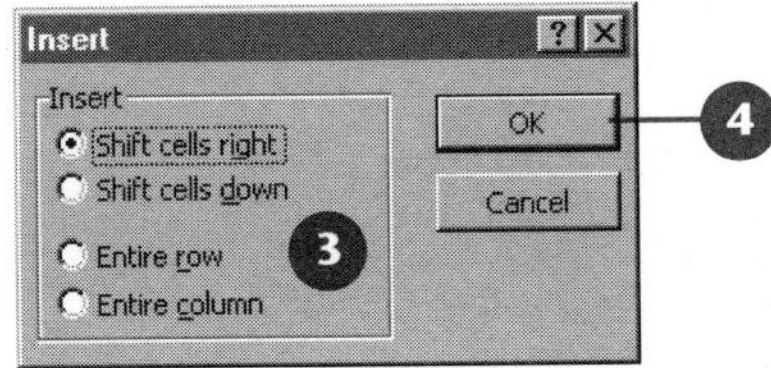

TIP

Deleting a cell vs. clearing a cell. *Deleting a cell is different from clearing a cell; deleting removes the cells from the worksheet, and clearing removes only the cell content or format or both.*

SEE ALSO

See "Clearing Cell Contents" on page 36 for more information on removing the contents of cells.

Delete a Cell

1. Select the cell or cells you want to delete.
2. Click the Edit menu, and then click Delete.
3. Click the option you want. If you want the remaining cells to move left, click the Shift Cells Left option button, or if you want the remaining cells to move up, click the Shift Cells Up option button.
4. Click OK.

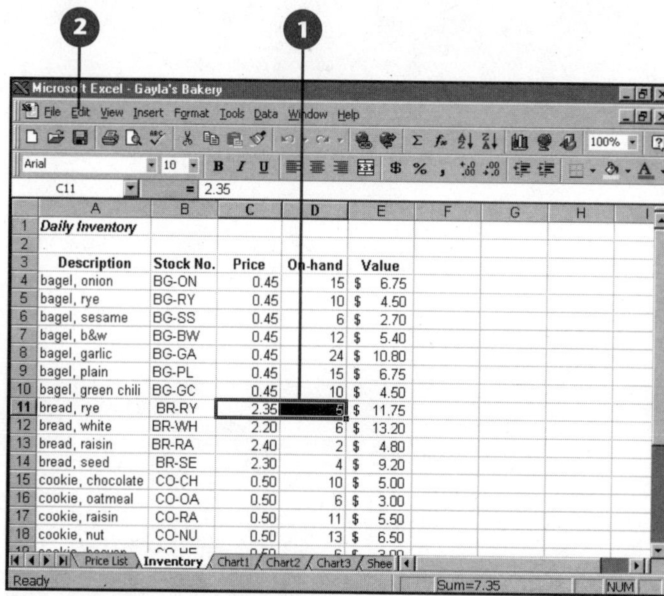

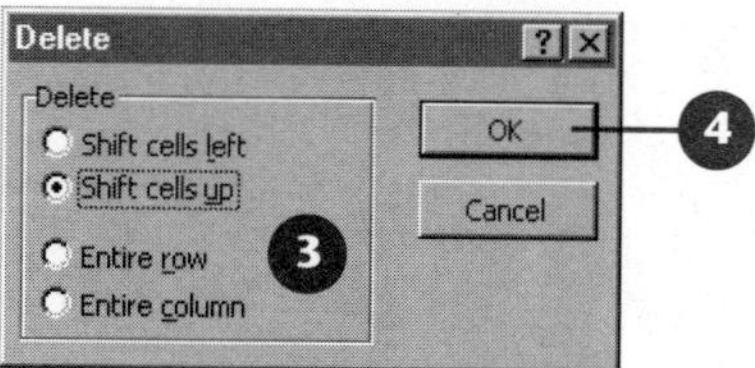

4

Working with Formulas

IN THIS SECTION

Creating a Simple Formula

Editing a Formula

Understanding Relative Cell Referencing

Using Absolute Cell References

Simplifying a Formula with Ranges

Using AutoCalculate

Performing Calculations Using Functions

Creating Functions

Once data is entered into worksheet cells, you'll want to enter formulas in other cells and make calculations. The results are always up-to-date no matter how often you change the data because Excel automatically recalculates the formulas. For complex computations, Excel includes built-in formulas, called *functions*, and a feature called the *Paste Function* helps you complete the functions, so you don't have to memorize each function.

Cell references within formulas generally change when that formula is copied to a new location. Sometimes, however, you'll want cell references to remain the same. Excel gives you the option of controlling how cell references are treated when they're copied.

Create a Simple Formula

A *formula* calculates values to return a result. In an Excel worksheet, you use values (such as *147* or *$10.00),* arithmetic operators (shown in the table), and cell references to create formulas. An Excel formula always begins with the equal sign (=). Although the formulas in the worksheet cells don't display, by default, you can change the view of the worksheet to display them.

TIP

Select a cell to enter its address to avoid careless typing mistakes. *Click a cell to insert its cell reference in a formula rather than typing its address.*

Enter a Formula

1. Click a cell where you want to enter a formula.
2. Type = (an equal sign) to begin the formula. If you do not begin a formula with an equal sign, Excel will display the information you type; it will not calculate it.
3. Enter the first argument. An *argument* can be a number or a cell reference. If it is a cell reference, you can type the reference or click the cell in the worksheet.
4. Enter an arithmetic operator.
5. Enter the next argument.
6. Repeat steps 4 and 5 to add to the formula.
7. Click the Enter button on the formula bar, or press Enter. Notice that the result of the formula appears in the cell and the formula appears in the formula bar.

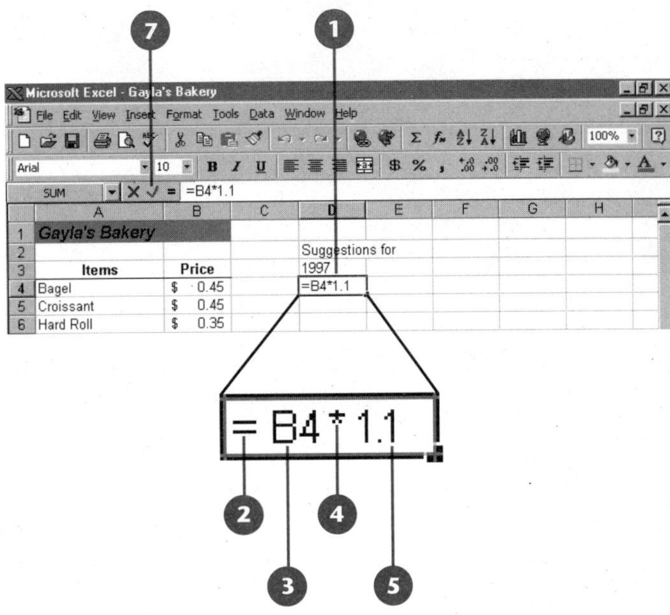

ARITHMETIC OPERATORS		
Symbol	**Operation**	**Example**
+	addition	=E3+F3
-	subtraction	=E3-F3
*	multiplication	=E3*F3
/	division	=E3/F3

TIP

Use the Order of Precedence to create correct formulas. *Formulas containing more than one arithmetic operator follow the order of precedence. Excel performs its calculations based on the following order: exponentiation, multiplication and division, and finally, addition and subtraction. For example, in the formula 5 + 2 * 3, Excel performs multiplication first (2*3) and addition after (5+6) for a result of 11. To change the order of precedence, use parentheses in a formula—Excel will calculate operations within parentheses first. Using parentheses, the result of (5 + 2) * 3 is 21.*

Display Formulas

1. Click the Tools menu, and then click Options.
2. Click the View tab.
3. Click to select the Formulas check box.
4. Click OK.

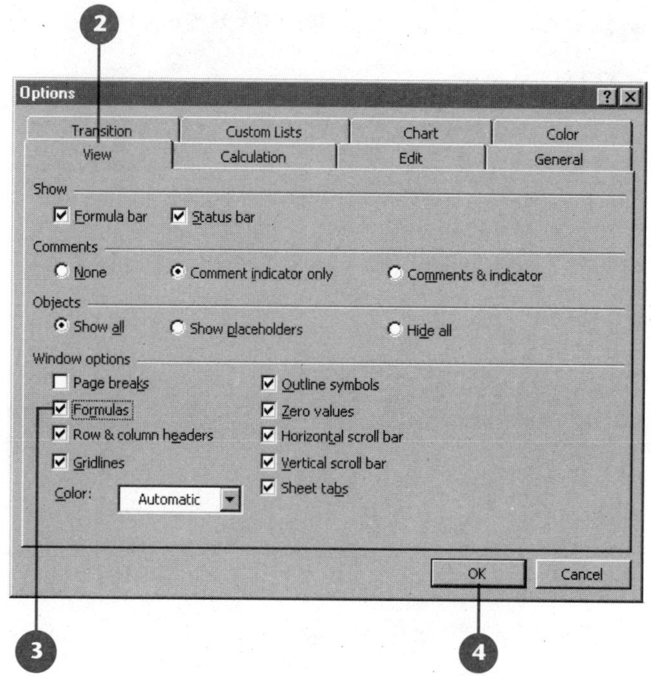

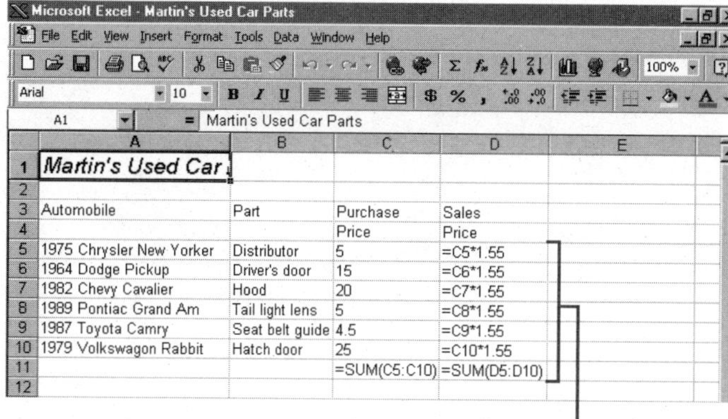

The formulas appear here.

4

Editing a Formula

You edit formulas just as you do other cell contents, using the formula bar or working in-cell. You can select, cut, copy, paste, delete, and format cells containing formulas just as you do cells containing labels or values. A special feature called the *fill handle* makes copying formulas to adjacent cells even easier than using the Clipboard.

TRY THIS

Copy a formula down a column. *If you're creating a worksheet, such as a budget, that contains several similar calculations, use the fill handle to copy a formula down a column, and watch how each formula adjusts to refer to the correct cells.*

Edit a Formula Using the Formula Bar

1. Select the cell that contains the formula you want to edit.
2. Press F2 to change to Edit mode.
3. Use the Backspace, Delete, Home, End, or arrow keys to move within the formula bar.
4. Make your corrections using the keyboard.
5. Click the Enter button on the formula bar, or press Enter.

An outline appears around the range in the formula.

		1996	1997	Total
15	1st Quarter	47,532	62,991	=SUM(B15:C15)
16	2nd Quarter	35,020	54,070	89,090
17	3rd Quarter	86,500	96,831	183,331
18	4th Quarter	52,060	42,009	94,069

Sheet1 / Sheet2 / Sheet3 / Locator / Payroll

Edit

2 The status bar indicates the edit mode.

Copy a Formula Using the Fill Handle

1. Select the cell that contains the formula you want to copy.
2. Point to the lower right corner of the selected cell until the pointer changes to a black plus sign.
3. Drag the mouse down until the adjacent cells where you want the formula pasted are selected, and then release the mouse button.

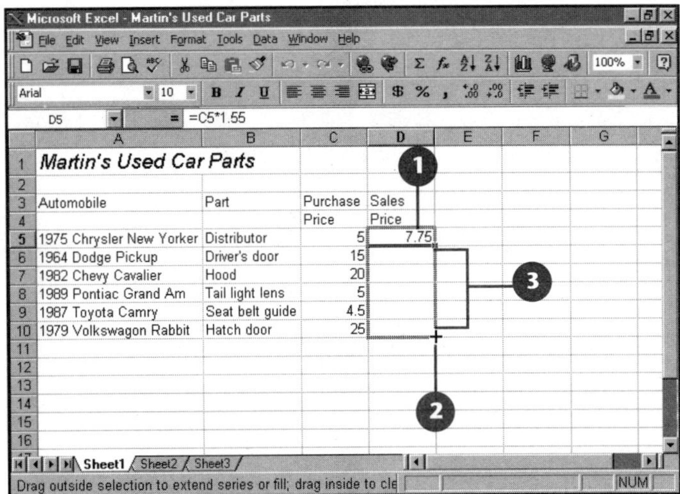

SEE ALSO

See "Editing Cell Contents" on page 32 for more information on editing the contents of a cell.

SEE ALSO

See "Copying Cell Contents" on page 38 or "Moving Cell Contents on page 40 for more information on copying and moving cell contents.

Copy a Formula Using the Clipboard

1. Select the cell that contains the formula you want to copy.
2. Click the Copy button on the Standard toolbar.
3. Select one or more cells where you want to paste the formula.
4. Click the Paste button on the Standard toolbar.

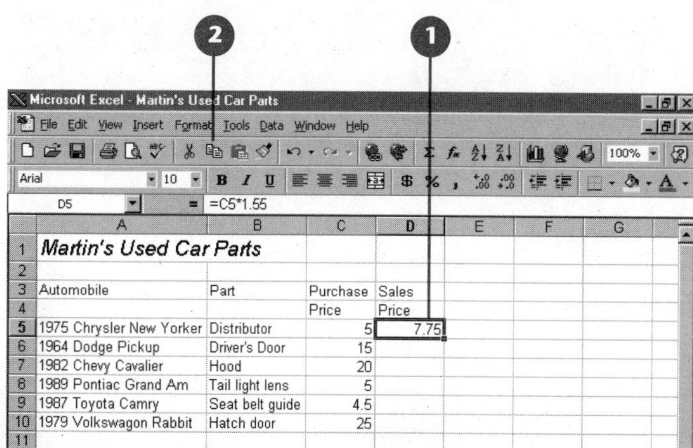

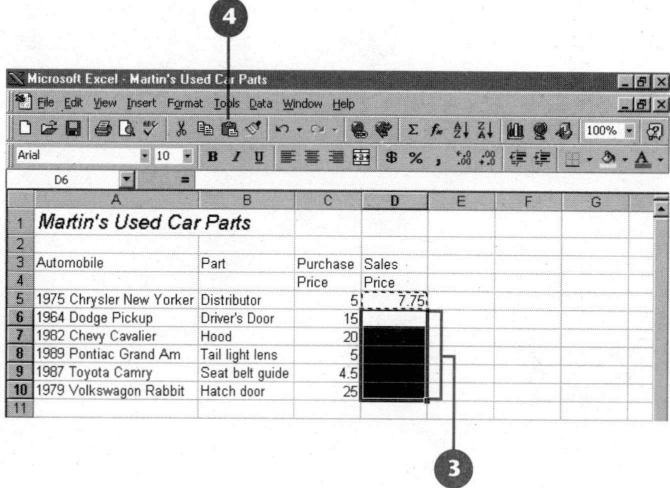

Understanding Relative Cell Referencing

By default, cell addresses in formulas change when you copy or move them to new locations. When you paste or drag a formula to a new location, the cell references in the formula adjust automatically relative to their new locations to calculate the same formula with the information in the new cells. For example, when you copy the formula =D3+D4 in cell D5 to cell E5, the cell references change automatically to =E3+E4. This automatic adjustment is called *relative addressing*. Relative addressing can save you the trouble of creating new formulas for each row or column in a worksheet filled with repetitive information.

D6 = =SUM(B6:C6)

	A	B	C	D	E
1	*Martin's Used Car Parts*				
2	Sales Summary				
3					
4					
5		**1996**	**1997**	**Total**	
6	1st Quarter	47,532	62,991	110,523	
7	2nd Quarter	35,020	54,070	89,090	
8	3rd Quarter	86,500	96,831	183,331	
9	4th Quarter	52,060	42,009	94,069	
10	Total	223,108	257,898	477,013	
11					

These formulas are identical to the one in D6, but one adjusted relative to their location.

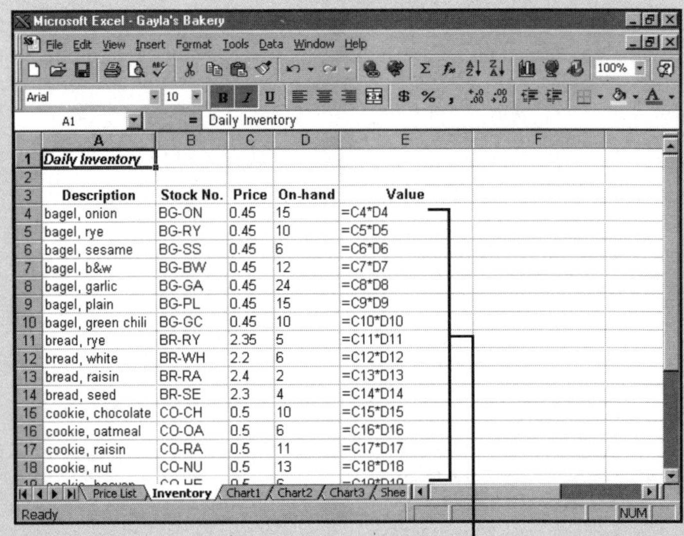

	A	B	C	D	E
1	*Daily Inventory*				
2					
3	**Description**	**Stock No.**	**Price**	**On-hand**	**Value**
4	bagel, onion	BG-ON	0.45	15	=C4*D4
5	bagel, rye	BG-RY	0.45	10	=C5*D5
6	bagel, sesame	BG-SS	0.45	6	=C6*D6
7	bagel, b&w	BG-BW	0.45	12	=C7*D7
8	bagel, garlic	BG-GA	0.45	24	=C8*D8
9	bagel, plain	BG-PL	0.45	15	=C9*D9
10	bagel, green chili	BG-GC	0.45	10	=C10*D10
11	bread, rye	BR-RY	2.35	5	=C11*D11
12	bread, white	BR-WH	2.2	6	=C12*D12
13	bread, raisin	BR-RA	2.4	2	=C13*D13
14	bread, seed	BR-SE	2.3	4	=C14*D14
15	cookie, chocolate	CO-CH	0.5	10	=C15*D15
16	cookie, oatmeal	CO-OA	0.5	6	=C16*D16
17	cookie, raisin	CO-RA	0.5	11	=C17*D17
18	cookie, nut	CO-NU	0.5	13	=C18*D18

Each section is identical, but modified for its row.

Using Absolute Cell References

When you need to refer to a particular cell in a formula, even if you copy or move the formula elsewhere in the worksheet, you need to use an *absolute cell reference*. An absolute cell reference contains a dollar sign ($) to the left of the column or row reference.

TIP

Use the F4 key to edit a formula. *When you edit a formula to make a cell reference absolute, position the insertion point in the cell reference you want to change, and then press the F4 key. The cell reference will become absolute.*

TRY THIS

Edit a cell reference in a formula. *Select a cell with an absolute reference, and then press the F4 key several times. The cell coordinates that are absolute will change. You can make the row or the column coordinate absolute, not necessarily the whole cell address.*

Use an Absolute Reference

1. Click a cell where you want to enter a formula.
2. Type = (an equal sign) to begin the formula. Use the formula in the figure as an example.
3. Select a cell, and then type + (an arithmetic operator).
4. Select another cell, and press F4 to make that cell reference absolute.
5. If necessary, continue entering the formula.
6. Click the Enter button on the formula bar, or press Enter.

Even if you move or copy this formula to another location, this cell reference will not change.

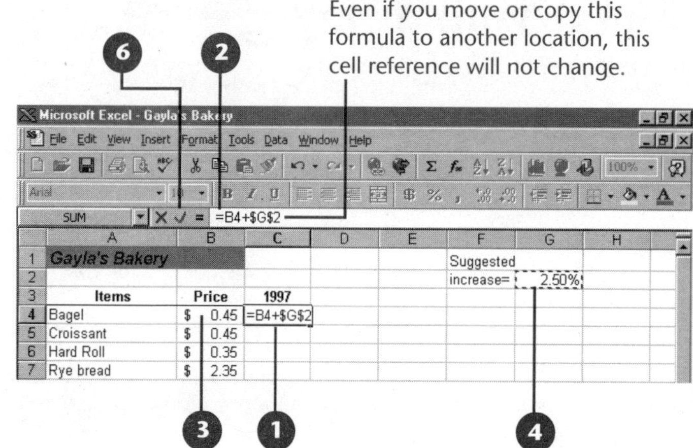

4

Simplifying a Formula with Ranges

You can simplify formulas by using ranges and range names. For example, if 12 cells in your worksheet contain monthly budget amounts, and you want to multiply each amount by 10%, you can insert one range address in a formula instead of inserting 12 different cell addresses, or you can insert a range name. Using a range name in a formula helps to identify what the formula does; the formula =1997 SALES * .10, for example, is more meaningful than =D7:O7*.10.

SEE ALSO

See "Selecting Multiple Cells" on page 34 for more information on selecting and naming a range.

SEE ALSO

See "Creating a Simple Formula" on page 46 for more information on creating a formula.

Use a Range in a Formula

1. Type an equal sign (=) to begin the formula.
2. Click the first cell of the range, and then drag to select the last cell in the range. Excel enters the range address for you.
3. Complete the formula, and then click the Enter button on the formula bar or press Enter.

Use a Range Name in a Formula

1. Type an equal sign (=) to begin the formula.
2. Press F3 to display a list of named ranges.
3. Click the name of the range you want to insert.
4. Click OK in the Paste Name dialog box.
5. Complete the formula, and then click the Enter button on the formula bar or press Enter.

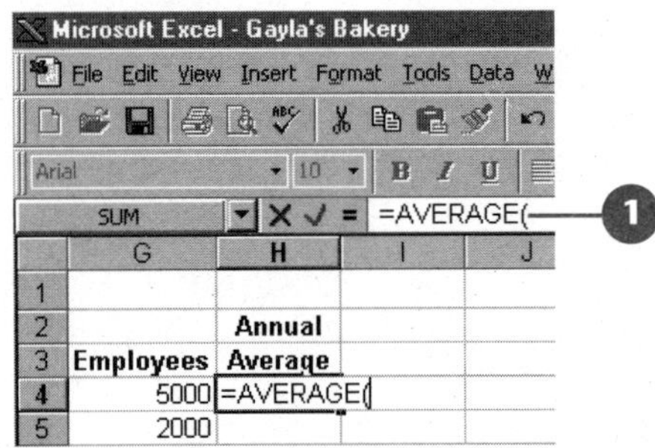

Using AutoCalculate

You can simplify your work using a feature called AutoCalculate when you don't want to insert a formula, you just want to see the results of a simple calculation quickly. *AutoCalculate* is a feature that automatically displays the sum, average, maximum, minimum, or count in the status bar of values in whatever cells you select. This result does not appear on the worksheet when printed but is useful for giving you a quick answer while you work.

TRY THIS

Calculate a result with AutoCalculate. *Use AutoCalculate on a range of cells to get a average without entering a formula.*

Calculate a Range Automatically

1. Select the range of cells you want to calculate. The sum of the selected cells appears in the status bar next to SUM=.
2. If you want to change the type of calculation AutoCalculate performs, right-click the AutoCalculate display in the status bar.
3. Click the type of calculation you want.

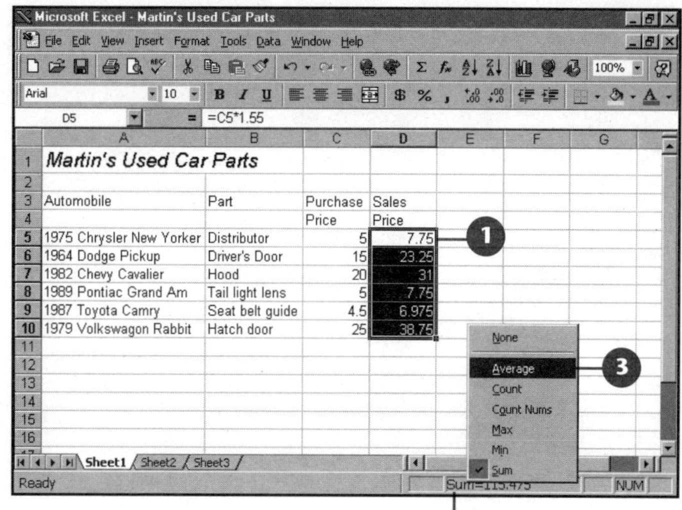

4

Performing Calculations Using Functions

Functions are predesigned formulas that save you the time and trouble of creating a commonly used equation. Excel includes hundreds of functions that you can use alone or in combination with other formulas or functions. Functions perform a variety of tasks from adding, averaging, and counting to more complicated tasks, such as calculating the monthly payment amount of a loan. You can enter a function manually if you know its name and all the required arguments, or you can easily insert a function using the Paste Function.

SEE ALSO

See "Creating Functions" on page 55 for more information on entering a function using the Paste Function.

Enter a Function

1. Click the cell where you want to enter the function.
2. Type = (an equal sign), type the name of the function, and then type (, an opening parenthesis. For example, to insert the SUM function, type =SUM(.
3. Type the argument or click the cell or range you want to insert in the function.
4. Click the Enter button on the formula bar or press Enter. Excel will automatically add the closing parenthesis to complete the function.

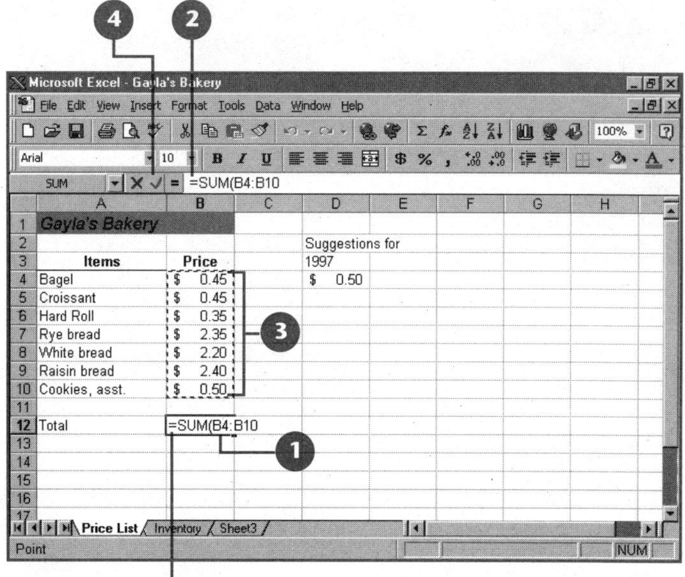

A function always begins with an equal sign.

COMMONLY USED EXCEL FUNCTIONS		
Function	**Description**	**Sample**
SUM	Displays the sum of the argument	=SUM(*argument*)
AVERAGE	Displays the average value in the argument	=AVERAGE(*argument*)
COUNT	Calculates the number of values in the argument	=COUNT(*argument*)
MAX	Determines the largest value in the argument	=MAX(*argument*)
MIN	Determines the smallest value in the argument	=MIN(*argument*)
PMT	Determines the monthly payment in a loan	=PMT(*argument*)

Creating Functions

Trying to write a formula that calculates various pieces of data, such as calculating payments for an investment over a period of time at a certain rate, can be difficult and time-consuming. The Paste Function feature makes it easy to create complicated formulas by providing built-in formulas called functions. A function defines all the necessary components you need to produce a specific result; all you have to do is supply the values, cell references, and other variables. You can even combine one or more functions if necessary.

Paste Function button

Enter a Function Using the Paste Function

1. Click the cell where you want to enter the formula.
2. Click the Paste Function button on the Standard toolbar.
3. In the Function Category box, click a function category you want to use.
4. In the Function Name box, click a function you want to use.
5. Click OK.
6. Enter the cell addresses in the text boxes either by typing them or by clicking the Collapse Dialog button to the right of the text box, and then selecting the range using your mouse. In many cases, the Paste Function might try to "guess" which cells you want to include in the function.
7. Click OK.

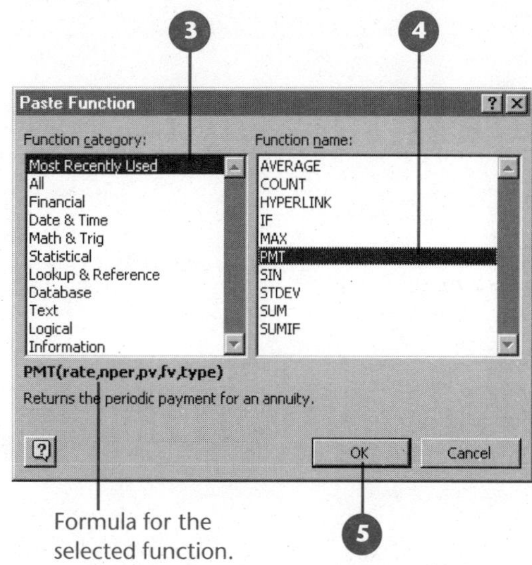

Formula for the selected function.

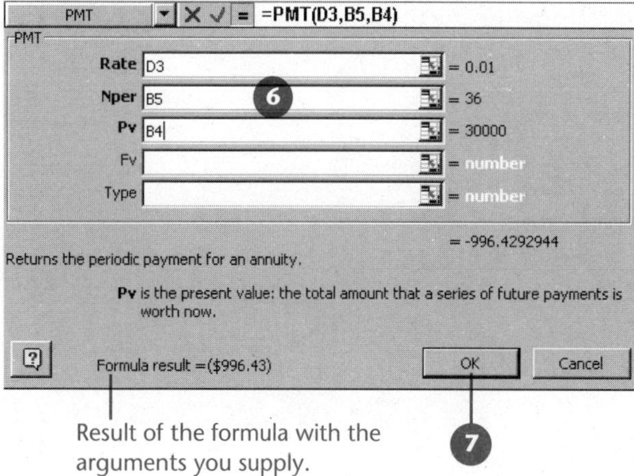

Result of the formula with the arguments you supply.

4

5

Modifying Worksheets and Workbooks

IN THIS SECTION

Selecting and Naming a Worksheet

Inserting and Deleting a Worksheet

Moving and Copying a Worksheet

Inserting a Column or Row

Deleting a Column or Row

Hiding a Column or Row

Adjusting Column Width and Row Height

Setting Up the Page

Adding a Header or Footer

Customizing Print Settings

Saving Print Settings

Making changes in a workbook is inevitable—it's just not possible to think of everything your workbook will need from the start. In addition to editing the data in a workbook, you can change the workbook itself as you work.

You can reorganize a workbook by adding, deleting, moving, and renaming worksheets. Within any worksheet, you can insert and delete cells, rows and columns, and adjust column width and row height, so that you can structure the worksheet exactly the way you want. It's easy to make as many changes as you want because Excel automatically updates existing formulas whenever you modify a worksheet.

A combination of print settings, such as margins, hidden columns and rows, paper orientation, and headers and footers, can be saved and then reused, saving time and adding to your efficiency.

Selecting and Naming a Worksheet

Each new workbook you open has three workbook sheets. You can switch from sheet to sheet by clicking the sheet tab. Clicking the sheet tab makes that sheet *active*. Each of the sheets is named consecutively—Sheet1, Sheet2, and Sheet3. You can give a sheet a more meaningful name, and the size of the sheet tab automatically accommodates the name's length.

TIP

Use short sheet tab names to save screen space. *Because the size of a sheet tab enlarges to accommodate a longer name, using short names means more sheet tabs will be visible. This is especially important if a workbook contains several worksheets.*

Select a Sheet

1. Click the sheet tab to make it the active worksheet.

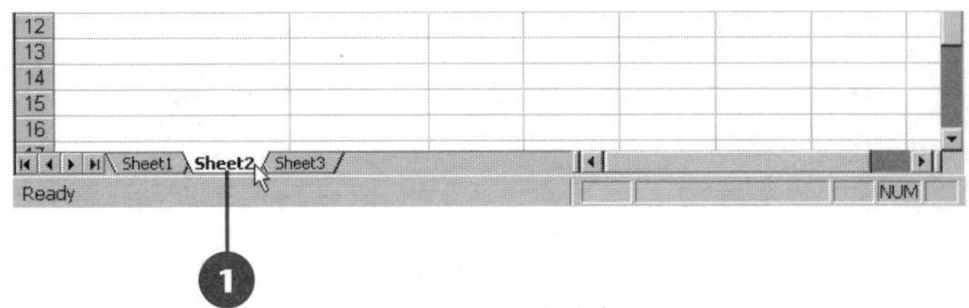

Name a Sheet

1. Double-click the sheet tab you want to name.
2. Type a new name. The current name, which is selected, is automatically replaced when you begin typing.
3. Press Enter.

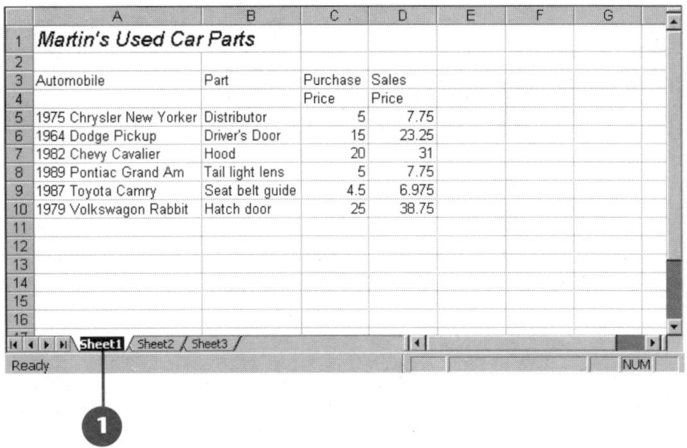

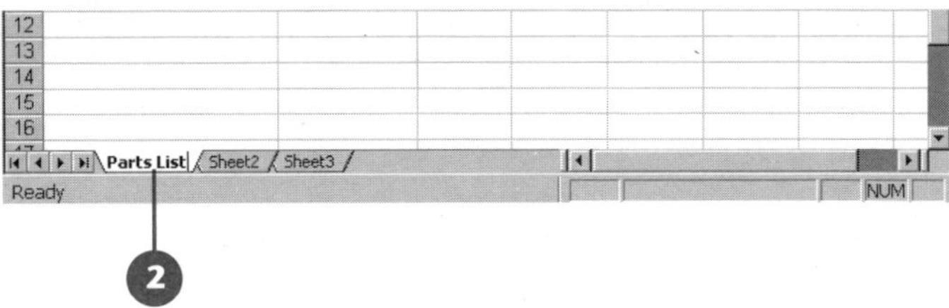

Inserting and Deleting a Worksheet

You can add or delete sheets in a workbook. If you were working on a project that involved more than three worksheets, you could add sheets to a workbook rather than use multiple workbooks. That way, all your related information would be in one file. Deleting unused sheets saves disk space.

SEE ALSO

See "Moving and Copying a Worksheet" on page 60 for information on reorganizing sheets in a worksheet.

Insert a Worksheet

1. Click the sheet tab (or select any cell in a worksheet) to the right, or *in front of,* where you want to insert the new sheet.
2. Click the Insert menu, and then click Worksheet. A new worksheet will be inserted to the left, or *behind,* of the selected worksheet.

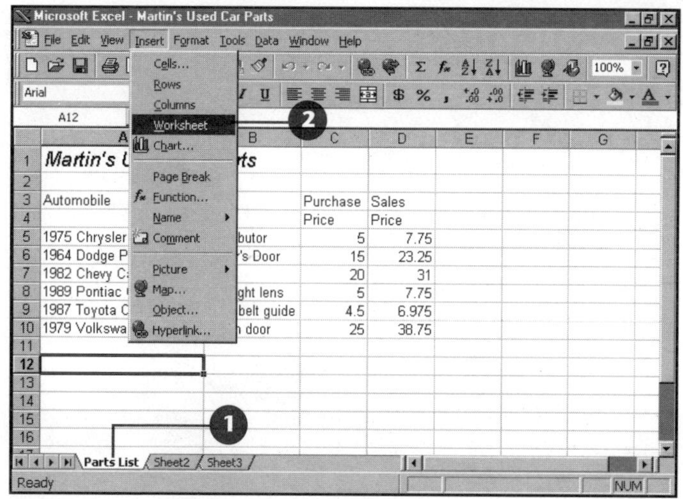

Delete a Worksheet

1. Select any cell in the worksheet you want to delete.
2. Click the Edit menu, and then click Delete Sheet.
3. Click OK to confirm the deletion.

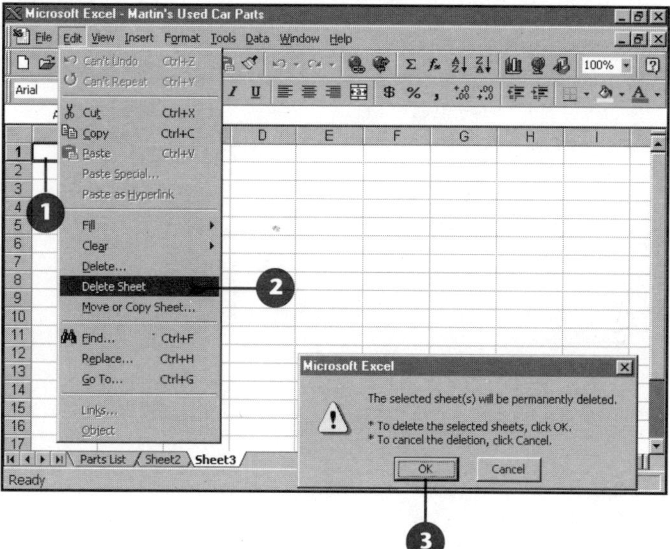

Moving and Copying a Worksheet

After adding several sheets to a workbook, you might want to reorganize them. You can easily move a sheet within a workbook or to another workbook by dragging it to a new location. You can also copy a worksheet within a workbook or to another workbook. Copying a worksheet is easier and often more convenient than having to reenter similar information in a new sheet. The ability to move and copy whole worksheets means you can have your workbooks set up exactly the way you want them, without having to do a lot of needless typing.

Move a Sheet

1. Click the sheet tab of the worksheet you want to move, and then press and hold the mouse button. The mouse pointer changes to a small sheet.
2. Drag the pointer to the right, or in front of the sheet tab where you want to move the worksheet.
3. Release the mouse button.

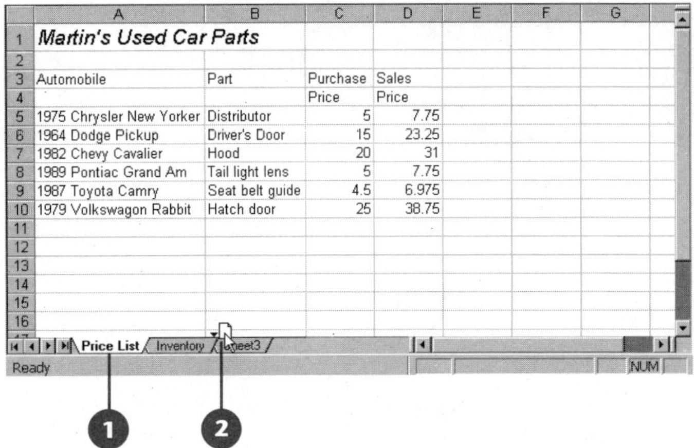

	A	B	C	D	E	F	G
1	*Martin's Used Car Parts*						
2							
3	Automobile	Part	Purchase	Sales			
4			Price	Price			
5	1975 Chrysler New Yorker	Distributor	5	7.75			
6	1964 Dodge Pickup	Driver's Door	15	23.25			
7	1982 Chevy Cavalier	Hood	20	31			
8	1989 Pontiac Grand Am	Tail light lens	5	7.75			
9	1987 Toyota Camry	Seat belt guide	4.5	6.975			
10	1979 Volkswagon Rabbit	Hatch door	25	38.75			
11							
12							
13							
14							
15							
16							

Inventory | **Price List** | Sheet3

Ready NUM

3

SEE ALSO

See "Copying Cell Contents" on page 38 and "Moving Cell Contents" on page 40 for additional information on copying and moving data in cells.

TIP

Use the Create A Copy check box to move a worksheet. *Deselect the Create A Copy checkbox in the Move or Copy dialog box to move a worksheet.*

Copy a Sheet

1. Click the sheet tab of the worksheet you want to copy.
2. Click the Edit menu, and then click Move Or Copy Sheet.
3. If you want to copy the sheet to another workbook, click the To Book drop-down arrow, and select that workbook. The sheets of the selected workbook appear in the Before Sheet box.
4. Click a sheet name in the Before Sheet list. The copy will be inserted before this sheet.
5. Click the Create A Copy check box to activate the function.
6. Click OK.

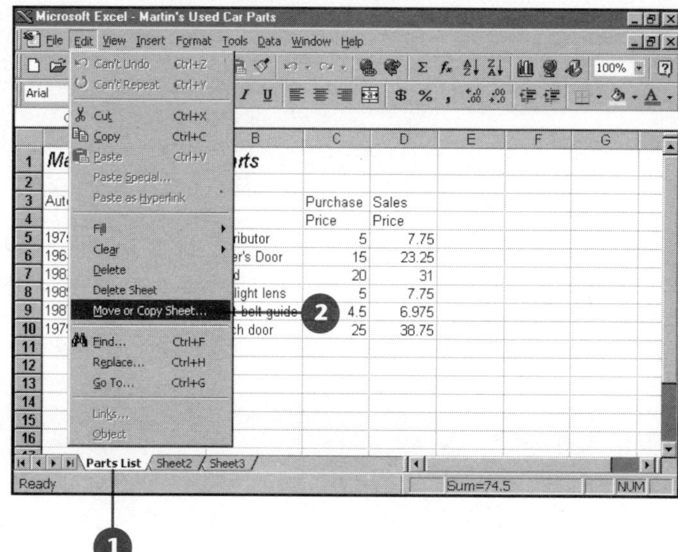

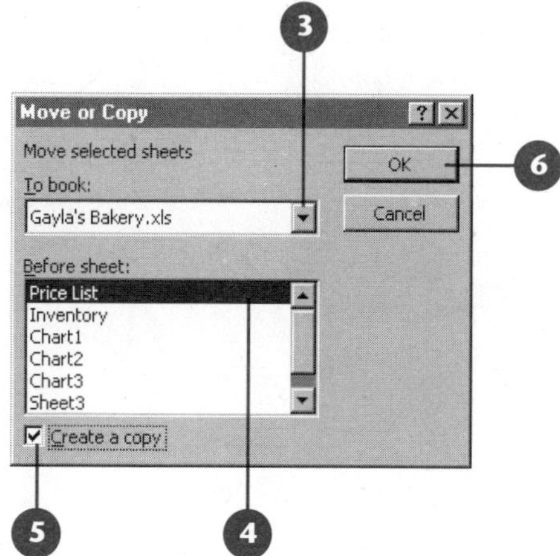

5

Inserting a Column or Row

You can insert blank columns and rows in a worksheet between columns or rows that are already filled without deleting and retyping anything. When you insert one or more columns, they are inserted to the left of the selected column. When you add one or more rows, they are inserted above the selected row. Excel repositions existing cells to accommodate the new columns and rows and adjusts any existing formulas so that they refer to the correct cells.

SEE ALSO

See "Inserting and Deleting a Cell" on page 42 for information about inserting individual cells.

Insert a Column

1. Click anywhere in the column to the right of the location of the new column you want to insert.
2. Click the Insert menu, and then click Columns.

   A column inserts to the left of the selected cell or column.

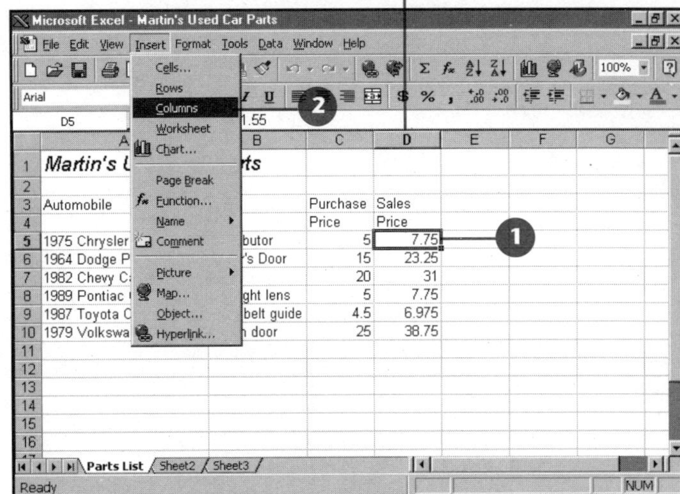

Insert a Row

1. Click anywhere in the row immediately below the location of the row you want to insert.
2. Click the Insert menu, and then click Rows.

   A row inserts above the selected cell or row.

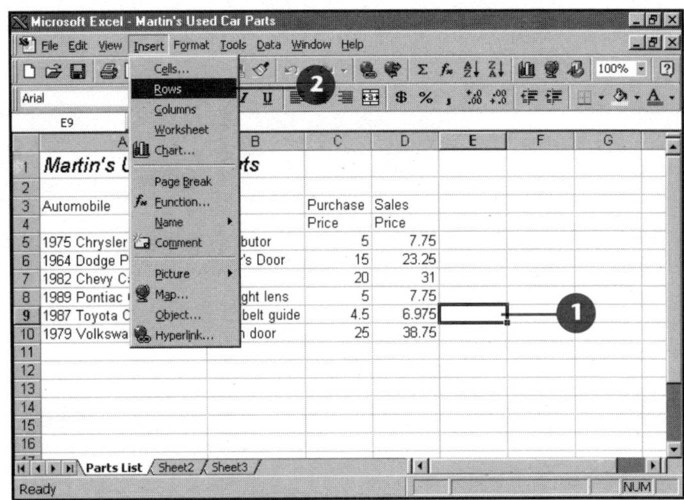

TIP

The Insert menu changes depending on what you select. *Clicking a column indicator button selects an entire column; then only the Columns command is available on the Insert menu. Clicking a row selector button selects an entire row; then only the Rows command is available on the Insert menu.*

Insert Multiple Columns or Rows

1. To add multiple columns, drag to select the *column indicator* buttons—the buttons containing the column letter in the worksheet frame—for the number of columns to be inserted.

   To add multiple rows, drag to select the *row indicator* buttons—the buttons containing the row number in the worksheet frame—for the number of rows to be inserted.

2. Click the Insert menu, and then Columns, or click the Insert menu, and then click Rows.

   The number of columns or rows selected are inserted.

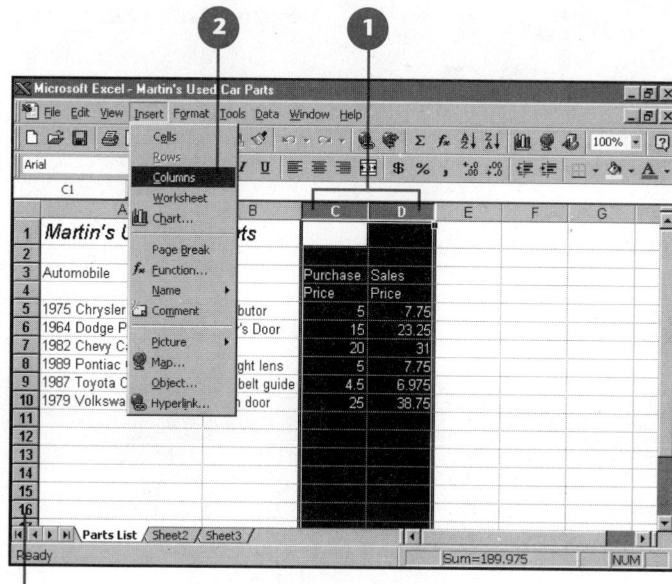

Row Indicator button

5

Deleting a Column or Row

At some time, you may find that you have information in a worksheet that is incorrect or irrelevant. When this happens, unnecessary columns or rows of data can be deleted. You can delete columns and rows just as easily as you can insert them. Remaining columns and rows move to left or up to join the other remaining cells.

SEE ALSO

See "Inserting and Deleting a Worksheet" on page 59 for more information about deleting a worksheet.

SEE ALSO

See "Inserting and Deleting a Cell" on page 42 for more information about using the Edit Delete command.

Delete a Column

1. Click the column indicator button of the column(s) you want to delete.
2. Click the Edit menu, and then click Delete.

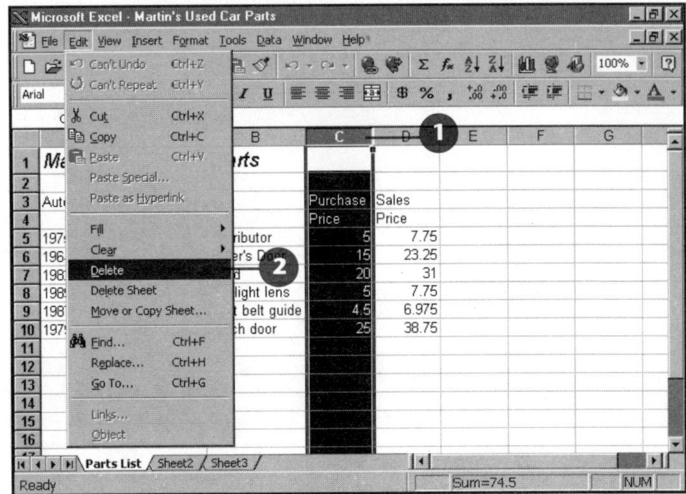

Delete a Row

1. Click the row indicator button for the row(s) you want to delete.
2. Click the Edit menu, and then click Delete.

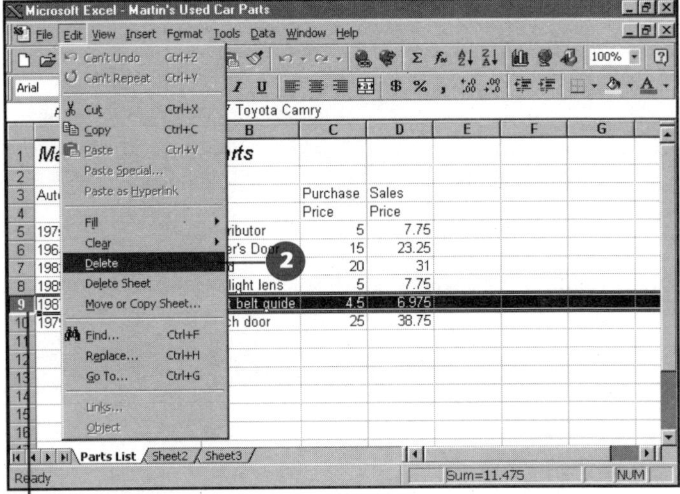

Hiding a Column or Row

Not all the data in a worksheet should be available to everyone. You can hide sensitive information without having to permanently delete it by hiding selected columns or rows. For example, if you have a worksheet that lists employee salaries, you can still use the worksheet without having to delete this information. You can hide columns and rows without affecting formulas within a worksheet; all data within hidden columns and rows are still referenced by formulas—they just aren't visible. (Hidden columns and rows do not appear in a printout, either.)

SEE ALSO

See "Inserting a Column or Row" on page 62 or see "Deleting a Column or Row" on page 64 for information about selecting rows and columns.

Hide a Column

1. Click the column indicator button of the column you want to hide. (Select multiple column indicator buttons to hide more than one column.)
2. Click the Format menu, point to Column, and then click Hide.

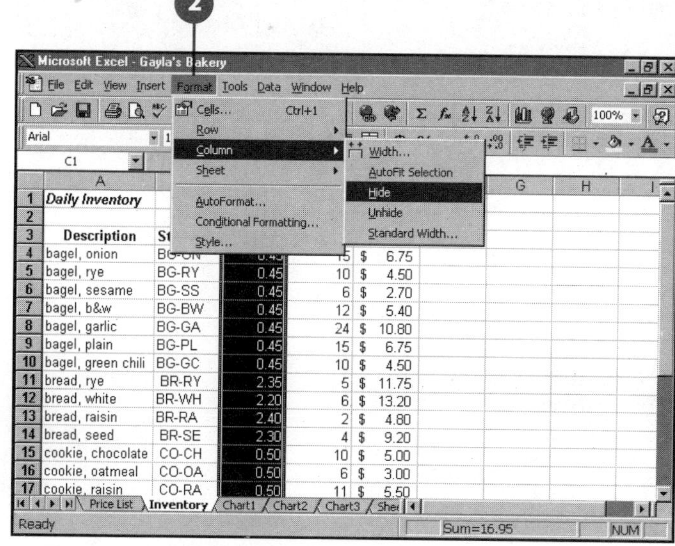

Hide a Row

1. Click the row indicator button for the row you want to hide. (Select multiple row indicator buttons to hide more than one row.)
2. Click the Format menu, point to Row, and then click Hide.

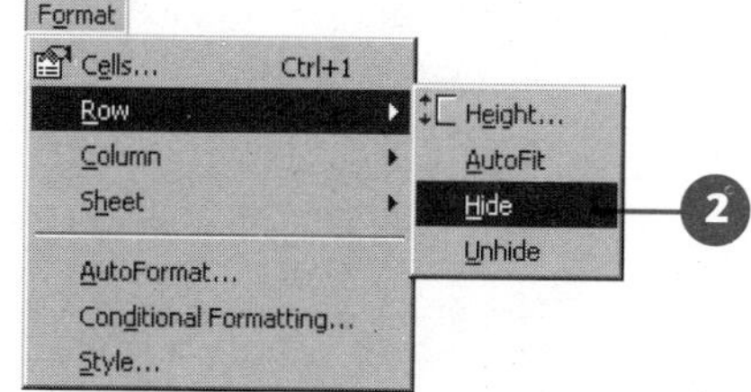

Adjusting Column Width and Row Height

As you're working with Excel, you'll want to change the default width of some columns or the default height of some rows to accommodate long strings of data or larger font sizes. You can use the *AutoFit* feature to have Excel adjust column or row size automatically to fit the data you have entered, or you can manually change column widths or row heights.

Change Column Width Using AutoFit

1. Position the mouse between the column indicator buttons of the column you want to change and the one to its right. The mouse pointer changes to a double-sided arrow.
2. Double-click the mouse button.

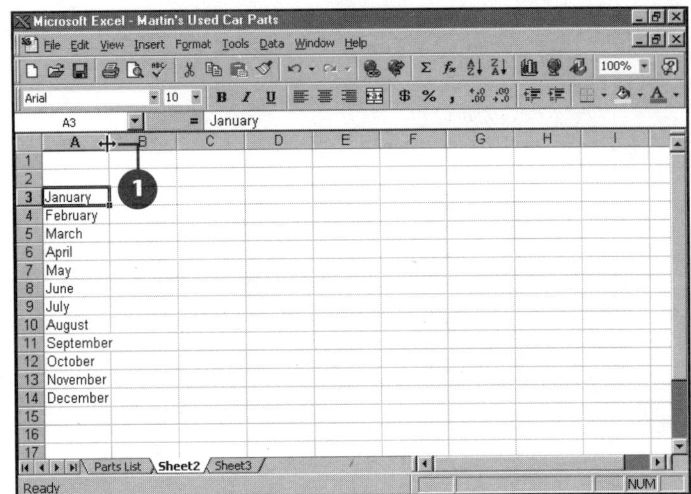

Change Row Height Using AutoFit

1. Position the mouse between the row indicator buttons of the row you want to change and the one beneath it. The mouse pointer changes to a double-sided arrow.
2. Double-click the mouse button.

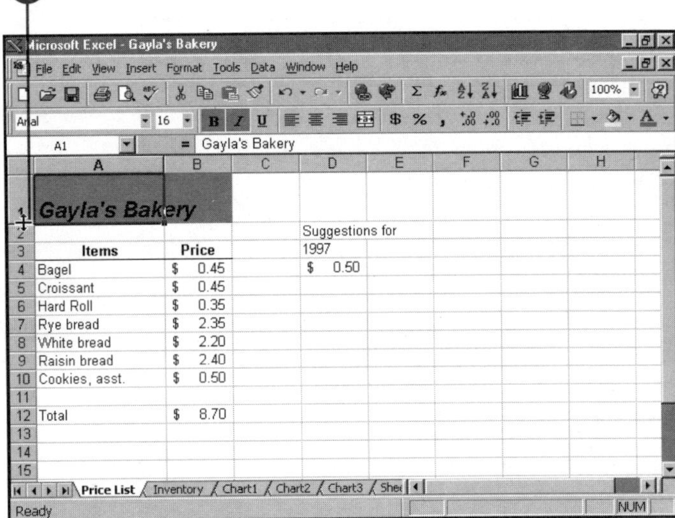

TIP

Default column width and row height. *By default, each column in each worksheet is 8.43 points wide, and each row is 12.75 points high.*

SEE ALSO

See "Formatting Data with AutoFormat" on page 88 for more information about formatting data quickly.

Adjust Column Width or Row Height Using the Mouse

1. To change a column width or row height, position the mouse pointer between the indicator buttons of the column or row you want to change. When the mouse pointer changes to a double-headed arrow, click and drag the pointer to a new width or height.

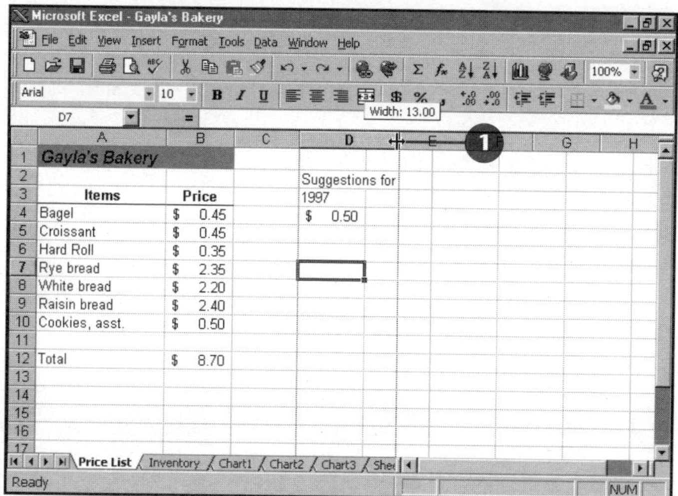

Change Column Width or Row Height Using the Menu

1. Click anywhere in the column or row you want to adjust.
2. Click the Format menu, point to Column, and then click Width or click the Format menu, point to Row, and then click Height.
3. Type a new column width or row height.
4. Click OK.

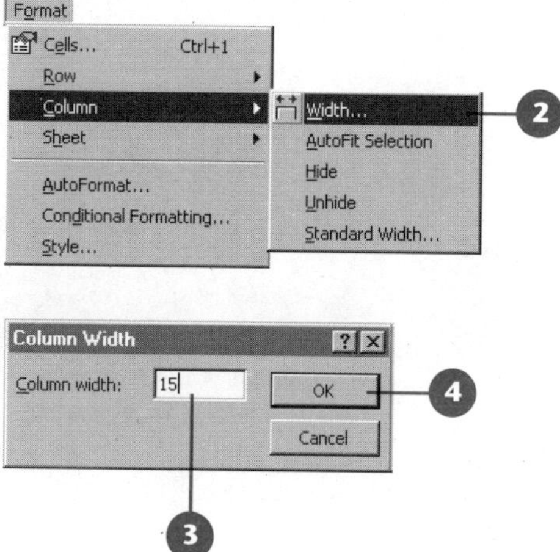

5

Setting Up the Page

You can set up the worksheet page so that it prints just the way you want. With the Page Setup dialog box, you can choose the *page orientation,* which determines how the worksheet data prints on a page, vertically or horizontally; change the *print scaling,* which reduces or enlarges the size of printed characters; choose the *paper size* to match the size of paper in your printer; specify the left, right, top, and bottom *margins,* which are the blank areas around the edges of the paper.

TIP

Changes made in the Page Setup dialog box are not reflected in the worksheet window. *You can only see them when previewing or printing the worksheet.*

Change the Page Orientation

1. Click the File menu, and then click Page Setup.
2. Click the Page tab.
3. Click the Portrait (8.5 x 11) option button (the default) or click the Landscape (11 x 8.5) option button to select page orientation.
4. Click OK.

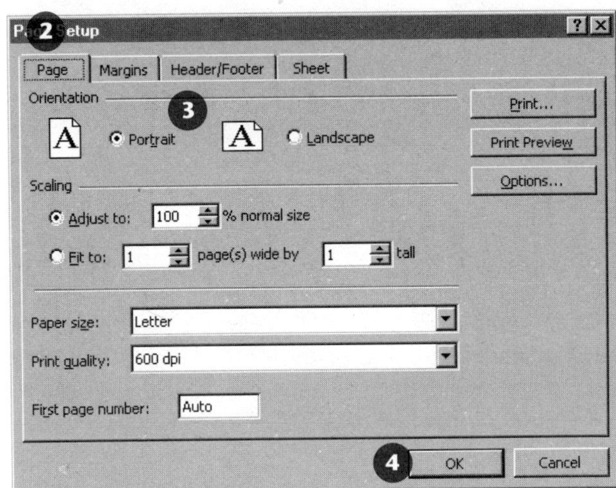

Change the Margin Settings

1. Click the File menu, and then click Page Setup.
2. Click the Margins tab.
   - Click the Top, Bottom, Left, and Right spin arrows to adjust the margins.
   - Click the Center On Page check boxes to automatically center data relative to the left and right margins (horizontally) or the top and bottom margins (vertically).
3. Click OK.

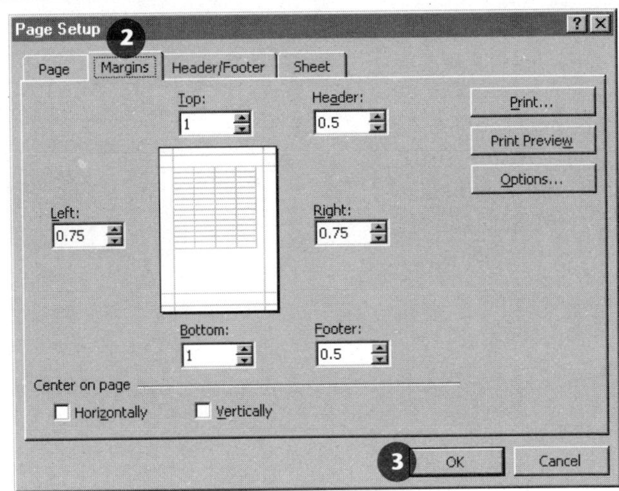

Adding a Header or Footer

Adding a header or footer to a workbook makes your work easier for readers to manage and look more professional. With the Page Setup command, you can add header and footer information such as the page number, worksheet title, or current date at the top and bottom of each page or section of a worksheet or workbook. Using header and footer buttons, your pages can include your computer's system date and time, the page number, the name of the workbook and sheet, and other custom information.

Change a Header or Footer

1. Click the File menu, and then click Page Setup.
2. Click the Header/Footer tab.
3. If the Header box doesn't contain the information you want, click Custom Header.
4. Type the information in the left, middle, or right text boxes, or click a button icon to insert built-in header information.

   If you don't want a header to appear at all, delete the text and codes in the text boxes.
5. Select any text you want to format, and then click the Font button.
6. Click OK.
7. If the Footer box doesn't contain the information that you want, click Custom Footer.
8. Type the information in the left, middle, or right text boxes, or click a button icon to insert the built-in footer information.
9. Click OK.
10. Click OK.

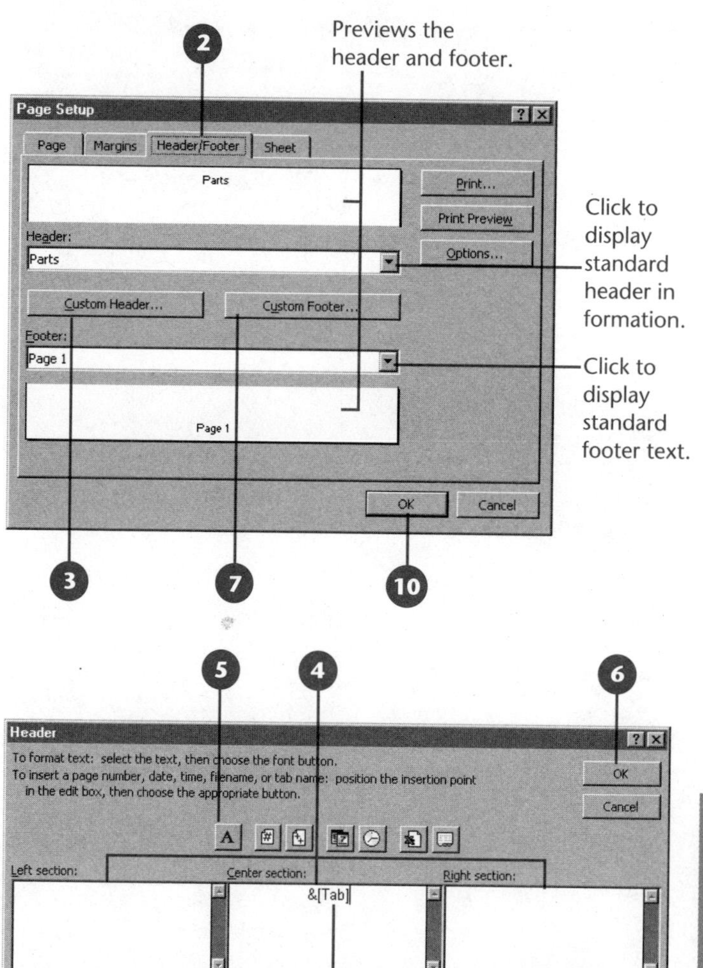

5

Customizing Print Settings

At some point you'll want to print out your work so you can distribute it to others, or use it for other purposes. You can print all or part of any worksheet, and control the appearance of many features, such as the gridlines that display on the screen, whether the column letters and row numbers display, or whether some columns and rows are repeated on each page.

SEE ALSO

See "Selecting Multiple Cells" on page 34 for more information about selecting a range of cells.

Print Part of a Worksheet

1. Click the File menu, and click Page Setup.
2. Click the Sheet tab.
3. Click in the Print Area text box, and then type the range you want to print, or click the Collapse dialog button, drag the mouse over the cells you want to print, then click the Collapse dialog button again to restore the dialog box.
4. Click OK.

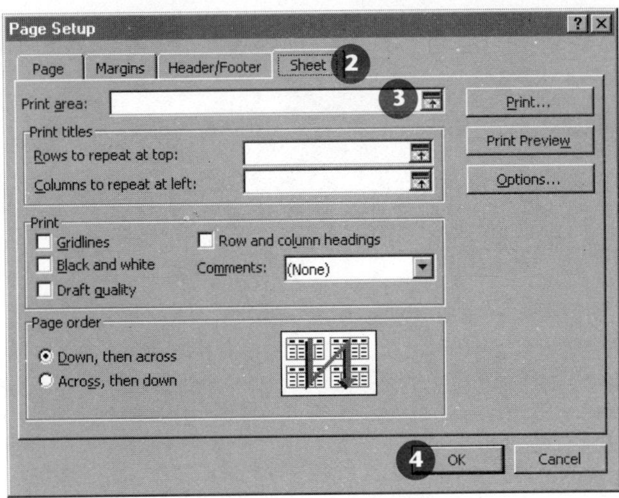

Print Row and Column Titles on Each Page

1. Click the File menu, and click Page Setup.
2. Click the Sheet tab.
3. In the Print Titles area, enter the number of the row or letter of the column letter that contains the titles, or click the appropriate Collapse dialog box, select the row or column with the mouse, then click the Collapse dialog box again to restore the dialog box.
4. Click OK.

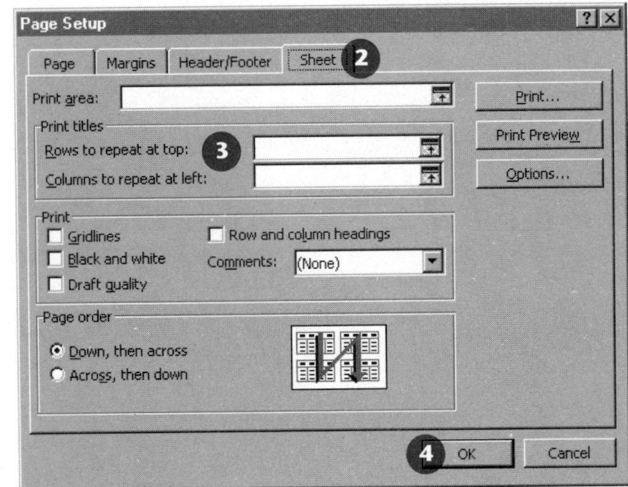

TIP

The Print Area should not include any columns or rows you want printed on every page. *Including this data in the Print Area will cause that data to print twice on the first page. Instead, use the Print Titles option.*

Print Gridlines, Column Letters, and Row Numbers

1. Click the File menu, and click Page Setup.
2. Click the Sheet tab.
3. Click to select the Gridlines check box.
4. Click to select the Row and Column Headings check box.
5. Click OK.

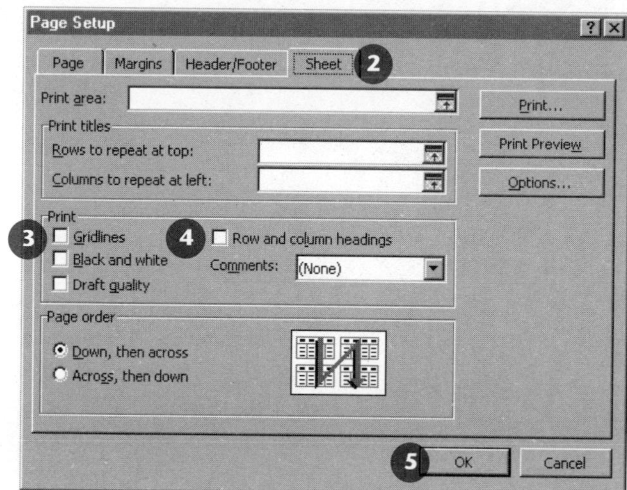

TIP

You can reduce or enlarge the size of the printed characters. *Click the Adjust To up or down arrow to set the percentage size of the printed characters. Click the Fit To up or down arrow to set the specificed number of pages you want to fit the printed characters.*

Fit Your Worksheet on a Specific Number of Pages

1. Click the File menu, and then click Page Setup.
2. Click the Page tab.
3. Select a scaling option. Click the Adjust To option to scale the worksheet using a percentage. Click the Fit To option to force a worksheet to print to a specific number of pages.
4. Click OK.

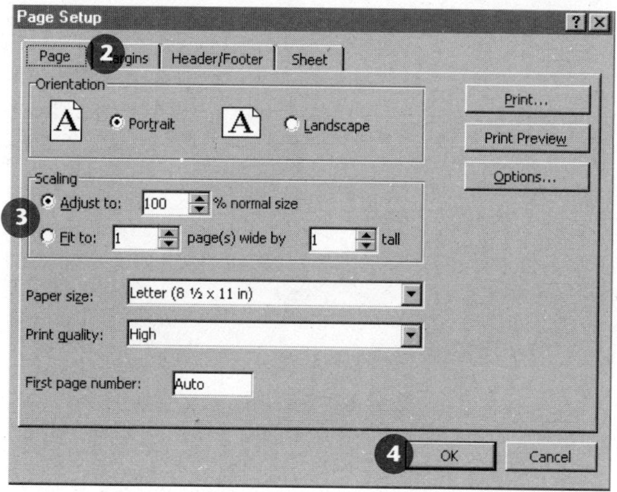

5

Saving Print Settings

You can print a single worksheet in a variety of ways. Perhaps your department heads need a worksheet printed with several columns hidden and special headers and footers in landscape orientation; your sales staff needs the same worksheet printed with different columns hidden and their own headers and footers in portrait orientation. Rather than having to change the print settings for each occasion, Excel lets you save these settings as a *Custom View*. Each view contains print settings, as well as hidden columns and rows, that you can access easily at any time.

SEE ALSO

See "Setting Up the Page" on page 68 for information on print settings.

Create a Custom View

1. Specify the print settings you want for a worksheet.
2. If necessary, hide any columns and rows.
3. Click the View menu, and then click Custom Views.
4. Click Add.
5. Type a name of the view.
6. If necessary, click to select the Print Settings check box and the Hidden Rows, Columns and Filter Settings check box to include them in the view.
7. Click OK.

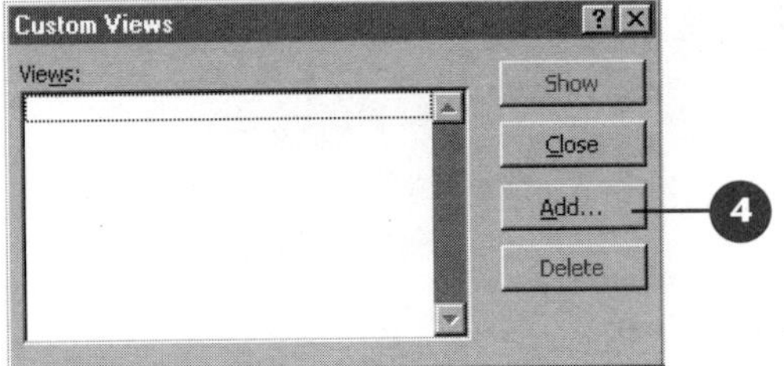

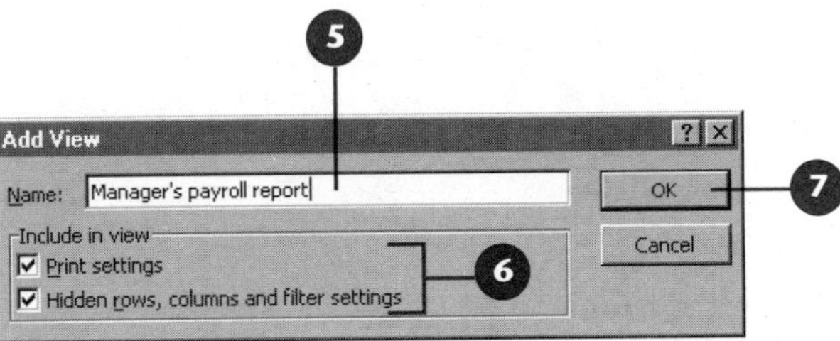

Display a Custom View

1. Click the View menu, and then click Custom Views.
2. Click the name of the view you want to use.
3. Click Show. The print settings you set in this view are in effect when you print.

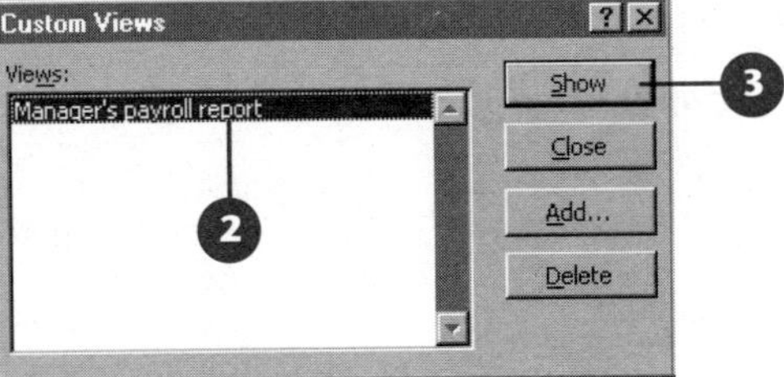

6

Formatting a Worksheet

IN THIS SECTION

Formatting Text and Numbers

Designing Conditional Formatting

Copying Cell Formats

Changing Font Styles

Changing Data Alignment

Controlling Text Flow

Changing Data Color

Adding Color and Patterns to Cells

Adding Borders to Cells

Formatting Data with AutoFormat

Modifying an AutoFormat

Creating and Applying a Style

Modifying a Style

Microsoft Excel 97 offers several tools for making your worksheets look more attractive and professional. The look of a worksheet does not affect its functionality—as long as the values and formulas are correct, you'll get the results you need—but the look of the worksheet can greatly affect the people reading its data. If you want to make the information you are presenting easier to understand, take the time to format your worksheet.

Formatting a Worksheet

Formatting a worksheet involves making cosmetic changes to cell contents and the worksheet grid. Without formatting, a worksheet full of data can look like a sea of meaningless data. To make important information stand out, you can change the appearance of the numbers and text in a worksheet by formatting them with boldface and italics, or by adding dollar signs and commas. You can select a new font and font size, adjust the alignment of the data in cells, and add colors, patterns, borders and pictures. Using these formatting elements wisely can also help reinforce your corporate image or personal style.

Formatting Text and Numbers

You can change the appearance of the data in the cells of a worksheet without changing the actual value in the cell. You can format text and numbers with *font attributes*, such as bolding, italics, or underlining, to enhance this data to catch the reader's eye and to focus the reader's attention. You can also apply *numeric formats* to the numbers in a worksheet to better reflect the type of information they present—dollar amounts, dates, decimals, and so on. For example, you can format a number to display up to 15 decimal places, or none at all.

SEE ALSO

See "Selecting Multiple Cells" on page 34 for more information about selecting cells before formatting them.

Change the Appearance of Text Quickly

1. Select a cell or range that contains the text you want to format.
2. Click the Bold, Italics, or Underline button on the Formatting toolbar to apply the attribute you want to the selected range. You can apply more than one attribute as long as the range is selected.

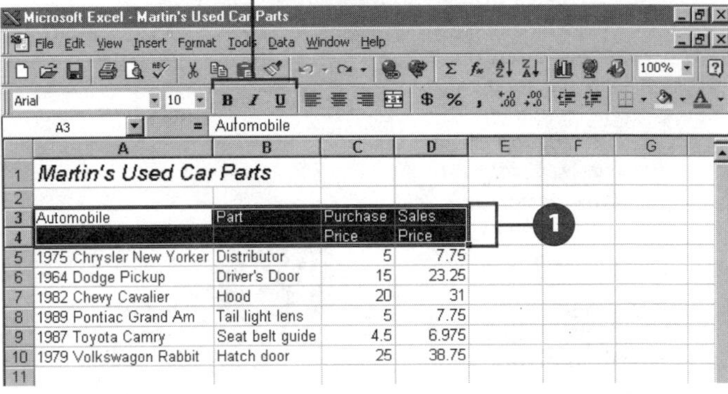

FORMATTING TOOLBAR BUTTONS

Icon	Button Name	Example
B	Bold	**Excel**
I	Italic	*Excel*
U	Underline	Excel
$	Currency Style	$5,432.10
%	Percent Style	54.32%
,	Comma Style	5,432.10
+.0 .00	Increase Decimal	5,432.10 becomes 5,432.100
.00 +.0	Decrease Decimal	5,432.10 becomes 5,432.1

TIP

Remove a numeric format or font attribute quickly. *The buttons on the Formatting toolbar are* toggle buttons, *which means you simply click to turn them on and off. To remove a numeric format or font attribute, select the cell or range, and then click the appropriate button on the Formatting toolbar to turn the format or attribute off.*

Change the Appearance of a Number Quickly

1. Select a cell or range that contains the number(s) you want to format.
2. Click the Currency Style, Percent Style, Comma Style, Increase Decimal, or Decrease Decimal button on the Formatting toolbar to apply the numeric attribute you want to the selected range. You can apply more than one attribute as long as the range is selected.

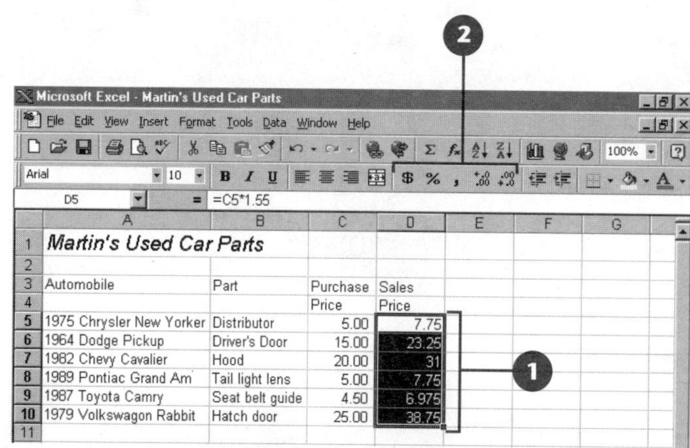

TIP

Open the Format Cells dialog box quickly. *Right-click a selected cell or range, and click Format Cells.*

Format a Number Using the Format Cells Dialog Box

1. Select a cell or range that contains the number(s) you want to format.
2. Click the Format menu, and then click Cells.
3. Click the Number tab, if necessary.
4. Click to select a category.
5. Select the formatting options you want to apply.
6. Preview your selections in the Sample box.
7. Click OK.

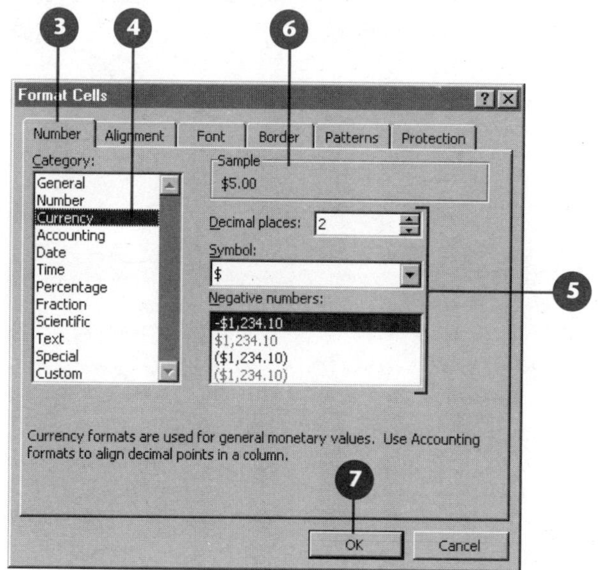

6

Designing Conditional Formatting

You can make your worksheets more powerful by setting up conditional formatting. *Conditional formatting* enables you to determine the formatting of cells based on their contents. For example, you might want this year's sales information to display in red and italics if it's lower than last years sales, but in green and bold if it's higher.

To establish conditional formatting, click Format on the menu bar, and then click Conditional Formatting to show the Conditional Formatting dialog box.

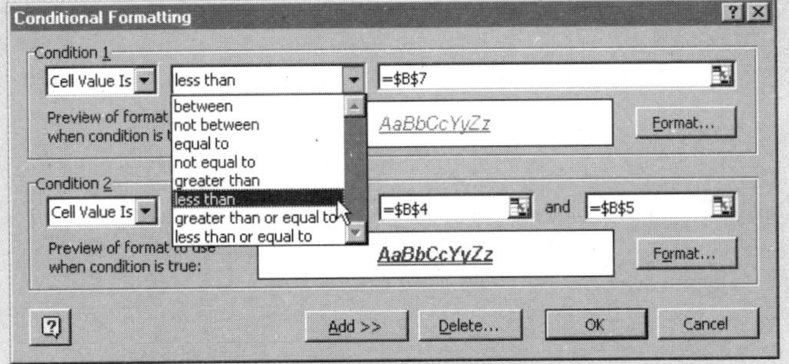

When the dialog box opens, you see option boxes for establishing one condition, a button for opening the Formatting dialog box, and a preview window showing how the formatting will look if this condition is true. To establish a condition, you select whether to test a cell value or a formula, and the cell or formula against which to test it. If you choose to test a cell value, you also specify a comparison operator to use in the test. Use the Format button to change the formatting that will be applied. You can establish up to two additional conditions by clicking the Add button. When you add a condition, the dialog box expands to display more option boxes, a Format button, and another preview window.

You can also delete conditions you no longer want by clicking the Delete button.

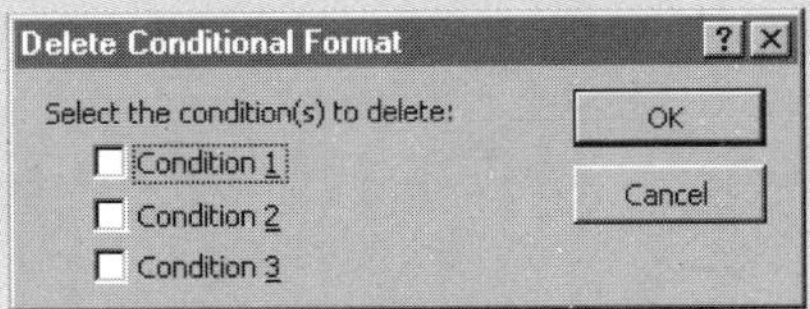

When the Delete Conditional Format dialog box opens, click to select the check boxes next to the condition you want to delete.

Copying Cell Formats

After formatting a cell in a worksheet, you might decide you want to copy its formatting to other cells in the worksheet. For example, you might want each subtotal in your worksheet to be formatted in italics, bold, 12-point Times New Roman, and with a dollar sign, commas, and two decimal places to the right. Rather than selecting each subtotal and applying the individual formatting to each cell you can *paint* (that is, copy) the formatting from the one cell to others.

Format Painter button

TIP

Use the Esc key to cancel format painting. *If you change your mind about painting a format, cancel the marquee by pressing the Esc key.*

Copy a Format From One Cell to Another

1. Select a cell or range that contains the formatting you want to copy to other cells.
2. Click the Format Painter button on the Standard toolbar.
3. Drag to select the cell(s) you want to paint. When you release the mouse button, the cells appear with the new formatting.

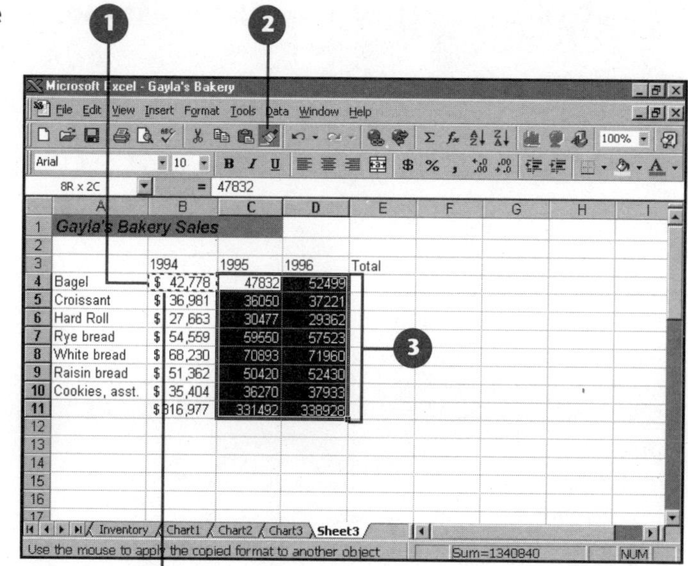

A marquee appears around the cell whose format you want to copy.

Changing Font Styles

A *font* is a collection of alphanumeric characters that share the same *typeface*, or design, and have similar characteristics. Most fonts are available in a number of sizes. The size of each font character is measured in *points* (approximately 1/72nd of an inch). You can use any font that is installed on your computer, but the default is a 10-point Arial font.

TIP

What is a TrueType font? *A TrueType font is a font that uses special software capabilities to print exactly what is seen on the screen.*

Change the Font and Font Size

1. Select a cell or range that contains the data you want to format with a new font or font size.
2. Right-click the mouse button, and then click Format Cells.
3. Click the Font tab, if necessary.
4. Select a font you want to use.
5. Select a font style.
6. Select a font size you want to use.
7. Select any additional effects.
8. Preview the selections you have made.
9. Click OK.

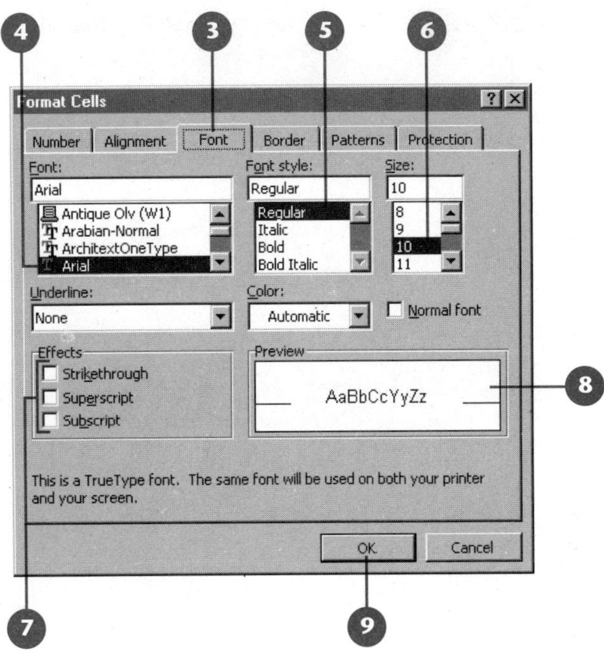

SEE ALSO

See "Selecting Multiple Cells" on page 34 for more information about selecting cells prior to changing fonts and point sizes.

SEE ALSO

See "Formatting Data with AutoFormat" on page 88 for more information about applying Excel's predesigned formats to worksheet cells.

Change the Font and Font Size Using the Formatting Toolbar

1. Select a cell or range that contains the data you want to format with a new font or font size.
2. Click the Font drop-down arrow on the Formatting toolbar.
3. If necessary, scroll to find the font you want to use, and then click to select it.
4. Click the Font Size drop-down arrow on the Formatting toolbar.
5. If necessary, scroll to find the font size you want to use, and then click to select it.

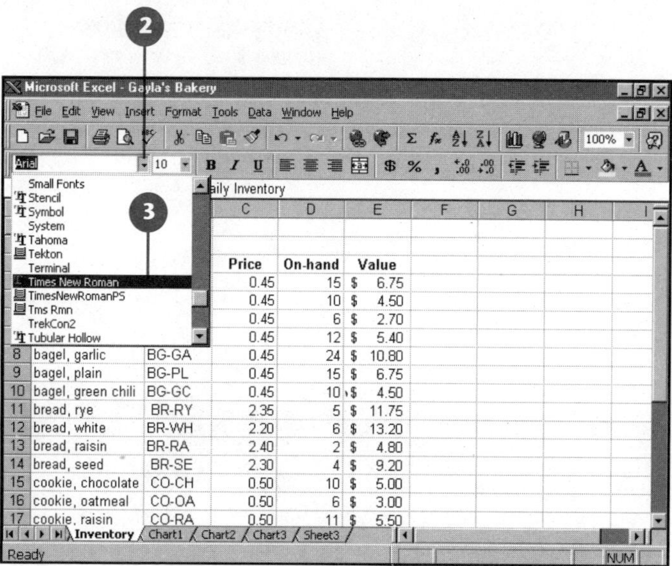

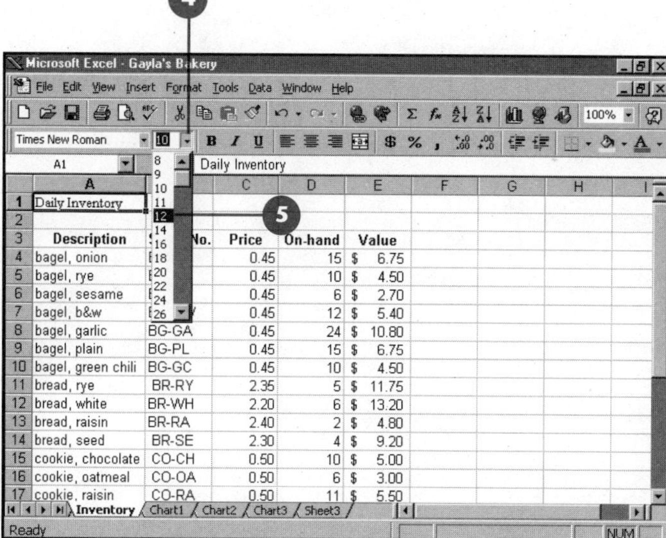

6

Changing Data Alignment

When you enter data in a cell, Excel aligns labels on the left edge of the cell and aligns values and formulas on the right edge of the cell. How Excels aligns the contents of a cell relative to the left or right edge of a cell is known as *horizontal alignment* and how Excel aligns cell contents relative to the top and bottom of a cell is called *vertical alignment*. You can change the alignment of the data you enter in each cell.

Excel also provides an option for changing the flow and angle of characters within a cell. The *orientation* of the contents of a cell is expressed in degrees. The default orientation is 0° in which characters appear horizontally within a cell.

SEE ALSO

See "Controlling Text Flow" on page 82 for information on text control.

Change Alignment Using the Format Cells Dialog Box

1. Select a cell or range that contains the data you want to realign.
2. Right-click the mouse button, and then click Format Cells.
3. If necessary, click the Alignment tab.
4. Click the Horizontal drop-down arrow, and then select an alignment.
5. Click the Vertical drop-down arrow, and then select an alignment.
6. Select an orientation by clicking a point on the orientation map or by clicking the Degrees up or down arrows.
7. If necessary, click one or more Text Control check boxes.
8. Click OK.

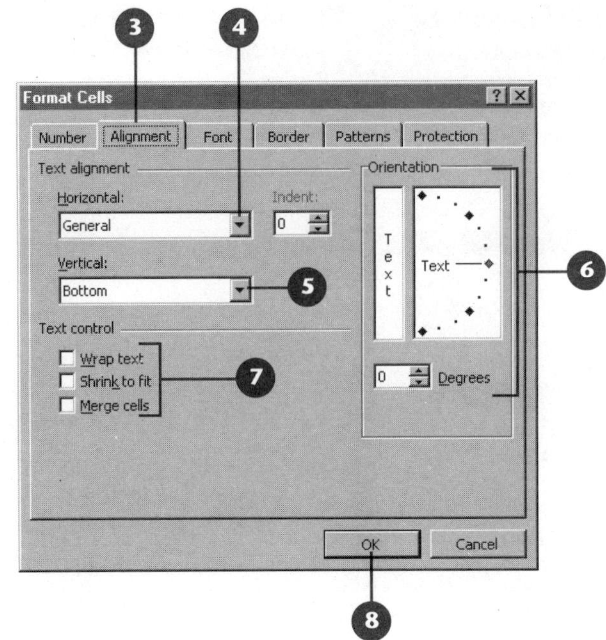

> **TIP**
>
> **Use the Format Cells dialog box to select more alignment options.** *Many more alignment options are available from the Format Cells dialog box, but for centering across columns, and simple left, right, and center alignment, it's easier to use the Formatting toolbar buttons.*

> **TRY THIS**
>
> **Merge and center a worksheet title.** *To center a title across the top of a worksheet, enter it in column A, and then select all the columns you plan to print and click the Merge And Center button.*
>
> 

Change Alignment Using the Formatting Toolbar

1. Select a cell or range that contains the data you want to realign.
2. Click the Align Left, Center, Align Right, or Center Across Columns button on the Formatting toolbar.

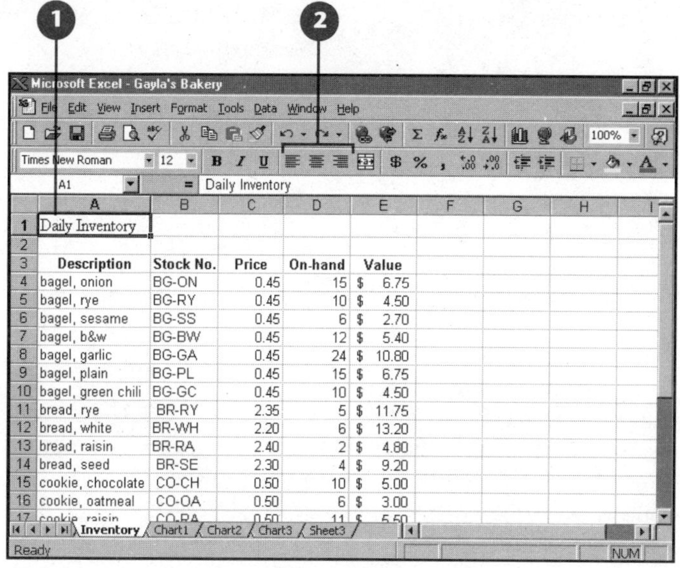

ALIGNMENT TOOLBAR BUTTONS

Icon	Button Name	Description
	Align Left	Aligns cell contents on left edge of cell
	Center	Centers cell contents in the middle of cell
	Align Right	Aligns cell contents on right edge of cell
	Merge and Center	Centers cell contents across the columns of a selected range

6

Controlling Text Flow

The length of a label might not always fit within the width you've chosen for a column. If the cell to the right is empty, a label spills over into it, but if that cell contains data, the label will be truncated (that is, cut off). You can format the cell to automatically wrap text to multiple lines so you don't have to widen the column. For example, you might want a label that says "1997 Division 1 Sales" to fit in a column that is only as wide as "Sales." The contents of cells can also be modified to fit within the space available in a cell, or to be combined with the contents of other cells.

Control the Flow of Text in a Cell

1. Select a cell or range that contains the text you want to wrap.
2. Right-click the mouse button, and then select Format Cells.
3. Click the Alignment tab, if necessary.
4. Click one or more Text Control check boxes.
    - Wrap Text wraps text to multiple lines within a cell.
    - Shrink To Fit reduces character size to fit within a cell.
    - Merge Cell combines selected cells into a single cell.
5. Click OK.

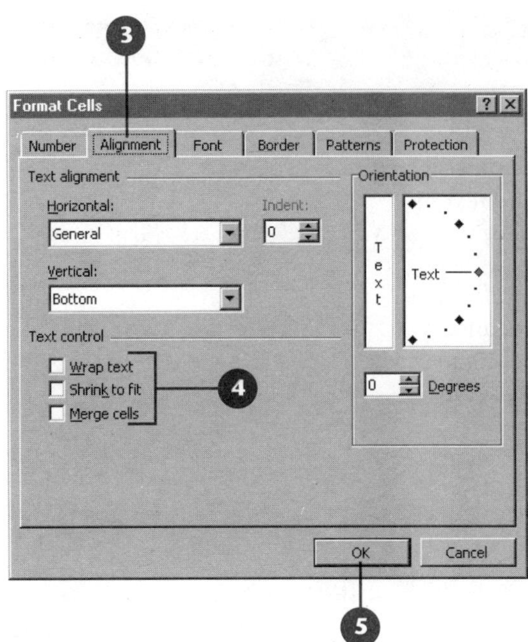

Changing Data Color

You can change the color of the numbers and text in a worksheet. Strategic use of a *font color* can be an effective way of tying similar values together. For instance, you can display sales figures in green and expenses in red.

Change Text Color with the Format Cells Dialog Box

1. Select a cell or range that contains the text whose color you want to change.
2. Right-click the mouse button, and then click Format Cells.
3. Click the Font tab, if necessary.
4. Click the Color drop-down arrow, and then click a color you want to use.
5. Preview your selection.
6. Click OK.

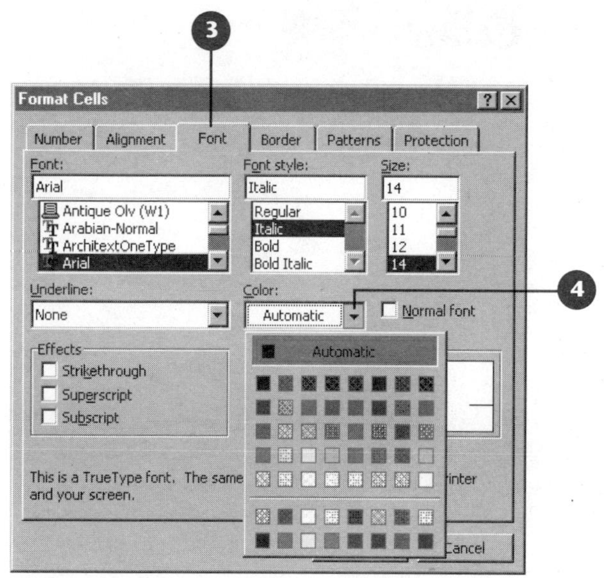

TIP

Use the Font Color button on the Formatting toolbar to display the last font color you selected. *To apply this color to another selection, simply click the button, not the drop-down button arrow.*

Change Font Color Using the Formatting Toolbar

1. Select a cell or range whose color you want to change.
2. Click the Font Color drop-down arrow on the Formatting toolbar.
3. Click a color that you want to use.

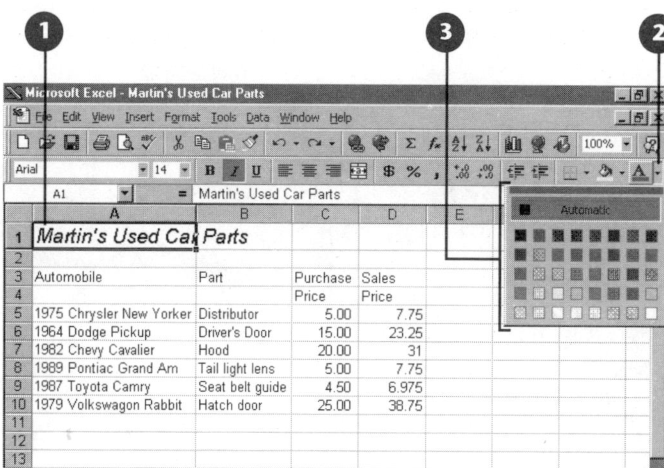

6

Adding Color and Patterns to Cells

You can add, or *fill,* the background of a cell with a color and a pattern to make its data stand out. Fill colors and patterns can also add uniformity to the information in your worksheet. You might, for example, want all the Fourth Quarter sales figures to have a blue background, and the Second Quarter sales figures to have a yellow background. You can use fill colors and patterns in conjunction with text attributes, fonts, and font colors to further enhance the appearance of your worksheet. When you paint a format, the fill colors and patterns get copied too.

SEE ALSO

See "Copying Cell Formats" on page 77 for more information about copying a format to other cells.

Choose a Fill Color and Pattern Using the Format Cells Dialog Box

1. Select a cell or range you want to format with a fill color or pattern.
2. Right-click the mouse button, and then click Format Cells.
3. Click the Patterns tab, if necessary.
4. Click a color that you want to use.
5. Click the Pattern drop-down arrow to display the available patterns, and then click the pattern you want to use or another color pallet.
6. Preview your selection in the Sample box.
7. Click OK.

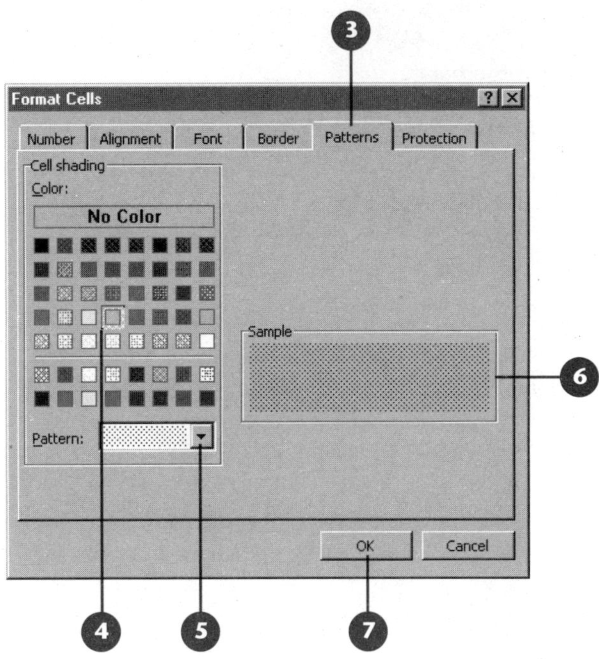

TIP

Use the Preview button on the Standard toolbar to save time. *Preview your worksheet, before you print it especially if you don't have a color printer. Some colors and patterns look great on screen but can make a worksheet difficult to read in black and white.*

Choose a Fill Color Using the Formatting Toolbar

1. Select a cell or range you want to add a background color to.
2. Click the Fill Color drop-down arrow on the Formatting toolbar.
3. Click a color that you want to use.

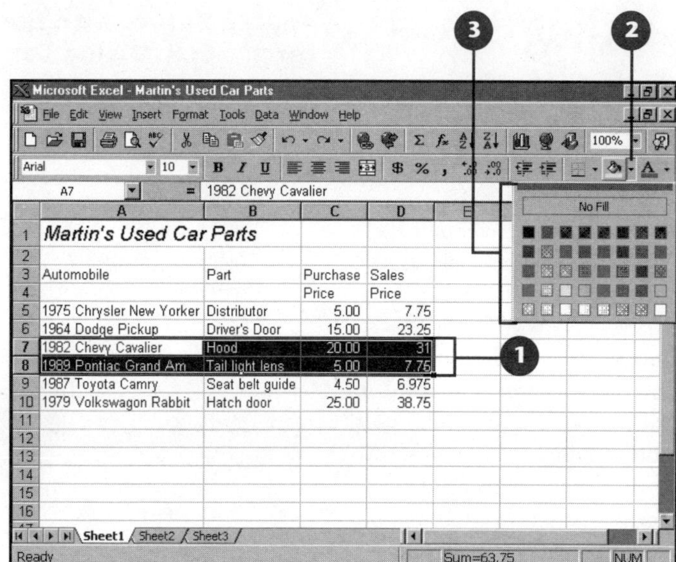

6

Adding Borders to Cells

You've probably found that the light gray grid that displays on the worksheet screen helps your eyes connect from cell to cell. However, Excel does not include this grid on printouts. You can choose to print gridlines using the Page Setup dialog box or improve on the grid pattern by adding different types of borders to a worksheet. You can add borders to some or all sides of a single cell or range. You can select borders of varying line widths and colors.

SEE ALSO

See "Setting Up the Worksheet Page" on page 68 for information about printing options.

Apply a Border with the Format Cells Dialog Box

1. Select a cell or range where you want to apply borders, or to select the entire worksheet, click the Select All button.
2. Right-click the mouse button, and then click Format Cells.
3. Click the Border tab, if necessary.
4. Select a line type from the Style list.
5. If you want a border on the outside of a cell or range, or lines inside a range of cells, click the Outline or Inside option. If you want to remove a border, click the None option.
6. To choose the other available Border options, click a Border button, or click in the Border box at the location where you want the border to appear.
7. Click the Color drop-down arrow, and then click a color for the border you have selected.
8. Click OK.

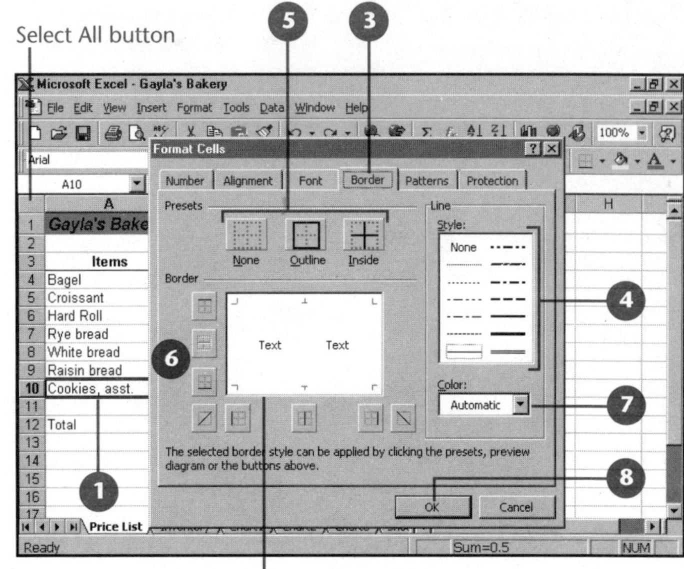

> **TIP**
>
> **Use the Format Cells command to format a border.** *To apply a border color other than the default (black), select the range that either has an existing border or is where you want a border to appear, right-click the range, click Format Cells, and then click the Border tab. Select the color you want for the border from the palette of available colors, and then click OK.*

> **SEE ALSO**
>
> *See "Formatting Data with AutoFormat" on page 88 for information on predesigned formats that include borders and can be applied quickly.*

Apply a Border Quickly

1. Select a cell or range where you want a border.
2. Click the Borders drop-down button on the Formatting toolbar to select from a list of border styles or click the Borders button to select the default border style.
3. Select a border from the palette of available borders. The border sytle you have chosen appears as the default Borders button on the Formatting toolbar.

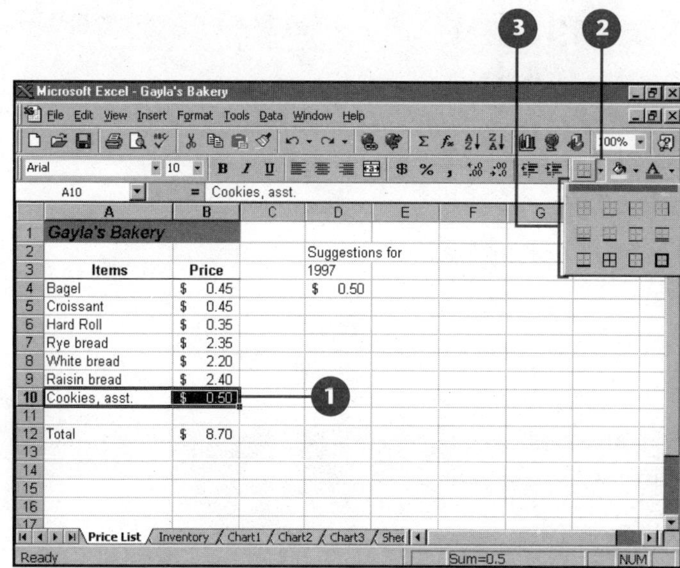

6

Formatting Data With AutoFormat

Formatting worksheet data can be a lot of fun but also very time consuming. To make formatting data more efficient, Excel includes 18 AutoFormats. An *AutoFormat* includes a combination of fill colors and patterns, numeric formats, font attributes, borders, and font colors, professionally designed to enhance your worksheets. And to make formatting even easier, Excel will "guess" which data should be formatted if you don't select the data before choosing the AutoFormat option.

TIP

Use AutoFormats to override previous formatting. *When you apply an AutoFormat, any existing formatting is erased.*

Apply an AutoFormat

1. Select a cell or range where you want to apply the AutoFormat.
2. Click the Format menu, and then click AutoFormat.
3. Click a format style you want to apply from the Table Format list.
4. Preview you selection in the Sample box.
5. Click OK.

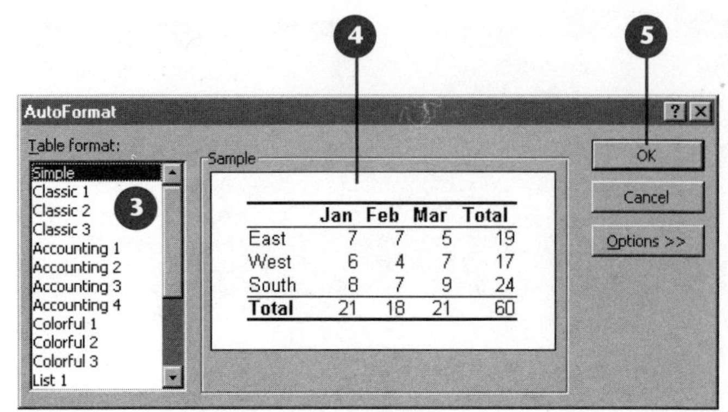

Modifying an AutoFormat

Although the Excel AutoFormats are designed to give your worksheet a professional look, you might need to modify an AutoFormat to better suit your needs. You can change an AutoFormat, but the changes are temporary; you can't permanently alter an AutoFormat.

TIP

You can let Excel choose the range to format. *If you don't select the cells you want to apply the AutoFormat to, Excel will guess which cells you want formatted.*

Modify an AutoFormat

1. Select a cell or range you want to apply an AutoFormat to.
2. Click the Format menu, and then click AutoFormat.
3. Click Options. The Formats To Apply pane appears at the bottom of the AutoFormat dialog box.
4. Click any of the Formats To Apply check boxes to turn a feature on or off.
5. Preview your selections in the Sample box.
6. Click OK.

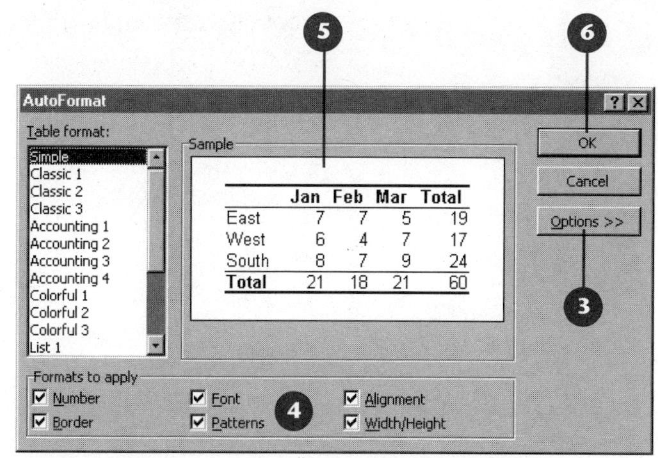

Creating and Applying a Style

A *style* is a defined collection of formats—font, font size, attributes, numeric formats, and so on—that you can store as a set and later apply to other cells. For example, if you always want sales figures to display in blue 14-point Times New Roman, bold, italic, with 2 decimal places and commas, you could create a style that include all these formats. Styles can also be copied from one workbook to another, meaning you can share styles among workbooks.

Once you create a style, it is available to you no matter what workbook you open.

Create a New Style

1. Select a cell or range in which you want to create a new style.
2. Click the Format menu, and then click Style.
3. Type the name of the new style in the Style Name box. For example, this style will be named "Sales data."
4. Clear the check boxes to turn off any option you do not want to include in the style.
5. Click Modify to make changes to any of the options you want to include in the style.
6. Make any necessary changes in the Format Cells dialog box.
7. Click OK.
8. Click OK.

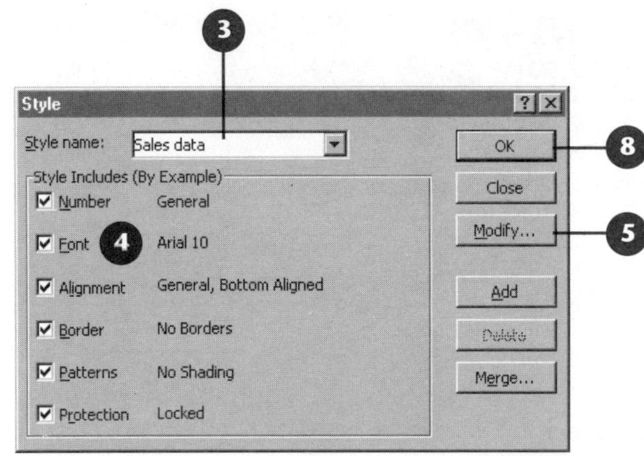

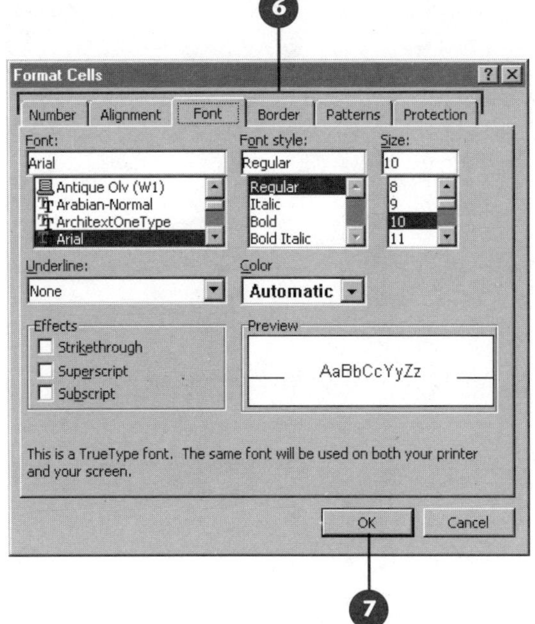

TIP

You can apply styles before you enter data. *If you plan to enter repetitive information, such as a list of dollar amounts, in a row or column, its often easier to apply the desired style to the range before you enter the data. That way, you can simply enter each number, and Excel formats it as soon as you press Enter.*

SEE ALSO

See "Selecting Multiple Cells" on page 34 for information on selecting a range.

Apply a Style

1. Select a cell or range in which you want to apply a style.
2. Click the Format menu, and then click Style.
3. Click the Style Name drop-down arrow.
4. Click the style you want to apply.
5. Click OK.

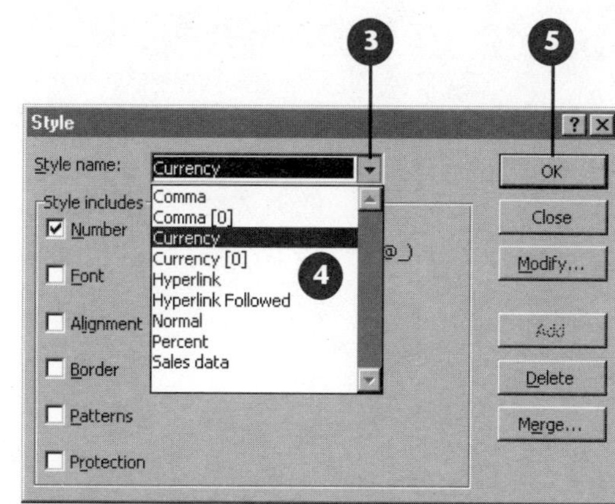

6

Modifying a Style

Any style—whether it was supplied by Excel or created by you or someone else—can be modified. The same dialog box used to create a style is also used to permanently make modifications. If you want to use styles created or modified in another workbook, you can merge the styles into the open workbook. If you no longer use a style, you can delete the style from the workbook.

TIP

Use the Add button to create a new style based on a current style. *You never know when you might want to use an original style supply by Excel. To keep the original intact, modifying the formatting in the Style dialog box as desired, but then click the Add button and give the modified style a new name.*

Modify a Style

1. Click the Format menu, and then click Style.
2. Click the Style Name drop-down arrow.
3. Click the style you want to modify.
4. Click Modify.
5. Make any necessary changes in the Format Cells dialog box.
6. Click OK.
7. Click OK.

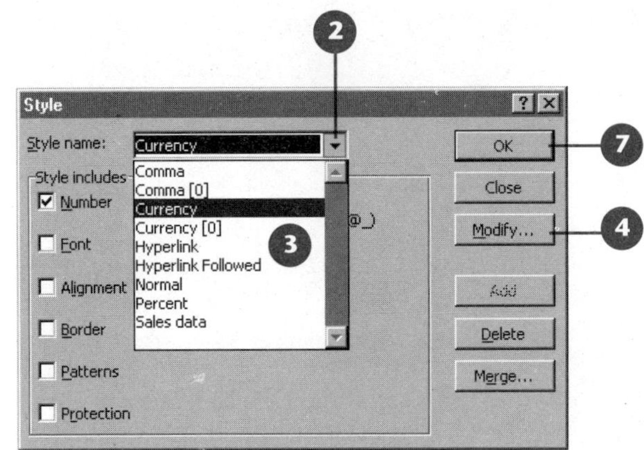

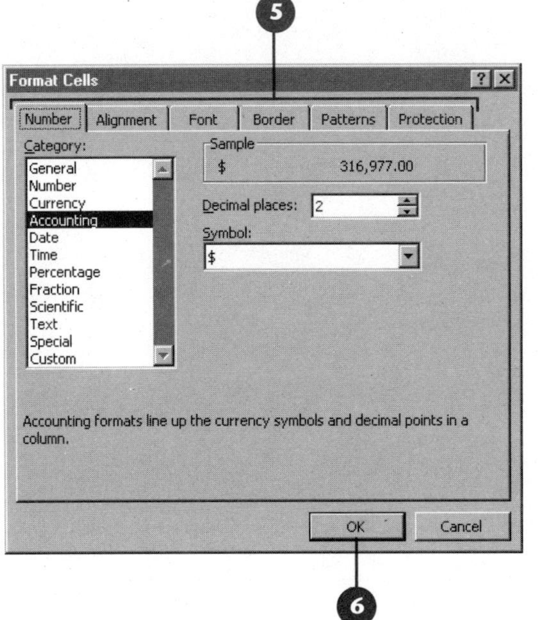

Merge Styles

1. Click the Format menu, and then click Style.
2. Click Merge.
3. Click the workbook that contains the styles you want to merge with the current workbook.
4. Click OK.
5. Click OK.

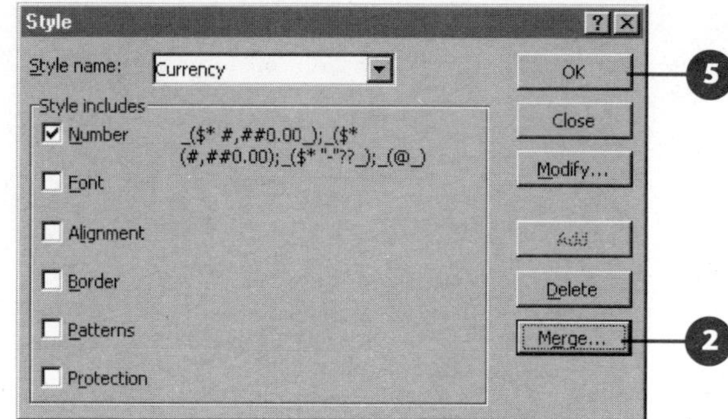

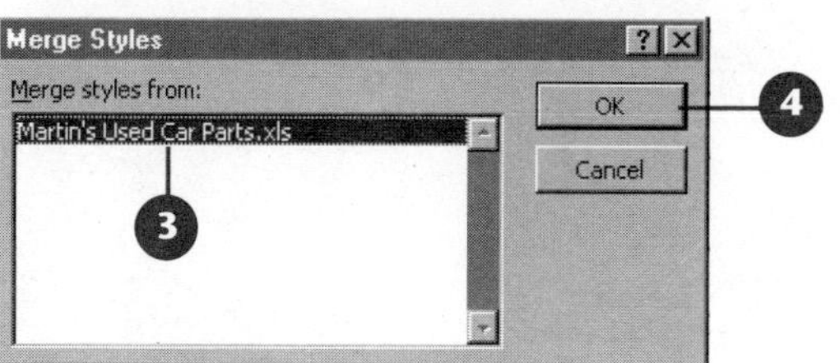

Delete a Style

1. Click the Format menu, and then click Style.
2. Click the Style Name drop-down arrow.
3. Click the style you to delete.
4. Click Delete.
5. Click OK.

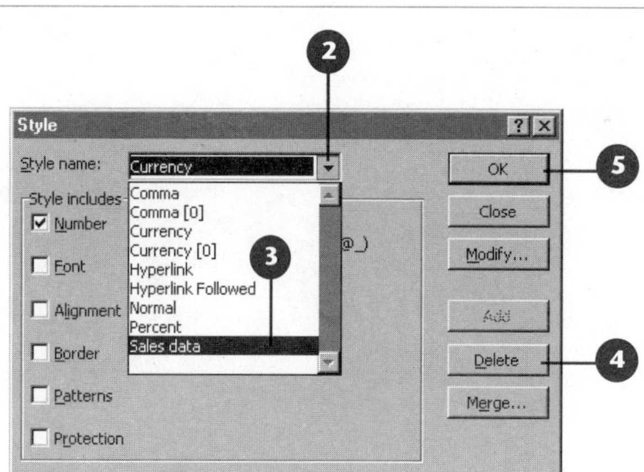

6

7

Inserting Graphics and Related Material

IN THIS SECTION

Inserting Pictures

Accessing the Office 97 CD-ROM for Extras

Stylizing Text with WordArt

Editing WordArt Text

Applying WordArt Text Effects

Inserting an Organization Chart

Modifying an Organization Chart

Correcting Text with AutoCorrect

Creating and Reading a Cell Comment

Editing and Deleting a Cell Comment

Looking Up Reference Material

Spice up an otherwise drab worksheet using colorful graphic images—that are included with Excel, purchased by you or your company, or created by you using separate graphics software. Graphic images can be used to reinforce a corporate identity or to display the subject of a worksheet, and only serve to make your work look more professional. You can add several different types of graphics ,such as pictures, stylized text, or organization chart, to your worksheet.

As you enter information in worksheets, Excel's AutoCorrect feature automatically corrects misspelled words as you type them. You can add your own abbreviations, or unusual, frequently used words to AutoCorrect.

You can attach notes to cells—just as you might attach a sticky tag to a piece of paper. These notes can include information you want others to have, or comments that serve as reminders to yourself. If you have reference material on CD-ROM, such as Microsoft Bookshelf, you can look up information directly from Excel and insert it into your worksheet.

Inserting Pictures

You can add pictures to a worksheet. Your company might have a logo that it includes in all worksheets. Or you might want to use *clip art,* copyright-free graphics, in your worksheet for a special presentation you need to give. In Excel, a picture is any *graphic object* that you insert as a single unit. You can insert pictures that you've created in a drawing program or scanned in, or you can insert clip art provided with Excel or that you've purchased separately. After you insert a graphic object, you can resize or move it with its selection *handles,* the little squares that appear on the edge of the object when you click the object to select it.

Insert Clip Art from the Clip Gallery

1. Select the cell or range where you want a picture to appear. The image will appear in the approximate area of the selected cells, but may overlap other information.
2. Click the Insert menu, point to Picture, and then click Clip Art.
3. Click the Clip Art tab, if necessary.
4. Click a category in the list on the left.
5. Click a picture in the box. If necessary, scroll to see the available pictures in the category you selected.
6. Click Insert.

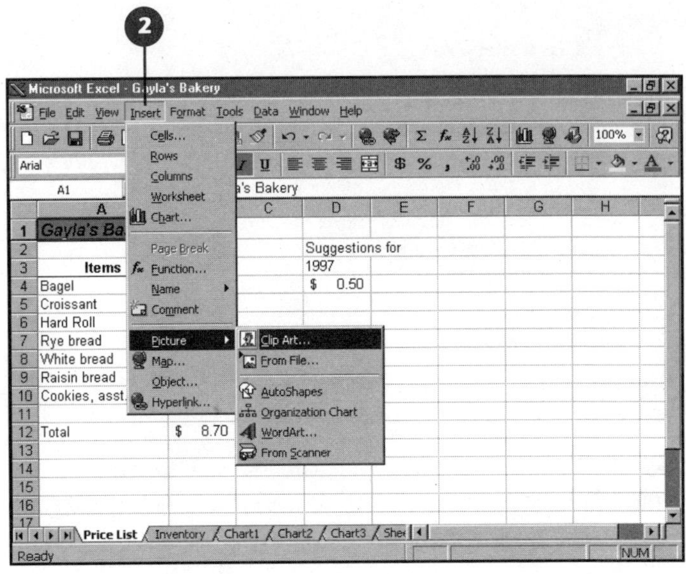

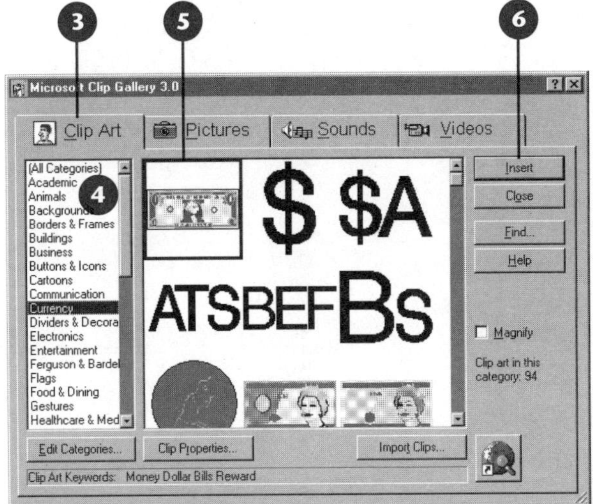

TIP

Use the Clip Gallery to insert pictures, sounds, and videos. *Use the same steps as described in "Inserting Clip Art From the Clip Gallery," but click the Pictures, Sounds, or Videos tab instead of the Clip Art tab.*

SEE ALSO

See "Accessing the Office 97 CD-ROM for Extras" on page 98 for more information about using additional clip art.

Insert a Picture From an Existing File

1. Click the cell or range where you want the picture to appear.
2. Click the Insert menu, point to Picture, and then click From File.
3. Click the Look In drop-down arrow, and then select the graphic image file you want to insert.
4. Click the Preview button to view the file before you insert it.
5. Click Insert.

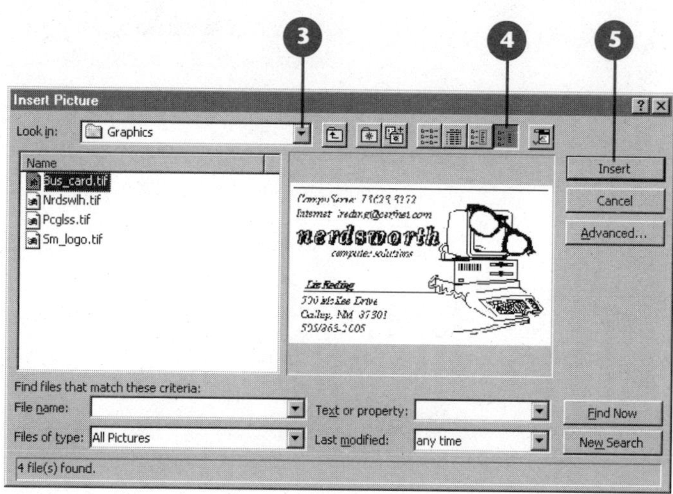

Delete a Picture

1. Click the object to display its handles.
2. Click the Cut button on the Standard toolbar if you want to move the picture to the Clipboard, or press Delete to delete it completely.

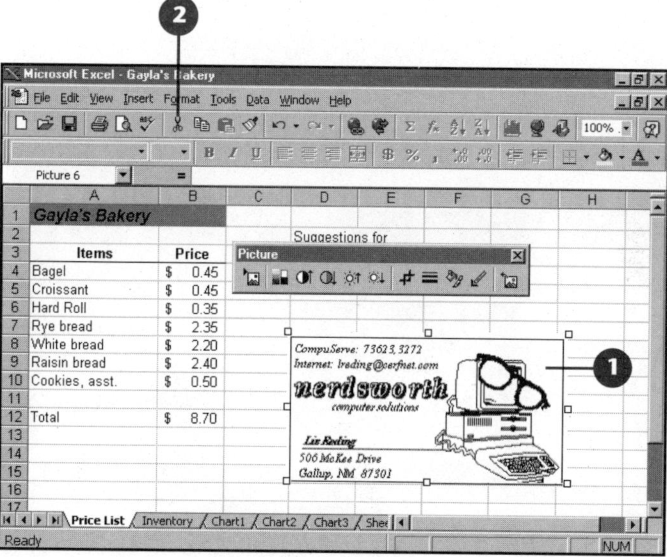

Accessing the Office 97 CD-ROM for Extras

The Office 97 CD-ROM includes extra programs, files, and resource material that are not automatically installed when you install Office 97. These extra features can be found in the ValuPack folder on the Office 97 CD-ROM. The ValuPack includes extra templates for specialized tasks, additional sound and video files, and additional programs to enhance your Office documents. The Office 97 CD-ROM also includes additional clip art found in the Clip Art folder.

> **TIP**
>
> **You can add additional fonts to your computer with the ValuPack.** *The ValuPack includes 150 extra fonts that you can install on your computer if you have the space.*

Insert a ValuPack Overview Presentation Object

1. Display the slide on which you want to insert the ValuPack object.
2. Click the Insert menu and then click Object.
3. Click the Create From File option button.
4. Click Browse.
5. Locate your CD-ROM drive and then double-click the Valupack folder.
6. Double-click Overview, a presentation that gives you an overview of ValuPack features.
7. Click OK.
8. Double-click the presentation object to start the slide show, and then click to advance through each slide to find out what's in the Office 97 ValuPack.

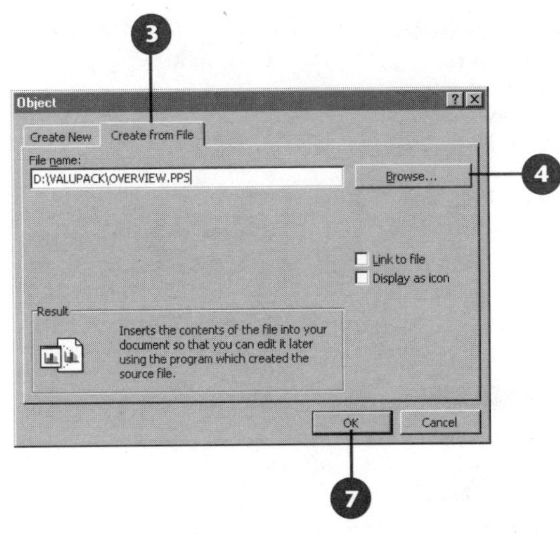

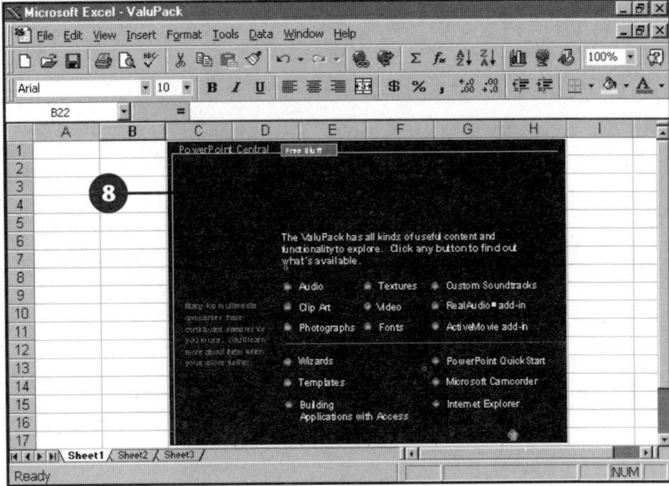

7

TIP

Connect to the Web for access to additional clip art. *Click the Connect To Web For Additional Clips button to open a Web broswer and connect to a clip art Web site to download files.*

SEE ALSO

See "Getting Data from the Web" on page 228 for information on getting Gallery clips from the Web.

Access Additional Clips

1. Click the Insert menu, point to Picture, and then click Clip Art.
2. In the Clip Gallery, click the tab for the clip type you want.
3. Click the clip you want.
4. Click Insert.

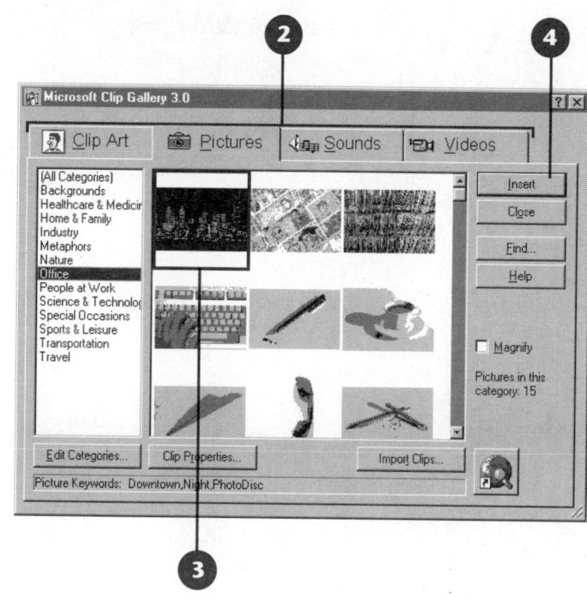

Stylizing Text with WordArt

WordArt is a Microsoft program that provides a wide variety of predesigned text images that have various patterns and effects, which you can use to stylize the text on your worksheet. For example, if you don't have a logo for your company, you can easily create your own using the predesigned WordArt examples. Like any other object on your Excel worksheet, you can move or resize your WordArt, even though it might contain many components.

Create WordArt

1. Click the Insert menu, point to Picture, and then click WordArt.
2. Click a the WordArt style of text you want to insert.
3. Click OK.
4. Type the text you want in the Edit WordArt Text dialog box.
5. If you want, click the Font drop-down arrow to select a new font, and click the Size drop-down arrow to select a new font size to increase or decrease the size of the lettering.
6. If you want to add font attributes, click the Bold or Italic buttons or both.
7. Click OK.

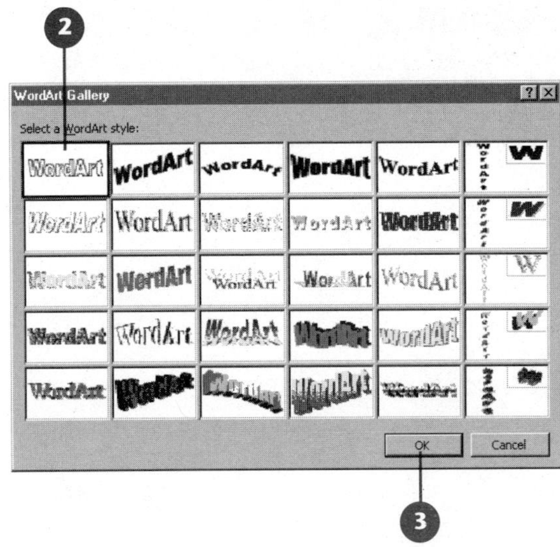

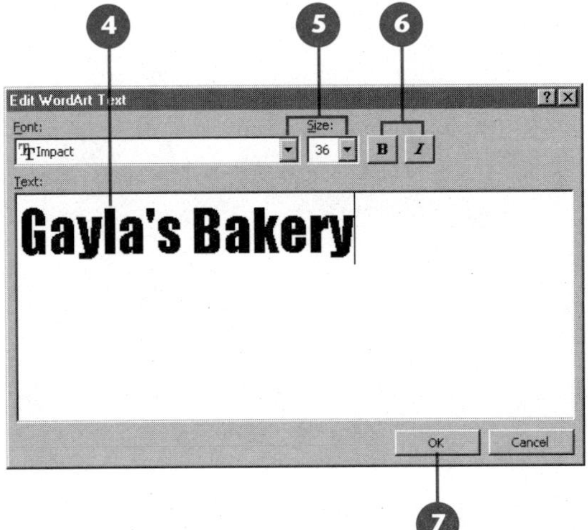

SEE ALSO

See "Editing WordArt Text" on page 102 for information about modifying WordArt text and using the WordArt toolbar.

8. If desired, click the WordArt toolbar buttons to make additional modifications.

9. To deselect the WordArt, click anywhere on the worksheet, or press Esc.

USING WORDART TOOLBAR BUTTONS

Icon	Button Name	Description
	WordArt	Create new WordArt
Edit Text...	Edit Text	Edit the existing text in a WordArt object
	WordArt Gallery	Choose a new style for existing WordArt
	Format WordArt	Change the attributes of existing WordArt
Abc	WordArt Shape	Modify the shape of an existing WordArt object
	Free Rotate	Rotate an existing object
Aa	WordArt Same Letter Heights	Makes upper and lower case letters the same height
Ab b	WordArt Vertical Text	Changes horizontal letters into a vertical formation
	WordArt Alignment	Allows the alignment of an existing object to be modified
AV	WordArt Character Spacing	Allows the spacing between characters to be changed

Editing WordArt Text

With WordArt, in addition to applying one of the preformatted styles, you can create your own style by shaping your text into a variety of shapes, curves, styles, and color patterns. When you select the WordArt object edit the text, the WordArt toolbar opens. The WordArt toolbar gives you tools for coloring, rotating, and shaping your text. You can also format your WordArt using the tools that are available through the Format dialog box that you have learned about in other sections, including positioning and sizing your WordArt. After editing the WordArt text, deselect the object to close the WordArt toolbar.

Change the Shape of WordArt Text

1. Click the WordArt object.
2. Click the WordArt Shape button on the WordArt toolbar.
3. Click the shape you want to apply to the text.
4. Click a blank area of the worksheet to deselect the WordArt object.

Rotate WordArt Text

1. Click the WordArt object.
2. Click the Free Rotate button on the WordArt toolbar.
3. Drag one of the rotate handles that appear in the four corners to rotate the object in any direction you want.
4. When you are finished, click the Free Rotate button to deselect the object.
5. Click a blank area of the worksheet to deselect the WordArt object.

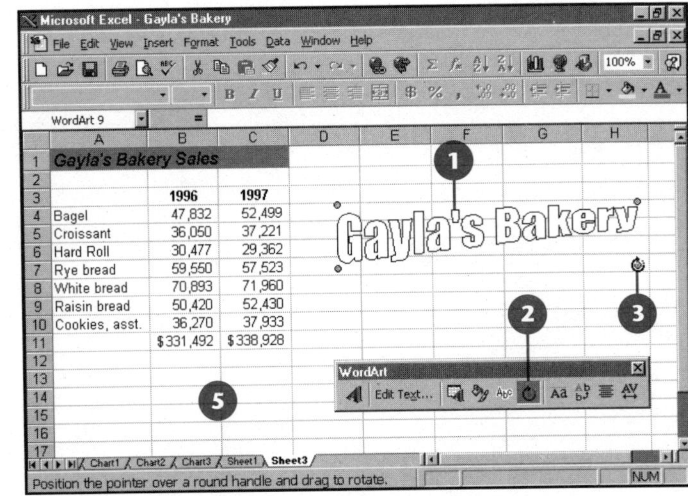

Color WordArt Text

Format WordArt button

1. Click the WordArt object.
2. Click the Format WordArt button on the WordArt toolbar.
3. Click the Colors And Lines tab.
4. Click the Fill Color drop-down arrow and then click a color or fill effect.
5. Click OK.
6. Click a blank area of the worksheet to deselect the WordArt object.

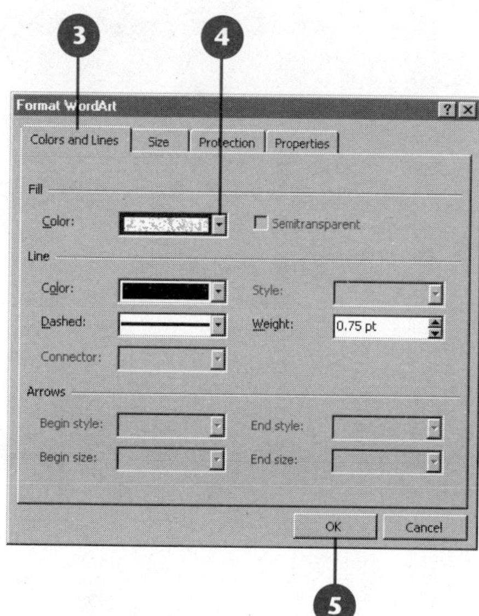

SEE ALSO

See "Applying WordArt Text Effects" on page 104 for information about enhancing WordArt text.

Edit WordArt Text

Edit Text...

Edit Text button

1. Click the WordArt object.
2. Click the Edit Text button on the WordArt toolbar.
3. Click the Text box to place the insertion, and then edit or format the text.
4. Click OK.
5. Click a blank area of the worksheet to deselect the WordArt object.

SEE ALSO

See "Stylizing Text with WordArt" on page 100 for information on using the Edit WordArt Text dialog box.

Applying WordArt Text Effects

You can apply a number of text effects to your WordArt objects that determines letter heights, justification, and spacing. The effect of some of the adjustments you make will be more pronounced for certain WordArt styles than others. Some of these effects will make the text unreadable for certain styles, so apply these effects carefully.

Make Letters the Same Height

1. Click the WordArt object.
2. Click the WordArt Same Letter Heights button on the WordArt toolbar.
3. Click a blank area of the worksheet to deselect the WordArt object.

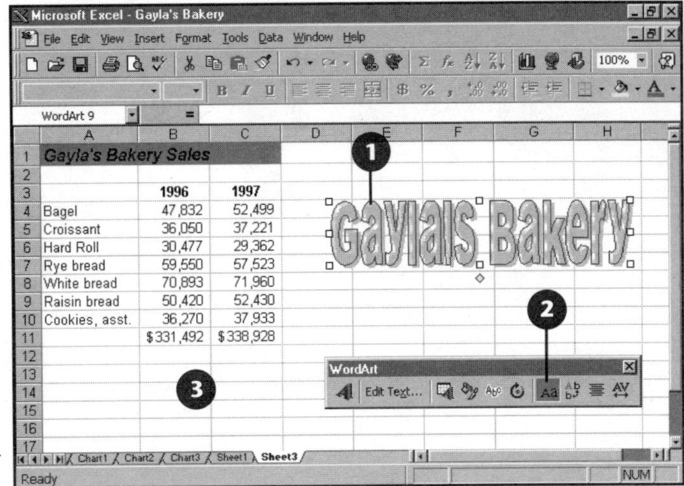

Format Text Vertically

1. Click the WordArt object.
2. Click the WordArt Vertical Text button on the WordArt toolbar.
3. Click a blank area of the worksheet to deselect the WordArt object.

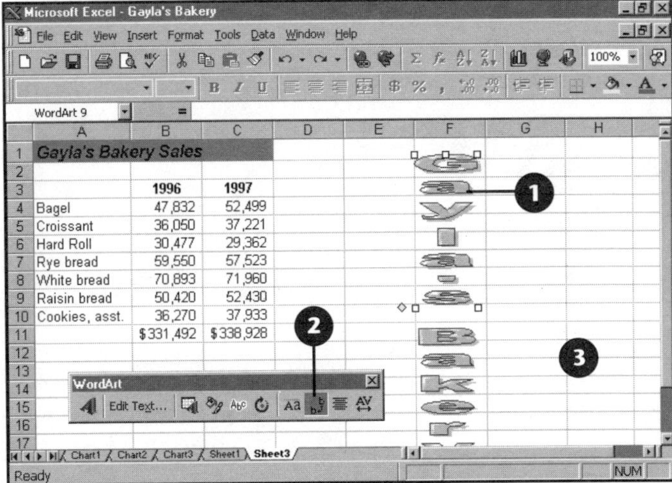

SEE ALSO

See "Editing WordArt Text" on page 102 for information about modifying WordArt text and using the WordArt toolbar.

Align WordArt

1. Click the WordArt object.
2. Click the WordArt Alignment button on the WordArt toolbar.
3. Click the alignment you want.
4. Click a blank area of the worksheet to deselect the WordArt object.

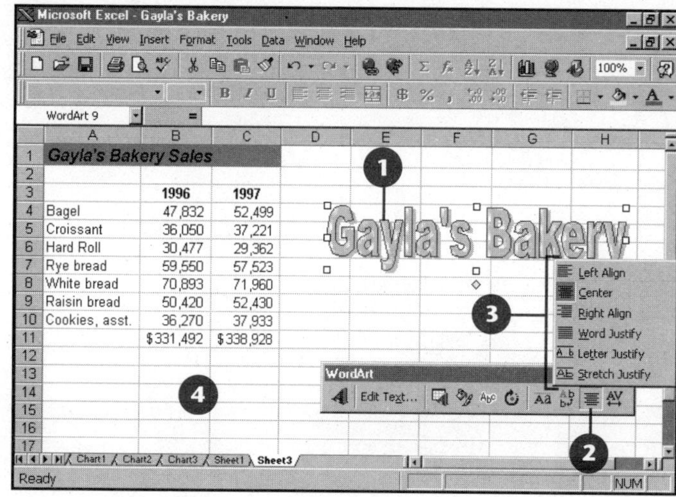

Adjust Character Spacing

1. Click the WordArt object.
2. Click the WordArt Character Spacing button on the WordArt toolbar.
3. Click a spacing setting to determine the amount of space between characters.
4. If necessary, select or deselect the Kern Character Pairs option to adjust the space between characters.
5. Click a blank area of the worksheet to deselect the WordArt object.

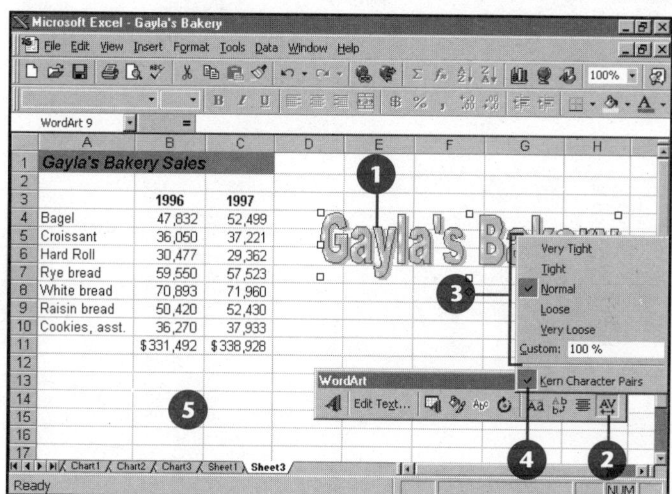

7

Inserting an Organization Chart

An *organization chart*, also known as an *org chart*, shows the personnel structure in an organization. You can include an organization chart in a worksheet using Microsoft Organization Chart, a program that comes with the Office 97 suite. When you start Organization Chart, chart boxes appear into which you enter company personnel. Each chart box is identified by its position in the chart. Managers, for example, are at the top, while Subordinates are below, Co-Workers to the sides, and so on.

Create an Organization Chart

1. Click the Insert menu, point to Picture.
2. Click Organization Chart.
3. Use the Organization Chart tools and menus to design your organization chart.
4. Click the File menu, and then click Exit And Return To [File Name] to return to your worksheet.
5. Click Yes to update the worksheet.
6. Double-click the Organization Chart object in the worksheet to re-open it.

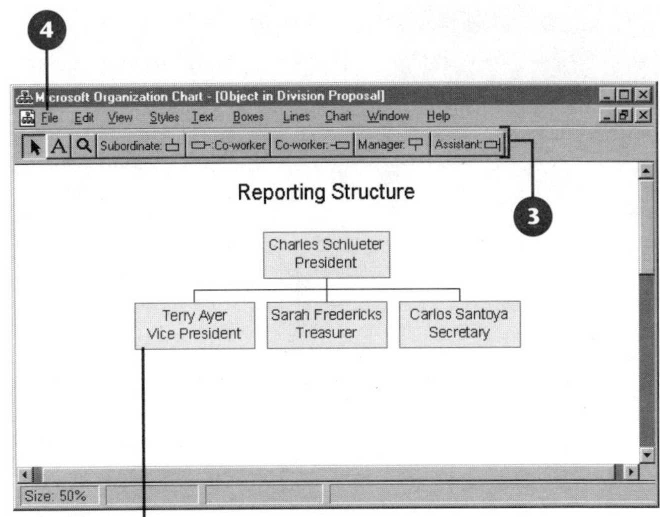

Each chart box represents one person or group in your company's structure. You can enter up to 4 lines of information.

SEE ALSO

See "Modifying an Organization Chart" on page 108 for information about changing an Organization chart.

Enter Text into a Chart Box

1. Click a chart box in which you want to enter text. (After you start Microsoft Organization Chart, the first chart box is selected for you, and you can just start typing.)
2. Type a person's name, and then press Enter.
3. Type a person's title, and then press Enter.
4. Type up to two lines of comments. If you don't want to include comments, leave the comment line placeholders blank.
5. When you are finished, click outside the chart box.

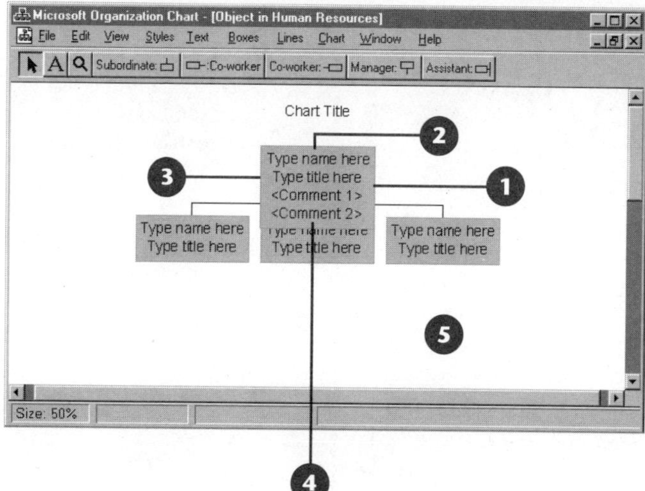

Add a Title

1. Highlight the sample title text "Chart Title" at the top of the organization chart.
2. Type a title you want for your org chart.
3. When you are finished, click outside the title area.

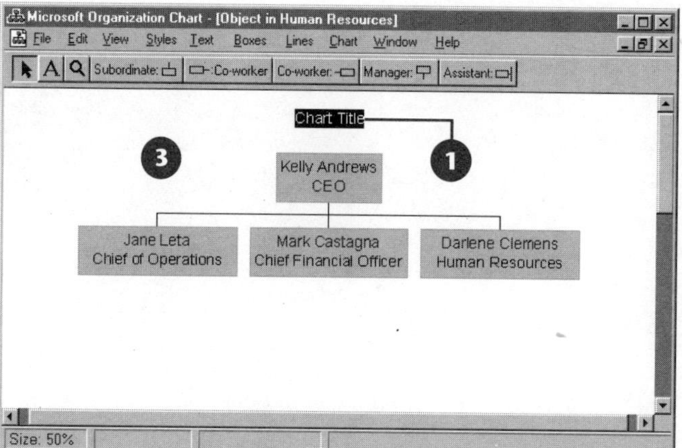

Modifying an Organization Chart

Before you can modify an organization chart, you need to open the object in Microsoft Organization Chart. Just double-click the object. Chart boxes exist in relation to each other. For example, if you want to add a Subordinate chart box, you must select the chart box to which it will be attached. The buttons on the toolbar show the relationship between the different chart boxes you can add. When you add a Subordinate, it is automatically placed below the selected chart box. You can, however, display the chart box levels in a different structure, and you can customize the organization chart's appearance using the formatting options.

Add a Chart Box

1. Click the chart box button on the Organizational Chart toolbar you want to add, such as Subordinate or Co-Worker.
2. Click the chart box in the chart to which you want to attach the new chart box.
3. Enter the information for the box you just added.
4. Click outside the box.

Clicking the Subordinate button allows you to add a box below an existing box.

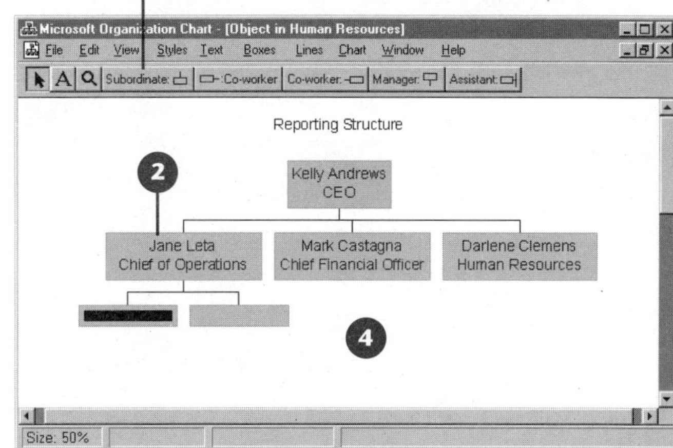

Change the Structure Style

1. Select the chart box or chart boxes whose style you want to change.
2. Click the Styles menu.
3. Click the button that provides the structure you want to use.

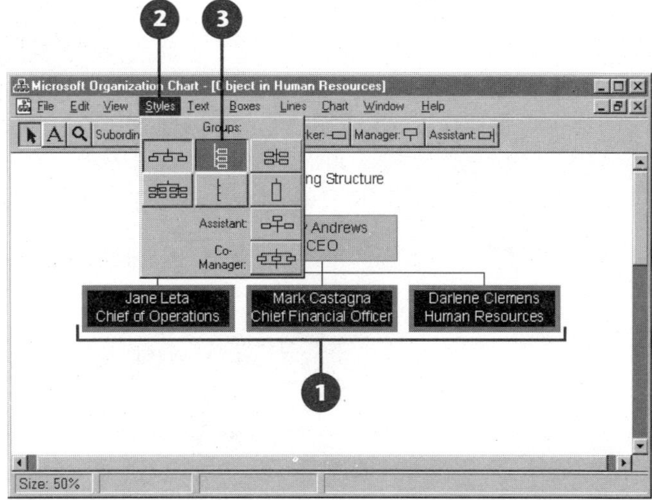

Rearrange a Chart Box

1. Make sure the chart box you want to move is deselected.
2. Drag the chart box over an existing chart box. The pointer changes to a four-headed arrow.
3. Continue to drag the chart box in the direction you want, and notice that the pointer changes to:
   - A left arrow when you drag over the left side of a box
   - A right arrow appears when you drag over the right side of a box
   - A double-headed arrow and a small chart box appears when you drag over the bottom of a box
4. Release the mouse button when the chart box is in the correct position.

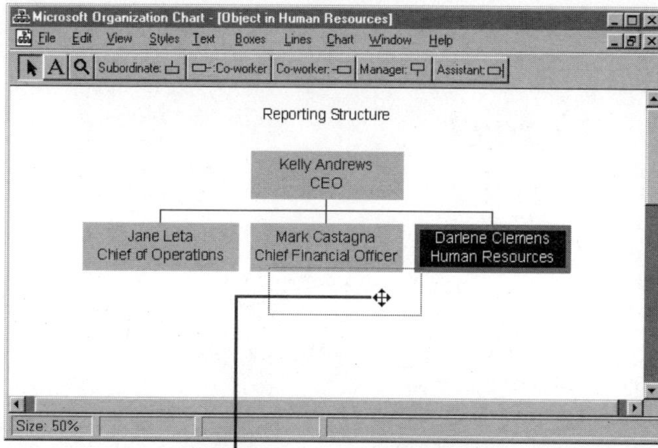

2 This pointer appears when you move the chart box below the highlighted chart box.

7

Correcting Text with AutoCorrect

Excel's AutoCorrect feature automatically corrects misspelled words as you type them. AutoCorrect comes with hundreds of entries, consisting of text and symbols that you can edit or delete, or you can add your own entries.

To get the most out of this feature, add words to the AutoCorrect dictionary that you frequently misspell, or add strings of words that you often type, so you can save time by just typing their initials. For example, you could use AutoCorrect to automatically change the initials EPA to Environmental Protection Agency. Use the AutoCorrect Exceptions dialog box to control how Excel handles capital letters.

Add an AutoCorrect Entry

1. Click the Tools menu, and then click AutoCorrect.
2. In the Replace box, type a misspelled word or an abbreviation.
3. In the With box, type the replacement entry.
4. Click Add.
5. Repeat steps 2 through 4 for each AutoCorrect entry you want to add.
6. Click OK.

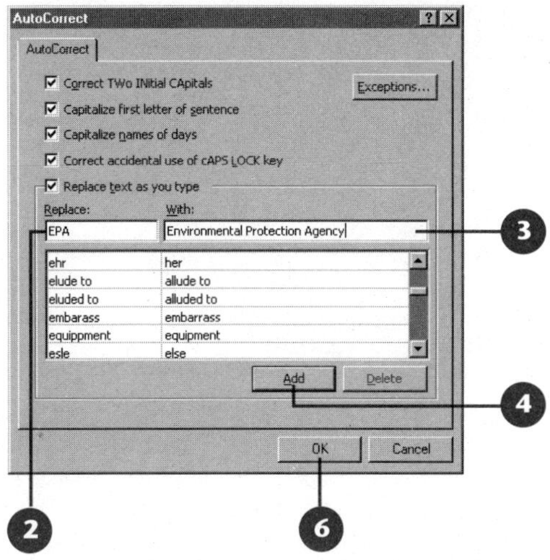

Edit an AutoCorrect Entry

1. Click the Tools menu, and then click AutoCorrect.
2. Select the AutoCorrect entry you want to change. You can either type the first few letters of the entry to be changed in the Replace box, or use the scroll bar to locate an entry and then click to select it.
3. In the With box, type the replacement entry.
4. Click Replace.
5. Click OK.

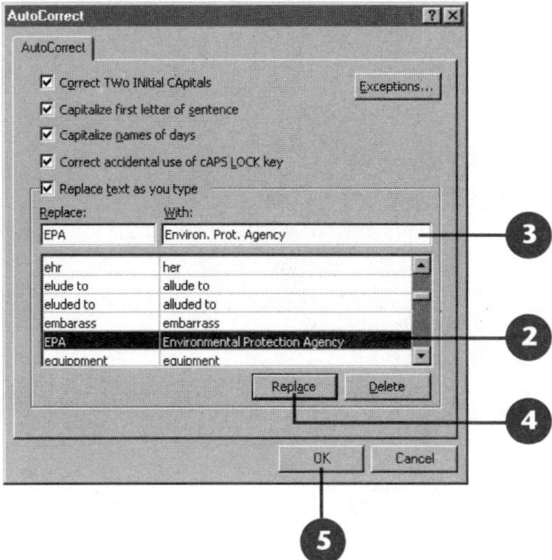

TIP

Delete an AutoCorrect Entry. *In the AutoCorrect dialog box, select the AutoCorrect entry you want to delete and click Delete.*

Change AutoCorrect Exceptions

1. Click the Tools menu, and then click AutoCorrect.
2. Click Exceptions.
3. Click the First Letter or INitial CAps tab. The First Letter list contains words that end with a period (.) but whose following word is never capitalized. The INitial CAps list contains words that have multiple capital letters; adding words to this list means that Excel will not try to correct them.
4. In the Don't Capitalize After box, type the entry you want to add.
5. Click Add.
6. Click OK to close the AutoCorrect Exceptions dialog box.
7. Click OK to close the AutoCorrect dialog box.

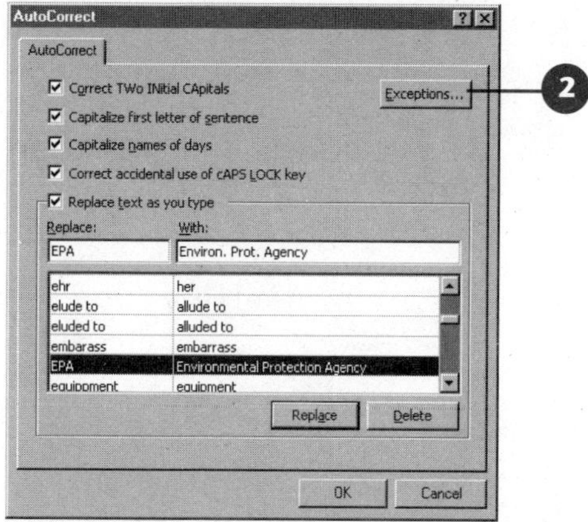

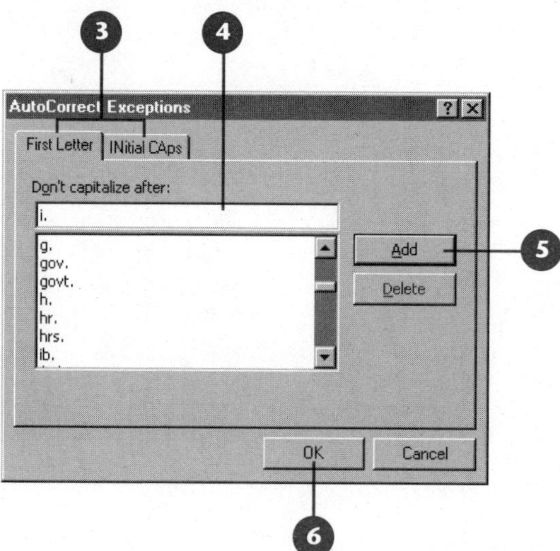

Creating and Reading a Cell Comment

Each cell within a worksheet can contain a *comment*—information you might want to share with co-workers or include as a reminder to yourself without making it a part of the worksheet. (Think of a comment as a nonprinting sticky note attached to an individual cell.) A cell that contains a comment displays a red triangle in the upper right corner of the cell. By default, comments are hidden.

TIP

Add and modify comments with the Reviewing toolbar. *Right-click any toolbar and click Reviewing to display the toolbar. Position the mouse pointer over a button to display its function.*

Add a Comment

1. Click the cell to which you want to add a comment.
2. Click the Insert menu, and then click Comments.
3. Type the comment in the comment box.
4. Click outside the comment box when you are finished, or press Esc twice to close the comment box.

Red triangle indicates a comment in a cell.

3	Employee	Rate	Hours	Gross Pay
4	Adams, Gail	$10.50		
5	Burns, Rachel	$12.50		
6	Carnoff, Joseph	$ 6.50		
7	Selkirk, Camaron	$12.75		
8	Tarson, Phillip	$10.50		
9	Total			$1,986.88

Perspection:
This rate was given during the last quarter.

Show a Comment

1. Position the mouse pointer over a red triangle in a cell to read its comment and then move the mouse pointer off the cell to hide the comment.

To show all the comments on the worksheet, click the View menu, and then click Comments. The Reviewing toolbar appears with the Show All Comments button depressed.

3	Employee	Rate	Hours	Gross Pay
4	Adams, Gail	$10.50		
5	Burns, Rachel	$12.50	3	
6	Carnoff, Joseph	$ 6.50	3	
7	Selkirk, Camaron	$12.75	4	
8	Tarson, Phillip	$10.50	3	
9	Total			$1,986.88

Perspection:
This rate was given during the last quarter.

7

Editing and Deleting a Cell Comment

You can edit or delete cell comments just as frequently as you edit or delete data in a worksheet. You can use common editing tools, such as the Backspace and Delete keys, as well as the Formatting toolbar buttons to edit the comment text.

TRY THIS

Format a comment. *Right-click the cell containing the comment you want to format, select the comment text, and click Bold, Italic, Underline, or Alignment buttons.*

Edit a Comment

1. Right-click the cell containing the comment you want to edit.
2. Click Edit Comment.
3. Make your changes.
4. Press Esc twice to close the comment box.
5. Click the Close button on the Reviewing toolbar.

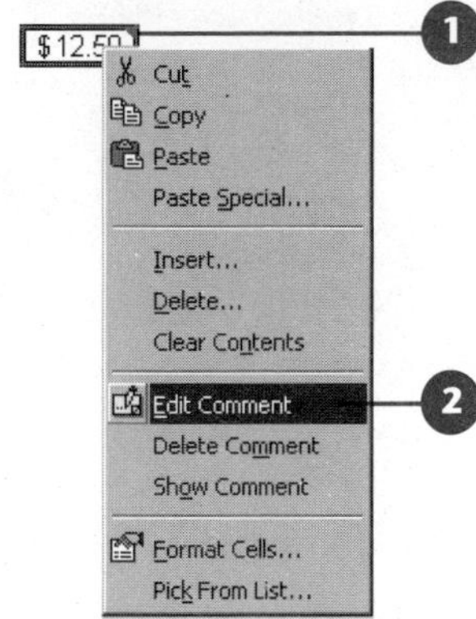

3	Employee	Rate	Hours	Gross Pay
4	Adams, Gail	$10.50		
5	Burns, Rachel	$12.50		
6	Carnoff, Joseph	$ 6.50		
7	Selkirk, Camaron	$12.75		
8	Tarson, Phillip	$10.50		
9	Total			$1,986.88

Perspection:
This rate was given during the last quarter.

3

Delete a Comment

1. Right-click the cell containing the comment you want to delete.
2. Click Delete Comment.

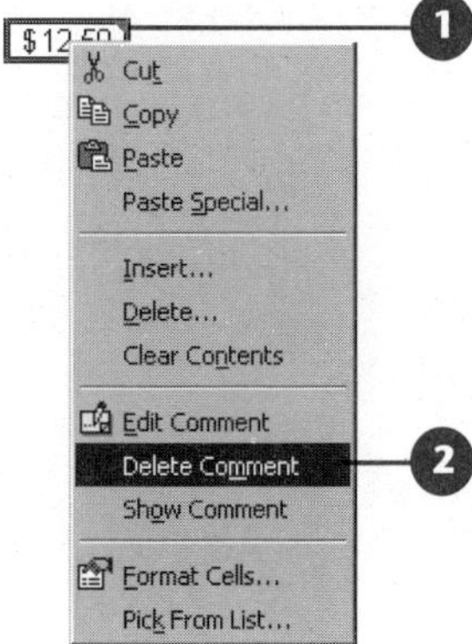

Looking Up Reference Material

Excel offers an assortment of textual tools. If you are searching for just the right word or for background information on a word or a concept, you can look it up right from Excel using Microsoft Bookshelf, available on your Office 97 CD.

TIP

You can insert additional reference titles. *If you have other reference resources, they might appear in the Available Reference Titles list. If you insert the appropriate CD, you can select it instead of Microsoft Bookshelf.*

Look up a Reference

1. Select the word or phrase you want to look up.
2. Click the Tools menu, and then click Look Up Reference.
3. Click Microsoft Bookshelf Basics to use the reference tools that accompany Office 97.
4. View the information that appears.
5. Click a topic to explore further.
6. Click the Close button when you are finished.

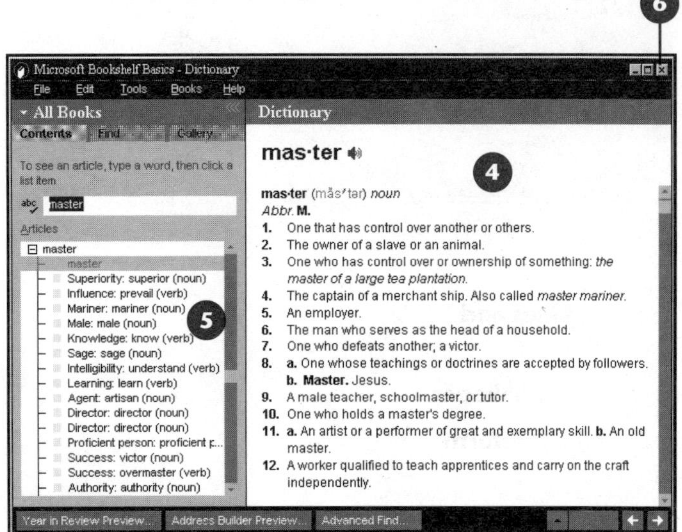

8

Drawing and Modifying Objects

IN THIS SECTION

- Drawing Lines and Arrows
- Drawing AutoShapes
- Drawing a Freeform Object
- Editing a Freeform Object
- Moving and Resizing an Object
- Rotating and Flipping an Object
- Choosing Object Colors
- Adding Object Shadows
- Creating a 3-D Object
- Aligning and Distributing Objects
- Arranging and Grouping Objects

When you need to be able to create your own pictures, you can use Excel 97 to get the job done. You can choose from a set of predesigned shapes, or you can use tools that allow you to draw and edit your own shapes and forms. Excel provides drawing tools that help you control how objects are drawn and placed on your worksheet in relation to one another.

Drawing Objects

Drawing objects can be classified into three categories: lines, AutoShapes, and freeforms. *Lines* are simply the straight or curved lines (arcs) that connect two points. *AutoShapes* are preset shapes, such as stars, circles, or ovals. A *freeform* is an irregular curve or polygon that you can create as a freehand drawing. To create a shape that is not included with the list of AutoShapes, you create it as a freeform.

Once you have created a drawing object, you can manipulate it in many ways, such as rotating it, coloring it, or changing its style. Excel also provides a formatting commands that allows you more precise control over all aspects of your drawing object's appearance.

Drawing Lines and Arrows

The most basic drawing objects you create on your worksheets are lines and arrows. Excel includes several tools for this purpose. The Line tool creates line segments. The Drawing toolbar's Line Style and Dash Style tools let you determine the type of line used in any drawing object—be it solid, dashed, or a combination of solid and dashed lines. The Arrow tool lets you create arrows that you can use to emphasize key features of your worksheet. The Drawing toolbar does not appear on the screen when you first open Excel, so to access the drawing tools, you'll need to open the Drawing toolbar.

SEE ALSO

See "Customizing a Toolbar" on page 184 for information on displaying and hiding a toolbar.

Draw a Straight Line

1. If necessary, click the Drawing button on the Standard toolbar.
2. Click the Line tool on the Drawing toolbar.
3. Drag the pointer to draw a line on your slide. The endpoints of the line are where you started and finished dragging.

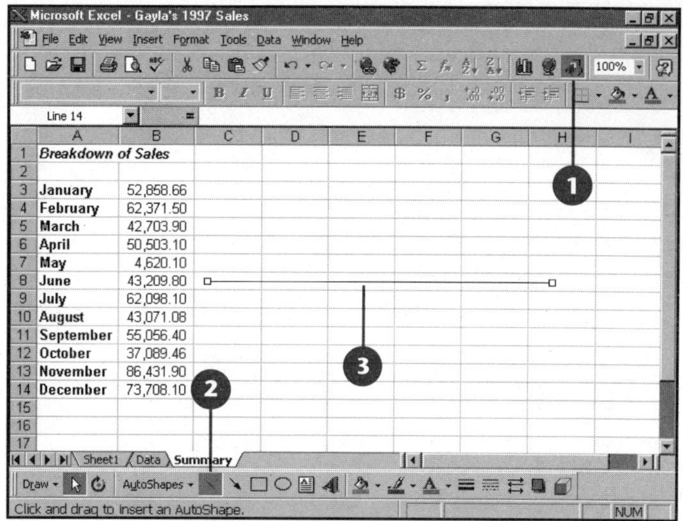

Edit a Line

1. Click the line you want to edit.
2. Click the Line Style tool on the Drawing toolbar to select a line thickness.
3. Click the Dash Style tool on the Drawing toolbar, to select a dash style.
4. Click the Line Color tool on the Drawing toolbar, to select a line color.
5. Drag the sizing handle at either end to a new location to change the size or angle of the line.

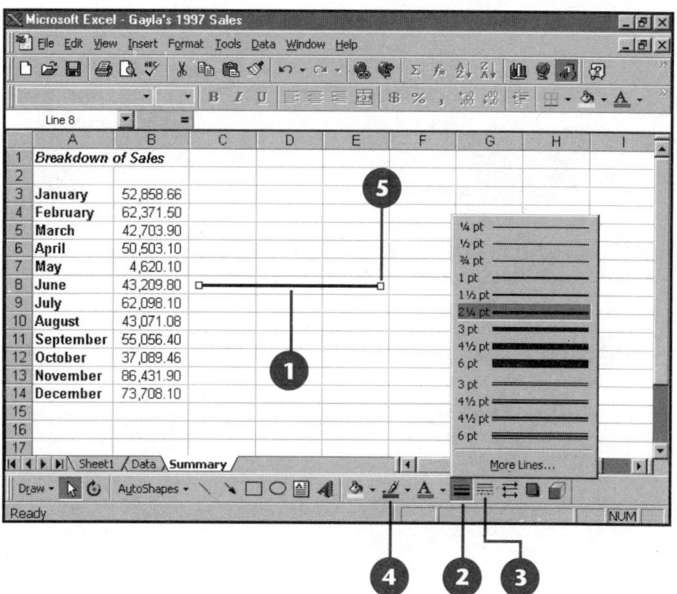

> **TRY THIS**
>
> **Use keyboard controls as you draw your arrow.** *Press and hold the Shift key as you drag the pointer to constrain the angle of the line to 15 degree increments. Press and hold the Ctrl key as you drag the pointer to draw the line from the center out, rather than from one endpoint to another.*

Draw an Arrow

1. Click the Arrow tool on the Drawing toolbar.
2. Drag the pointer from the base of the arrow to the arrow's point.
3. Release the mouse button when the arrow is correct length and angle.

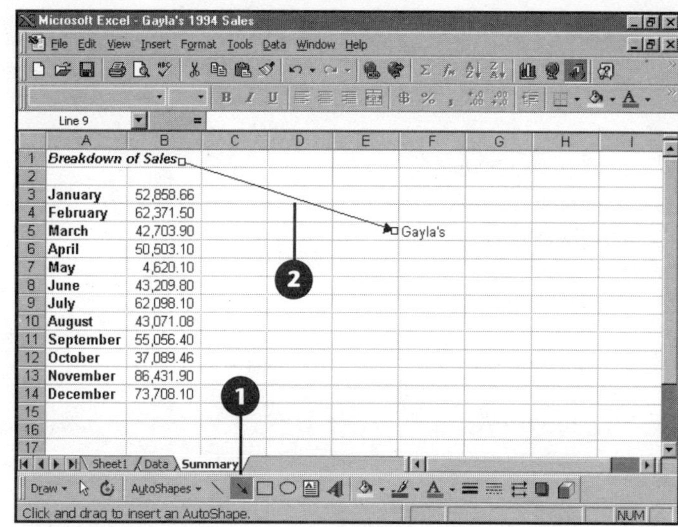

> **SEE ALSO**
>
> *See "Drawing AutoShapes" on page 118 for information on creating block arrows using the AutoShape drawing tool.*

> **TIP**
>
> **Use shared drawing tools in Office 97 programs.** *If you use other Office 97 programs, you might notice that the Drawing toolbar is available in most of them. These shared drawing tools, called* Office Art, *give you superior graphics capabilities when working in Office 97 programs.*

Edit an Arrow

1. Click the arrow you want to edit.
2. Click the Arrow Style tool on the Drawing toolbar.
3. Click the arrow type you want to use, or click More Arrows.
4. If you clicked More Arrows, modify the arrow type in the Format AutoShape dialog box as necessary, and click OK when you are finished.

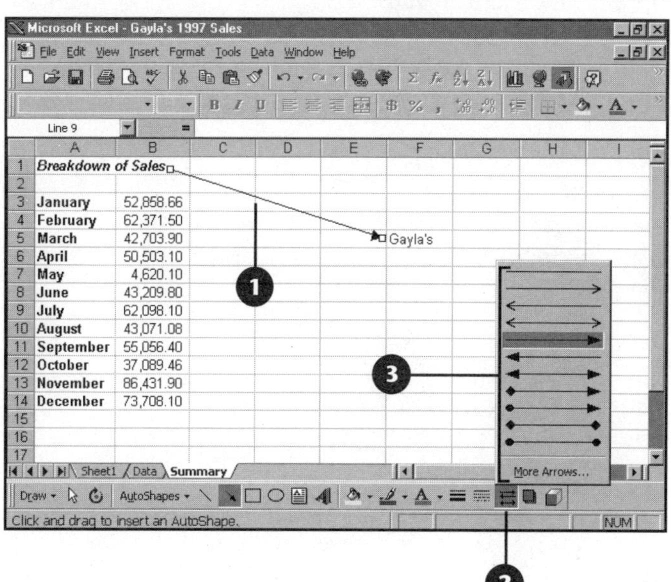

Drawing AutoShapes

You can choose from 155 different AutoShapes, ranging from hearts to lightening bolts, to draw on your worksheets. The two most common AutoShapes, the oval and the rectangle, are available directly on the Drawing toolbar. The rest of the AutoShapes are organized into categories that you can view and select from the AutoShapes menu off the Drawing toolbar. Once you have placed an AutoShape on a slide, you can resize it using the sizing handles. Many AutoShapes have an *adjustment handle*, a small yellow diamond, located near a resize handle, that you can drag to alter the shape of the AutoShape.

TIP

You can Draw a circle or square. *To draw a perfect circle or square, click the Oval or Rectangle tool on the Drawing toolbar, and then press and hold the Shift key as you drag the pointer.*

Draw an Oval or Rectangle

1. Click the Oval or Rectangle tool on the Drawing toolbar.
2. Drag over the slide where you want to place the oval or rectangle. The shape you drew takes on the line color and fill color defined by the presentation's color scheme.

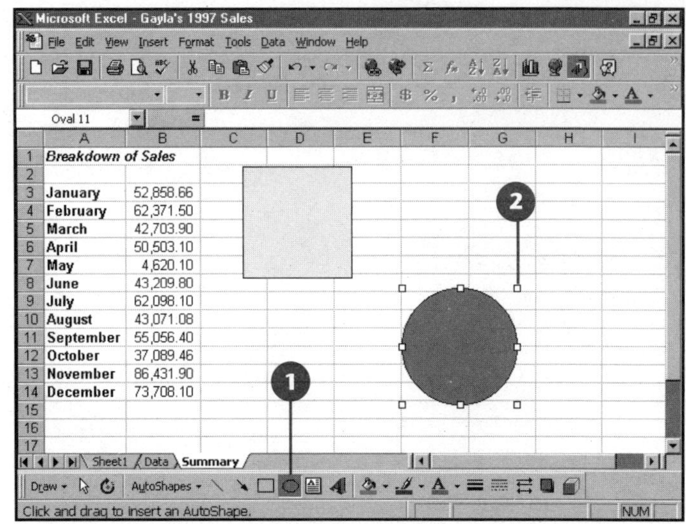

Draw an AutoShape

1. Click the AutoShapes tool on the Drawing toolbar, and then point to the AutoShape category you want to use.
2. Click the symbol you want.
3. Drag the pointer across the slide until the drawing object is the shape and size that you want.

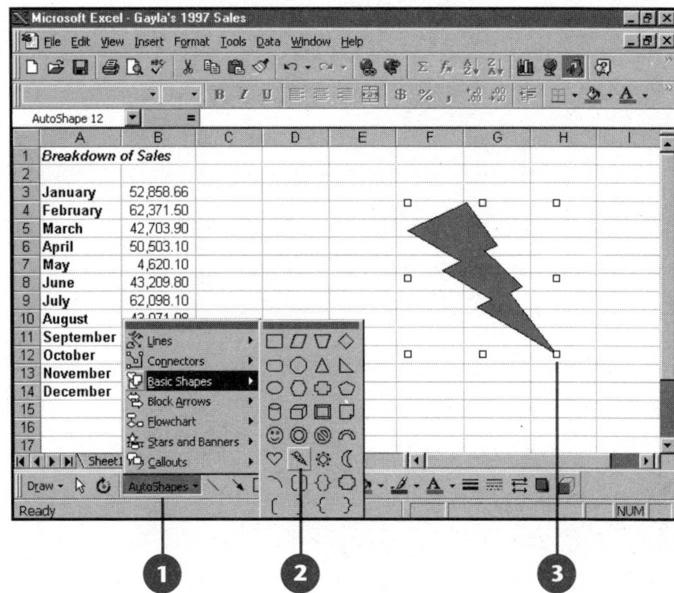

TRY THIS

Replace an AutoShape. *You can replace one AutoShape with another, while retaining the size, color, and orientation of the AutoShape. Click the AutoShape you want replace, click the Draw tool on the Drawing toolbar, point to Change AutoShape, and then select the new AutoShape you want.*

Adjust an AutoShape

1. Click the AutoShape you want to adjust.
2. Click one of the adjustment handles, and then drag the handle to alter the form of the AutoShape.

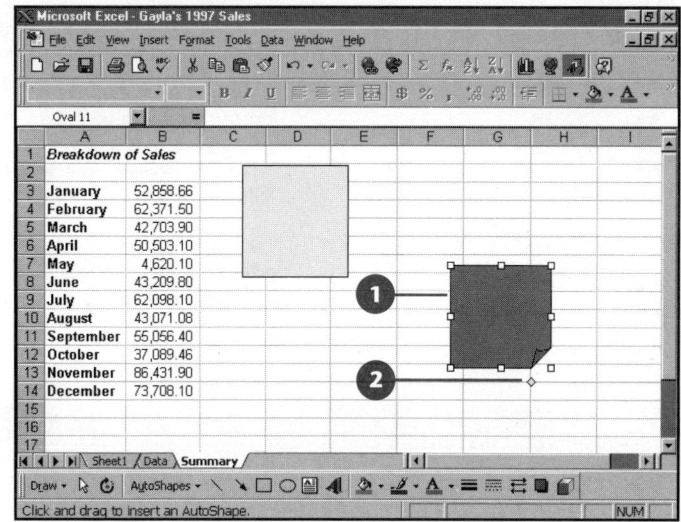

8

Drawing a Freeform Object

When you need to create a customized shape, you use the Freeform tools. They are all located in the Lines category in the list of AutoShapes. Freeforms are like the drawings you make yourself with a pen and paper, except that you have more control over the accuracy and length of the lines you draw. A freeform can either be an open curve or a closed curve.

Draw an Irregular Polygon

1. Click the AutoShapes tool on the Drawing toolbar, and then point to Lines.
2. Click the Freeform tool.
3. Click the spot on the slide where you want to place the first vertex of the polygon.
4. Move the pointer to second point of your polygon, and then click the left mouse button. A line joins the two points.
5. Continue moving and clicking the mouse pointer to create additional sides of your polygon.
6. To close the polygon, click near the starting point.

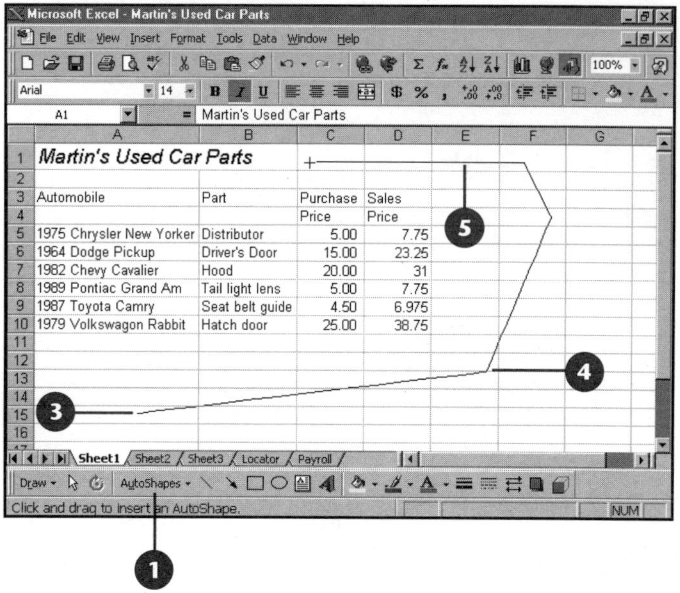

Draw an Irregular Curve

1. Click the AutoShapes tool on the Drawing toolbar, and then point to Lines.
2. Click the Curve tool.
3. Click the spot on the slide where you want to place the curve's starting point.

TIP

Switch Between a Closed Curve and an Open Curve. *Right-click the freeform drawing. To switch from an open curve to a closed curve, click Close Curve, or to switch from a closed curve to an open curve, click Open Curve.*

4. Move the pointer to the spot where you want your irregular curve to bend and then click. Repeat this step as often as you need to create bends in your curve.

5. Finish the curve.
   - For a closed curve, click near the starting point.
   - For an open curve, double-click the last point in the curve.

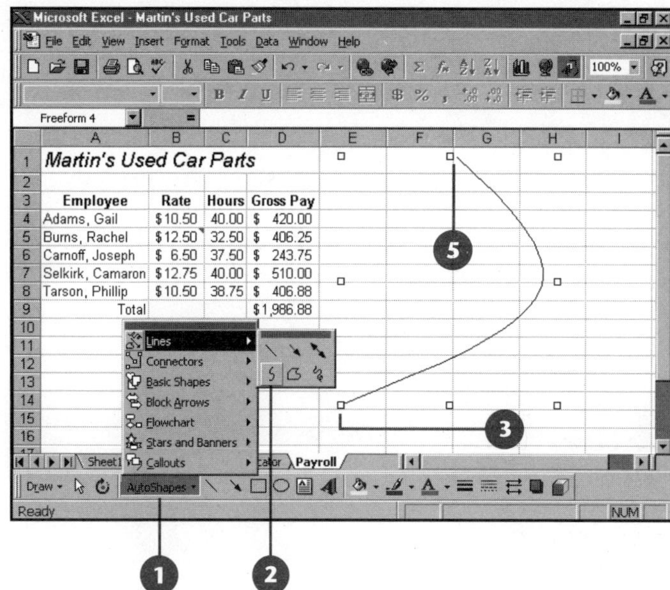

8

Scribble

1. Click the AutoShapes tool on the Drawing toolbar, and then point to Lines.
2. Click the Scribble tool.
3. Drag the pointer across the screen to draw freehand.

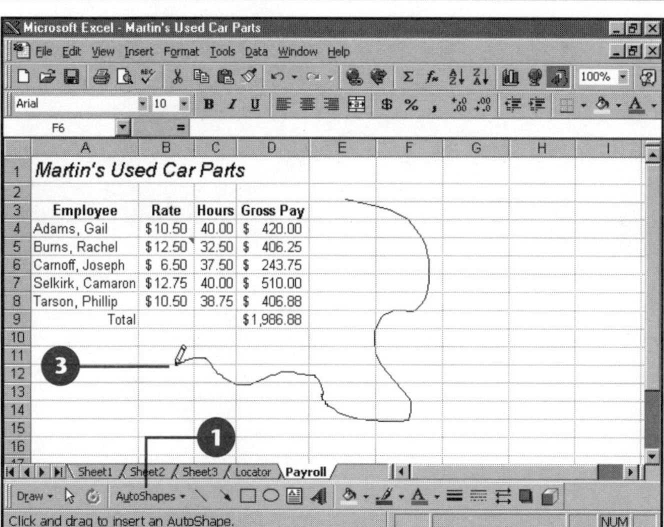

Editing a Freeform Object

You can edit a freeform by altering the vertices that create the shape using the Edit Points command. Each vertex (a corner in an irregular polygon and a bend in a curve) has two attributes: its position and the angle at which the curve enters and leaves it. You can move the position of each vertex and also control the corner or bend angles. Additionally, you can add or delete vertices. When you delete a vertex, Excel recalculates the freeform and smoothes it among the remaining points. Similarly, if you add a new vertex, Excel adds a corner or bend in your freeform.

Move a Vertex in a Freeform

1. Click the freeform object.
2. Click the Draw tool on the Drawing toolbar, and then click Edit Points.
3. Drag one of the freeform vertices to a new location.
4. Click outside the freeform when you are finished.

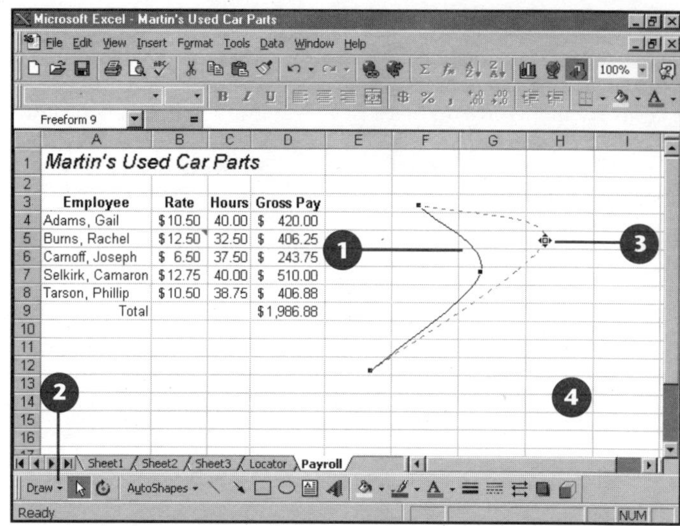

Insert a Freeform Vertex

1. Select the freeform object.
2. Click the Draw tool on the Drawing toolbar, and then click Edit Points.
3. Position the pointer on the curve or polygon border (not on a vertex), and then drag in the direction you want the new vertex.
4. Click outside the freeform to set the new shape.

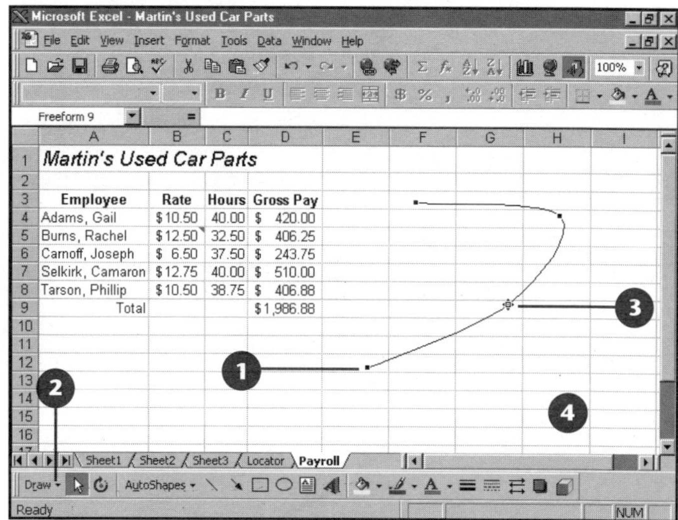

TRY THIS

Gain control over your freeform. *After you click Edit Points, right-click a vertex. PowerPoint displays a pop-up menu with options for other types of vertices you can use to refine the shape of the freeform. These commands let you specify, for example, a smooth point, a straight point, or a corner point.*

Delete a Freeform Vertex

1. Click the freeform object.
2. Click the Draw tool on the Drawing toolbar, and then click Edit Points.
3. Press the Ctrl key while clicking the point you want to delete.
4. Click outside the freeform to set the shape of the freeform.

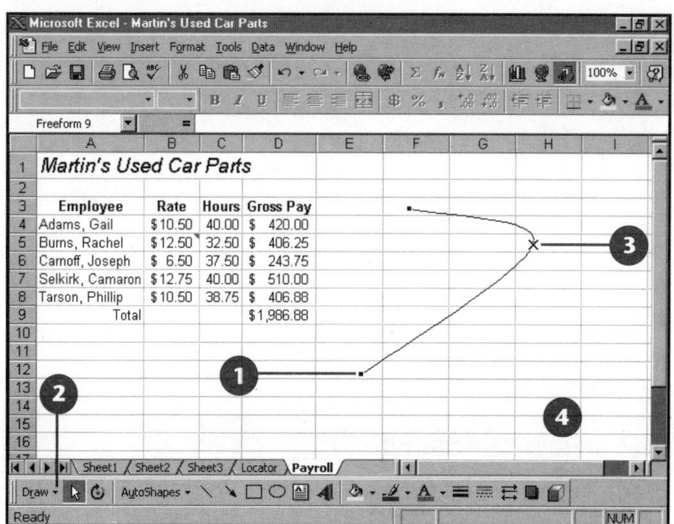

8

Modify a Vertex Angle

1. Click the freeform object.
2. Click the Draw tool on the Drawing toolbar, and then click Edit Points.
3. Right-click a vertex and click Smooth Point, Straight Point, or Corner Point. Angle handles appear.
4. Drag one or both of the angle handles to modify the shape of the line segments going into and out of the vertex.
5. Click outside the freeform to set its shape.

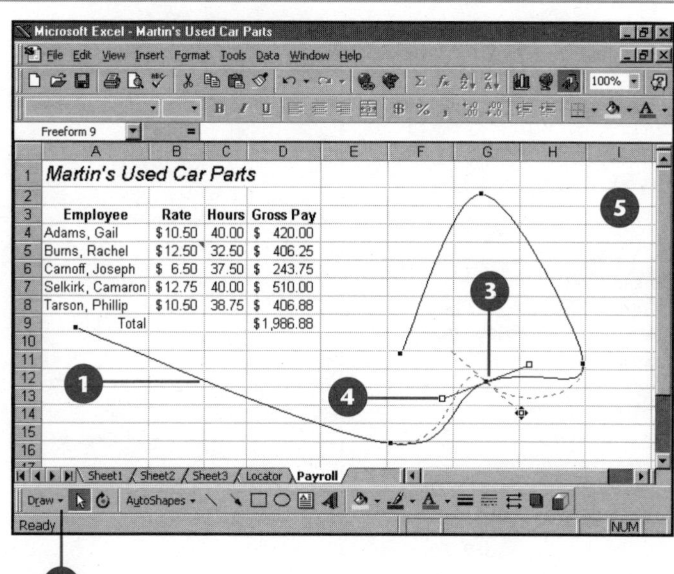

Moving and Resizing an Object

After you create a drawing object, you might need to resize it or move it to a different location on your worksheet. Although you can move and resize objects using the mouse, if you want more precise control over the object's size and position, use the AutoShape command on the Format menu to exactly specify the location and size of the drawing object. You can also use the Nudge command to move drawing objects in tiny increments, up, down, left, or right.

TIP

You can retain the proportions of the object you're resizing. *Press and hold the Shift key as you drag the pointer to the new size.*

Move an Object

1. Drag the object to a new location on the slide. Make sure you aren't dragging a sizing handle or adjustment handle. If you are working with a freeform and you are in Edit Points mode, drag the interior of the object, not the border, or you will end up resizing or reshaping the object, not moving it.

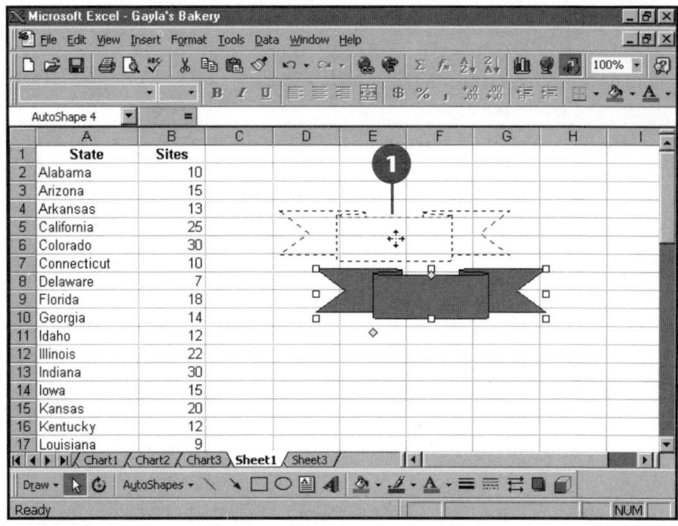

Nudge an Object

1. Click the object you want to nudge.
2. Click the Draw tool on the Drawing toolbar.
3. Point to Nudge and then click the direction: up, down, left or right.

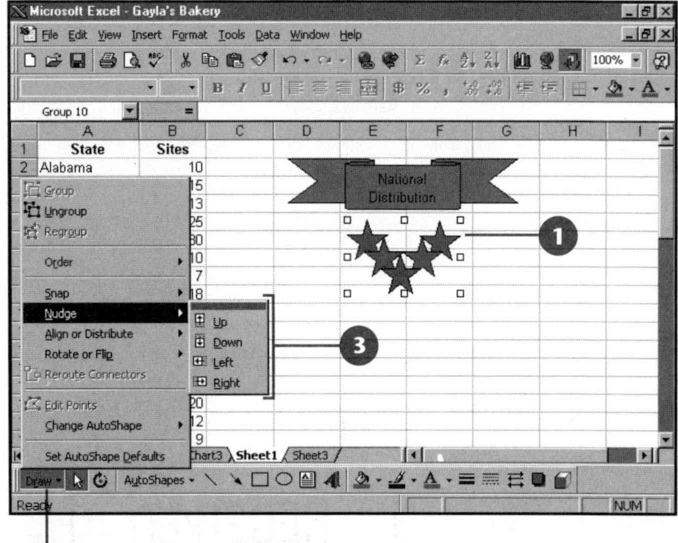

SEE ALSO

See "Moving and Resizing a Chart" on page 147 for more information on moving and resizing.

Resize a Drawing Object with the Mouse

1. Click the object to be resized.
2. Drag one of the sizing handles:
   - To resize the object in the vertical or horizontal direction, drag a sizing handle on the side of the selection box.
   - To resize the object in both the vertical and horizontal directions, drag a sizing handle on the corner of the selection box.

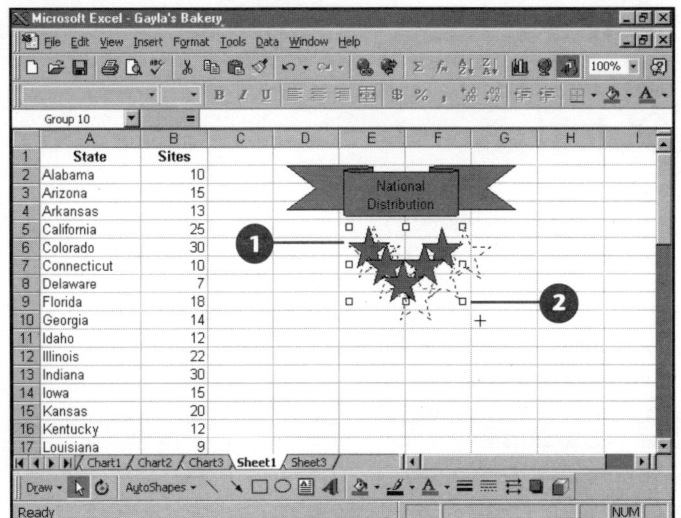

Resize an Object Precisely

1. Click the object to be resized.
2. Click the Format menu, and then click AutoShape.
3. Click the Scale Height and Width spin arrows to resize the object.
4. Click OK.

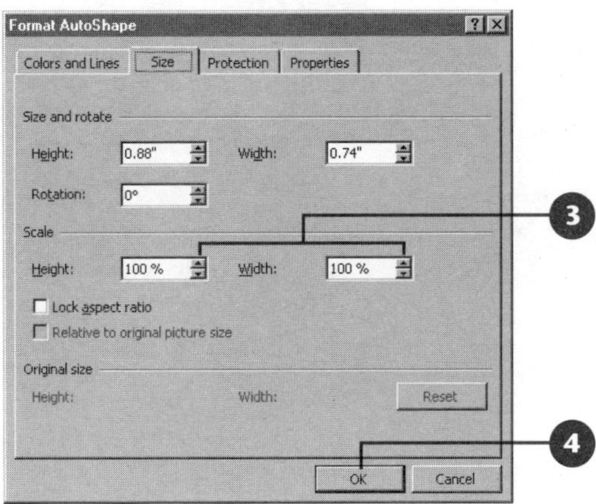

Rotating and Flipping an Object

If you need to change the orientation of a drawing object, you can rotate or flip it. For example, if you want to create a mirror image of your object you can flip it. To turn an object on its side, you can rotate it 90°. Rotating and flipping tools work with drawing and text objects. You won't usually be able to rotate or flip objects such as charts and pictures.

Rotate an Object to any Angle

1. Click the object you want to rotate.
2. Click the Free Rotate tool on the Drawing toolbar.
3. Drag a rotation handle to rotate the object.
4. Click outside the object to set the rotation.

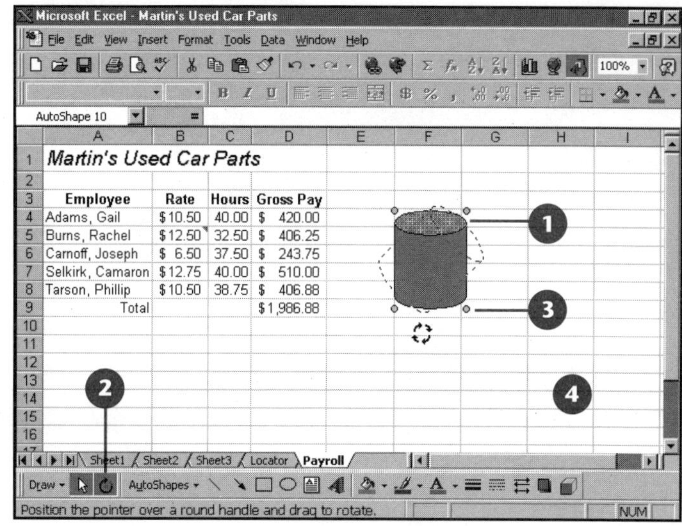

Rotate or Flip a Drawing Using Preset Increments

1. Click the object you want to rotate.
2. Click the Draw tool on the Drawing toolbar.
3. Point to Rotate Or Flip, and then click one of the Rotate or Flip commands.

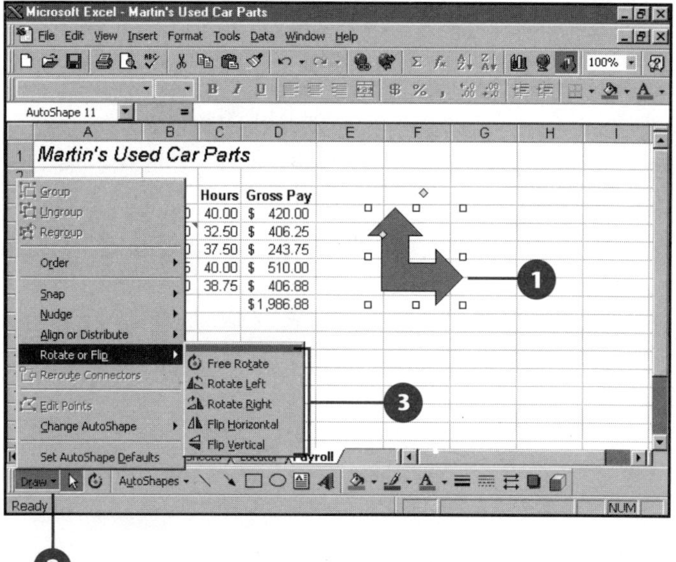

TIP

You can rotate an object 90 degrees. *To rotate an object 90 degrees to the left, click Rotate Left. To rotate an object 90 degrees to the right, click Rotate Right.*

TIP

You can constrain the rotation to 15-degree increments. *Press and hold the Shift key when rotating the object.*

Rotate a Drawing Object Around a Fixed Point

1. Click the object you want to rotate.
2. Click the Free Rotate tool on the Drawing toolbar.
3. Click the rotate handle opposite the point you want to rotate, and then press and hold the Ctrl key as you rotate the object.
4. Click outside the object to set the rotation

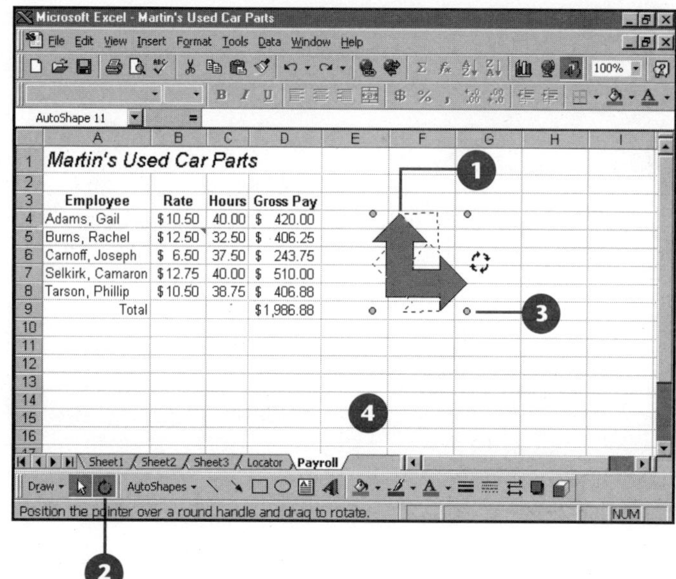

8

Rotate a Drawing Precisely

1. Right-click the object you want to rotate, and then click Format AutoShape.
2. Click the Size tab.
3. Enter the angle of rotation.
4. Click OK.

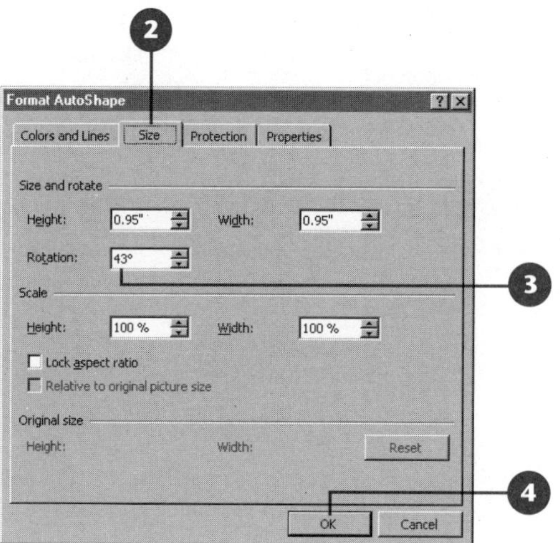

Choosing Object Colors

When you create a closed drawing object, you can choose the Fill color and the Line color. When you create a drawing object, it uses a default color. You can change the Fill and Line color settings for drawing objects using the same color tools you use to change a text color. These tools include the ability to use patterns . You can use fill effects as well, including gradients, patterns, and even clip art pictures.

Change a Drawing Object's Fill Color

1. Click the drawing object whose fill color you want to change.
2. Click the Fill Color tool on the Drawing toolbar.
3. Select the fill color or fill effect you want.

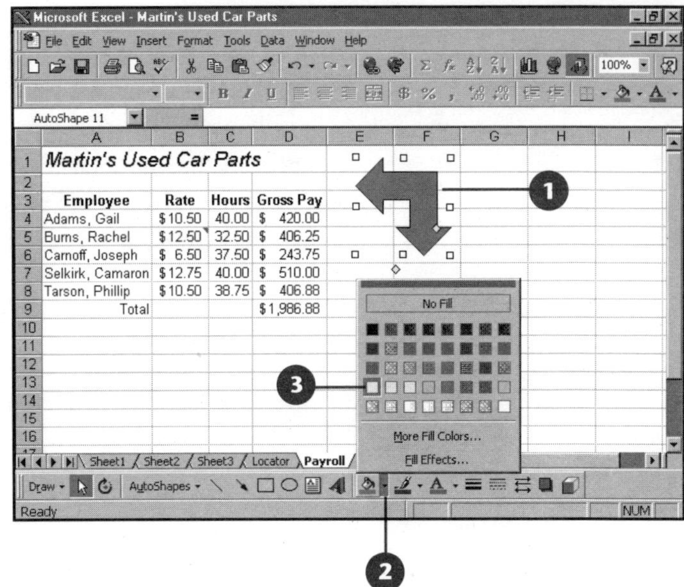

Change Colors and Lines in the Format Dialog Box

1. Right-click the object you want to modify, and then click Format AutoShape.
2. Click the Colors and Lines tab.
3. Set your color, line, and arrow options.
4. Click OK.

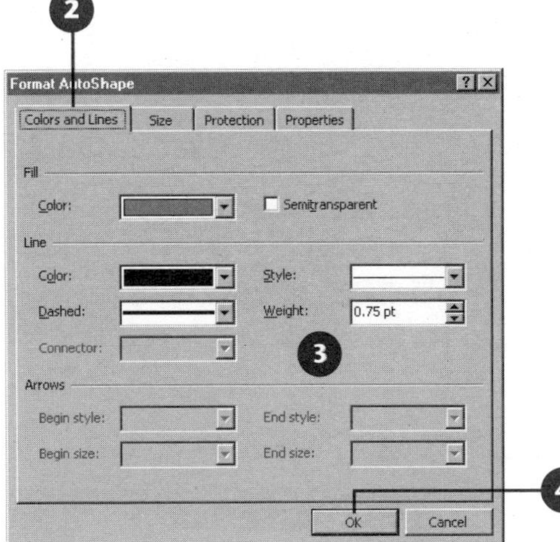

TIP

You can set the color and line style for an object as the default for future drawing objects. *Right-click the object and click Set Object Defaults. Any new objects you create will use the same styles.*

SEE ALSO

See "Choosing Data Color" on page 83 for information on selecting colors and see "Adding Color and Patterns to Cells" on page 84 for information on using fill effects and patterns.

Create a Line Pattern

1. Right-click the line you want to change, and then click Format AutoShape.
2. Click the Color drop-down arrow.
3. Click Patterned Lines.
4. Click the Foreground drop-down arrow, and then click the color you want as a foreground.
5. Click the Background drop-down arrow, and then click the color you want as a background.
6. Click the pattern you want in the Pattern grid.
7. Click OK twice.

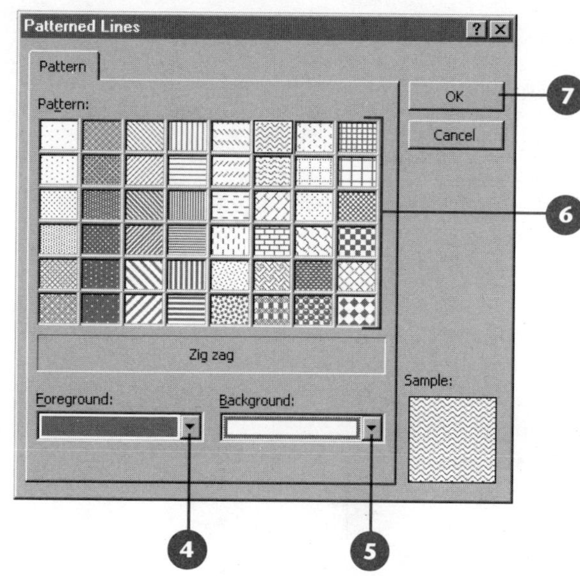

8

Adding Object Shadows

You can give objects on your worksheet the illusion of depth by adding shadows. Excel provides several preset shadowing options, or you can create your own by specifying the location and color of the shadow. If the shadow is falling on another object in your worksheet, you can create a semitransparent shadow that blends the color of the shadow with the color of the object underneath it.

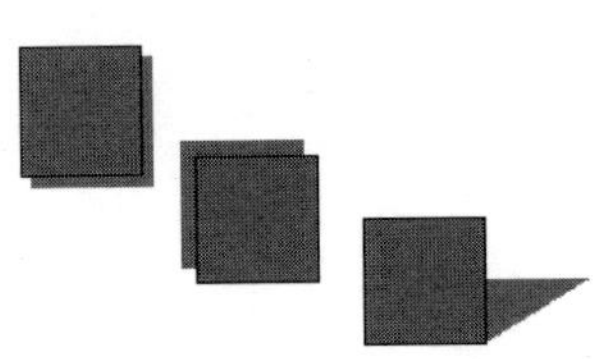

Use a Preset Shadow

1. Click the drawing object.
2. Click the Shadow tool on the Drawing toolbar.
3. Click one of the 20 preset shadow styles.

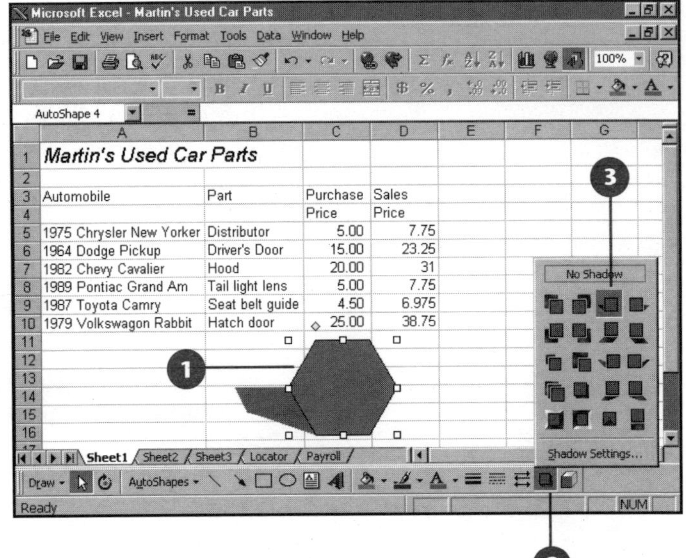

Change the Location of a Shadow

1. Click the drawing object that has the shadow.
2. Click the Shadow tool on the Drawing toolbar, and then click Shadow Settings.
3. Click the tool that will give the effect you want.

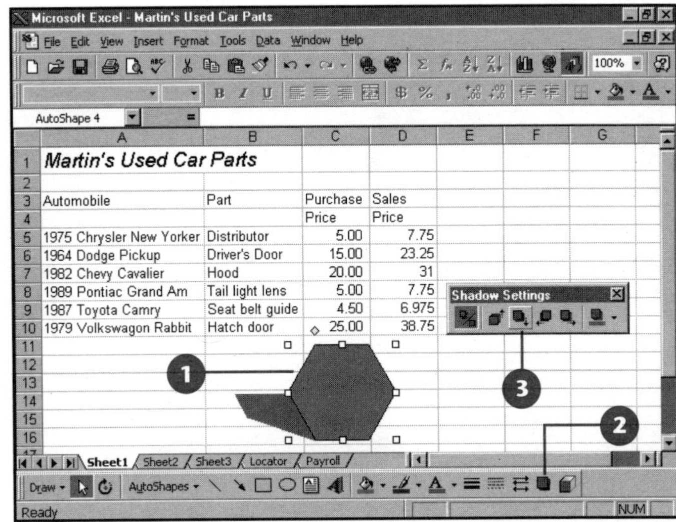

SEE ALSO

See "Adding Borders to Cells" on page 86 for information on adding and formatting borders to cells.

Change the Color of a Shadow

1. Click the drawing object that has the shadow.
2. Click the Shadow tool on the Drawing toolbar, and then click Shadow Settings.
3. Click the Shadow Color tool on the Shadow Settings toolbar, and then select a new color.

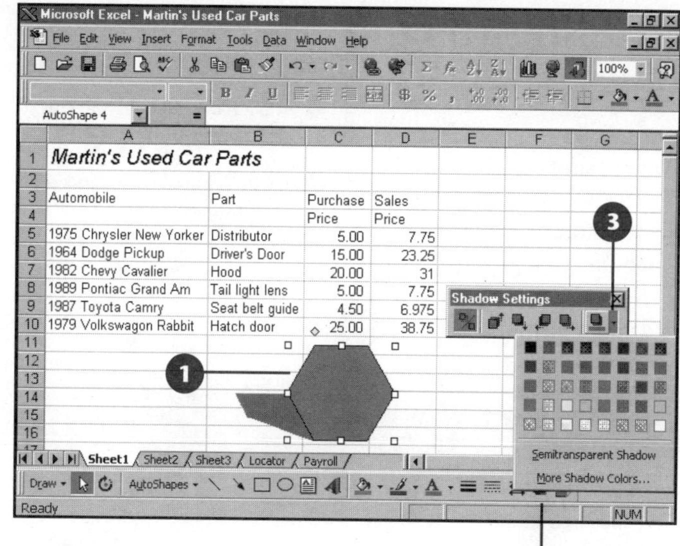

8

Creating a 3-D Object

You can add the illusion of depth to your worksheets by giving your drawings a three-dimensional appearance using the 3-D tool. Although not all objects can be turned into 3-D objects, most of the AutoShapes can. You can create a 3-D effect using one of the 20 preset 3-D styles, or you can use the 3-D tools to customize your own 3-D style. With the customization tools you can control, among other things, the angle at which the 3-D object is tilted and rotated, the depth of the object, and the direction of light falling upon the object.

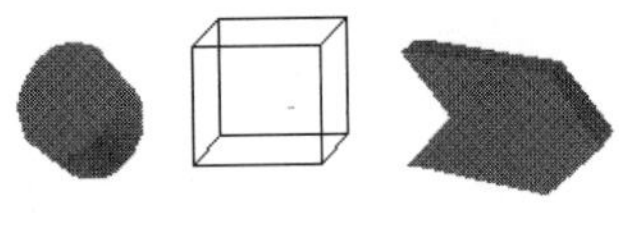

Apply a Preset 3-D Style

1. Click the drawing object.
2. Click the 3-D tool on the Drawing toolbar.
3. Click one of the 20 preset 3-D styles

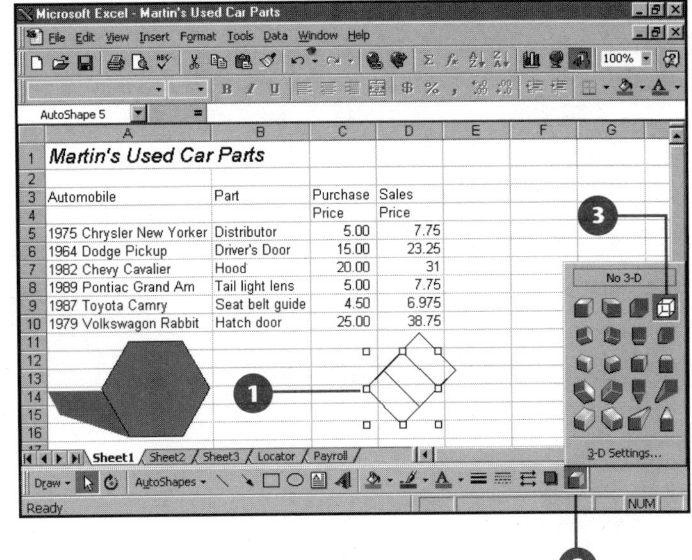

Spinning a 3-D Object

1. Click the 3-D object.
2. Click the 3-D tool on the Drawing toolbar, and then click 3-D Settings.
3. Click the spin setting you want.

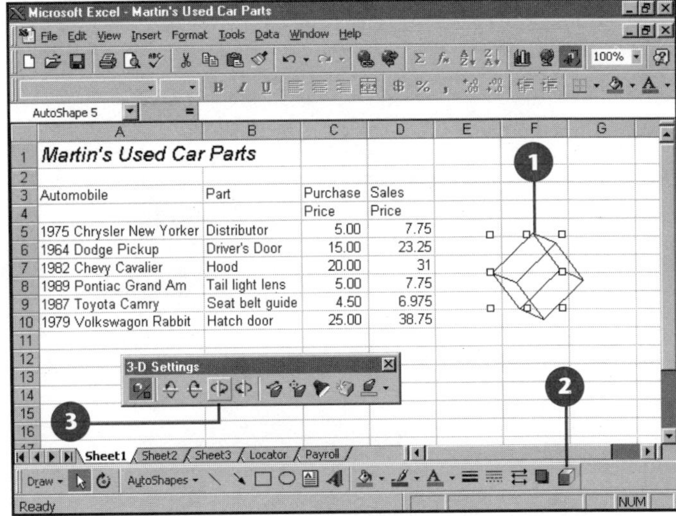

TIP

You cannot use both drop shadows and 3-D effects on the same object.

Set Lighting

1. Click the 3-D object.
2. Click the 3-D tool on the Drawing toolbar, and then click 3-D Settings.
3. Click the Lighting tool.
4. Click the spotlight that creates the effect you want.

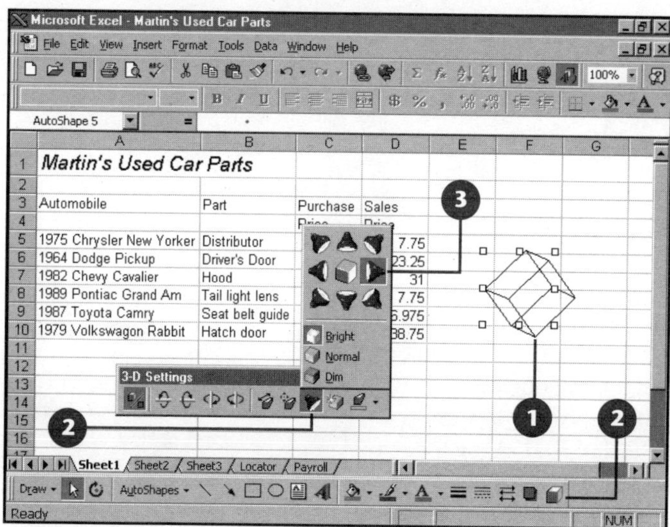

Set 3-D Depth

1. Click the 3-D object.
2. Click the 3-D tool on the Drawing toolbar, and then click 3-D Settings.
3. Click the Depth tool.
4. Click the size of the depth in points, or enter the exact number of points you want in the Custom box.

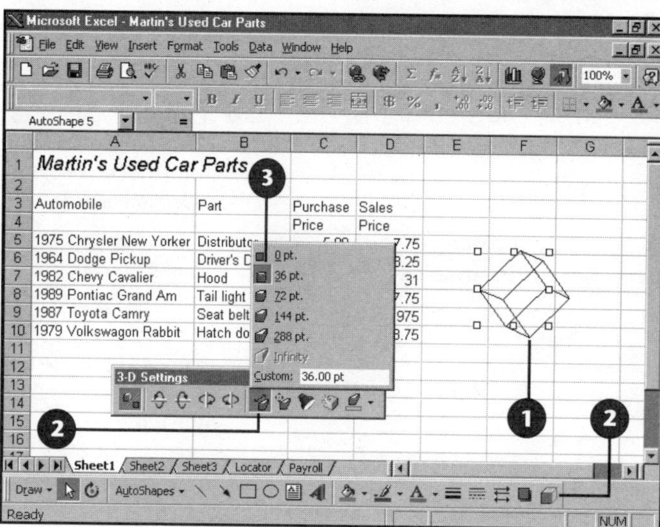

Aligning and Distributing Objects

Often when you work with three similar or identical objects, they look best when aligned in relation to each other. For example, you can align three objects with the leftmost object in the selection so that the tops of all three objects match along an invisible line. Sometimes your task will not be alignment but to distribute your objects evenly across a space. Excel includes commands to distribute your items horizontally and vertically. You can specify whether the distribution should occur for only the space currently occupied by the objects or across the entire slide.

Align Objects

1. Select the objects that you want to align. You can press Shift to select multiple objects.
2. Click the Draw tool on the Drawing toolbar, and point to Align Or Distribute.
3. Decide whether you want the objects to align relative to the slide or relative to each other, and then make sure that Relative To Slide is selected or deselected, based on your decision.
4. Click the alignment option you want.
   - Click Align Left to line up the objects with the left edge of the selection or slide.
   - Click Align Center to line up the objects with the center of the selection or slide.
   - Click Align Right to line up the objects with the right edge of the selection or slide.
   - Click Align Top to line up the objects with the top edge of the selection or slide.

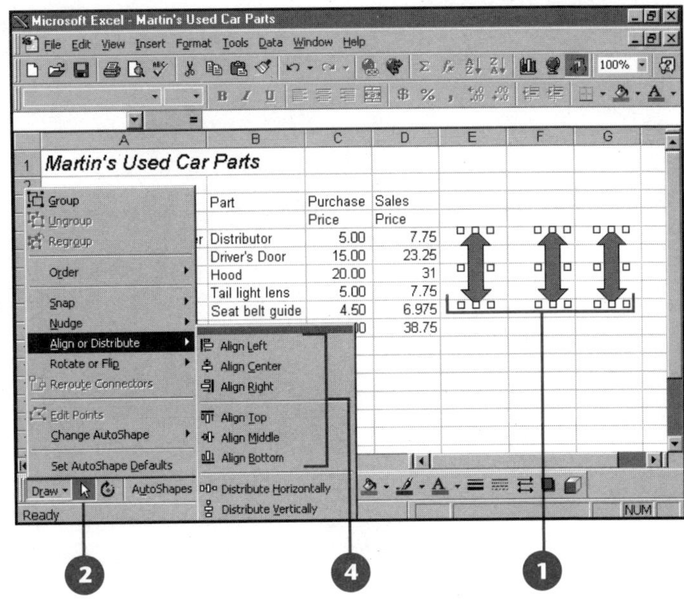

- Click Align Middle to line up the objects vertically with the middle of the selection or slide.
- Click Align Bottom to line up the objects with the bottom of the selection or slide.

8

SEE ALSO

See "Moving and Resizing an Object" on page 124 for information on moving and resizing distributed objects.

Distribute Objects

1. Select the objects that you want to distribute. You can press Shift to select multiple objects.
2. Click the Draw tool on the Drawing toolbar, and then point to Align Or Distribute.
3. Click the Distribution option you want.
   - Click Distribute Horizontally to distribute the objects evenly horizontally.
   - Click Distribute Vertically to distribute the objects evenly vertically.

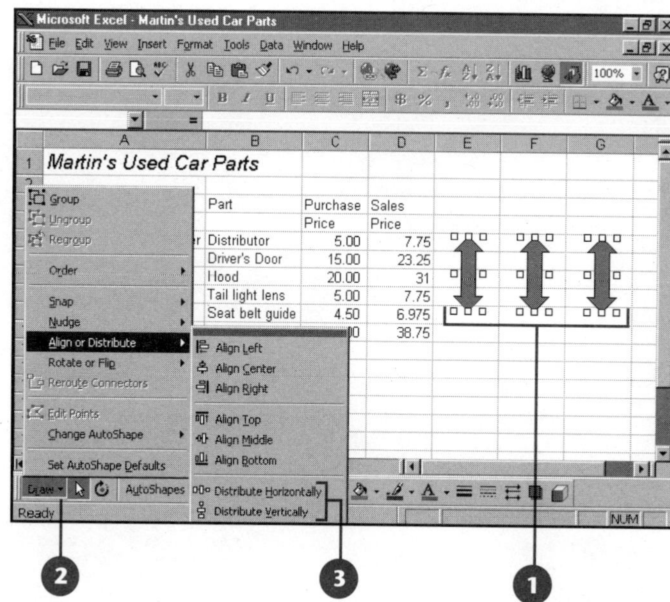

Arranging and Grouping Objects

When a worksheet contains multiple objects you might need to consider how they interact with each other. If the objects overlap, the most recently-created drawing will be placed on top of older drawings, but you can change how the stack of objects is ordered. If you have created a collection of objects that work together, you might want to group them to create a new drawing object that you can move, resize or copy as a single unit.

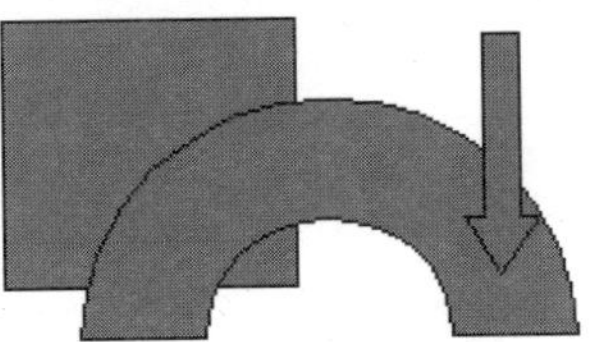

Arrange a Stack of Objects

1. Click the drawing object you want to place.
2. Click the Draw tool on the Drawing toolbar, and then point to Order.
3. Click Bring to Front to move the drawing to the top of the stack. Click Send to Back to move a drawing to the bottom of the stack. Click Bring Forward to move a drawing up one location in the stack. Click Send Backward to move a drawing back one location in the stack.

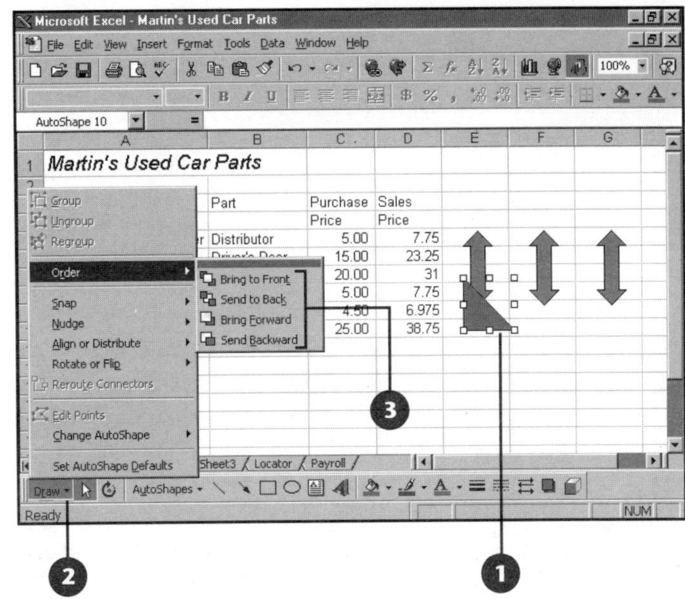

Group Objects Together

1. Select the drawing objects you want to group together. You can press Shift to select multiple objects.
2. Click the Draw tool on the Drawing toolbar.
3. Click Group.

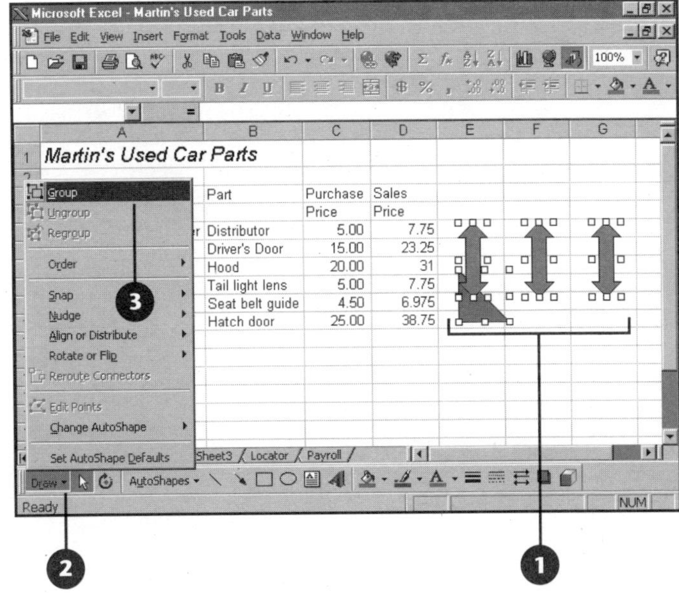

SEE ALSO

See "Moving and Resiging an Object" on page 124 for information on moving and resizing grouped objects.

Ungroup a Drawing

1. Select the object you want to ungroup.
2. Click the Draw tool on the Drawing toolbar.
3. Click Ungroup.

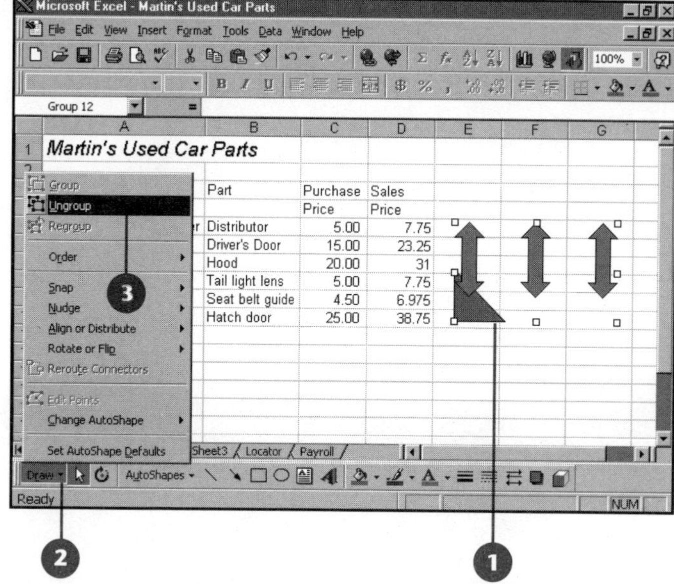

Regroup a Drawing

1. Click the Draw tool on the Drawing toolbar.
2. Click Regroup.

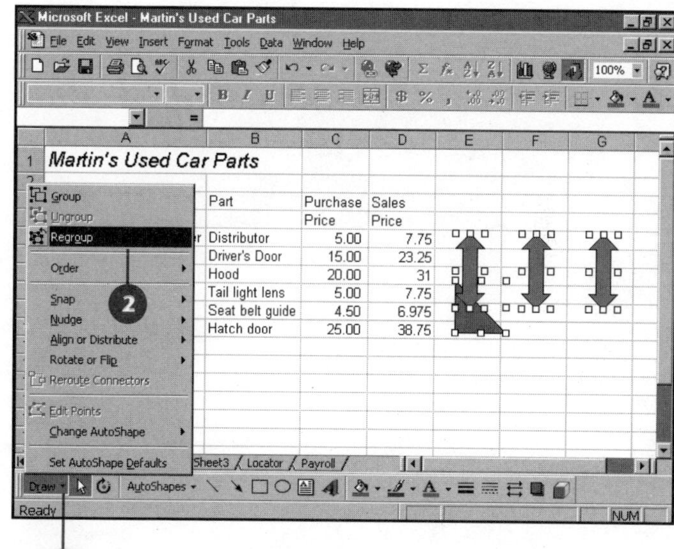

8

9

Creating Charts and Maps

IN THIS SECTION

Understanding Chart Terminology

Choosing the Right Type of Chart

Creating a Chart

Editing a Chart

Selecting a Chart

Changing a Chart Type

Moving and Resizing a Chart

Pulling Out a Pie Slice

Adding and Deleting a Data Series

Enhancing a Data Series

Enhancing a Chart

Drawing on a Chart

Changing Chart Fonts

Creating a Map

Modifying a Map

When you're ready to share data with others, showing the worksheet you created might not be the best way to present the information. A page full of numbers, if even formatted attractively, can be hard to understand and perhaps even a little boring. To help you present information more effectively, Microsoft Excel 97 makes it easy to create and modify charts and maps based on worksheet data.

Creating Charts and Maps

A *chart*, sometimes called a graph, is a visual representation of selected data in your worksheet. A well-designed chart draws your reader's attention by illustrating trends and highlighting significant relationships between numbers. Once readers grasp the basic idea conveyed in a chart, they're more likely to read and understand the detailed information contained in your worksheet.

A *map* displays geographic data—such as population values in the United States—within an actual map. A variety of maps are included with Excel; including the United States and other countries, and you can have a great deal of freedom to show only those states or countries you need.

Understanding Chart Terminology

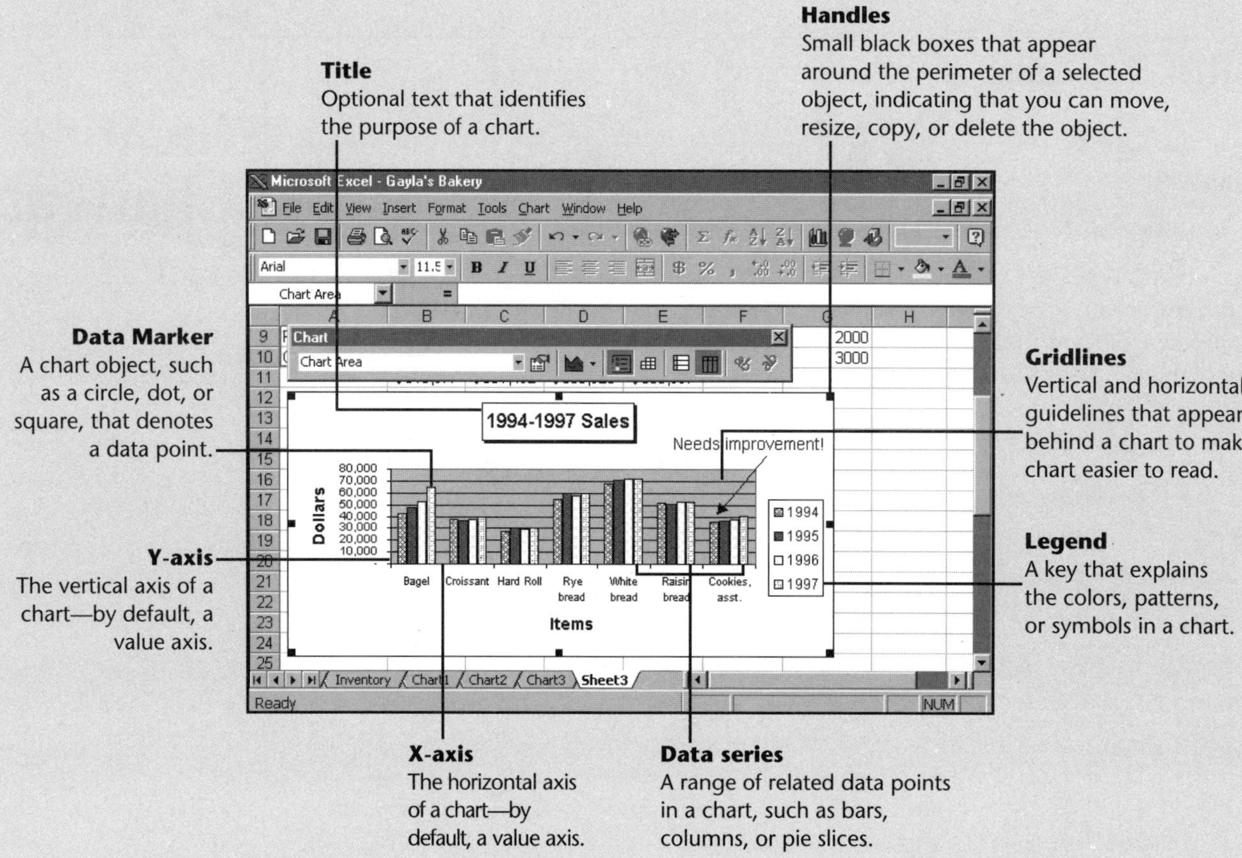

Choosing the Right Type of Chart

When you create a chart in Excel, you can choose from a variety of chart types. Each type interprets data in a slightly different way. For example, use a pie chart when you want to compare parts of a whole, such as regional percentages of a sales total, and a column chart when you want to show how different sales regions performed through the course of a year. Although there is some overlap among types, each is best for conveying a certain type of information.

Regardless of the stated purpose of each chart, you'll evaluate whether the chosen chart type suits the data being plotted. Sometimes a fancy 3-D chart is just what data needs to draw attention to it; other times, it might be a distraction.

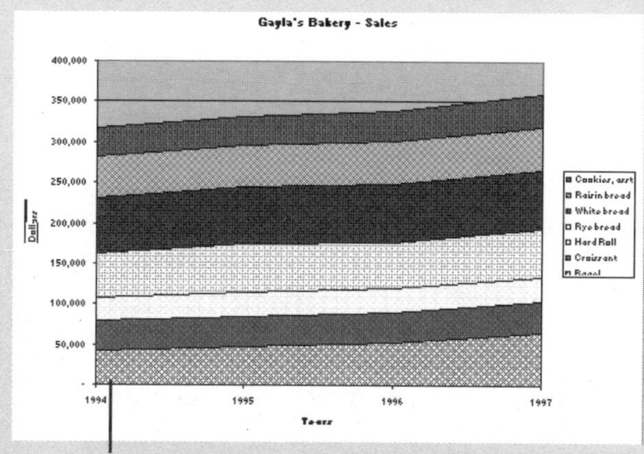

An **area chart** shows how volume changes over time.

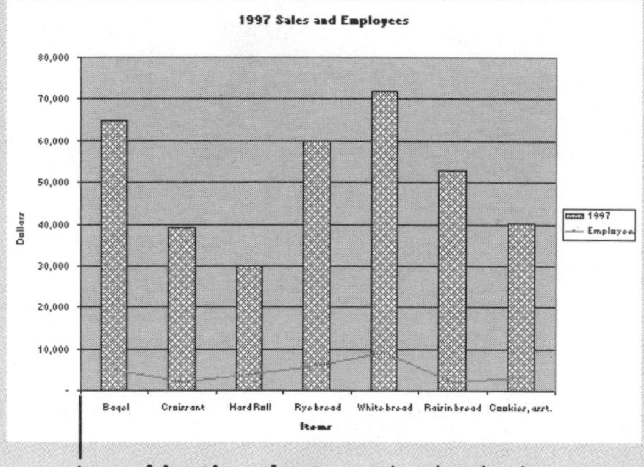

A **combination chart** contains data having different scales.

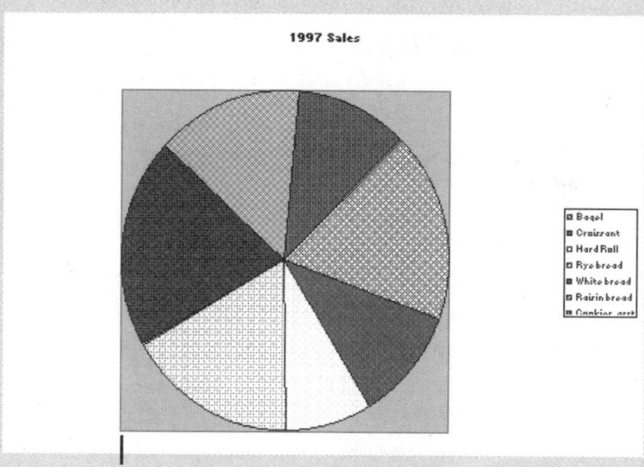

A **pie chart** compares elements of a whole unit.

Creating a Chart

You have many choices to make when you create a chart, from choosing the chart type you want to use to choosing the objects you want to include and the formatting you want to apply. Excel simplifies the chart-making process with a feature called the Chart Wizard. The *Chart Wizard* is a series of dialog boxes that leads you through all the steps necessary to create an effective chart. You pick and choose from different chart types and styles and select any options you might want to apply while the Chart Wizard is open. Any options you don't add while the Chart Wizard is open can always be added later.

Chart Wizard button

Create a Chart Using the Chart Wizard

1. Select the data range you want to chart. Make sure you include the data you want to chart *and* the column and row labels in the range. The Chart Wizard expects to find this information and automatically incorporates it in your chart.
2. Click the Chart Wizard button on the Standard toolbar.
3. Select a chart type.
4. Select a chart sub-type.
5. Click the Press And Hold To View Sample button to preview your selection.
6. Click Next.
7. Make sure the correct data range is selected.
8. Select the appropriate option button to plot the data series in rows or in columns.
9. Click Next.

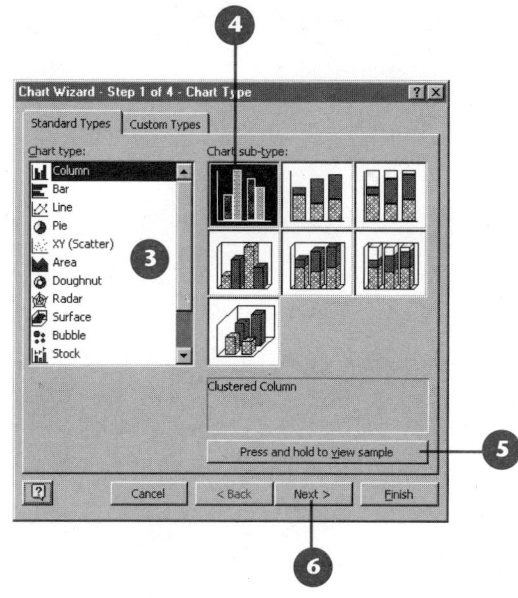

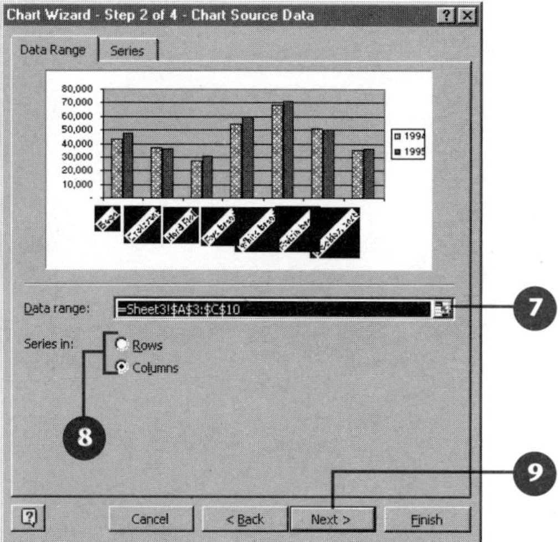

Place Chart As Object

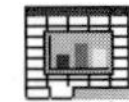

Place Chart As Sheet

TIP

You can make changes to the Chart Wizard. *Click the Back button to make changes before clicking the Finish button.*

SEE ALSO

See "Linking and Embedding files" on page 216 for more information on embedding a chart.

SEE ALSO

See "Moving and Resizing a Chart" on page 147 for more information on chaning the location or size of a chart.

10 To identify the data in the chart, type the titles in the appropriate text boxes.

11 Click Next.

12 Select the option you want to place the chart on a new sheet or on an existing sheet. If you choose to place the chart on an existing sheet rather than on a new sheet, the chart is called an *embedded object*.

13 Click Finish.

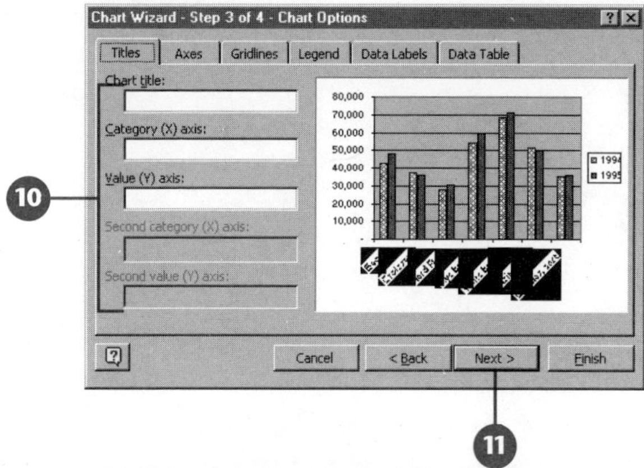

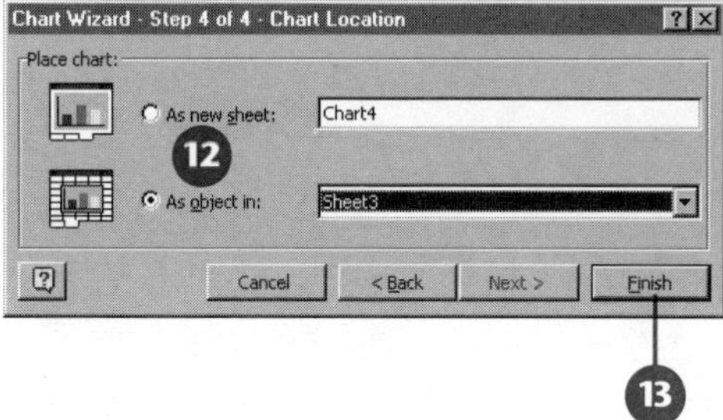

9

Editing a Chart

Editing a chart means changing the features of a chart. To change a chart's type or any element within it, you must select the chart or element. When a chart is selected, handles display around the window's perimeter, and the Chart toolbar displays: all buttons on this toolbar function when the chart is selected. As the figure below illustrates, you can point to any object or area on a chart to see what it is called.

Point to any chart object to see its type.

When you select an object, its name appears in the Chart Objects list box in the Chart toolbar and you can edit it.

Editing a chart has no effect on the data used to create it. You don't need to worry about updating a chart if you change worksheet data because Excel does it for you. The only chart data you might need to edit is a data range. If you decide you want to plot more or less data in a range, you can select the data series in the worksheet, as shown in the figure below, and drag the outline to include the range you want in the chart.

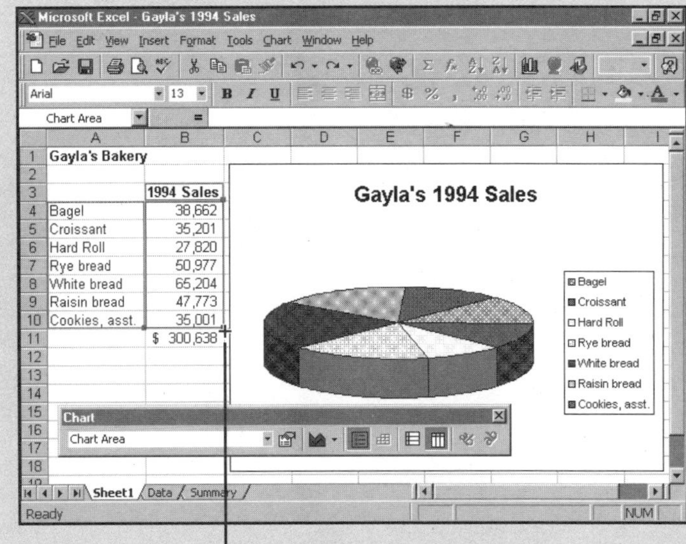

Change the plotted data by dragging the outline.

Selecting a Chart

You need to select a chart object before you can move, resize, and make formatting changes to it. When an object is selected, handles appear around its perimeter. You can also see which object is currently selected by clicking the Chart Object drop-down arrow on the Chart toolbar.

> **TIP**
>
> **Use the mouse button or keyboard to deselect a chart object.** *Click in another area of the chart or press the Esc key.*

> **TIP**
>
> **Use ScreenTips to find out about an object.** *If you can't remember the name of the chart object you want to format, position the mouse pointer over the object, and a message will display beneath the pointer.*

Select a Chart Object

1. Select a chart.
2. Position the mouse pointer over a chart object, and then click to select it, or click the chart object drop-down arrow on the Chart toolbar, and then click the name of the object you want to select.

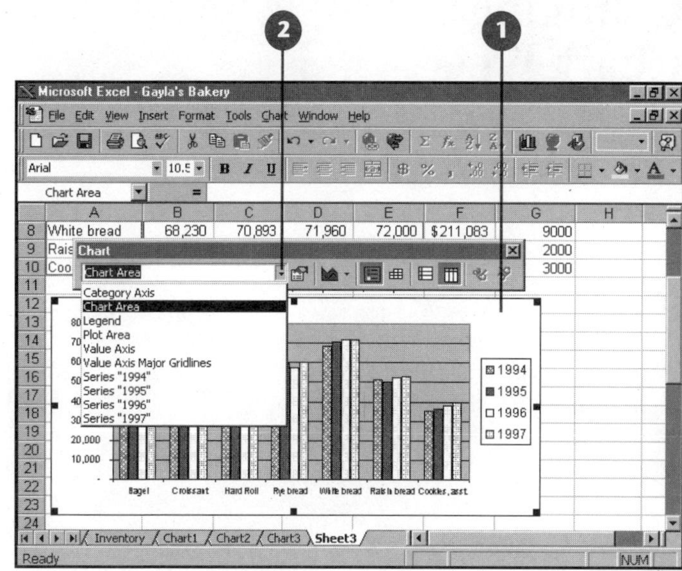

Changing a Chart Type

Excel's default chart type is the column chart, although there are many other types from which to choose. A column chart might adequately display your data, but you can experiment with a variety of chart types to find the one that shows the data in the most effective way.

Change a Chart Type Quickly

1. Select a chart whose chart type you want to change.
2. Click the Chart Type drop-down arrow on the Chart toolbar.
3. Select a chart type. Excel automatically changes the chart type when you release the mouse button.

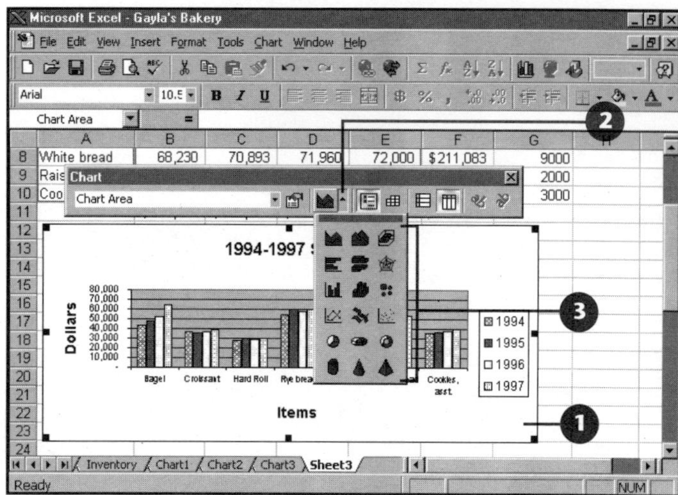

TIP

Use the Chart Wizard to change a chart type. *If you finish creating a chart and don't like the result, simply click the chart to select it, and then click the Chart Wizard button and choose a different chart type.*

Change a Chart Type Using the Chart Dialog Box

1. Select a chart whose chart type you want to change.
2. Click the Chart menu, and then click Chart Type.
3. Click a new chart type.
4. Click a new chart sub-type.
5. Click the Press And Hold To View Sample button to preview your chart in its new layout, and then release the mouse button when you are finished previewing.
6. When you've chosen a chart type, click OK.

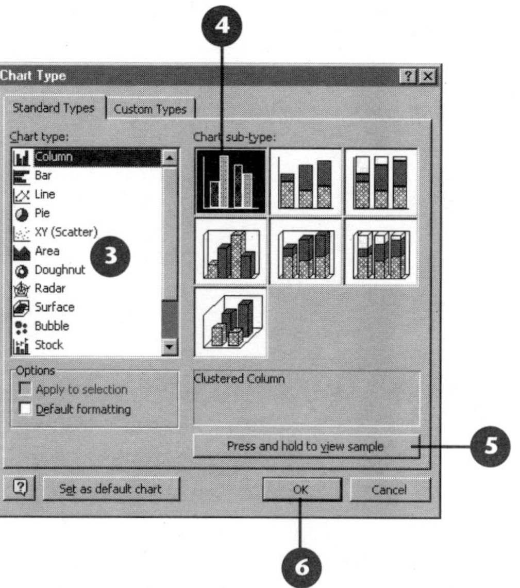

Moving and Resizing a Chart

You can move or resize an embedded chart after you select it. You know a chart is selected when it is surrounded by small black squares, called *handles*. If you've created a chart as a new sheet instead of an embedded object in an existing worksheet, the chart's size and location are fixed by the sheet's margins. You can change the margins to resize or reposition the chart.

SEE ALSO

See "Linking and Embedding files" on page 216 for more information on embedding a chart.

SEE ALSO

See "Setting Up the Page" on page 68 for more information on adjusting margins.

Move an Embedded Chart

1. Select a chart you want to move.
2. Position the mouse pointer over a blank area of the chart, and then click and drag the pointer to move the outline of the chart to a new location. (Do not click a handle or you will resize the chart.)
3. Release the mouse button.

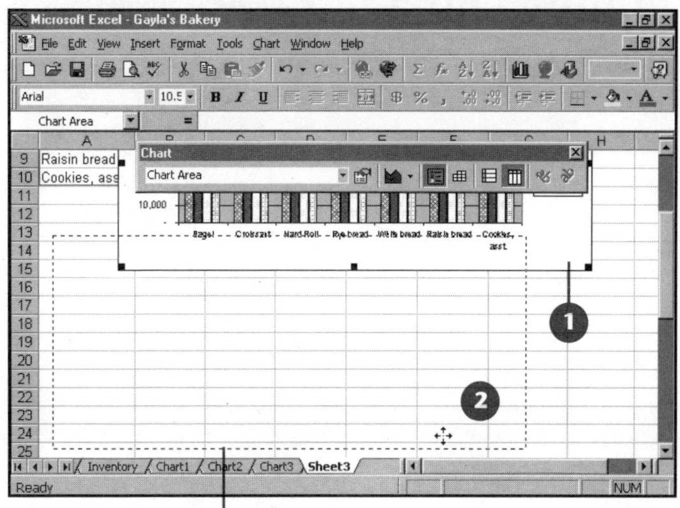

Outline indicates new position.

Resize an Embedded Chart

1. Select a chart you want to resize.
2. Position the mouse pointer over one of the handles.
3. Drag the handle to the size you want the chart to be.
4. Release the mouse button.

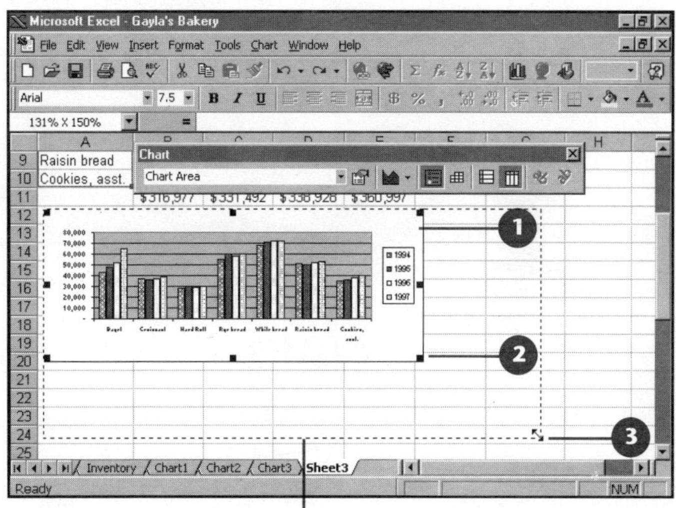

Outline indicates new chart size.

9

Pulling Out a Pie Slice

A pie chart is an excellent chart type choice for comparing parts that make up a whole entity, such as departmental percentages of a company budget. You can call attention to individual pie slices that are particularly significant in a pie by moving them away from the other pieces, or *exploding* the pie.

SEE ALSO

See "Changing a Chart Type" on page 146 for information on about changing a chart type to a pie.

Explode a Single Pie Slice

1. Select a pie chart.
2. Click the pie slice you want to explode. Clicking a pie slice selects its data series. Since a pie chart has only one data series, clicking any pie slice selects the entire data series.
3. Drag the slice away from the pie.
4. Release the mouse button.

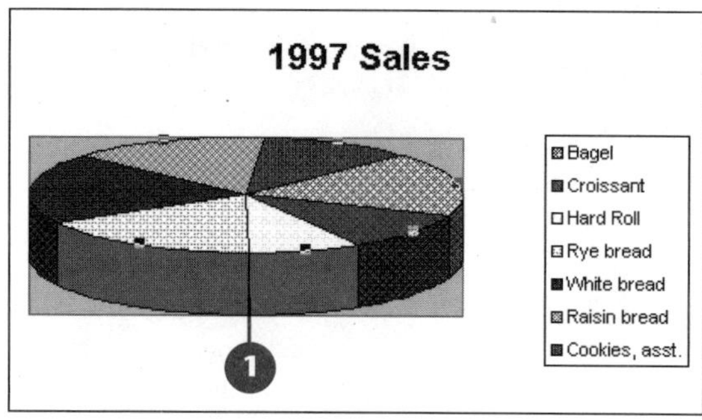

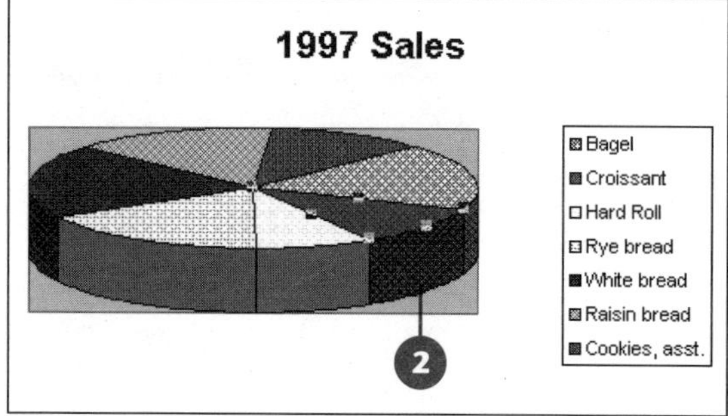

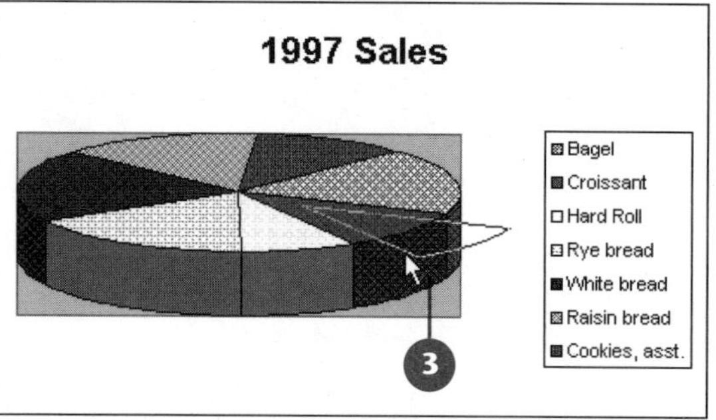

TIP

Use the ScreenTip to help identify a chart object. *When you position the mouse pointer over any area or object within the chart, a ScreenTip shows you the name of the area or object.*

Explode an Entire Pie

1. Select a pie chart.
2. Click a pie slice to select the data series.
3. Drag the pie slice away from the center of the pie.
4. Release the mouse button.

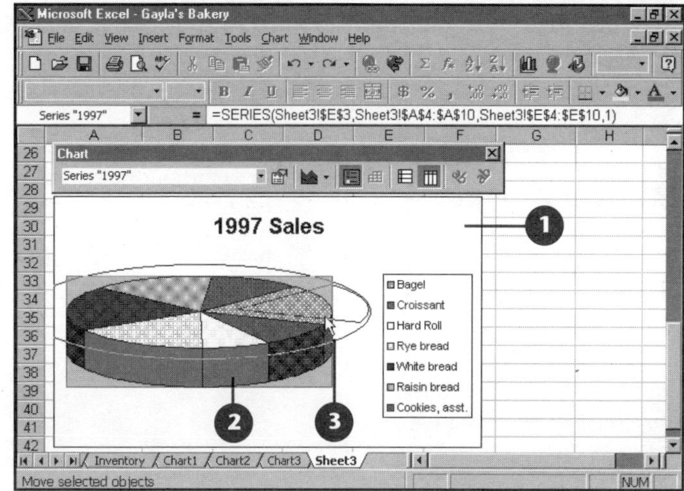

Undo a Pie Explosion

1. Select a pie chart.
2. Click a pie slice to select the data series.
3. Drag a slice towards the center of the pie.
4. Release the mouse button.

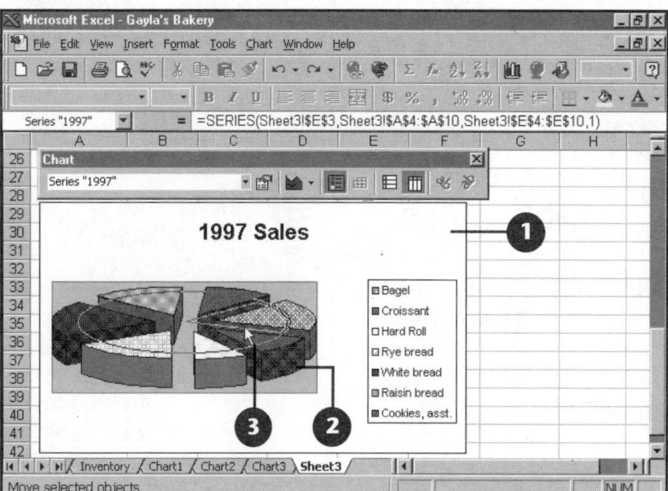

Adding and Deleting a Data Series

Each range of data that comprises a bar, column, or pie slice is called a *data series;* each value in a data series is called a *data point*. The data series is defined when you select a range and then open the Chart Wizard. But what happens if you want to add a data series once a chart is complete? Using Excel, you can add a data series by changing the data range information in the Chart Wizard, by using the Chart menu, or by dragging a new data series into an existing chart.

As you create and modify more charts, you might also find it necessary to delete one or more data series. You can easily delete a data series by selecting the series and pressing the Delete key.

Add a Data Series to a Chart Quickly

1. Select the range that contains the data series you want to add to your chart.
2. Drag the range into the existing chart.
3. Release the mouse button.

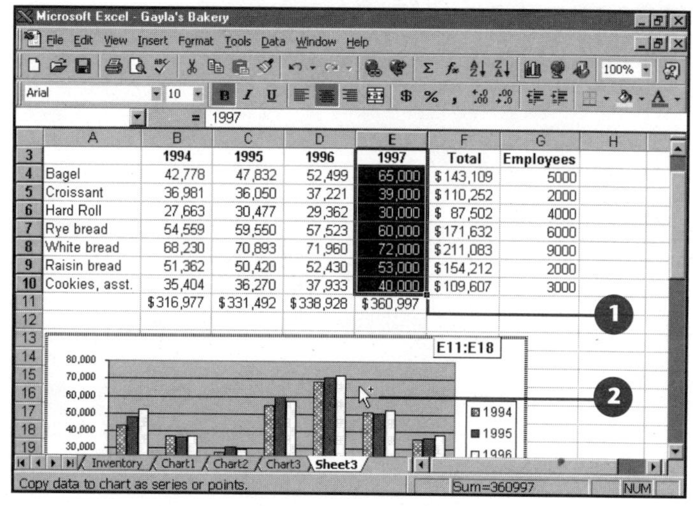

Add a Data Series Using the Add Data Dialog Box

1. Select the chart to which you want to add a data series.
2. Click the Chart menu, and then click Add Data.
3. Type the range in the Range box, or click the Collapse Dialog button and then drag the pointer over the new range you want to add. When you release the mouse button, the Add Data dialog box reappears.
4. Click OK.

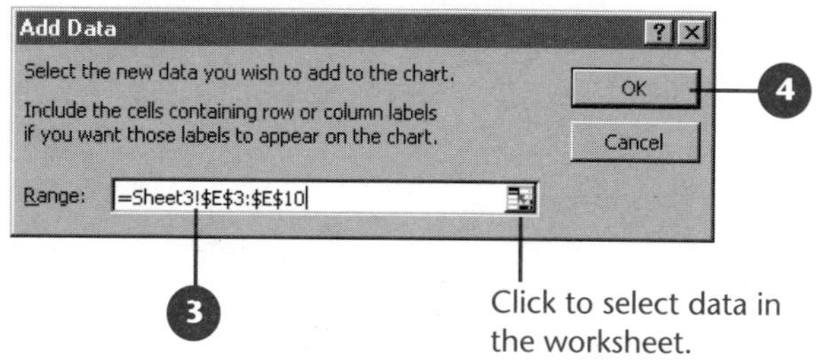

TIP

You can choose to delete one data point in a chart. *To delete one data point, but keep the rest of the series in the chart, click the data point twice so that it is the only point selected, and then press the Delete key.*

TIP

Use the Undo button to reverse a deletion. *Click the Undo button on the Standard toolbar to restore the deleted data series or data point in the chart.*

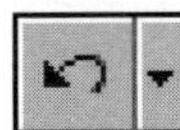

Delete a Data Series

1. Select the chart that contains the data series you want to delete.
2. Click any data point in the data series.
3. Press Delete.

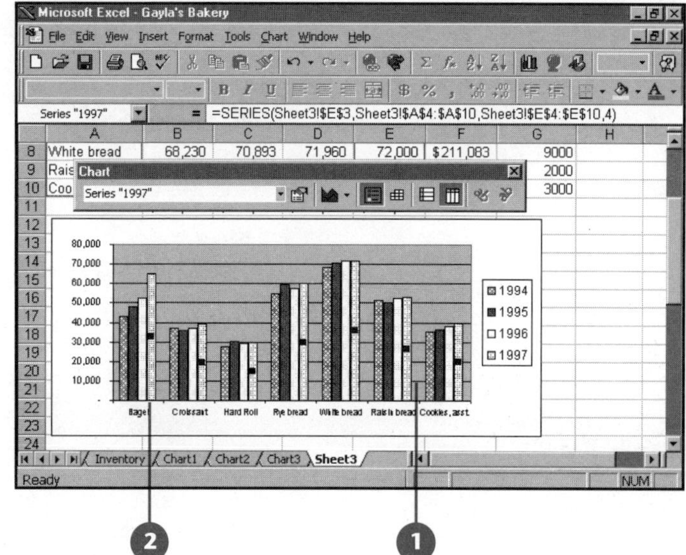

Enhancing a Data Series

When you create a chart using the Chart Wizard, Excel automatically decides which colors should be used to represent each data series. Sometimes these colors are not to your liking. Perhaps you want more dynamic colors—adding patterns and texture to further enhance a data series—or maybe you'll be printing your charts in black and white, and you want to control the appearance of each data series. You can change also choose to insert a picture in a chart so that its image could be seen in a bar or column.

TIP

Use the mouse button to format a chart object quickly. *Double-clicking an object opens a corresponding Format dialog box, which you can use to change the object's attributes.*

Change a Data Series Color or Pattern

1. Click any data point in a data series to select it.
2. Double-click a data point in the selected data series.
3. If necessary, click the Patterns tab.
4. Select a color from the Area palette. By default, data series colors are automatically selected. The selected color displays in the Sample box.
5. If you want to add effects, such as textures, patterns, gradients, or pictures, click Fill Effects.
6. Click the Gradient, Texture, or Pattern tabs to change the qualities of the data series color.
7. When you're done, click OK.
8. Click OK if you're satisfied with the results shown in the Sample box.

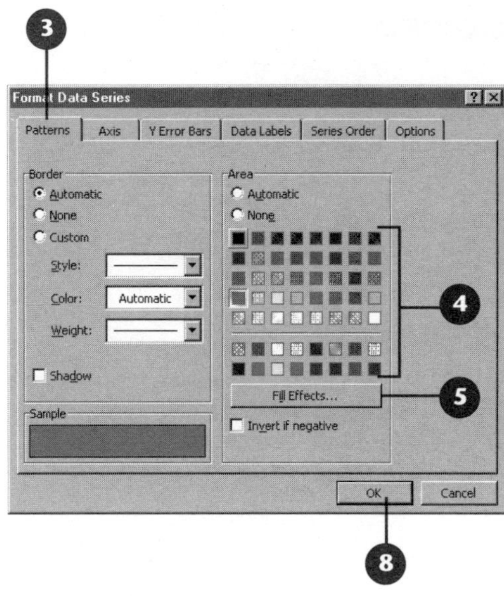

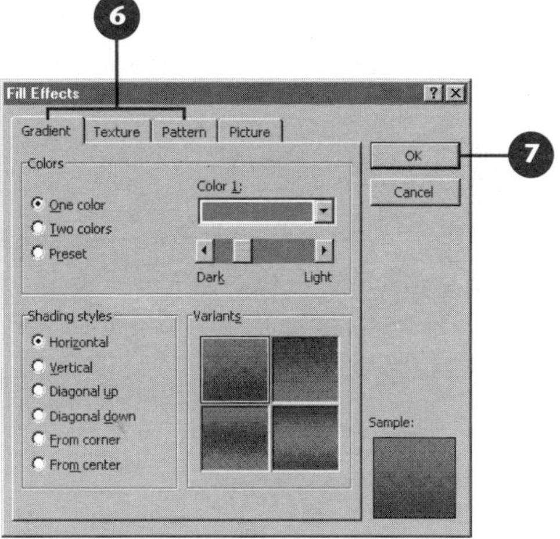

SEE ALSO

See "Editing a Chart" on page 144 for more information on modifying a chart.

SEE ALSO

See "Inserting Pictures" on page 96 for more information on inserting pictures and clip art.

Add a Picture to a Data Series

1. Select a data series.
2. Double-click a data point in the selected series.
3. Click Fill Effects.
4. Click the Picture tab.
5. Click Select Picture.
6. Locate and select the graphics file.
7. Click OK.
8. If you want the data point to contain one copy of the image stretched to fill it, click the Stretch option, or if you want the data point to contain duplicate iterations of the image, click the Stack option.
9. Click OK.
10. Click OK.

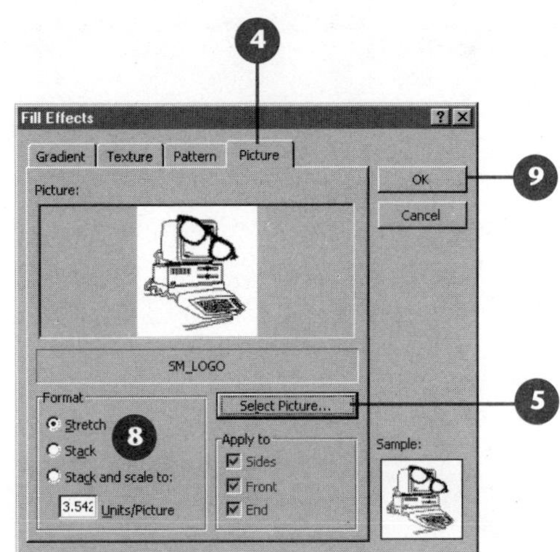

9

Enhancing a Chart

You can add *chart objects,* such as titles, legends, and text annotations, and *chart options* such as gridlines to a chart to enhance the appearance of the chart and increase its overall effectiveness. A *chart title* helps to identify the primary purpose of the chart and a title for each axis further clarifies the data that is plotted. Titles can be more than one line, and formatted just like other worksheet text. You can also add a *text annotation,* additional text not attached to a specific axis or data point, to call attention to a trend or some other area of interest. A *legend* helps the reader connect the colors and patterns in a chart with the data they represent.

Gridlines are horizontal and vertical lines you can add to help the reader determine data point values in a chart that without the gridlines would be difficult to read.

Add a Title

1. Select a chart to which you want to add a title or titles.
2. Click the Chart menu, and then click Chart Options.
3. Click the Titles tab.
4. Type the text you want for the title of the chart.
5. To add a title for the x-axis, press Tab and type the text.
6. To add a title for the y-axis, press Tab and type the text.
7. If you want a second line for the x- or y-axis, press Tab to move to the Second Category or Value box, and then type the title text (if available).
8. Preview the title(s) you are adding.
9. Click OK.

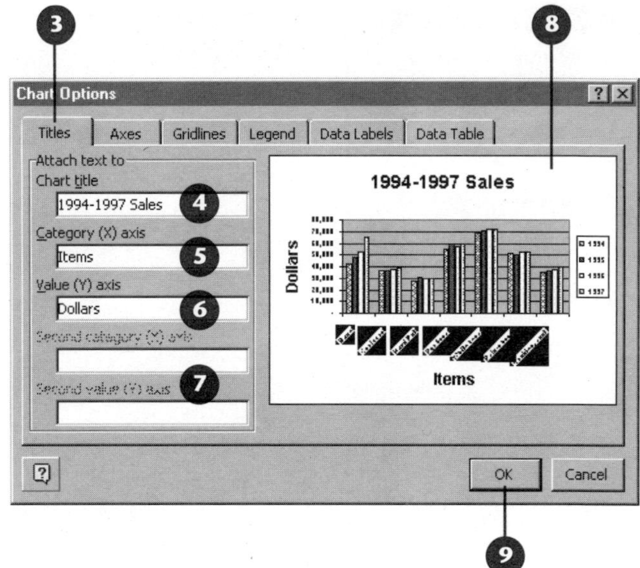

Add or Delete a Legend

1. Select the chart to which you want to add or delete a legend.
2. Click the Legend button on the Chart toolbar. You can drag the legend to move it to a new location.

TIP

Resize the text box to create a multiple line title. *Type the tile text, and then resize the text box.*

Add a Text Annotation

1. Select a chart to which you want to add a text annotation.
2. Type the text for the annotation.
3. When you're finished, press Enter and the text annotation appears in a text box within the plot area. Then position the mouse pointer over the text box until the pointer changes shape.
4. Drag the selected text box to a new location.
5. Press Esc to deselect the text box.

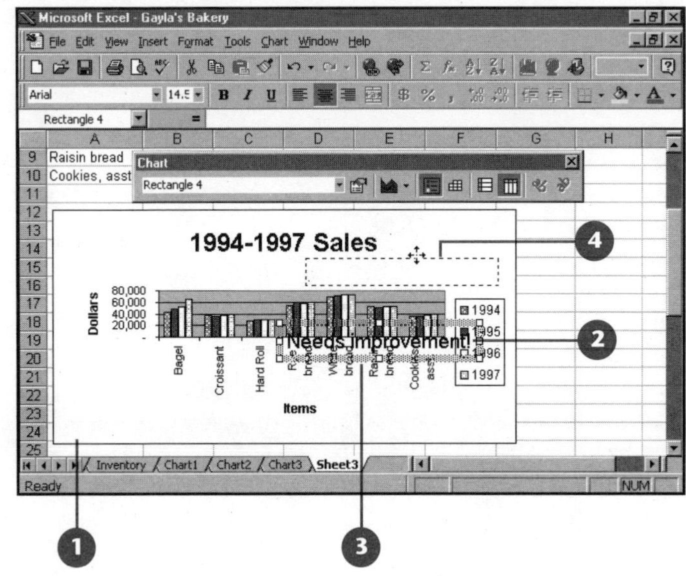

TIP

Major guidelines vs. minor guidelines. *Major gridlines occur at each value on an axis; minor gridlines occur between values on an axis. Use gridlines sparingly and only when they improve the readability of a chart.*

Add Gridlines

1. Select a chart to which you want to add gridlines.
2. Click the Chart menu, and then click Chart Options.
3. Click the Gridlines tab.
4. Select the type of gridlines you want to the x-axis (vertical) and y-axis (horizontal).
5. Click OK.

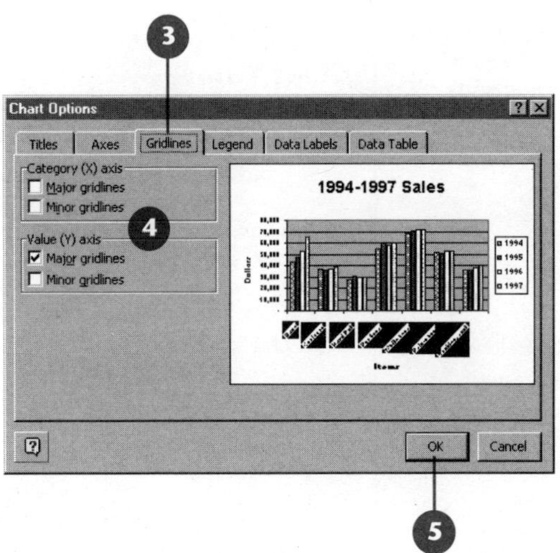

9

Drawing on a Chart

Once titles and text have been added and the chart is fine-tuned, you might want to accentuate information in it using tools on the Drawing toolbar. For example, a drop shadow adds dimension to the chart's title; an arrow helps to show a connection between annotated text and specific data in your chart.

Add a Drop Shadow to a Text Annotation

1. Select a chart that contains a text annotation you want to enhance.
2. Select the text annotation.
3. Click the Drawing button on the Chart toolbar.
4. Click the Shadow button on the Drawing toolbar.
5. Select a shadow based on the effect you want. You can experiment until you find the one you want.

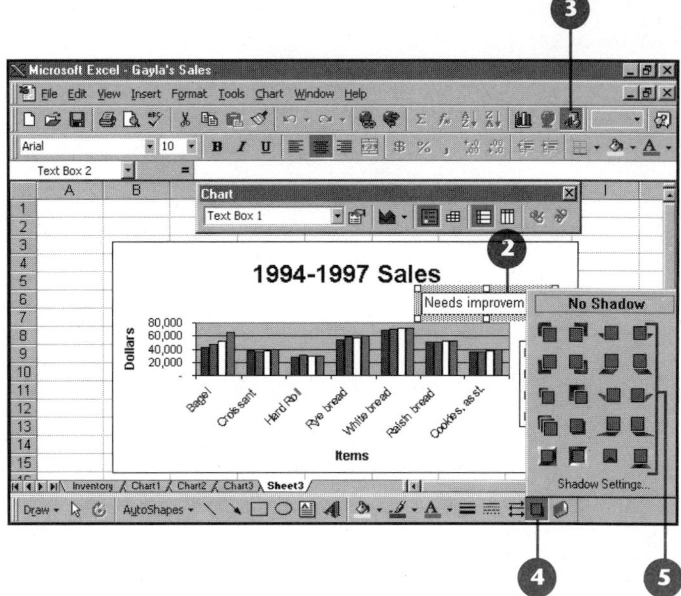

TIP

Use the Drawing toolbar to draw objects on a chart. *Click the Drawing button on the Standard toolbar to display or hide the toolbar.*

SEE ALSO

See "Drawing AutoShapes" on page 118 for more information on about drawing other objects in a chart.

Add a Drop Shadow to a Chart Title

1. Select the chart.
2. Double-click the title.
3. Click the Patterns tab, if necessary.
4. Click to select the Shadow check box.
5. Click OK.

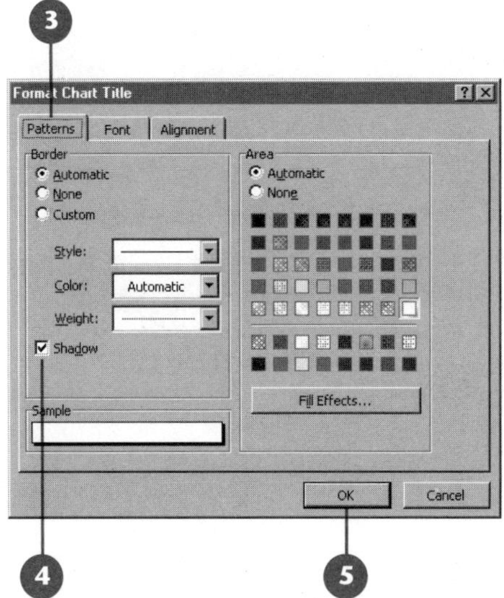

TIP

Use the Shift key to draw straight lines. *Press and hold the Shift key while you drag to create a vertical, horizontal or diagonal arrow.*

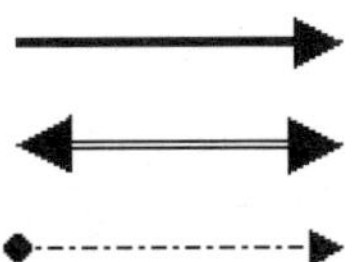

TIP

Use the Drawing toolbar to modify the arrow object. *Click the Line Style, Dash Style, or Arrow Style buttons on the Drawing toolbar to modify the arrow object.*

 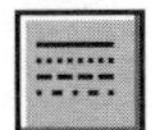 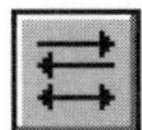

SEE ALSO

See "Moving and Resizing an Object" on page 124 for more information on about moving and resizing graphic objects.

Draw an Arrow on a Chart

1. Select the chart.
2. Click the Drawing button on the Standard toolbar.
3. Click the Arrow button on the Drawing toolbar.
4. Position the mouse pointer near the object that you want as the starting point or base of the arrow.
5. Click and drag the pointer from the base object to another object. The arrowhead appears at the point of the second object.

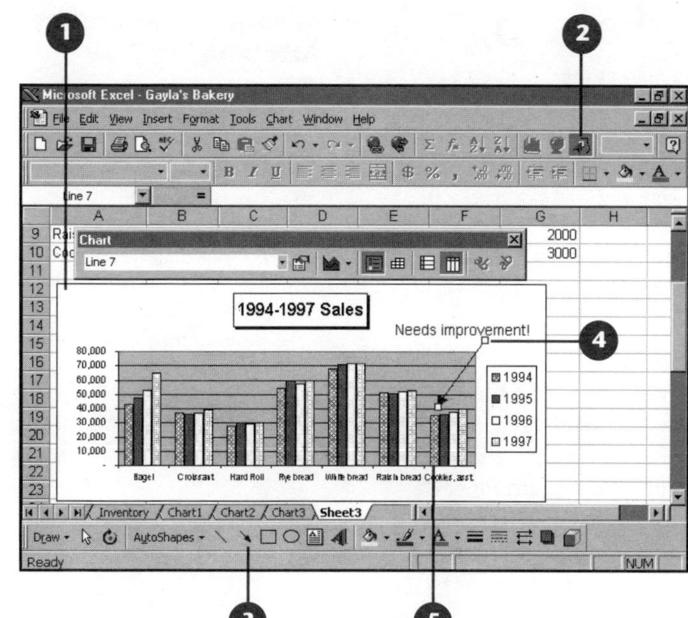

9

Changing Chart Fonts

Objects such as annotated text, data labels, and titles contain *chart text*. To make chart text easier to read, you can change the font the chart text is displayed in. You can also change the attributes available with a font, such as the size of the font or options such as underlining, bold, or italics. For example, if the labels along an axis are too long, making them unreadable, you might want to reduce the font size to make the labels fit better within a small space.

TIP

Use a TrueType font to print high quality charts. *Choosing a TrueType font ensures that the font you see on the screen is the font that you'll see in your print out.*

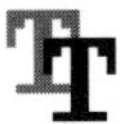

Change a Font and Its Attributes

1. Select the chart that contains the text you want to change.
2. Double-click the object that contains the text. A Format dialog box opens. This dialog box is *context-sensitive;* its options vary depending on the object you selected.
3. Click the Font tab.
4. Select a font.
5. Select a font style.
6. Select a size.
7. Select any combination of the Underline, Color, Background, or Effects options.
8. Preview your selections.
9. Click OK.

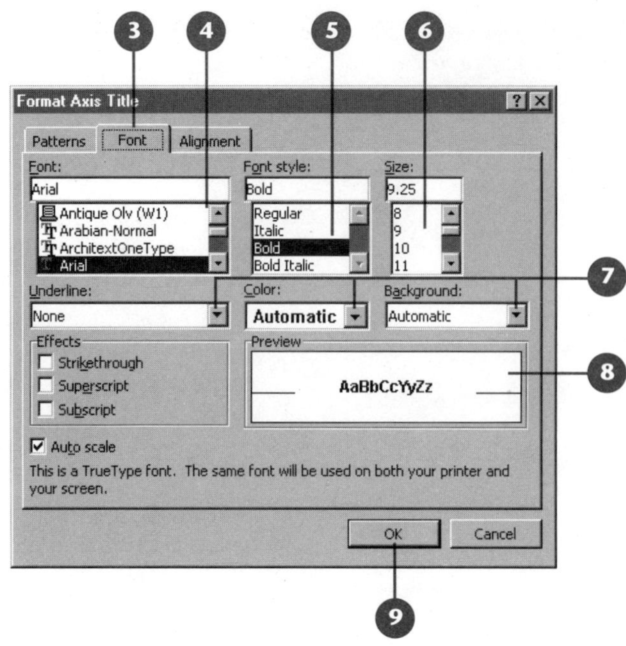

Creating a Map

Data for geographic locations can be charted using any existing chart type, but you can add real impact by using Excel's special mapping feature. This mapping feature analyzes and charts your data in an actual geographic map containing countries or states and helps readers understand the relationship of geographic data when viewed within a map. For example, seeing population data displayed within a map of the United States would probably have more meaning for you than to see the same information displayed in a column chart.

SEE ALSO

See "Modifying a Map" on page 160 for more information on about changing a map.

Create a Geographic Map

1. Select a range that contains the geographic data you want to map.
2. Click the Map button on the Standard toolbar.
3. Select the map you want to use.
4. Click OK.
5. Press Esc to deselect the map.

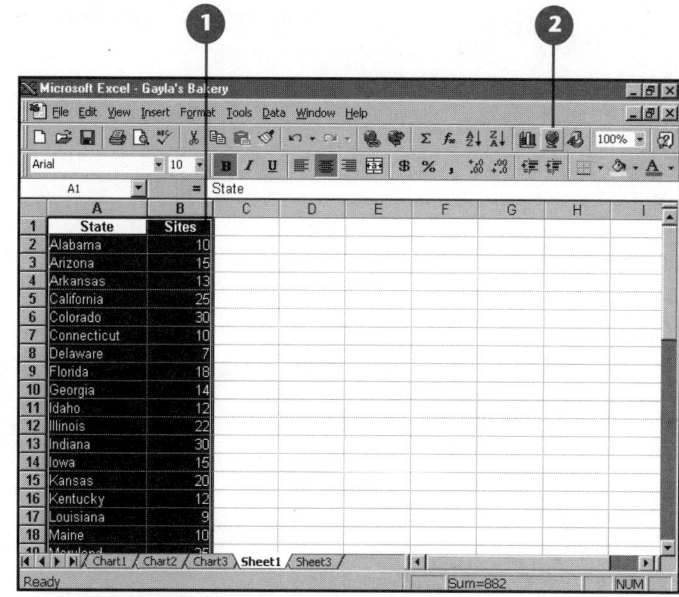

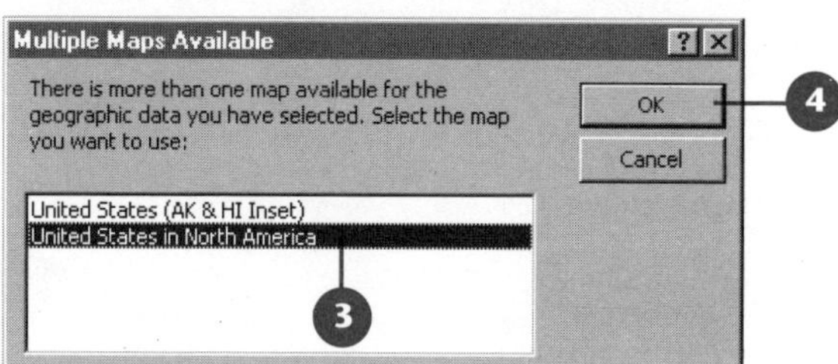

Modifying a Map

An existing geographic map can be modified to reflect updated data. You must update the geographic map when you change the data. In addition, the colors and patterns used to display the data within the map can also be changed.

TIP

Always refresh a map after changing worksheet data. *Unlike chart data, Excel does not automatically update map data whenever the worksheet data changes.*

SEE ALSO

See "Moving and Resizing a Chart" on page 124 for more information about moving and resizing a map.

Modify a Geographic Map

1. Make the necessary changes to the worksheet data that is used in your geographic map.
2. Double-click the map.
3. If necessary, click the Map Refresh button on the Microsoft Map toolbar.
4. Change data and the way it is displayed in the map using buttons in the Microsoft Map Control dialog box.
5. Press Esc to deselect the map.

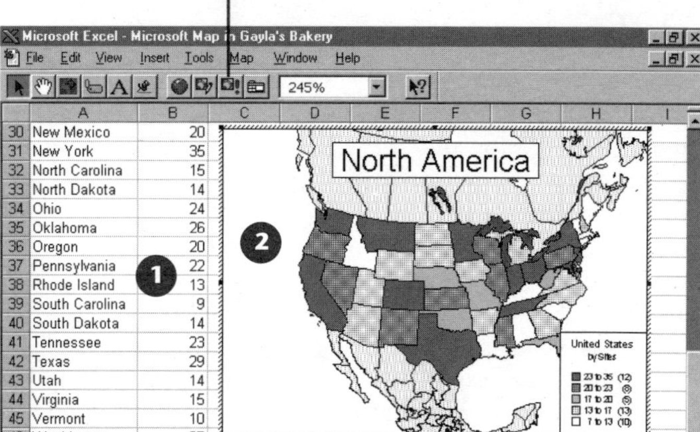

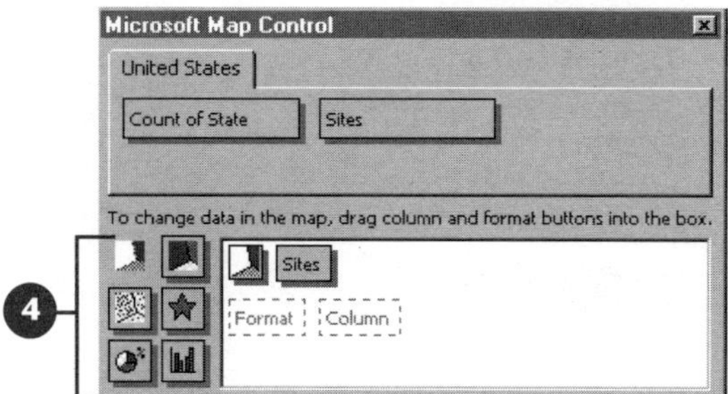

10

Analyzing Worksheet Data

IN THIS SECTION

Understanding List Terminology

Creating a List

Understanding a Data Form

Adding Records Using a Data Form

Managing Records Using a Data Form

Sorting Data in a List

Displaying Parts of a List with AutoFilter

Creating Complex Searches

Entering Data in a List Quickly

Analyzing Data Using a PivotTable

Updating a PivotTable

Charting a PivotTable

In addition to using a worksheet to calculate values, you can also use it to manage a list of information, sometimes called a *database*. You can use a Microsoft Excel 97 worksheet to keep an inventory list, a school grade book, or a customer database. Excel provides a variety of tools that make it easy to keep lists up to date and analyze them to get the information you want quickly. For Example, you can use these tools to find out how many inventory items are out of stock, which students are earning an A average, or which product is the best selling item.

Analyzing Worksheet Data

Excel's data analysis tools includes alphanumeric organizing (called *sorting*), displaying information that meets specific criteria (called *filtering*), and summarizing of data within a table (called a *PivotTable*).

You can analyze data directly in a worksheet, or use a feature called a *Data Form*, an on-screen data entry tool similar to a paper form. A Data Form lets you easily enter data by filling in blank text boxes, and then it adds the information to the bottom of the list. This tool makes entering information in a lengthy list a snap!

Understanding List Terminology

A database is a collection of related records. Examples of databases are an address book, a list of customers or products, or a telephone directory. In Excel, a database is referred to as *list*.

Record
One set of related fields, such as all the fields pertaining to one customer or one product. In a worksheet, each row represents a unique record.

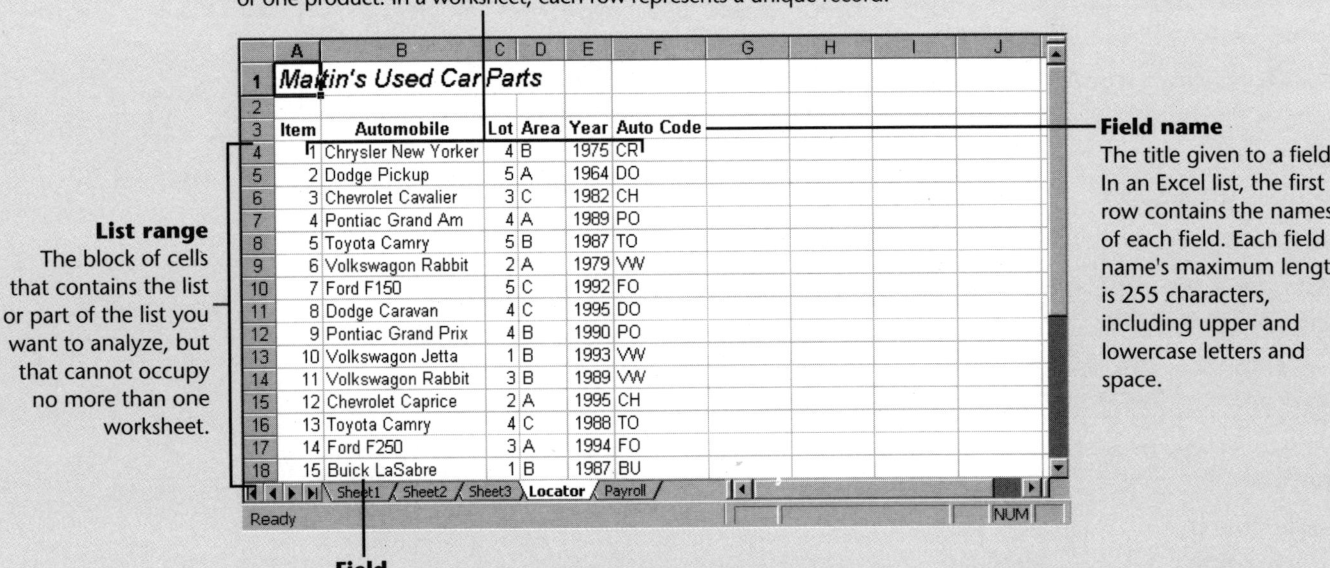

List range
The block of cells that contains the list or part of the list you want to analyze, but that cannot occupy no more than one worksheet.

Field name
The title given to a field. In an Excel list, the first row contains the names of each field. Each field name's maximum length is 255 characters, including upper and lowercase letters and space.

Field
One piece of information, such as customer's last name, or an item's code number. In a worksheet, each column represents a field.

Creating a List

To create a list in Excel, you can enter data in worksheet cells, just as you do any other worksheet data, but the placement of the field names and list range must follow these rules:

- Field names must occupy a single row and be the first row in the list.
- Enter each record in a single row, with each field in the column corresponding to the correct field name.
- Do not include any blank rows within the list range.
- Do not use more than one worksheet for a single list range.

Don't worry about entering records in any particular order; Excel offers several tools for organizing an existing list alphabetically, by date, or in almost any order you can imagine.

Create a List

1. Open a blank worksheet, or use a worksheet that has enough empty columns and rows for the list.
2. Enter a name for each field in adjacent columns across the first row of the list.
3. Enter the field information for each record in a separate row, starting with the row directly beneath the field names. Take advantage of features such as AutoComplete, that make data entry easier.

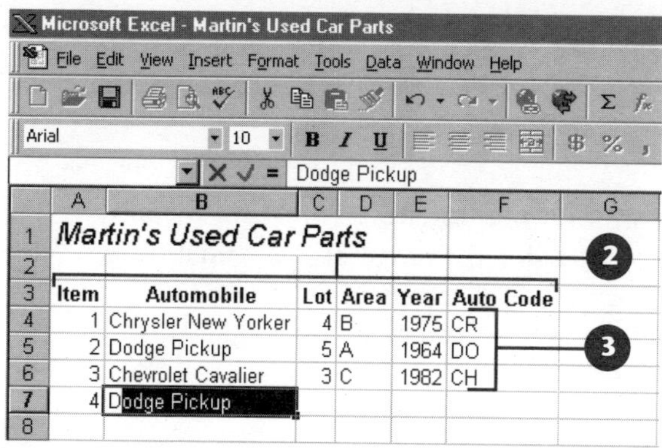

10

Understanding a Data Form

The Data Form is an optional tool for entering and searching for data in a list range. It is automatically generated by Excel, and makes it easy to enter repetitive information one record at a time. Each Data Form is customized for the selected list, containing a text box for each field. It also offers several commands for moving around in the list.

The Data Form dialog box is customized for the currently selected list in the worksheet, containing a text box for each field.

A Data Form dialog box

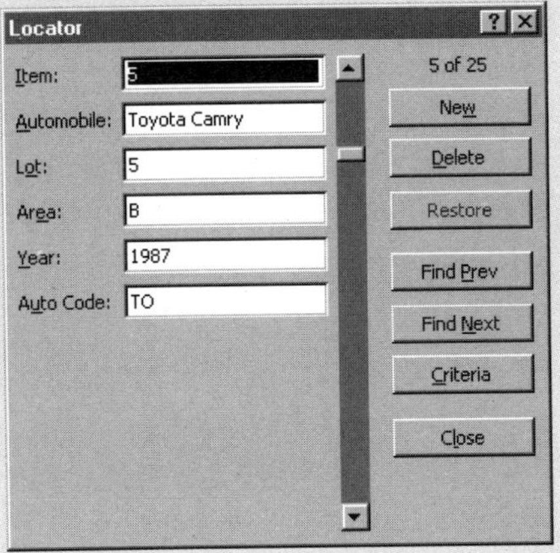

To use the Data Form, you select a list range, click the Data menu, and then click Form. All field names in the list range are displayed. You cannot change field names from within a Data Form. Data for the currently selected record appears in the text boxes (if the list already contains data). You can enter new data in text boxes of a blank record, and can edit existing records by clicking in the text box of the field you want to change and modify the text. The Data Form also contains buttons to help you perform related tasks.

- Click the New button to enter a new record.
- Click the Delete button to remove an existing record.
- Click the Restore button to undo the previous action.
- Click the Find Prev button to locate the closest previous record matching the criteria.
- Click the Find Next button to locate the closest record matching the criteria.
- Click the Criteria button to display the Data Form with all fields blank. Enter the field items you want to find.
- Click the Close button to close the Data Form and return to the worksheet.

Adding Records Using a Data Form

A *Data Form* is an optional method of entering information in a list range. Once field names are entered, you access a Data Form using the Data menu. You don't even need to select the list range first; as long as the active cell is somewhere within the list range when the Data Form is opened, Excel will automatically locate the list.

As you add new records to the form, the list range is constantly updated to include the new rows. This means that as new records are added, Excel automatically enlarges the list range.

SEE ALSO

See "Entering Data in a List Quickly" on page 172 for information on using the AutoComplete and PickList features for quick and easy data entry.

Add Records Using a Data Form

1. Click any cell within the list range. If you have not entered any records for the list yet, click one of the field names.
2. Click the Data menu, and then click Form.
3. Click New.
4. Type each field entry in the appropriate text box. Move from field to field by pressing the Tab key or by clicking in each field.
5. Click Close.

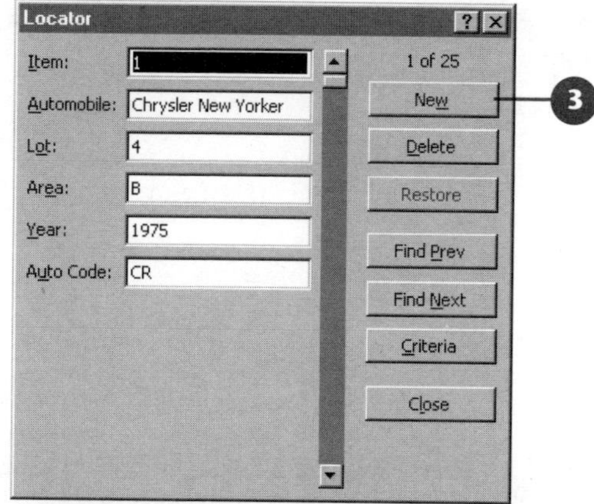

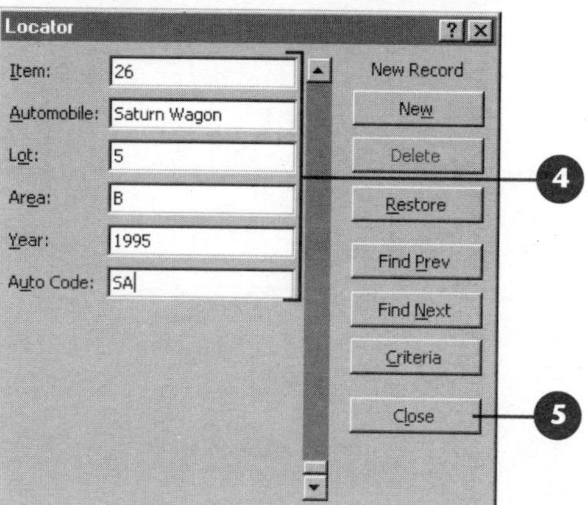

10

Managing Records Using a Data Form

You can use a Data Form to display, edit, or delete selected records within a list. To display only selected records in the Data Form, you specify the search *criteria*—the information a record must contain—in the Data Form, and Excel uses that criteria to find and display matching records. Although the Data Form only shows the records that match your criteria, the other records still exist in the list. If more than one record matches your criteria, you can use the Data Form buttons to move through the records, editing or deleting them.

TIP

You can return to the complete list of records at any time. *Return to the initial Data Form by clicking the Form button.*

Display Selected Records

1. Click anywhere within the list range.
2. Click the Data menu, and then click Form.
3. Click Criteria.
4. Type the information you want matching records to contain. You can fill in one or more fields.
5. Click Find Prev or Find Next to advance to a matching record.
6. Repeat step 5 until Excel beeps, or enough records have been viewed.
7. Click Close.

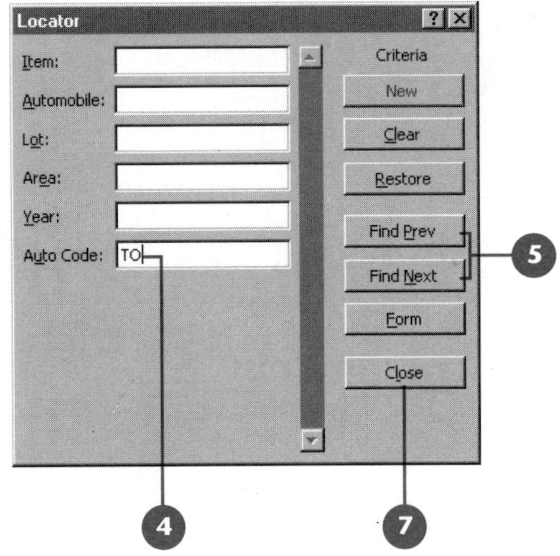

Edit a Record

1. Click anywhere within the list range.
2. Click the Data menu, and then click Form.
3. Find a record that requires modification.
4. Click in the field you want to edit to position the insertion point, and then use the Backspace or Delete keys to modify the text.
5. Click Close.

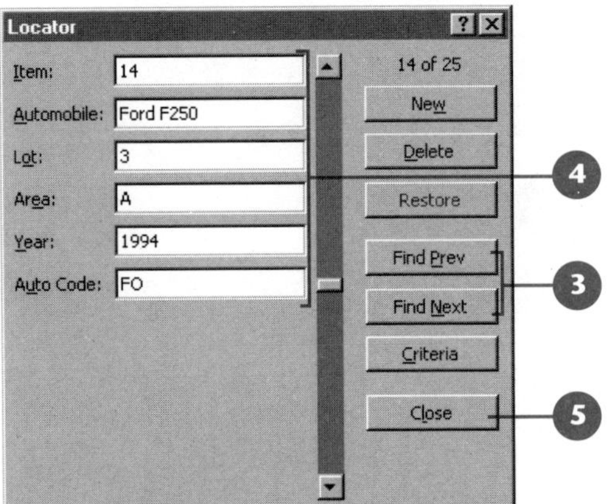

TIP

Use wildcards to find data in a list quickly. *The wildcard "?"stands for any single character, while "*" stands for many characters. R?N might find RAN or RUN while R*N might find RUN, RAN, RUIN, or RATION.*

TRY THIS

Experiment using wildcards to locate specific records. *Find data using the single character wildcard (?), then try finding the same characters using the asterisk (*). See how the results differ.*

Delete a Record

1. Click anywhere within the list range.
2. Click the Data menu, and then click Form.
3. Click Criteria.
4. Type the information you want matching records to contain. You can fill in one or more fields.
5. Click Find Prev or Find Next to advance to a matching record.
6. Click Delete.
7. Click OK in the warning dialog box.
8. Click Close.

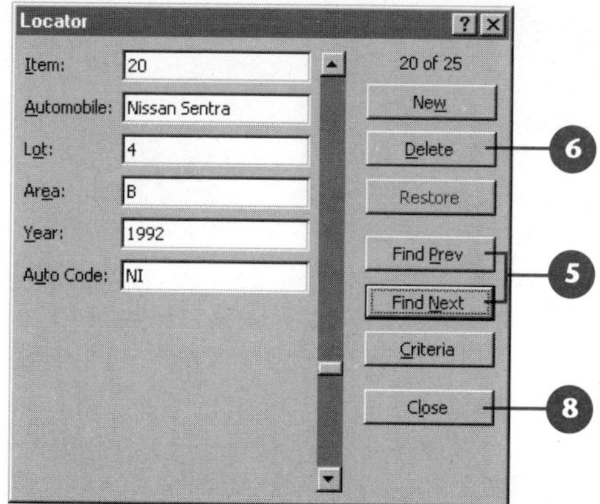

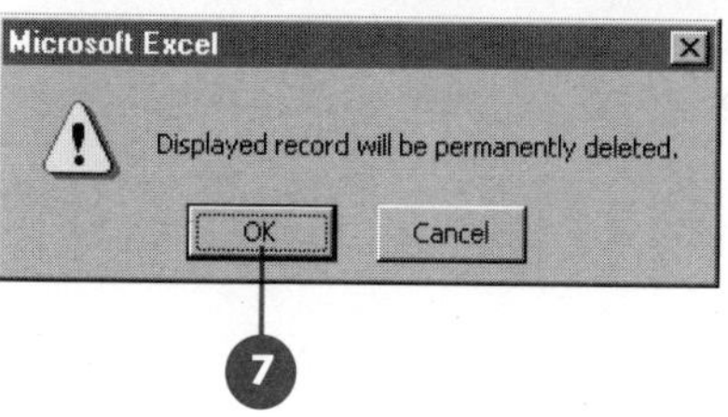

10

Sorting Data in a List

Once you enter records in a list, you can reorganize the information by *sorting* the records. Sometimes, you might want to sort records in a client list alphabetically by last name or numerically by date of their last invoice. You can sort a list alphabetically or numerically, in ascending or descending order using a field or fields you choose as the basis for the sort. You can sort a list on one field using the Standard toolbar, or on multiple fields using the Data menu. A simple sort—such as organizing a telephone directory alphabetically by last name—can be made complex by adding more than one *sort field* (a field used to sort the list).

Sort Data Quickly

1. Click a field name you want to sort on.
2. Click the Sort Ascending or the Sort Descending button on the Standard toolbar.

   In a list sorted in ascending order, records beginning with a number in the sort field are listed before records beginning with a letter (0-9, A-Z).

   In a list sorted in descending order, records beginning with a letter in the sort field appear first (Z-A, 9-0).

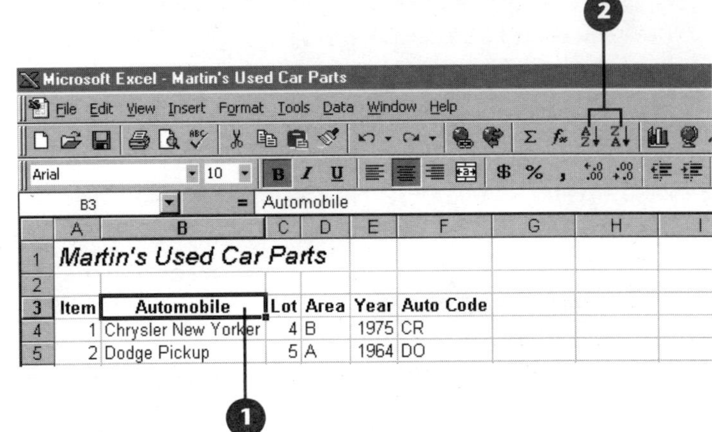

TIP

Protect your original list order with an index field. *Before sorting a list for the first time, try to include an index field, a field that contains ascending consecutive numbers (1, 2, 3, etc.). That way, you'll always be able to restore the original order of the list.*

TIP

You can sort data in rows. *If the data you want to sort is listed across a row instead of down a column, click the Options button in the Sort dialog box, and then click the Sort Left To Right option button in the Sort Options dialog box.*

Sort a List Using More than One Field

1. Click anywhere within the list range.
2. Click the Data menu, and then click Sort.
3. Click the Sort By drop-down arrow, and then click the field on which the sort will be based (the *primary sort field*).
4. Click the Ascending or Descending option button.
5. Click the first Then By drop-down arrow, and then click the Ascending or Descending option button.
6. If necessary, click the second Then By drop-down arrow, and then click the Ascending or Descending option button.
7. Click the Header Row option button to *exclude* the field names (in the first row) from the sort, or click the No Header Row option button to *include* the field names (in the first row) in the sort.
8. Click OK.

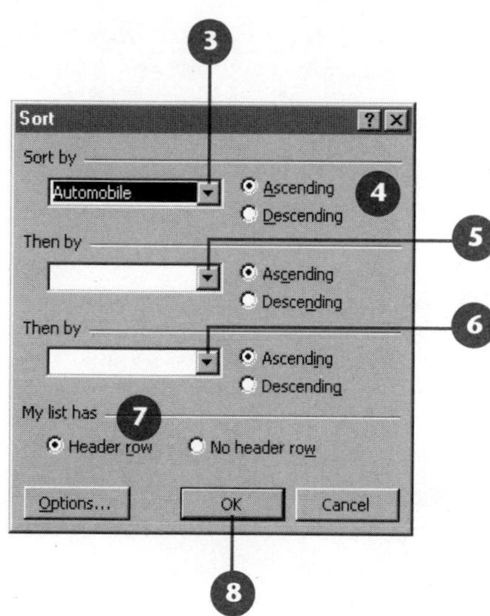

10

Displaying Parts of a List with AutoFilter

A list containing numerous records can be difficult to work with—unless you can narrow your view of the list when you need to. For example, rather than looking through an entire inventory list, you might want to see records that come from one distributor. The *AutoFilter* feature creates a list of the items found in each field. You select the items that you want to display in the column (that is, the records that meet certain criteria). Then you can work with a limited number of records. You can redisplay the records after you are finished.

Display Specific Records Using AutoFilter

1. Click anywhere within the list range.
2. Click the Data menu, point to Filter, and then click AutoFilter.
3. Click the drop-down arrow of the field you want to use to specify search criteria.
4. Select the item that records must match in order to be included in the list.
5. Repeat steps 3 and 4, as necessary, to filter out more records using additional fields.
6. Click the Data menu, point to Filter, and then click AutoFilter to turn off AutoFilter and redisplay all records in the list.

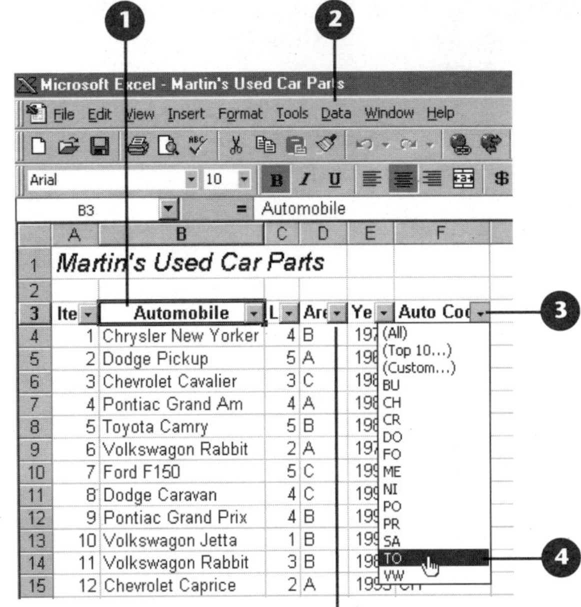

A drop-down arrow appears to the right of the field name when you turn on Auto Filter.

> **TIP**
>
> **Speed up your work with the Top 10 list.** *The AutoFilter offers a Top 10 command in the drop-down list of every field. Click this command to quickly create a filter for the top or bottom 10 items in a list.*

Creating Complex Searches

There are many times you'll want to search for records that meet more than one criteria. For example, you might want to see records of only those orders purchased from a particular distributor that are out of stock. Using the AutoFilter and the Custom command, you can create complex searches.

You use *logical operators* to measure whether an item in a record qualifies as a match with the selected criteria. You can also use the *logical conditions* AND and OR to join multiple criteria into a single search. The result of any search is either true or false; if a field matches the criteria, the result is true. The OR condition requires that only one criteria be true in order for a record to qualify. When multiple criteria are combined with the logical condition AND, both the criteria to the left and right of the condition must be true in order for the record to qualify.

Create a Complex Search Using AutoFilter

1. Click anywhere within the list range.
2. Click the Data menu, point to Filter, and then click AutoFilter.
3. Click the drop-down arrow next to the first field you want to include in the search.
4. Click Custom.
5. Click the Auto Code drop-down arrow (on the left), and then select a logical operator.
6. Click the drop-down arrow (on the right), and then select a field choice.
7. Click the And or Or option button.
8. Click the drop-down arrow (on the left), and then select a logical operator.
9. Click the drop-down arrow (on the right), and then select a field choice.
10. Click OK.

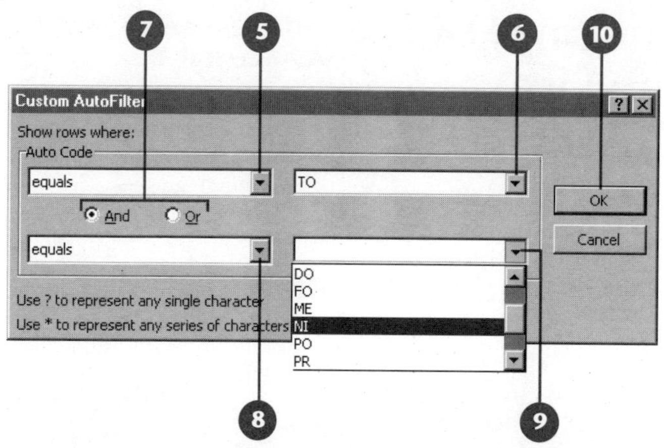

LOGICAL OPERATORS			
Symbol	**Operator**	**Symbol**	**Operator**
=	Equal to	<>	Not equal to
>	Greater than	<	Less than
>=	Greater than or equal to	<=	Less than or equal to

Entering Data in a List Quickly

Entering data in a list—whether you use the Data Form or worksheet—can be tedious and repetitive. Excel provides two tools that make the job easier in the worksheet: PickList and AutoComplete.

In order to use either of these features, you need to first enter at least one record in a list. Both features then use your previous entries to save you the trouble of typing repetitive information as you proceed through each field. The *PickList* displays previous entries made in the current field in a list format; *AutoComplete* automatically completes an entry when you type the first few letters of an entry you've made before. The PickList feature is available using the right mouse button; AutoComplete works automatically.

Enter Data with AutoComplete

1. Begin typing an entry in a cell. If a previous entry in that field begins with the same characters, AutoComplete displays the entry.
2. Press Enter or Tab to accept the entry. To make a different entry, resume typing and ignore the AutoComplete suggestion.

Auto Complete suggests this entry because an existing entry begins with "s."

Enter Data with the PickList

1. Right-click the cell in which you want to use the PickList.
2. Click Pick From List.
3. Click a selection from the list.
4. Press Enter or Tab to accept the entry, or press Esc to cancel the entry.

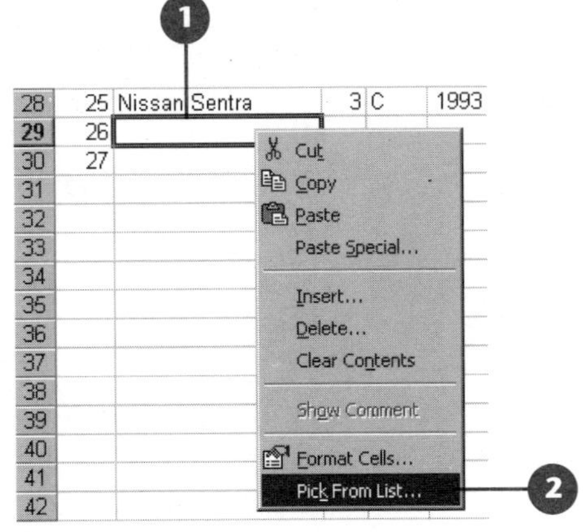

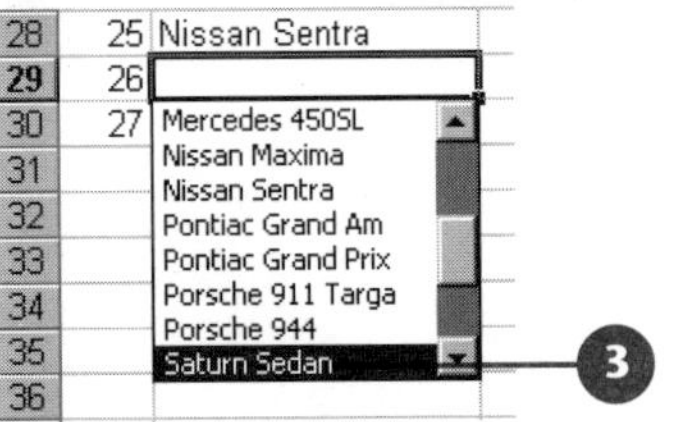

Analyzing Data Using a PivotTable

When you want to summarize information in a lengthy list using complex criteria, use the PivotTable to simplify your task. Without the PivotTable, you would have to manually count or create a formula to calculate which records met certain criteria, and then create a table to display that information for a report or presentation. Once you determine what fields and criteria you want to use to summarize the data, and how you want the resulting table to look, the PivotTable Wizard does the rest.

TIP

Use the Office Assistant to get help. *Click the Office Assistant button in the lower left corner of the dialog box for help using the PivotTable wizard.*

Create a PivotTable

1. Click any cell within the list range.
2. Click the Data menu, and then click PivotTable Report.
3. If using the list range, make sure the Microsoft Excel List Or Database option button is selected.
4. Click Next.
5. If the range you want is "Database" (the active list range), then skip to step 8.
6. If the range does not include the correct data, click the Collapse Dialog button.
7. Drag the pointer over the list range, including the field names, to select a new range, and then click the Expand Dialog button.
8. Click Next.
9. Drag field name(s) to the ROW and COLUMN and DATA areas.
10. Click Next.
11. Specify the location of the worksheet you want to use in the text box, and then click Finish.

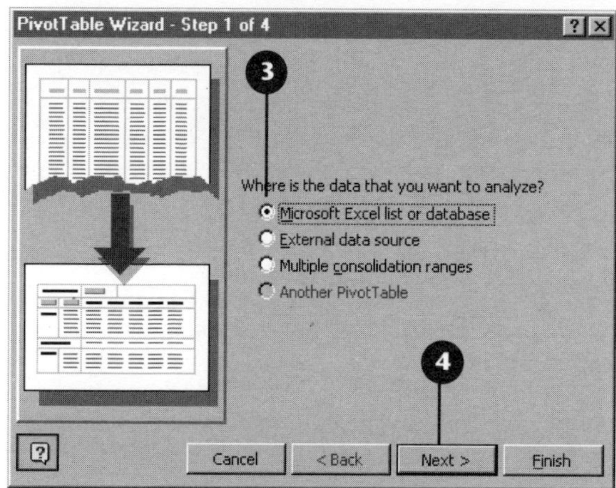

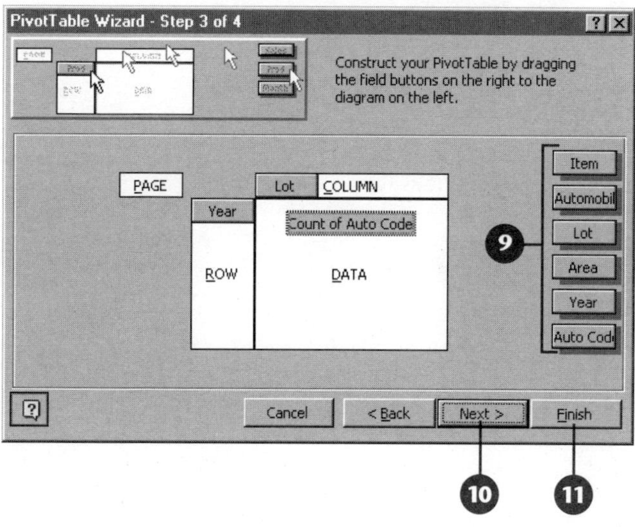

10

Updating a PivotTable

You can quickly update a PivotTable report using the PivotTable toolbar, which displays whenever a PivotTable is active. This saves you from having to re-create a PivotTable every time you add new data to a list.

> **TIP**
>
> **Access PivotTable functions several ways.** *All the functions of the PivotTable toolbar buttons are also available on the PivotTable drop-down arrow (the first button on the PivotTable toolbar).*

Update a PivotTable Report

1. Make any necessary change(s) in the list range data.
2. Click any cell in the PivotTable Report.
3. Click the Refresh Data button on the PivotTable toolbar, or click the PivotTable drop-down arrow on the PivotTable toolbar, and then click Refresh Data.

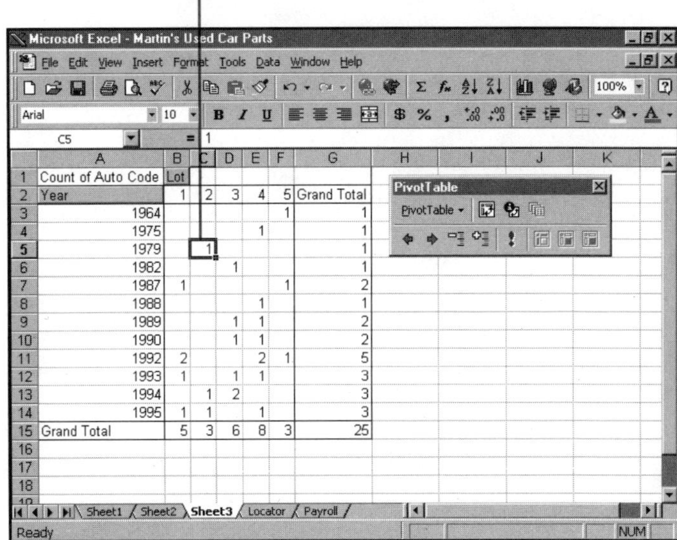

Count of Auto Code	Lot					
Year	1	2	3	4	5	Grand Total
1964					1	1
1975				1		1
1979		1				1
1982			1			1
1987	1				1	2
1988				1		1
1989			1	1		2
1990			1	1		2
1992	2			2	1	5
1993	1		1	1		3
1994		1	2			3
1995	1	1		1		3
Grand Total	5	3	6	8	3	25

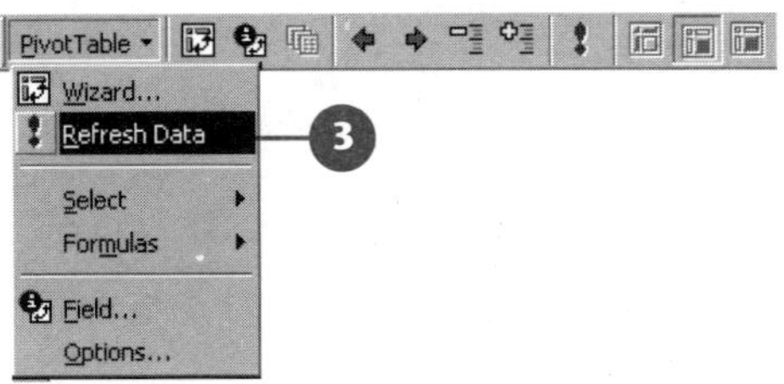

Charting a PivotTable

Data summarized in a PivotTable is an ideal candidate for a chart, since the table itself represents an overwhelming amount of difficult-to-read data. Once you select data within the PivotTable (using buttons on the PivotTable toolbar), then you can chart it like any other worksheet data using the Chart Wizard.

SEE ALSO

See "Creating a Chart" on page 142 for more information about using the Chart Wizard.

Create a Chart from a PivotTable

1. Click the Select Label And Data button on the PivotTable toolbar, or click the PivotTable drop-down arrow on the PivotTable toolbar, point to Select, and then click Label And Data.
2. Click the Chart Wizard button on the Standard toolbar.
3. Make selections from each of the four Chart Wizard dialog boxes.
4. Click Finish.

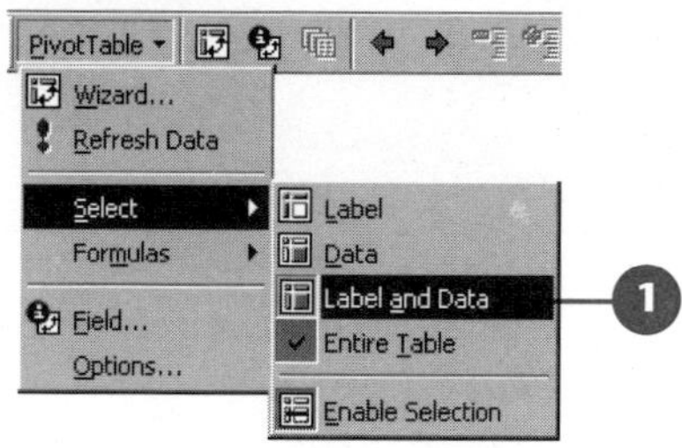

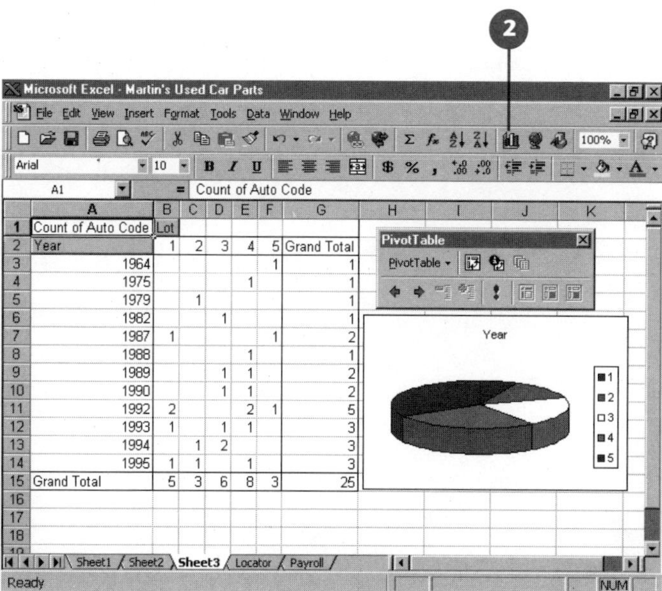

	A	B	C	D	E	F	G
1	Count of Auto Code	Lot					
2	Year	1	2	3	4	5	Grand Total
3	1964					1	1
4	1975				1		1
5	1979		1				1
6	1982			1			1
7	1987	1				1	2
8	1988				1		1
9	1989			1	1		2
10	1990			1	1		2
11	1992	2			2	1	5
12	1993	1		1	1		3
13	1994		1	2			3
14	1995	1	1		1		3
15	Grand Total	5	3	6	8	3	25

11

Tools for Working More Efficiently

IN THIS SECTION

- Viewing Multiple Workbooks
- Changing Your Worksheet View
- Customizing Your Excel Work Environment
- Freezing Columns and Rows
- Creating a Toolbar
- Customizing a Toolbar
- Adding a Macro to a Toolbar
- Saving Time with Templates
- Creating a Template
- Working with Templates
- Tracking Changes in a Worksheet
- Protecting Your Data

You might be surprised by all the tools Excel offers for saving time and effort while you work. These tools enable you to see more of the worksheet you're working on, to use and create customized worksheets, and to rearrange the desktop environment. By taking advantage of any or all of these tools, you can create a more efficient working environment to suit your personal preferences and speed up your work.

Working More Efficiently

You can increase your efficiency by customizing the way the Excel window looks, the way you execute commands, and even the way you create a worksheet.

No matter how large your monitor, it's impossible to see the entire worksheet at once. And if you're using more than one worksheet or workbook, it's that much more difficult to see all your work. There are several ways you can arrange the Excel worksheet window to see as much of your work area as possible, so you spend less time scrolling through a sheet and switching from sheet to sheet.

Viewing Multiple Workbooks

As you use many worksheets, it's only natural that you'll want to work in more than one workbook at a time. Multiple workbooks, like multiple worksheets, can be arranged on your monitor in a variety of ways to best suit your needs. For example, when working with workbooks from more than one fiscal year, it might be helpful to be able to view worksheets from each side-by-side.

TIP

You can arrange multiple views of one workbook. *To view different parts of the active workbook in multiple windows, select the Windows Of Active Workbook check box in the Arrange Windows dialog box.*

SEE ALSO

See "Changing Your Worksheet View" on page 179 for more information on modifying your worksheet's appearance.

View Multiple Workbooks

1. Open as many workbooks as you need to work with.
2. Click the Window menu. Notice that the names of all open files are listed at the bottom of this menu.
3. Click Arrange.
4. To choose the arrangement you want for viewing your multiple workbooks:
   - Click the Tiled option button to arrange the workbook windows clockwise starting in the top left position.
   - Click the Horizontal option button to arrange the workbook windows one beneath another.
   - Click the Vertical option button to arrange the workbook windows side-by-side.
   - Click the Cascade option button to arrange the workbook window one under another.
5. Click OK.

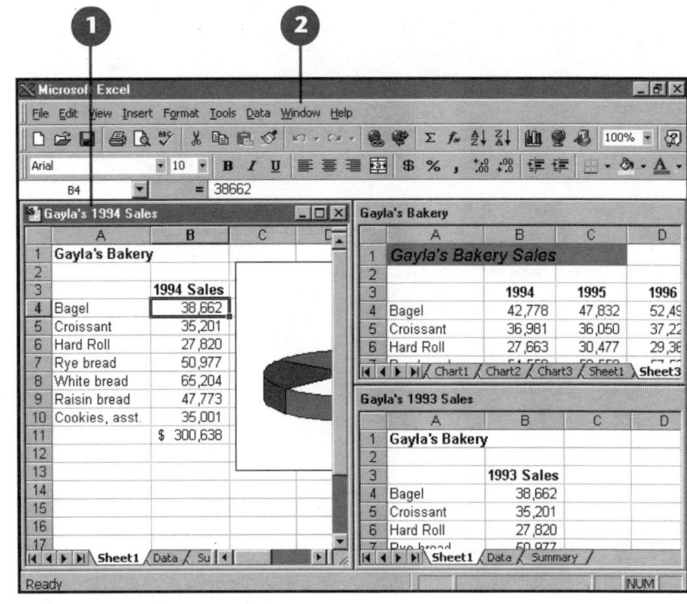

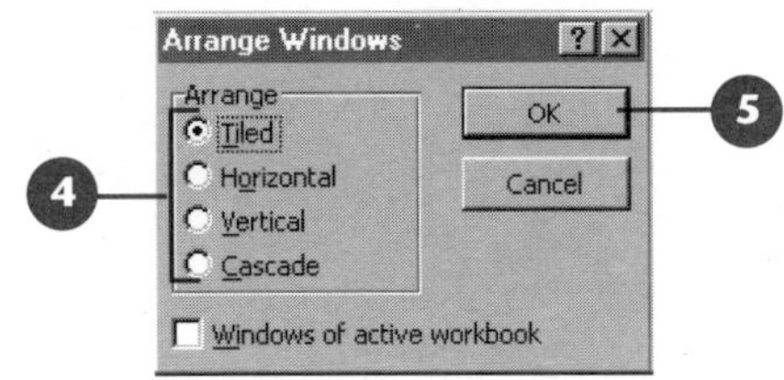

Changing Your Worksheet View

Changing your view of the worksheet window can improve your productivity. How you view a worksheet does not affect the printed document. To change the components of the worksheet window, you can select or deselect options in the Options dialog box. To open this dialog box, click the Tools menu, click Options, and then click the View tab.

The View tab allows you to display or hide almost any element in the worksheet window. By default, the formula bar and status bar both appear on the worksheet window. The formula bar shows the contents of the current cell, and the status bar displays information about selected or executed Excel commands and about special keys, such as the NUM Lock and Caps Lock keys.

The default display of a comment is a red triangle in the upper corner of a cell, but you can change the display. Graphic objects are automatically displayed within a worksheet, but you can change it to show placeholders or hide all to speed up the display. Although Windows options, such as Row & Column headers and scroll bars, provide valuable information, they also take up valuabe room on your screen.

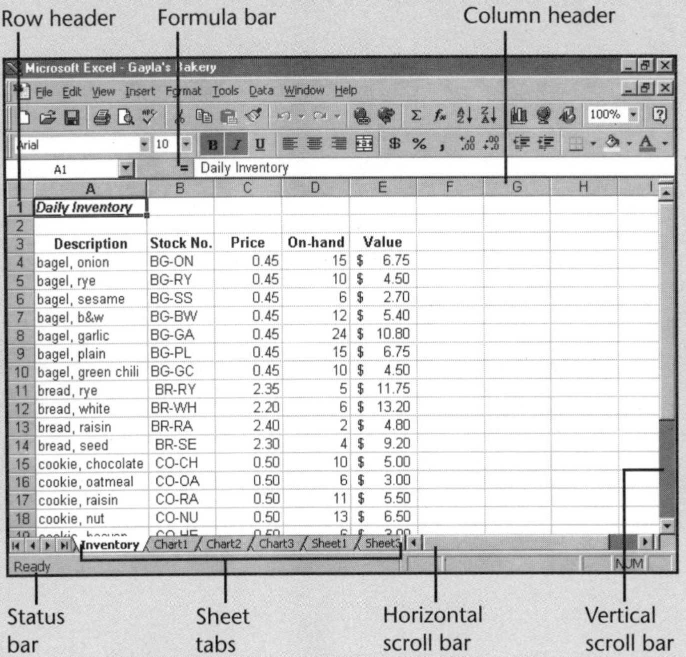

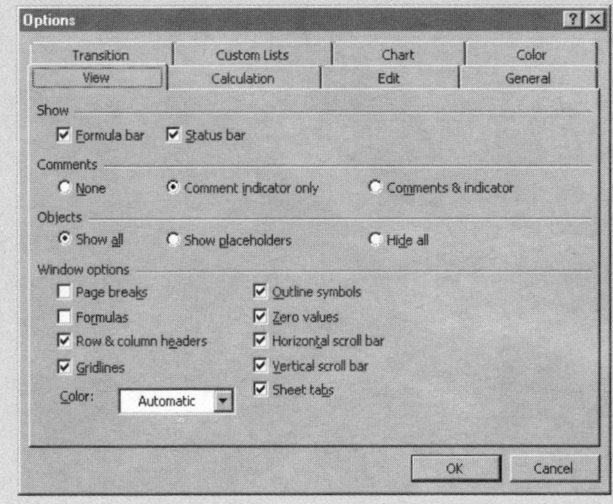

11

Customizing Your Excel Work Environment

To create a work environment that addresses your needs, Excel offers a variety of options that can be customized. The Options dialog box contains tabs for changing General options, such as the default font and the number of sheets in a new workbook, Edit options, such as where to move the active cell after you enter data and whether to allow drag and drop cell moving, Calculation options, such as whether you want Excel to automatically recalculate a worksheet whenever you change a value, and many more aspects of working in the program.

Change General Options

1. Click the Tools menu, and then click Options.
2. Click the General tab.
3. To turn on a setting in Excel, click the check box for the option you want.
4. To change the number of recently used files listed at the bottom of the File menu, click the spin arrows to set the number of files you want.
5. To change the default number of sheets in a new workbook, click the spin arrows to set a number.
6. To change the default font, click the Standard Font drop-down arrow, and then select a new font.
7. To change the default font size, click the Size drop-down arrow, and then select a new font size.
8. To specify where Excel should automatically look for existing files or newly saved files, enter the location of your default folder.
9. Click the User Name text box and edit its contents.
10. Click OK.

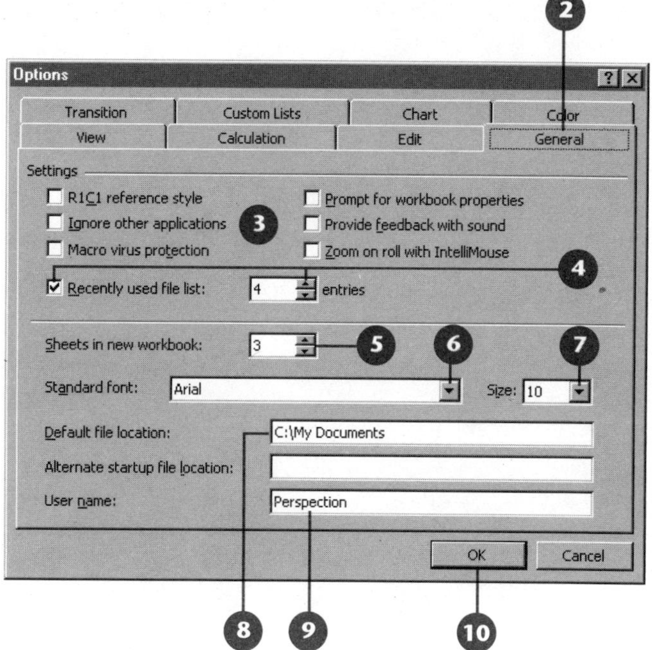

SEE ALSO

See "Changing Your Worksheet View" on page 179 for more information on customizing Excel.

TIP

Edit directly in a cell. *Turning on the Edit Directly In A Cell option allows you to make changes to a cell by double-clicking it.*

TIP

Alert before overwriting cells. *Turning off the Alert Before Overwriting Cells option can save you time, but you can accidently lose data.*

TIP

Change cell selection after you press the Enter key. *You can click the Direction drop-down arrow and select a direction to change the direction of the cell pointer after you press the Enter key.*

Change Edit Options

1. Click the Tools menu, and then click Options.
2. Click the Edit tab.
3. Click any of the check boxes to change the editing options you want.
4. Click OK.

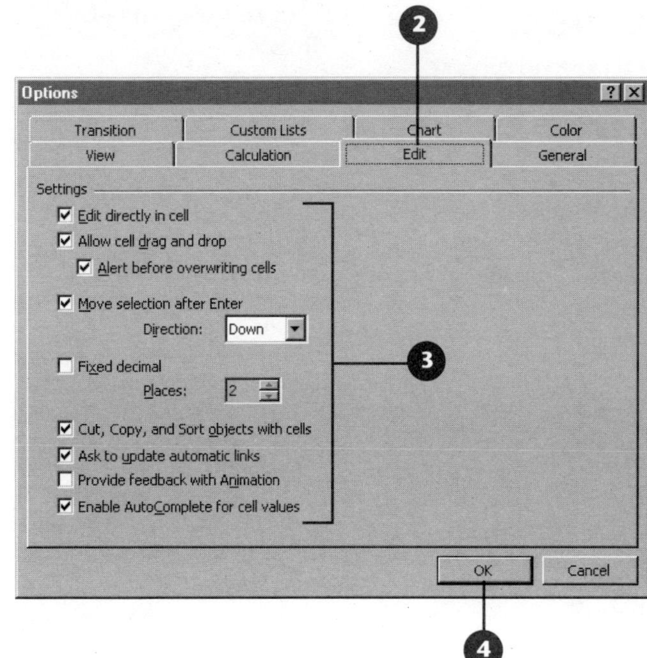

11

Freezing Columns and Rows

Large worksheets present a particular dilemma when it comes to working efficiently. If you scroll down to see the bottom of the list, you can no longer see the column names at the top of the list. Instead of repeatedly scrolling up and down, you can temporarily fix, or *freeze*, those column or row headings so that you can see them no matter where you scroll in the list.

When you freeze a row or column, you are actually splitting the screen into one or more *panes* (window sections) and freezing one of the panes. You can split the screen into up to four panes and can freeze up to 2 of these panes. You can edit the data in a frozen pane just as you do any Excel data, but the cells remain stationary even when you use the scroll bars; only the unfrozen part(s) of the screen scrolls.

Freeze Columns and Rows

1. Click any cell in the row below the rows you want to freeze, or in the column to the right of the columns you want to freeze.
2. Click the Window menu, and then click Freeze Panes.

- When you freeze a pane horizontally, all the rows *above* the active cell freeze. When you freeze a pane vertically, all the columns to the *left* of the active cell freeze.
- When you freeze a pane, it has no effect on how a worksheet looks when printed.

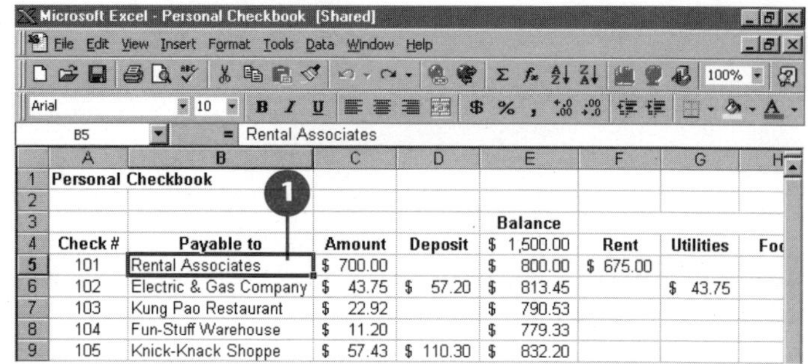

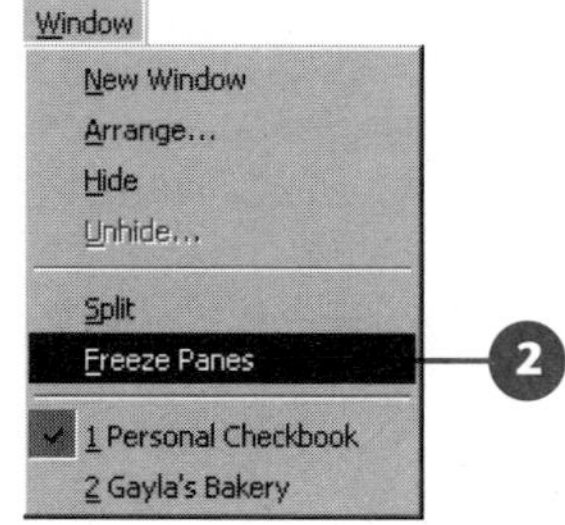

Unfreeze Columns and Rows

1. Click the Window menu.
2. Click Unfreeze Panes.

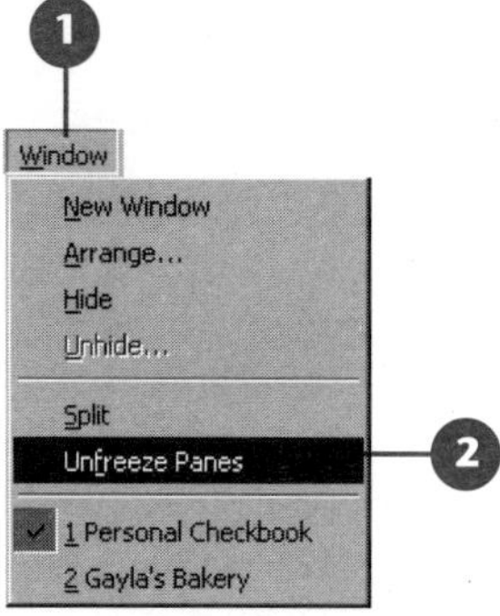

Creating a Toolbar

If none of the existing Excel toolbars fit your needs or if you just want a toolbar you can call your own, you can create a new toolbar. You might, for example, have several workbooks that involve specific tasks. Perhaps you have workbooks that require a lot of formatting; a special toolbar that contains a variety of formatting buttons would make it quick and easy to add those enhancements. Creating a toolbar that contains the buttons necessary for those common tasks can dramatically increase efficiency.

SEE ALSO

See "Working with Menus and Toolbar" on page 14 for more information on using toolbars or see "Customizing a Toolbar" on page 184 for information on modifying a toolbar.

Create a Toolbar

1. Click the View menu, point to Toolbars, and then click Customize.
2. Click New.
3. Type a name for the new toolbar.
4. Click OK.

   The new toolbar appears on your screen. The toolbar name may not fit in the title bar until the toolbar is long enough.
5. Click the Commands tab.
6. Click a category that contains the command(s) you want to add.
7. Click a command you want to add to the toolbar.
8. Drag the button to the new toolbar.
9. Repeat steps 6 through 8 until all buttons you want are added.
10. Click Close.

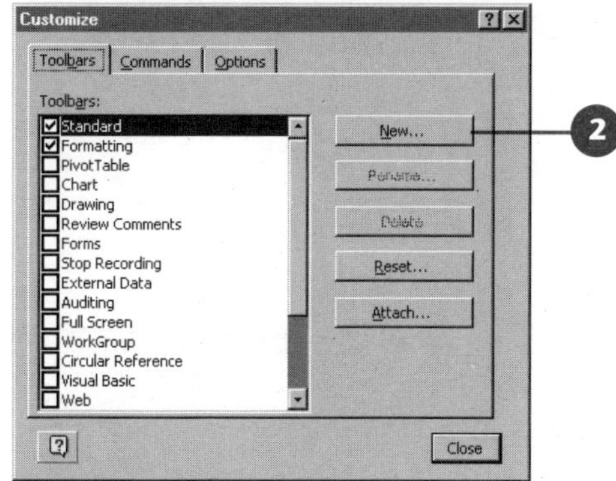

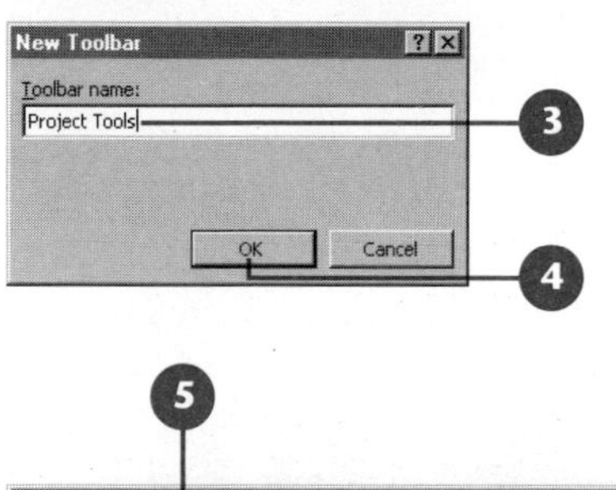

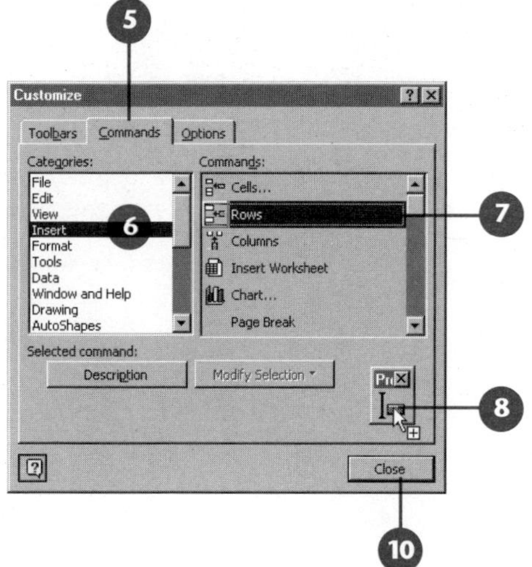

11

Customizing a Toolbar

Excel contains predesigned toolbars; by default, the Standard and Formatting toolbars appear on the screen at all times. These two toolbars contain the buttons for the most commonly used Excel commands. However, since everyone works differently, you may find that these toolbars take up space displaying some buttons you never use, while they do not display others you want available on your screen. Therefore, you can customize the toolbar display by choosing to display different Excel toolbars and by adding or deleting different toolbar buttons on any toolbar.

TIP

Use the Close button to hide a toolbar. *Click the Close button on a floating toolbars title bar to hide it.*

Display and Hide a Toolbar

1. Click the View menu, and then point to Toolbars.
2. Select the checked toolbar(s) you want to display or the unchecked toolbar(s) you want to hide.

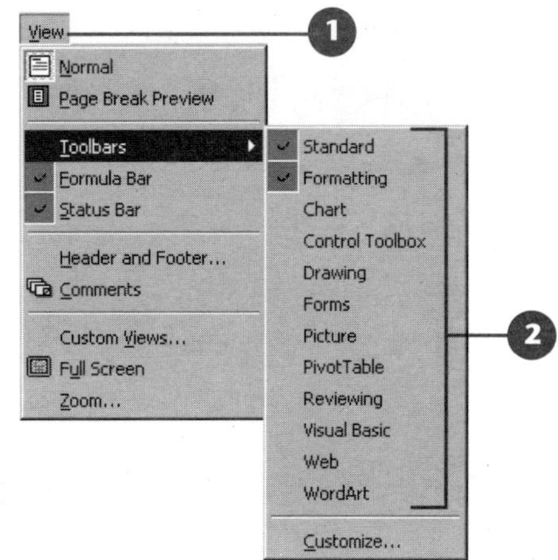

Delete a Button from a Toolbar

1. Click the View menu, point to Toolbars, and then click Customize.
2. Click the Toolbars tab, if necessary.
3. Make sure the toolbar you want to change is selected.
4. Drag the button you want to delete from the toolbar.
5. Click Close.

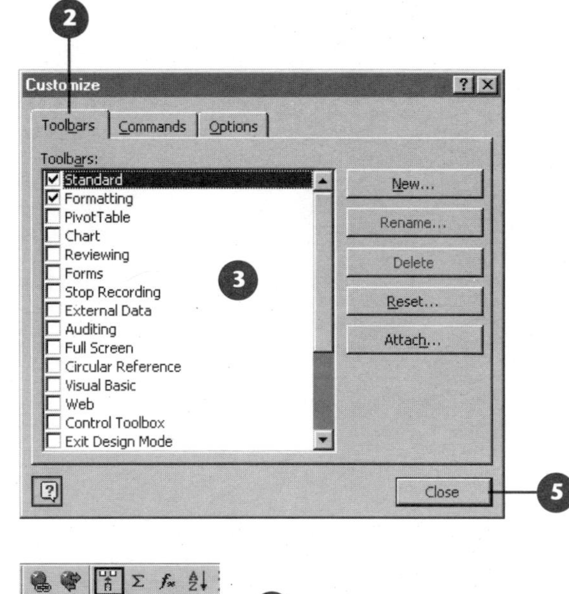

TIP

You can restore a toolbar to its original buttons. *In the Customize dialog box, click the toolbar you want to restore, and then click the Reset button.*

SEE ALSO

See "Adding a Macro to a Toolbar" on page 186 for more information on customizing a command or set of tasks.

Add a Button to a Toolbar

1. Click the View menu, point to Toolbars, and then click Customize.
2. Make sure the toolbar you want to change is selected.
3. Click the Commands tab.
4. Click the category that contains the command you want to add.
5. Click the command you want to add.
6. Drag the button you want to add to any location on the selected toolbar.
7. Repeat steps 4 through 6 until all the buttons you want are added.
8. Click Close.

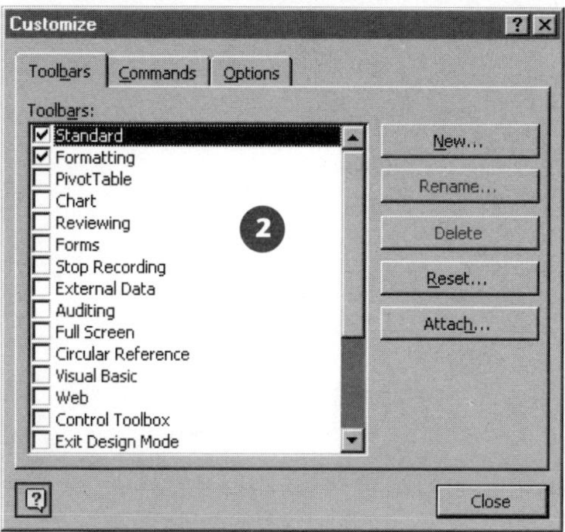

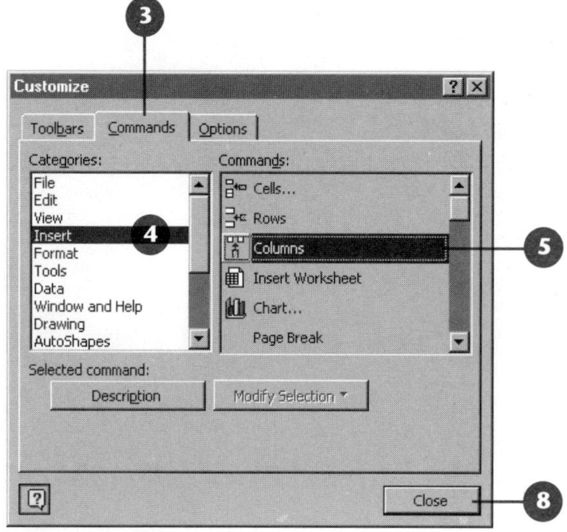

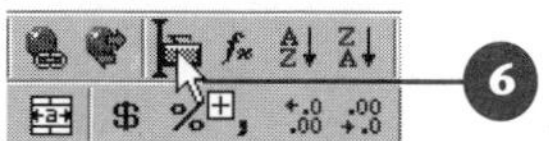

11

Adding a Macro to a Toolbar

If you use macros and you like using toolbar buttons to complete tasks, you can assign some of your favorite macros to toolbar buttons. Like menu commands, a toolbar button makes a macro just a button click away. Excel offers a choice of custom buttons you can assign to your macros to make it easier to remember what each represents.

SEE ALSO

See "Understanding How Macros Automate Your Work" on page 200 and "Recording a Macro" on page 201 for more information on macros and how to record them.

Assign a Button to a Macro

1. Click the View menu, point to Toolbars, and then click Customize.
2. Make sure the toolbar you want to add a button to is displayed.
3. Click the Commands tab.
4. Click Macros from the Categories list.
5. Click Custom Button from the Commands list.
6. Drag the button to a toolbar.
7. Click Modify Selection.
8. Click Assign Macro.
9. Click the macro you want to use in the Assign Macro dialog box.
10. Click OK.
11. Click Close.

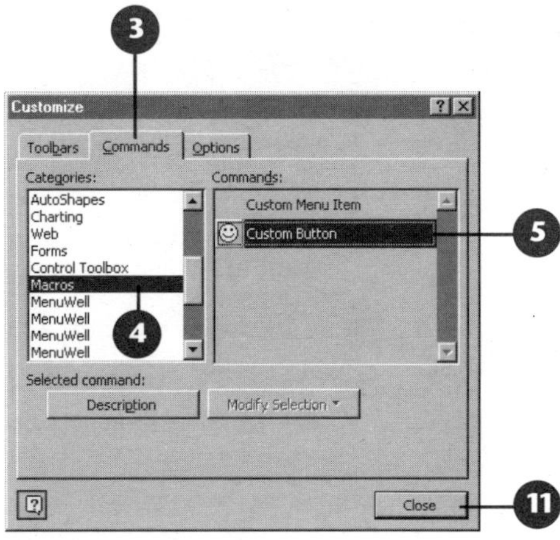

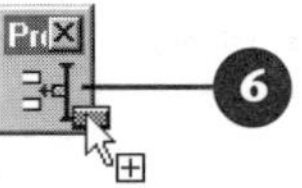

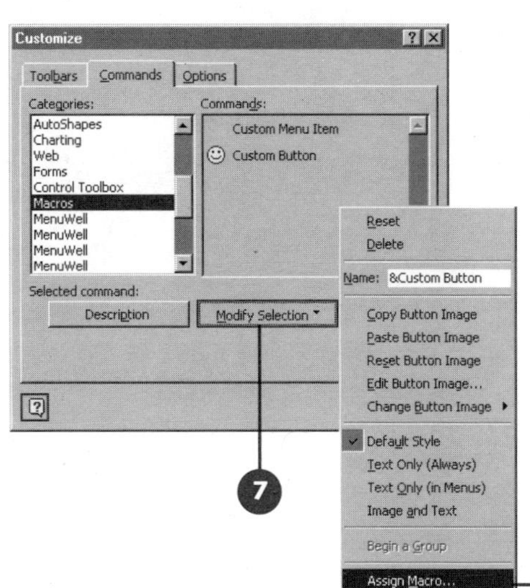

SEE ALSO

See "Creating a Toolbar" on page 183 for information on creating a new toolbar.

Change a Button's Appearance

1. Click the View menu, point to Toolbars, and then click Customize.
2. Make sure the toolbar you want is displayed.
3. Click the button on the toolbar you want to change.
4. Click the Commands tab.
5. Click Modify Selection.
6. Point to Change Button Image.
7. Click a new button on the palette.
8. Click Close.

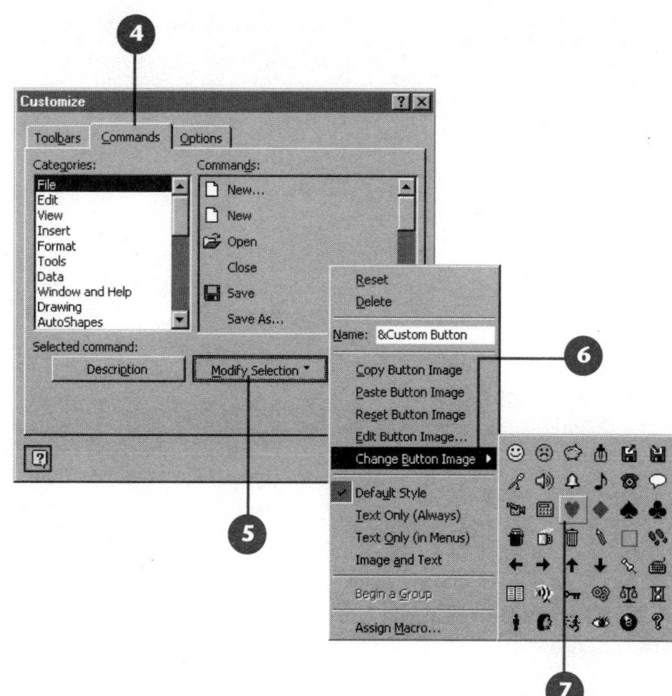

11

Saving Time with Templates

Many of the worksheets you create may be very similar. Perhaps each month you create a worksheet in which to record budget data. Each time you create the worksheet you have to enter the same formulas, labels, and formatting, and the only information that changes is the actual budget data. Wouldn't it be easier if you could open a new workbook that already contained all the repetitive information, so that all you would have to do was fill in the new data as if you were filling in a form? Excel templates make this possible.

A *template* is a workbook form that can contain formulas, labels, graphics, and formatting. When you start a new workbook, based on the template of your choice, your new workbook contains all the information from the template, so all you have to is fill in the blanks. Excel contains several built-in templates designed to be adapted for almost any business situation.

Start and Save a Workbook Using a Template

1. Click the File menu, then click New.
2. Click the Spreadsheet Solutions tab.
3. Click the name of the template you want to use.
4. Click OK.
5. Fill in the form with your own information.
6. Click Save. The Save As dialog box opens so that you can save the file as a workbook (not a new template).

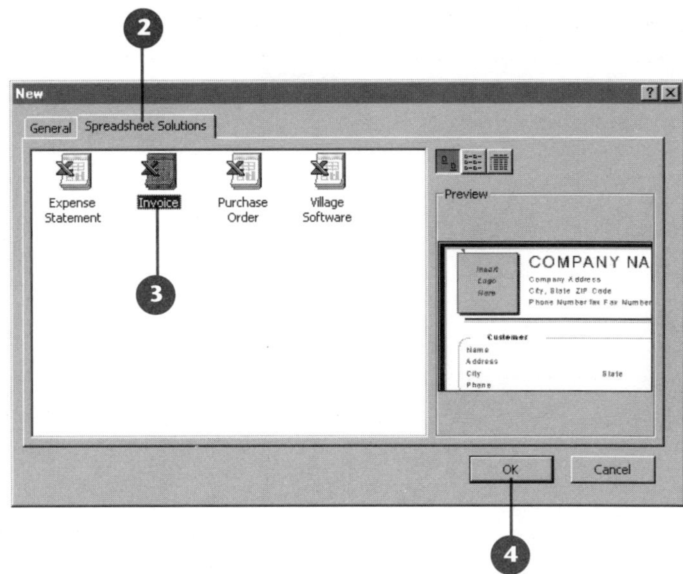

TEMPLATE	DESCRIPTION
Expense Statement	Creates an form for submitting business expenses.
Invoice	Creates a form containing customer and product information with unit and extended prices.
Purchase Order	Creates a purchase order form: similar to Invoice template.
Village Software	Contains a complex form that lets a user visit a web site, see software products, and view customer specials.

Creating a Template

You create a template in the same way you create any workbook. When you save the workbook you want to use as a template for the first time, you specify it as a Template rather than an Excel workbook.

TIP

Test your template as you work. *As you build a template, enter data in it to make sure the formulas work correctly. Then before saving it as a template, erase the data.*

TIP

When to use macros and templates. *Create a macro to make repetitive tasks more efficient; create a template for fill-in-the-blank data whose format rarely changes.*

SEE ALSO

See "Saving Time with Templates" on page 188 for more information on using Excel templates.

Create a Template

1. Enter all the necessary information in a new workbook—including formulas, labels, graphics, and formatting.
2. Click the File menu, and then click Save As.
3. Click the Save In drop-down arrow, and then select a location for the template.
4. Type a desired file name that will help you easily identify the purpose of the template.
5. Click the Save As Type drop-down arrow.
6. Click Template.
7. Click Save.

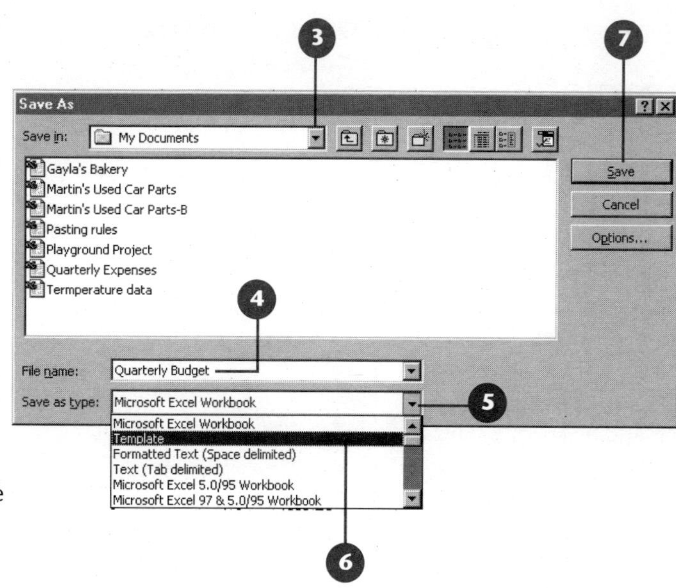

11

Working with Templates

You may not realize it, but every workbook you create is based on a template. When you start a new workbook without specifying a template, Excel creates a new workbook based on the *default template*, which includes three worksheets and no special formulas, labels, or formatting. When you specify a particular template in the New dialog box, whether it's one supplied by Excel or one you created yourself, Excel starts a new workbook that contains the formulas, labels, graphics, and formatting contained in that template. The template itself does not change when you enter data in the new workbook, because you are working on a new file, not with the template file. If you want to make changes to the template form itself, so that all new workbooks are based on its change, you need to open the template and make your changes there.

Open a Template

1. Click the Open button on the Standard toolbar.
2. Click the Look In drop-down arrow, and then select the drive and folder that contains the template you want to open.
3. Click the Files Of Type drop-down arrow.
4. Click Templates.
5. Click the filename of the template you want open.
6. Click Open.

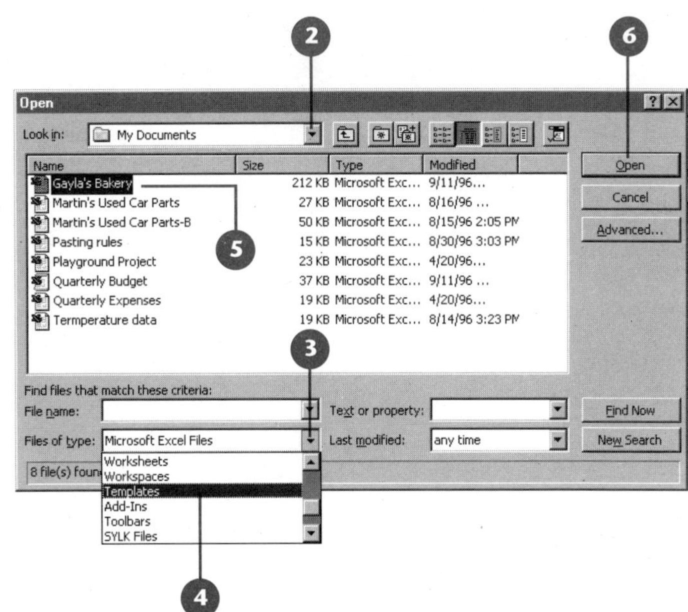

Change an Excel Template

1. Click the Open button on the Standard toolbar.
2. Click the Look In drop-down arrow, and change the location to drive C:/ Program Files/Microsoft Office/Templates/ Spreadsheet Solutions.
3. Click the template you want to use.
4. Click Open.

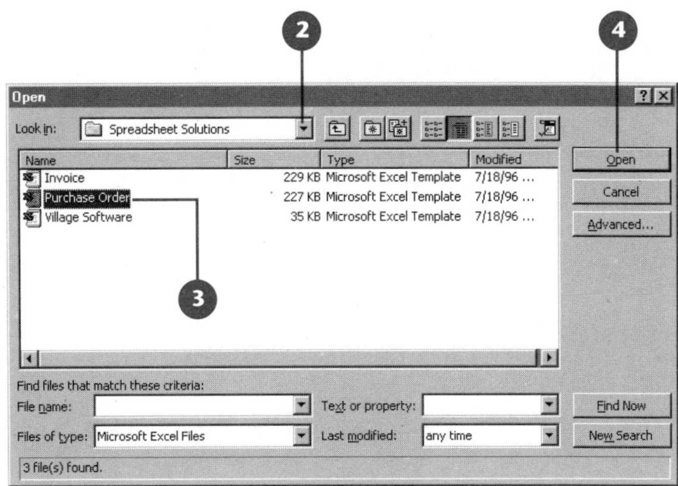

TIP

Use the New Workbook button to open a default workbook. *Clicking the New Workbook button on the Standard toolbar opens a workbook based on the default template.*

TIP

Changing the default template affects all new workbooks you create. *Be careful if you decide to make any changes to this template.*

5. Make the changes you want. Remember that these changes will affect all new workbooks you create using this template.
6. Click the Save button on the Standard toolbar.
7. Close the template before using it to create a new workbook.

Customize an Excel Template

1. Open the Excel template you want to customize. Excel templates are located in the Program Files/Microsoft Office/ Templates/Spreadsheet Solutions folder.
2. Click the Customize Your [Template Name] tab.
3. Point to cell notes for comments that help you customize the template.
4. Replace the placeholder text with your own information.
5. Click the Save button on the Standard toolbar.
6. Close the template before using it to create a new workbook.

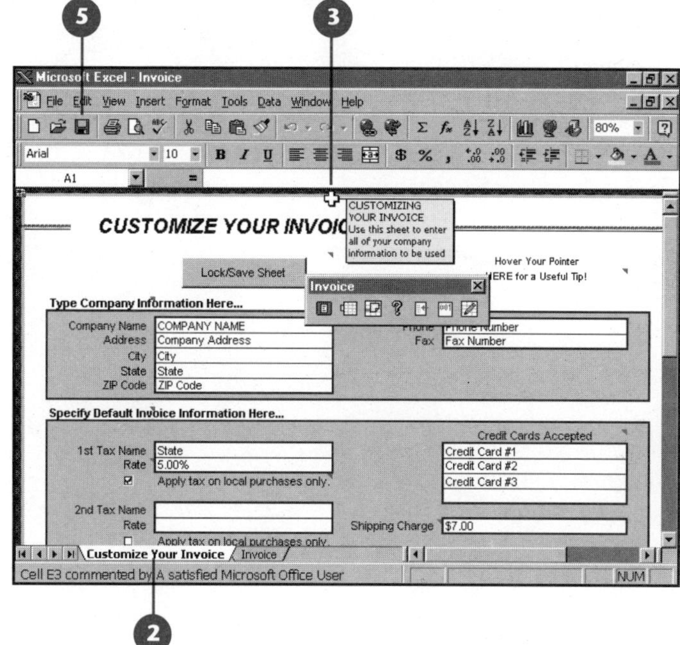

11

Tracking Changes in a Worksheet

As you build and fine tune a worksheet—particularly if you are sharing workbooks with co-workers—you can keep track of all the changes that are made at each stage in the process. The Track Changes feature makes it easy to know who has made what changes and when the changes were made. To take full advantage of this feature, turn it on the first time you, or a co-worker, edit a workbook. Then when it's time to review the workbook, all the changes will be recorded.

You can review a workbook at any point to see what changes have been made and who made them. Cells containing changes are surrounded by a blue border, and the changes made can be viewed instantly by moving your mouse pointer over any outlined cell. When you're ready to finalize the workbook, you can review it and either accept or reject the changes.

Turn On the Track Changes Feature

1. Click the Tools menu, point to Track Changes, and then click Highlight Changes.
2. Click the Track Changes While Editing check box.
3. Click OK.
4. Click OK to save the workbook.

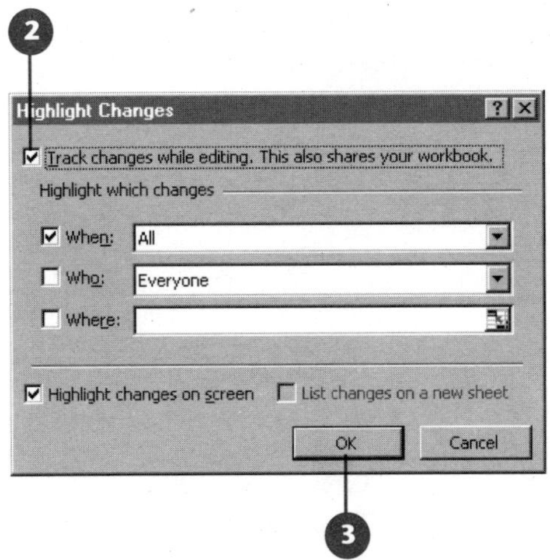

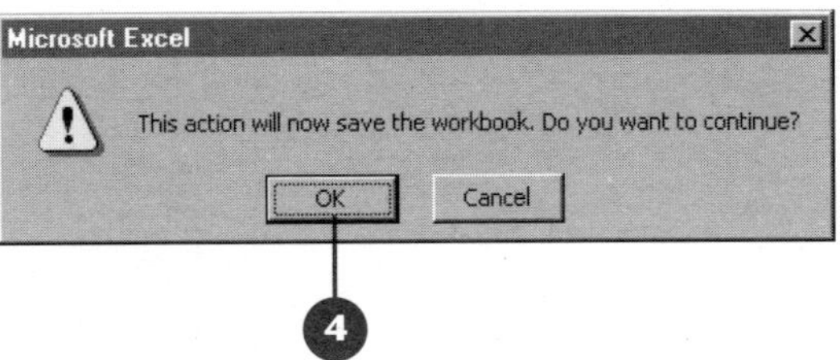

View Changes That Are Tracked

1. Position the mouse pointer over an edited cell.

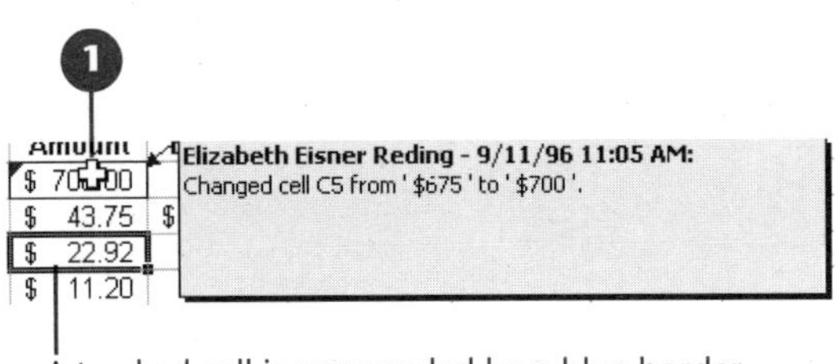

A tracked cell is surrounded by a blue border.

TIP

Title bar changes to alert you of shared status. *When you or another user applied the Track Changes command to a workbook, the message "[Shared]" displays in the title bar of the workbook to alert you that this feature is active.*

SEE ALSO

See "Editing Cell Contents" on page 32 for more information about editing cells.

SEE ALSO

See "Customizing Your Excel Work Environment" on page 179 for more information about changing the user name that displays when you track your changes.

Accept or Reject Tracked Changes

1. Click the Tools menu, point to Track Changes, and then click Accept Or Reject Changes. If necessary, click OK to the message box.
2. Click OK to begin reviewing changes.
3. If necessary, scroll to review all the changes, and then click:
   - Accept to make the selected change to the worksheet.
   - Reject to remove the selected change from the worksheet.
   - Accept All to make all the changes to the worksheet after you have reviewed them.
   - Reject All to remove all the changes to the worksheet after you have reviewed them.
4. Click Close.

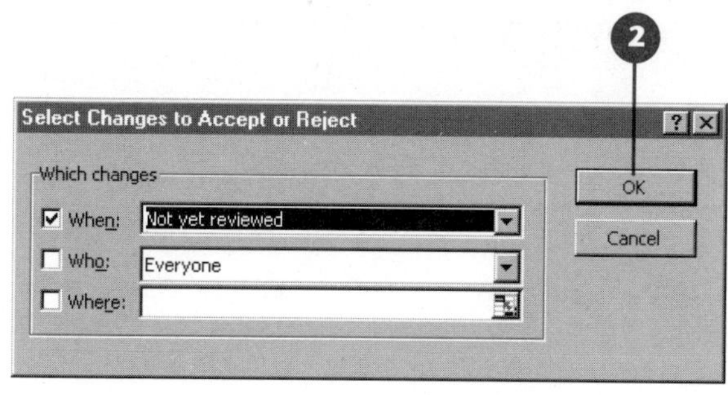

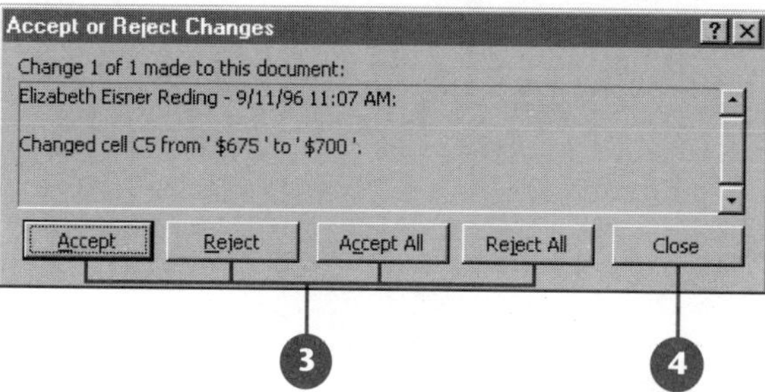

11

Protecting Your Data

You work very hard creating and entering information in a workbook. To preserve all your work—particularly if your files are being used by others—you can password protect its contents. You can protect a sheet or an entire workbook. In each case, you'll be asked to supply a password, and then enter it again when you want to work on the file.

TIP

Protect your password. *Make sure you keep your password in a safe place. Also, try to avoid obvious passwords like your name, your company, or your favorite pet.*

TIP

You need your password to unprotect a worksheet. *Turn off protection by clicking the Tools menu, point to Protection, and then click Unprotect Sheet. Enter the password, and then click OK.*

Protect Your Worksheet

1. Click the Tools menu, point to Protection, and then click Protect Sheet. Using the Tools menu, you can protect an individual sheet, the entire workbook, or you can protect and share a workbook. The steps for all are similar.
2. Click the check boxes for the options you want protected in the sheet.
3. Type a password.
4. Click OK.
5. Retype the password.
6. Click OK.

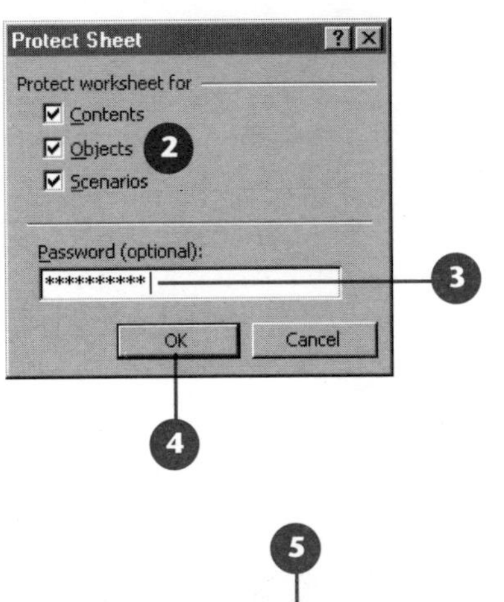

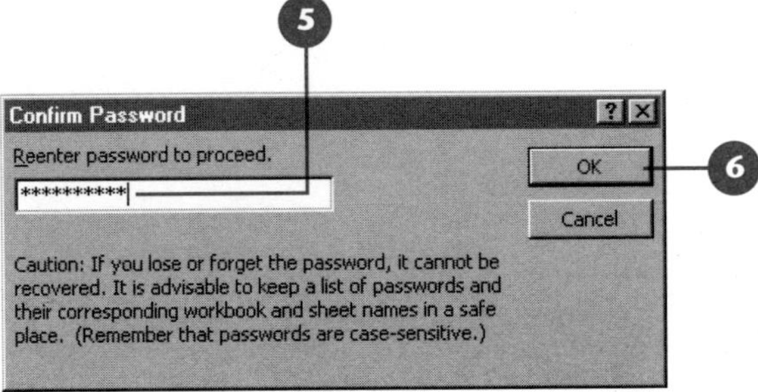

12

Building More Powerful Worksheets

IN THIS SECTION

Creating Links Between Worksheets and Workbooks

Consolidating Data

Understanding How Macros Automate Your Work

Recording a Macro

Running a Macro

Understanding Macro Code

Debugging a Macro Using the Step Mode

Editing a Macro

Adding Comments to a Macro

Understanding Excel Program Add-Ins

If your worksheet or workbook needs go beyond simple calculations, Microsoft Excel 97 offers several tools to help you create worksheets that address more specialized projects. With Excel's linking capabilities, you can share data among worksheets and workbooks.

Linking Data in Excel

For many projects, you may need to use more than one worksheet to record, analyze, or present information. If you run a small business, for example, you might use one Excel worksheet to maintain a price list for your products or services and another worksheet as an invoice form. When you generate an invoice, you need to enter the price for each product in the worksheet. You could check the price list and then enter the price for each product purchased, but what if your prices change often? You'd have to look up each price and enter it every time you generated an invoice. A better solution is to establish a *link*. You can link a formula that references a cell in the price list worksheet to a cell in the invoice worksheet, so that the invoice worksheet always reflects the most up-to-date prices. Like using cell references instead of values in a formula, linking makes it easy to calculate results no matter how often your worksheet changes, because it automatically updates values as necessary.

Creating Links Between Worksheets and Workbooks

A *link* can be as simple as a reference to a cell in another worksheet, or it can be part of a formula. You can link cells between sheets within one workbook or between different workbooks. The data in the cell that you want to link is called the *source data*. The cell or range to which you want to link the source data is called the *destination cell* or *destination range*. If you determine that linked data should no longer be continually updated, you can break a link easily.

TIP

Copy cells when you don't want the data to change. *If you want to use data from another worksheet or workbook but do not want the data to change, simply copy or move the cells by dragging them or using the Clipboard.*

Create a Link Between Worksheets

1. Select the destination cell or destination range.
2. Click the = button on the formula bar.
3. Click the sheet tab that contains the source data.
4. Select the cell or range that contains the source data.
5. Click OK or click the Enter button on the formula bar.

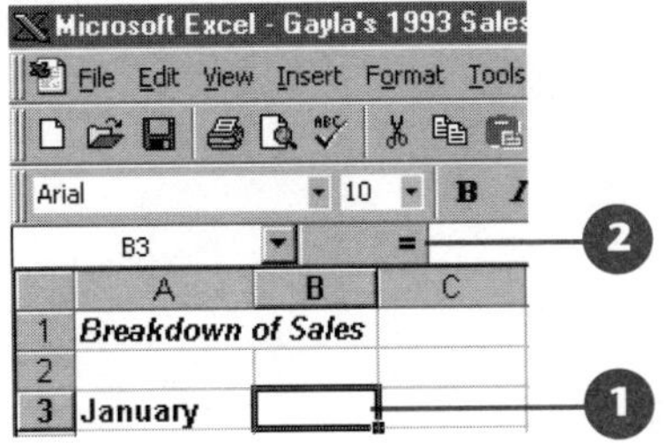

Sheet name indicates that the cell is on a different sheet.

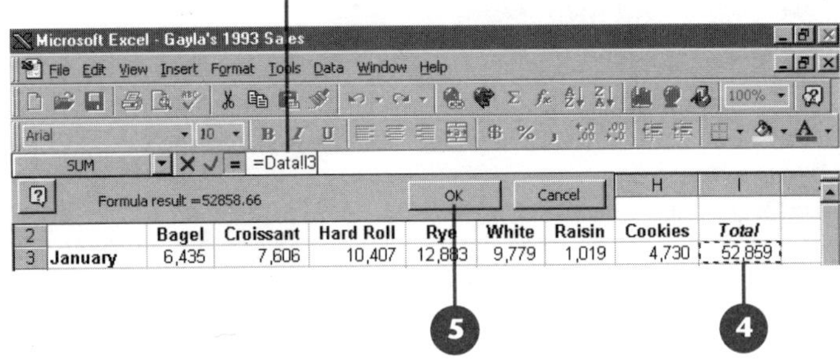

Break a Link

1. Click the cell containing the linked formula you want to break.
2. Click the Copy button on the Standard toolbar.
3. Click Edit, Paste Special.
4. Click the Values option button.
5. Click OK.

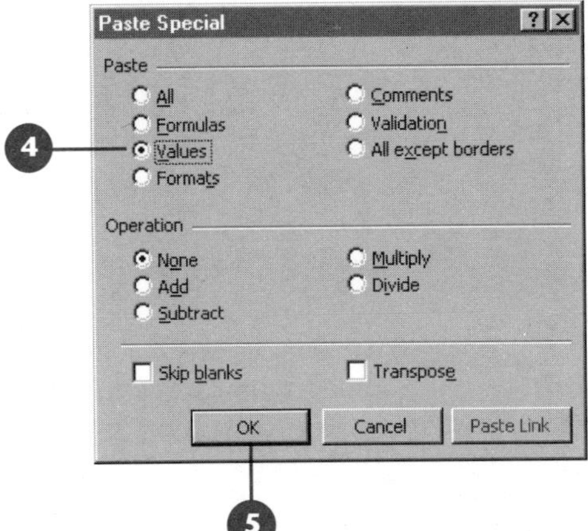

TIP

You can arrange worksheet windows to make linking easier. *To arrange open windows click the Window menu, click Arrange, and then click the option button for the window arrangement you want.*

TRY THIS

Create a link between two workbooks, and then close the workbook that contains the link. *In the open workbook, change the cell containing the source data. When you open the other workbook, watch how Excel updates the link to reflect the most up-to-date data.*

TIP

To include a link in a formula, treat the linked cell, as one argument in a larger calculation. *Enter the formula in the formula bar, and then enter the workbook, worksheet, and cell address of the data you want to link.*

SEE ALSO

See "Creating a Simple Formula" on page 46 for information about arithmetic operators.

Create a Link Between Workbooks

1. Open the workbooks that contains the data you want to link.
2. Click the destination cell or destination range.
3. Click the = button on the formula bar.
4. If the workbook that contains the data you want to link is visible, click anywhere within it to activate it. If it is not visible, click the Window menu, and then click the name of the workbook.
5. If necessary, click the sheet tab that contains the source data.
6. Select the cell or range that contains the source data.
7. Click OK or click the Enter button on the formula bar.

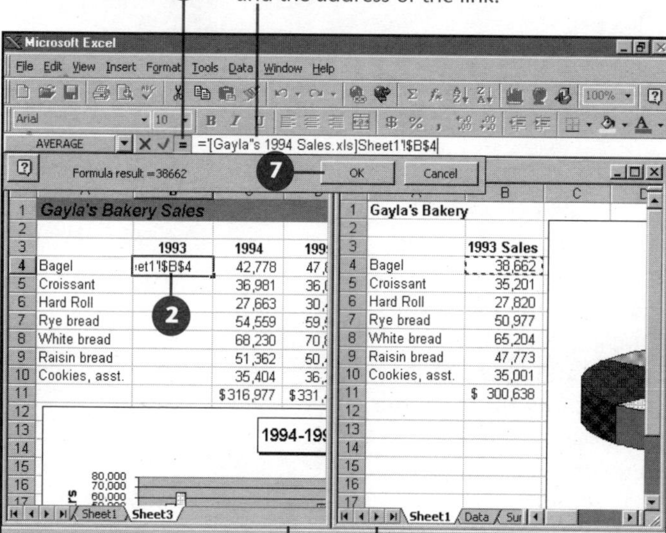

12

Consolidating Data

In some cases, you'll want to consolidate data from different worksheets or workbooks into a workbook rather than simply linking the source data. For instance, each division in your company is creating a budget, and your task is to pull together the totals for each line item into one company-wide budget. If each divisional budget is laid out in the same way, with the budgeted amount for each line item at the same cell address, you can very easily consolidate all the information without any retyping. And, if data in individual workbooks change—for example, one division decides to allot more funds to one item or fewer to another—the consolidated worksheet or workbook will always be correct.

Consolidate Data from Other Worksheets or Workbooks

1. Open all the workbooks that contain the data you want to consolidate.
2. Open or create the workbook that will contain the consolidated data.
3. Select the destination range. Make sure you select enough cells to accommodate any labels that might be included in the data you are consolidating.
4. Click the Data menu, and then click Consolidate.
5. Click the Function drop-down arrow, and then select the function you want to use to consolidate the data.
6. Type the location of the data to be consolidated, or click the Reference Collapse Dialog button and then select the cells to be consolidated. Use the Window menu to move between workbooks or to arrange them so they are visible at the same time.

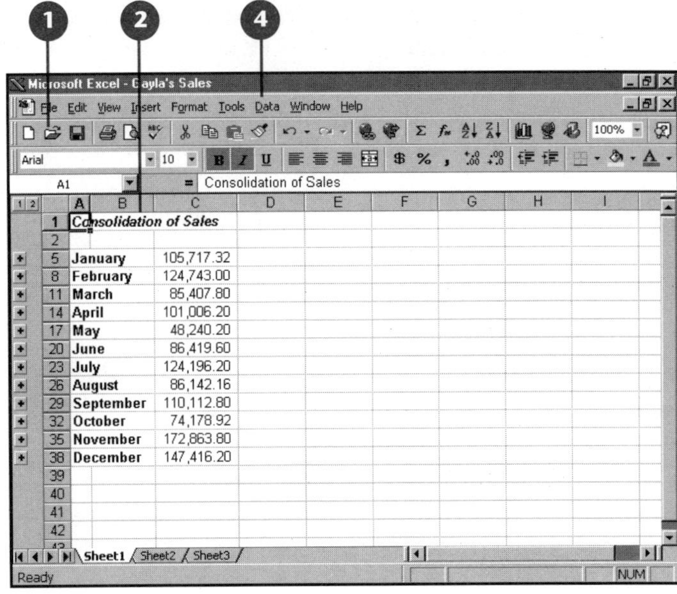

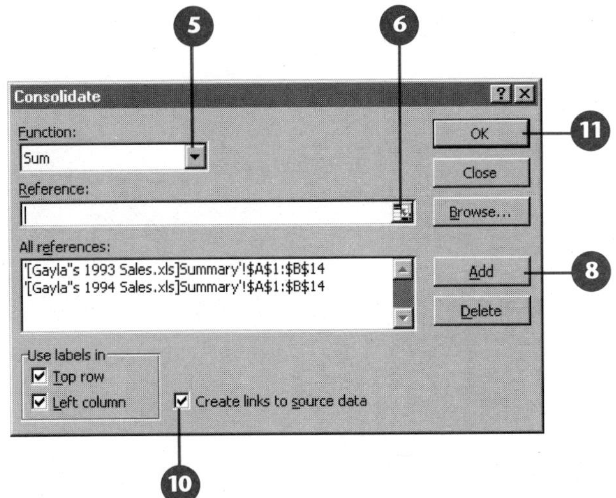

SEE ALSO

See "Creating Links Between Worksheets and Workbooks" on page 196 for information on breaking links.

TIP

You can often consolidate worksheets even if they are not laid out identically. *If the worksheets you want to consolidate aren't laid out with exactly the same cell addresses, but they contain identical types of information, select the Top Row and Left Column check boxes in the Consolidate dialog box, so that Excel uses labels to match up the correct data.*

7. Click the Expand Dialog button.
8. Click the Add button to add the reference to the list of consolidated ranges.
9. Repeat steps 6 through 8 until you have listed all references to consolidate.
10. Click the Create Links To Source Data check box.
11. Click OK.

Click the Plus button to see consolidated data.

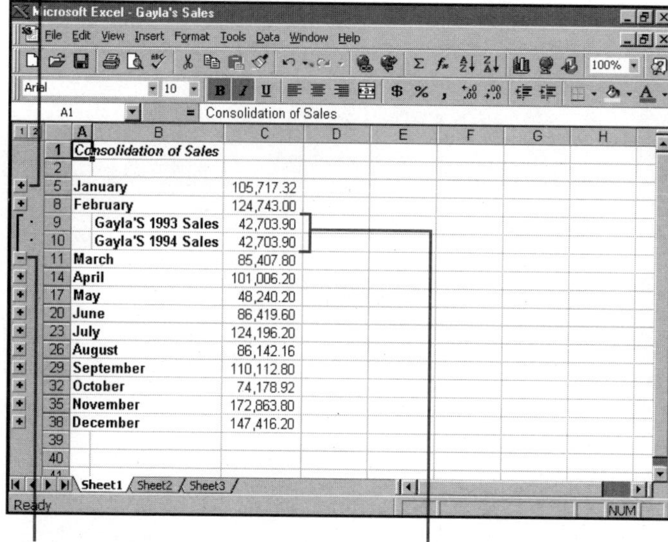

The Minus button indicates consolidated datea is displayed.

Consolidate data for March.

12

Understanding How Macros Automate Your Work

To complete many tasks in Excel, you need to execute a series of commands and actions. To print two copies of a selected range of Sheet2 of a worksheet, for example, you need to open the workbook, switch to Sheet2, select the print area, open the Print dialog box, and specify that you want to print two copies. If you often need to complete the same task, you'll find yourself repeatedly taking the same series of steps. It can become tiresome and irritating to continually repeat these same commands and actions when you can easily create a mini-program, or *macro*, that accomplishes all of them with a single command.

Creating a macro is easy and requires no programming on your part. Excel simply records the steps you want included in the macro while you use the keyboard and mouse. When you record a macro, Excel stores the list of commands with the name of your choice. You can store your macros in the current workbook, in a new workbook, or in Excel's Personal Macro workbook. Storing your macros in the Personal Macro workbook make the macros available to you from any location in Excel, even when no workbook is open.

Once a macro is created, you can make modifications to it, add comments so other users will understand its purpose, and find out if it runs correctly or not.

You can run a macro by choosing the Macro command on the Tools menu, or by using a shortcut key or clicking a toolbar button you've assigned to it. When you click the Tools menu, point to Macro, and then click Macros, the Macro dialog box.

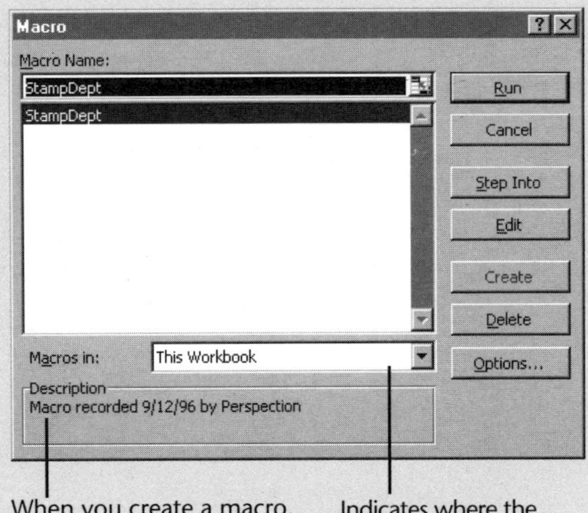

When you create a macro, you can add a description of what the macro does.

Indicates where the macro is stored.

From the Macro dialog box, you can create, edit, delete, or run a macro. If you have problems with a macro, you can step through the macro one command at a time, known as *debugging*.

Recording a Macro

Recording a macro is almost as easy as using a tape recorder. Once you turn on the macro recorder, Excel records every mouse click and keystroke action you execute until you turn off the recorder. Then you can "play" or run the macro whenever you want to repeat that series of actions. You don't even need to press a rewind button!

TRY THIS

Record a macro. *Create a macro that records a your name in a cell and includes attractive formatting.*

SEE ALSO

See "Understanding How Macros Automate Your Work" on page 200 for more information on where to save a macro.

Record a Macro

1. Click the Tools menu, point to Macro, and then click Record New Macro.
2. Type a name for the macro. This macro name appears in the list of available macros when you want to run a macro.
3. Assign a shortcut key to use a keystroke combination instead of a menu selection to run the macro.
4. Click the Store Macro In drop-down arrow, and then select a location. If you want the macro to be available for all your worksheet, save it in the Personal Macro workbook.
5. Type a description, if you want. The description appears at the bottom of the Macro dialog box.
6. Click OK.
7. Execute each command or action you need to complete the macro's task. Take the time to complete each action correctly, since the macro will repeat all moves you make, but at a much faster rate.
8. Click the Stop Recording button.

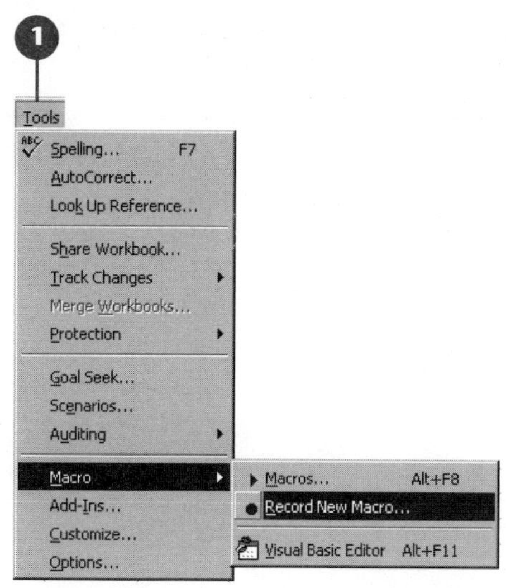

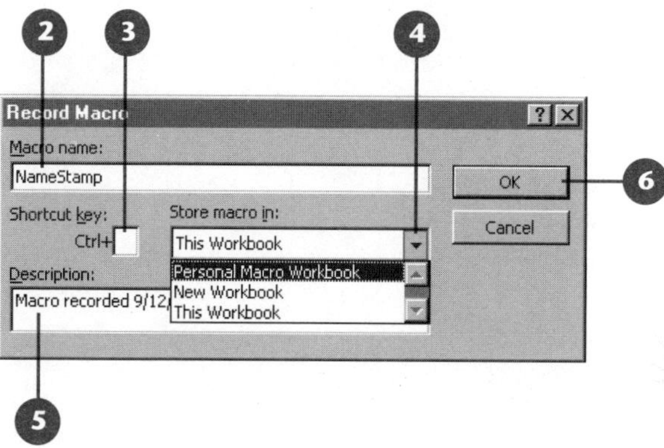

12

Running a Macro

Running a macro is similar to choosing a command in Excel. You can run a macro by selecting a menu command, issuing a keyboard combination, or by clicking a toolbar button, just as you might execute any Excel command.

When you record a macro, you can specify how you want to be able to play it back when you need it. You can also assign a toolbar button to a macro. Where you store a macro when you save it determines its availability later. Macros stored in the Excel Personal Macro workbook are always available, and macros stored in any other workbooks are only available when the workbook is open.

SEE ALSO

See "Adding a Macro to a Toolbar" on page 186 for information on adding a macro to a toolbar.

Run a Macro Using a Menu Command

1. Click the Tools menu, point to Macro, and then click Macros.
2. If necessary, click the Macros In drop-down arrow, and then select the workbook that contains the macro you want to run.
3. Click the name of the macro you want to run.
4. Click Run.

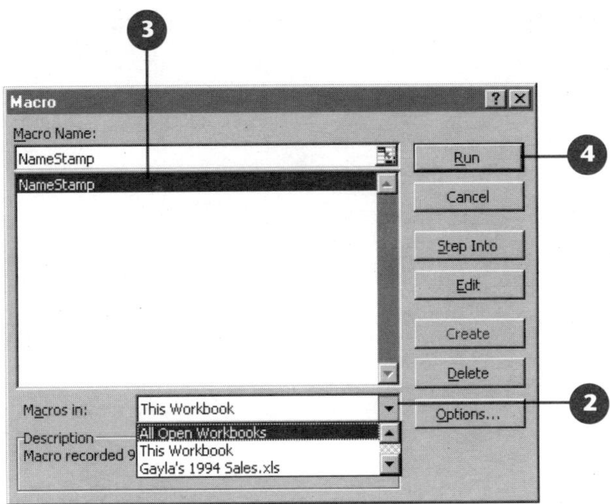

Run a Macro

1. Click the button assigned to the macro or issue the shortcut key you assigned to the macro.

Understanding Macro Code

Macro codes look cryptic and confusing, but they are the actual commands used within Excel. Back before tools such as the macro recorder existed, you'd create a macro by typing all the command code necessary to perform each action in the macro.

These comments tells the name of the macro, when the macro was created, and its purpose.

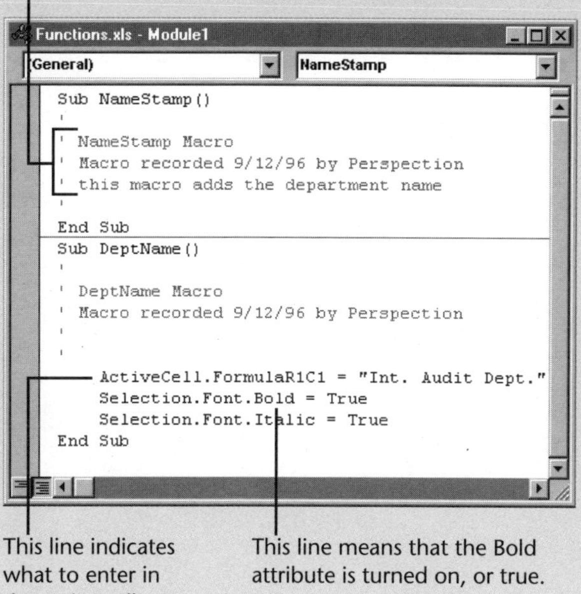

This line indicates what to enter in the active cell.

This line means that the Bold attribute is turned on, or true.

Each action listed in a macro either performs a step or states what attributes are turned on (true) or off (false). Quotation marks are used to indicate typed text, and the terms Sub and End Sub are used to indicate the beginning and ending of subroutines, respectively.

Because not everyone wants to read through macro code to figure out what a macro does, comments are often included within the code. The comments don't actually *do* anything, except clarify the purpose or actions of the macro. Comments can be used to help you remember why you took the steps you did, or help co-workers understand what is going on in the macro and how it should be used. A comment always begins with an apostrophe to distinguish it from command code.

To learn more about working with macro code, check out Visual Basic titles on the Microsoft Press Web site at http://www.microsoft.com/mspress/

12

Debugging a Macro Using the Step Mode

If a macro doesn't work exactly the way you want it to, you can fix the problem without re-creating the macro. Instead of recording the macro over again, Excel allows you to *debug*, or revise, an existing macro, so that you change only the actions that aren't working correctly. Excel's *step mode* shows you each action in a macro, such as a particular menu command, being executed one step at a time, and also shows you the programming code corresponding to the action in a separate window called a *Module sheet*. Using the step mode, you can determine which actions need modification, and then you make the necessary changes.

Debug a Macro Using the Step Mode

1. Click the Tools menu, point to Macro, and then click Macros.
2. Click the name of the macro you want to debug.
3. Click Step Into.
4. Proceed through each action by clicking Debug on the menu bar then clicking Step Into.
5. When you finish, click the File menu, and then click Close And Return To Microsoft Excel.

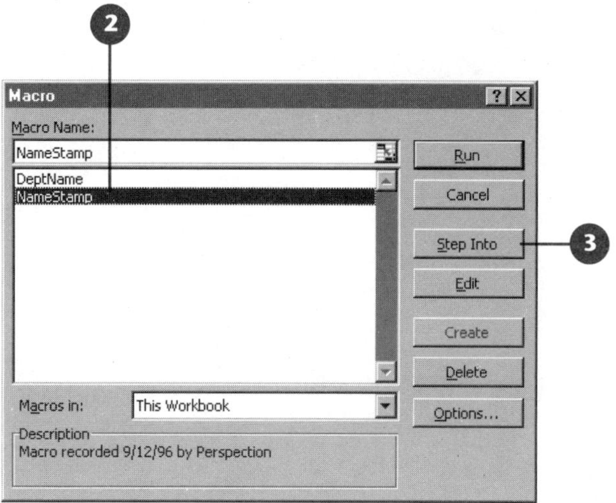

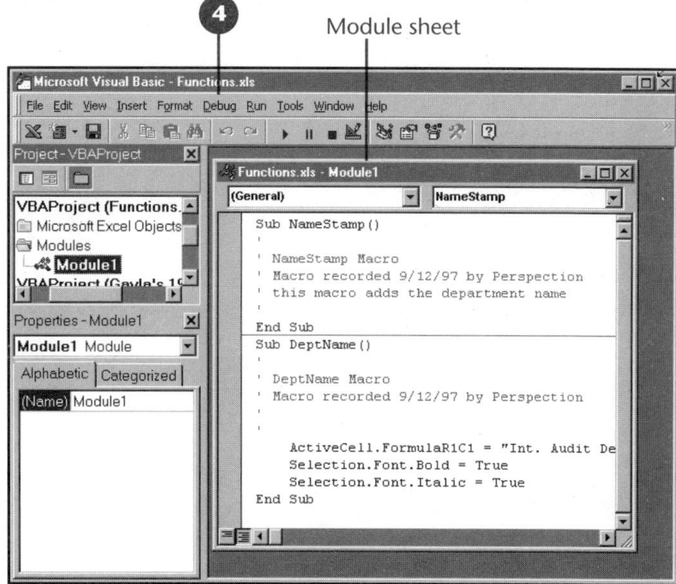

Editing a Macro

Even if a macro works correctly, you may sometimes find that you want to change the way it runs or the steps it contains. To do so, you can edit the existing code—the list of instructions Excel recorded when you turned on the macro recorder. As you recorded the macro steps, Excel kept track of each action in a separate location called a *Module sheet*. You can edit macro code by opening its Module sheet and using the keyboard to make changes just as you would a word processor document. You can use the Delete and Backspace keys to remove characters and then type the corrections. Using special macro commands, you can also record new steps in an existing macro.

Edit a Macro

1. Click the Tools menu, point to Macro, and then click Macros.
2. Click the macro you want to edit.
3. Click Edit.
4. Select the text to be edited, and then make the necessary corrections.
5. When you finish, click the File menu, and then click Close And Return To Microsoft Excel.

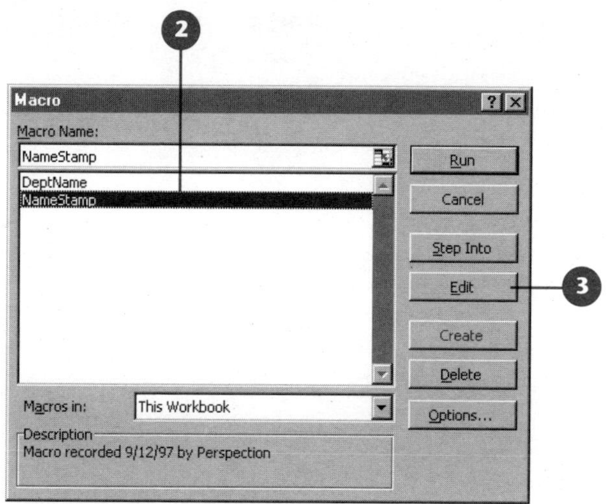

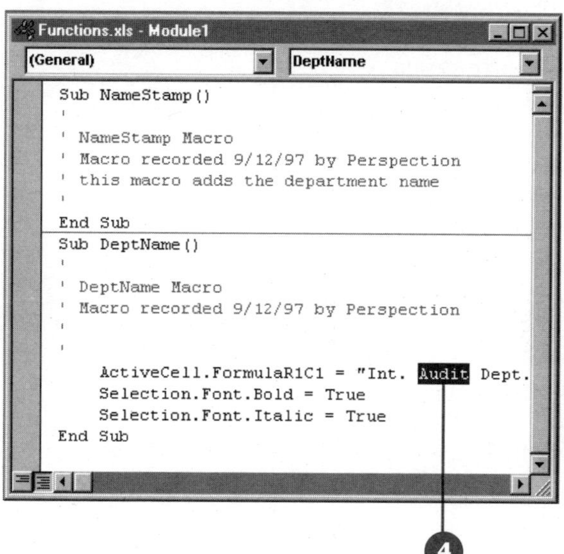

12

Adding Comments to a Macro

The programming code that makes up a macro looks somewhat cryptic because much of it is written in Visual Basic terminology instead of plain English. Consequently, a macro code listing may not have much meaning to you or other users. However, you can easily add helpful comments—in plain English—directly to a macro's code listing without affecting the way the macro runs. For example, you can add a comment about the purpose or intent of the macro, or you can provide instructions about when the macro should be used.

In a code listing, each line containing comments begins with an apostrophe, which prevents Excel from trying to execute it.

Add a Comment to a Macro

1. Click the Tools menu, point to Macro, and then click Macros.
2. Click the macro you want to add the comment to.
3. Click Edit.
4. Position the insertion point at the beginning of the line where you want to a comment.
5. Type an apostrophe ('), type the comment, and then press Enter.
6. Click the File menu, and then click Close And Return To Microsoft Excel.

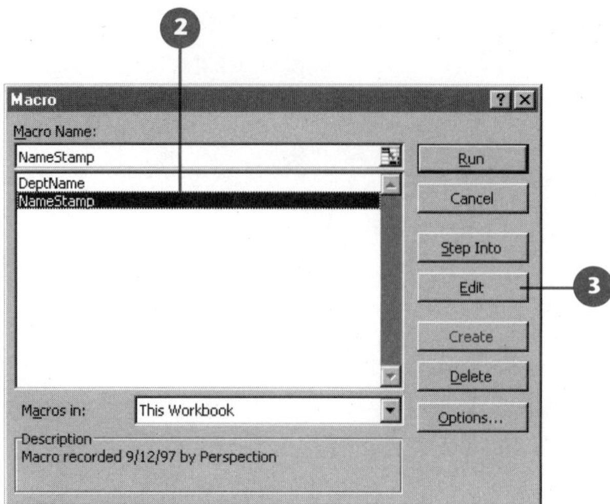

Excel automatically adds certain comments, such as the macro name.

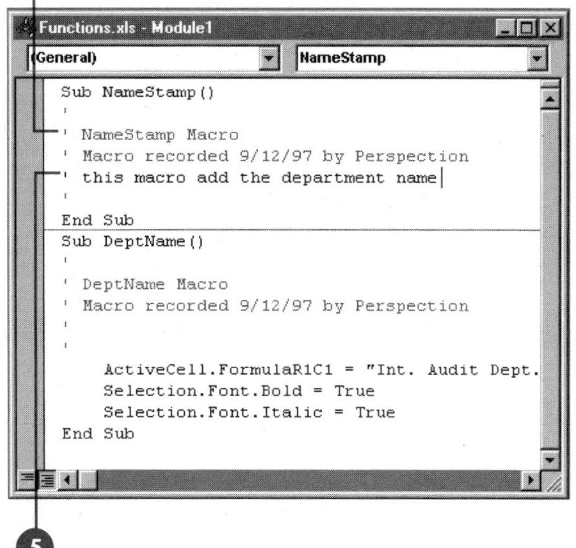

Understanding Excel Program Add-Ins

To increase your efficiency, Excel includes a variety of add-ins—programs that are included with Excel but not essential to its functionality. Some of these supplemental programs, such as AutoSave, are useful to almost anyone using Excel. Others, such as the Analysis ToolPak, add customized features, functions, or commands specific to use in financial, statistical, engineering or other highly specialized fields.

You might have installed one or more add-ins when you installed Excel. To see what add-ins are installed on your system, open the Add-Ins dialog box by clicking the Tools menu, and then clicking Add-Ins.

In the interest of conserving memory, Excel does not activate installed add-ins when you start the program, so you need to activate each one before you use it using the Tools Add-ins command. Then the add-in will be available either as a menu command or an option within a dialog box. The table below describes some of the more commonly used add-ins.

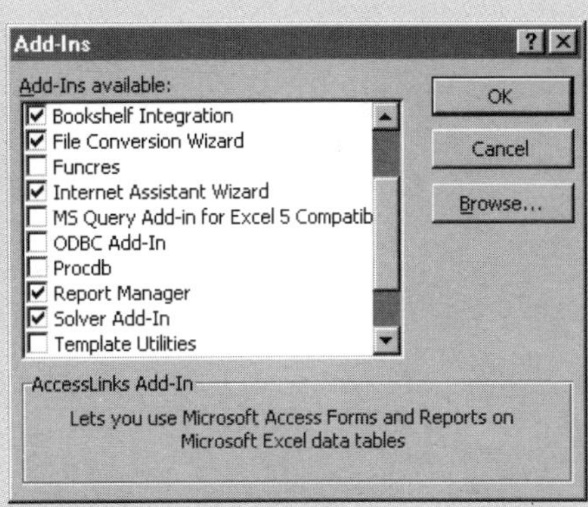

COMMONLY USED EXCEL ADD-INS

Add-In	What the Program Does	Location of Active Program
Analysis ToolPak	Contains additional financial, statistical, and engineering analysis functions	Tools menu
AutoSave	Saves an open workbook at timed intervals as you work	Automatic feature
Conditional Sum Wizard	Creates a formula that totals list data based on your criteria	Tools menu
File Conversion Wizard	Saves files created in other spreadsheet programs in the Microsoft Excel format.	Tools menu
Report Manager	Creates multi-page reports using sheets within a workbook, and can include views and scenarios	View menu
Solver	Calculates solutions to what-if scenarios.	Tools menu
Template Utilities	Provides useful utilities used in Excel's built-in templates	Data menu
Web Form Wizard	Sets up a form on a Web server	Tools menu

13

Tools for Working Together

IN THIS SECTION

Sharing Workbooks

Merging Workbooks

Sharing Information Among Documents

Exporting Data

Linking and Embedding Files

Creating Scenarios

Generating Multiple Page Reports

Getting Data from Another Program

Converting Excel Data into Access Data

Inserting an Internet Link

Creating HTML Internet Output

Getting Data from the Web

Creating successful workbooks is not always a solitary venture: in many offices, coworkers and their computers across the country are joined through *networks* (one or more computers connected to one another). These networks permit users to open each other's files, as well as to simultaneously make modifications. In addition to network sharing, people can also share workbooks globally, by adding Internet links to them. In a network, only those users whose computers are connected can share information: global sharing means anyone with Internet access can send and receive files, regardless of their actual location.

Working Together

The beauty of teamwork is that coworkers can combine their efforts to create a product that no one person could accomplish alone, at least not in as short an amount of time or with the same perspective. Excel has several tools you can use to enhance teamwork without losing control of your files. In a shared environment, however, users have to be more conscious of who controls the file, the version being used, what parts of the file can be updated, and its *routing order* (the order in which other users see the file).

Sharing Workbooks

When you're working with others on a network, you often want to enable them to share workbooks you have created, as well as the responsibilities of entering and maintaining the data in them. *Sharing* means users can add columns and rows, enter data, and change formatting, but allows you to review their changes. This type of work arrangement is particularly effective in a team situation in which many users have responsibilities for different types of data—all of which are included in the same workbook. Once a workbook is stored on a network, you can take advantage of tools enabling multiple users to share a single file. In cases in which the same cells are modified by multiple users, Excel can keep track of changes, and you can accept or reject them at a later date.

Enable Workbook Sharing

1. Open the workbook(s) you want to share.
2. Click the Tools menu, and then click Share Workbook.
3. Click the Editing tab, if necessary.
4. Click the Allow Changes By More Than One User At The Same Time check box.
5. Click OK, and then click OK again to save your workbook.

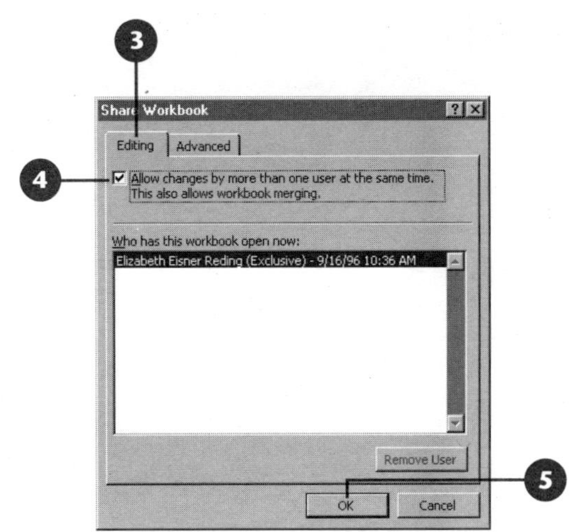

Change Sharing Options

1. Open the workbook(s) you want to share.
2. Click the Tools menu, and then click Share Workbook.
3. Click the Advanced tab, if necessary.
   - Changes made in a shared workbook can be discarded immediately or kept for any number of days using the Day spin boxes.

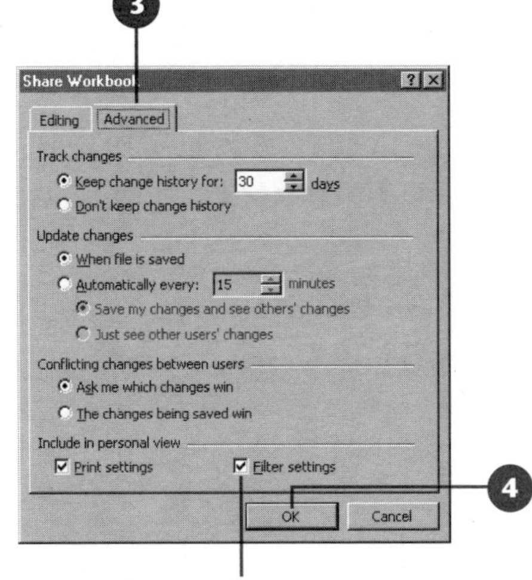

Saves settings made using the Filter submenu of the Data menu

TIP

Excel alerts you if you are working in a shared file. *When sharing is enabled, "[Shared]" appears in the title bar of the shared workbook.*

SEE ALSO

See "Working with the Excel Window" on page 7 for information about arranging worksheets.

SEE ALSO

See "Customizing Your Excel Environment" on page 180 for information about seeing more worksheet data on the screen.

- All changes can be saved only when the workbook is saved, or in any combination of your changes and others, in a time interval you specify.
- When conflicting changes are made, you can choose to automatically have the last change saved (The Changes Being Saved Win option), or you can be asked by Excel which changes you want to keep (Ask Me Which Changes Win option).
- You can choose to save none, either, or both of the personal view settings. Depending on which options are chosen, these are saved with your copy of the shared workbook.

4. Click OK.

Indicates that the workbook is shared

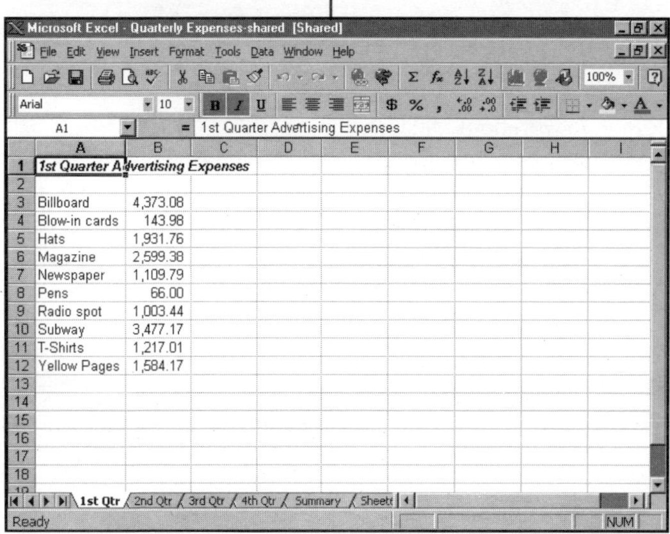

13

Merging Workbooks

To merge workbook data, Excel automates the process with the Template Wizard. The Template Wizard takes data from a list template within a worksheet and consolidates the data in a list. The Template Wizard lets you make individual entries in a worksheet that are actually compiled in a database. For example, if you are a manager at a local trucking company that requires each driver to file a daily run report, each entry would be added to a central database that contains all the reports. The template created by the Wizard ensures that each driver supplies the same information; the template is actually linked to the database.

SEE ALSO

See "Creating Links between Worksheets and Workbooks" on page 196 for information on working with workbook data.

Merge Workbook Data with the Template Wizard

1. Open the workbook that you want to use as the template.
2. Click the Data menu, and then click Template Wizard.
3. Enter the name of the workbook that you want to use as the template if it is not already displayed.
4. If you are not satisfied with the template name and location assigned by Excel, enter the name and location where you want the template stored.
5. Click Next.
6. Click Next to accept the type of database as an Excel workbook and the default location of the database.
7. Click in the Cell 1 box, click a cell, and then press Tab.
8. Repeat step 7 until all cells are identified.
9. Click Next.

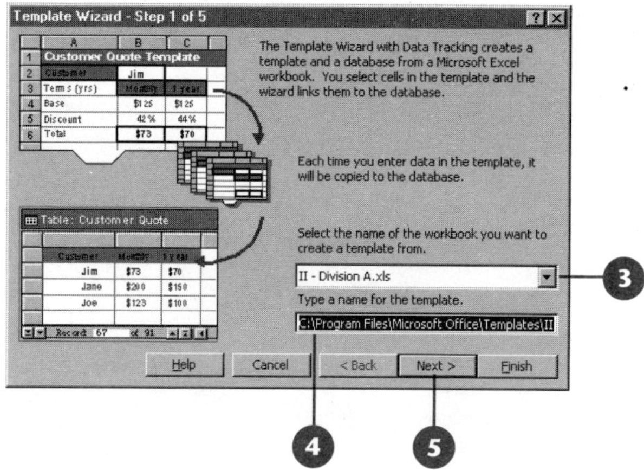

Click to change the type of database

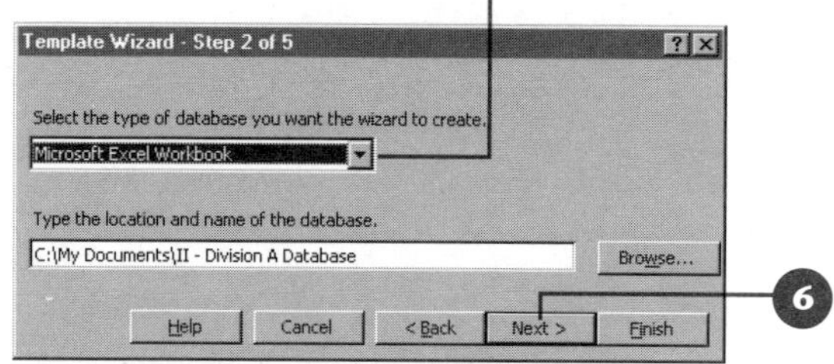

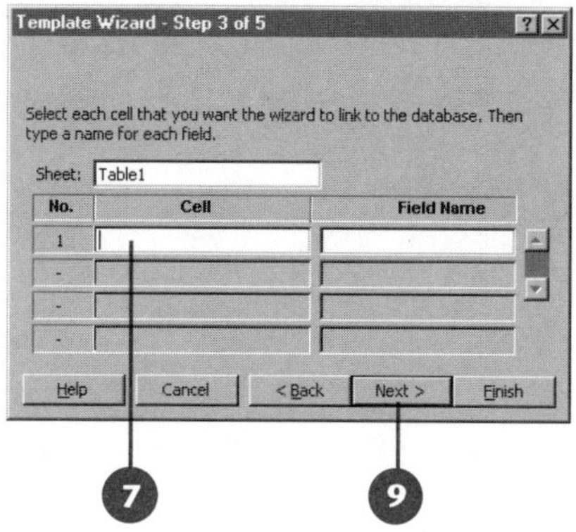

TIP

The Template Wizard may not be installed. *If you don't see the Template Wizard on the Data menu, you'll need to install it by running Setup from the Microsoft Office 97 CD.*

TIP

Data in existing workbooks can be added to the Template Wizard's database. *Before including it, just make sure the location of the data in the existing workbook matches the locations of the cells selected as data fields.*

10. Click the Yes, Include option button if you want to add information from existing workbooks, or click the No, Skip It option button if you don't want to add any data.
11. Click Next.
12. If you chose the Yes, Include option button in step 10, click Select to add any files whose data will be added.
13. Click Next.
14. Click Finish to complete the Template Wizard.

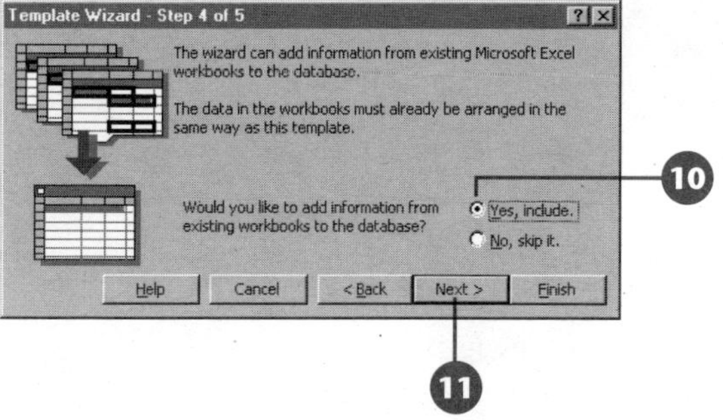

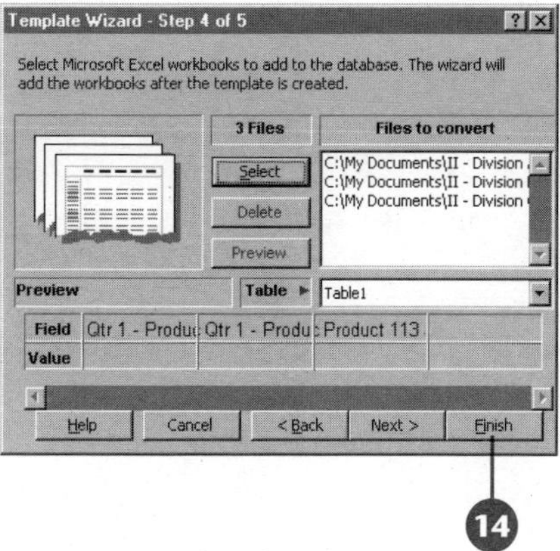

Sharing Information Among Documents

One of the great technological steps forward in recent years in personal computing has been the ability to insert an object created in one program into a document created in another program. Terms that you'll find useful in understanding how you can share objects among documents include:

TERM	DEFINITION
source program	The program that created the original object.
source file	The file that contains the original object.
destination program	The program that created the document into which you are inserting the object.
destination file	The file into which you are inserting the object.

For example, if you place an Excel chart into a PowerPoint presentation, Excel is the source program, and PowerPoint is the destination program. The chart is the source file; the presentation is the destination file.

There are three ways to share information in Windows programs: pasting, embedding, and linking.

Pasting

You can cut or copy an object from one document and then paste it into another using the Cut, Copy, and Paste buttons on the source and destination program toolbars.

Embedding

When you *embed* an object, you place a copy of the object in the destination file, and when you select the object, the tools from the source program become available in your worksheet. For example, if you insert an Excel chart into a PowerPoint presentation, the Excel menus and toolbars become available, replacing the PowerPoint menus and toolbars, so you can edit the chart if necessary. With embedding, any changes you make to the chart in the presentation do not affect the original file.

Linking

When you *link* an object, you insert a representation of the object itself into the destination file. The tools of the source program are available, and when you use them to edit the object you've inserted, you are actually editing the source file. Moreover, any changes you make to the source file are reflected in the destination file.

Exporting Data

In cases where it's of no importance that data be constantly updated, the most expedient way of getting data from one worksheet to another is to copy it. In cases where you want to copy data from one program to another, you can convert the data to a format that the other program accepts.

SEE ALSO

See "Selecting Multiple Cells" on page 34 and "Moving Cells" on page 40 for information on copying cell ranges.

TIP

Excel can only save a file to a format with an installed converter. *If the format you want to save a file in does not appear in the Save As type list, you'll need to install it by running Setup from the Microsoft Office 97 CD.*

Export Data to Another Program

1. Select the cell or range that you want to copy.
2. Click the Copy button on the Standard toolbar.
3. Open the destination file, or click the program's taskbar button if it's already open.
4. Position the insertion point where you want the data to be copied.
5. Click the Paste button on the Standard toolbar.

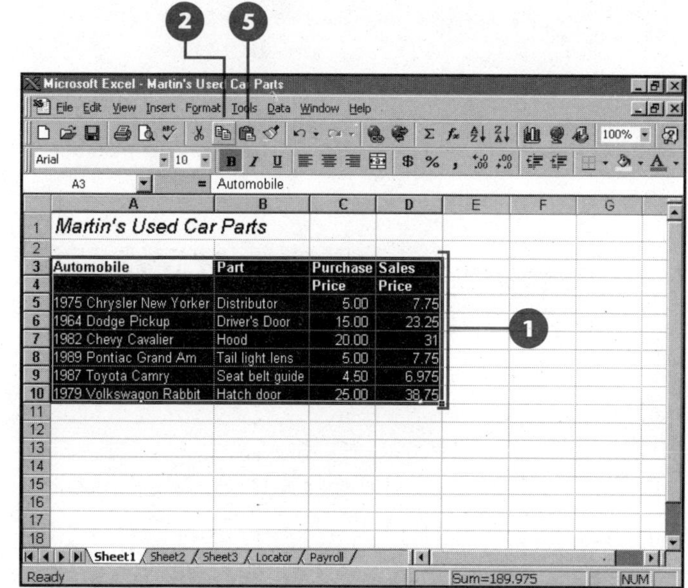

Export an Excel File to Another Program

1. Open the file that you want to save to another program.
2. Click the Save As Type drop-down arrow.
3. Click the file type you want.
4. Click Save.

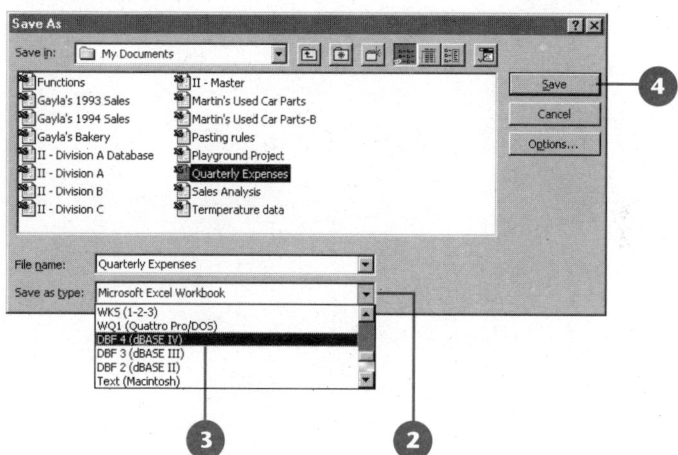

Linking and Embedding Files

Information created using other Office programs can be shared between them. This means that data created in an Excel workbook, for example, can be included in a Word document without being retyped. Information can either be linked or embedded.

SEE ALSO

See "Sharing Information Among Documents" on page 214 for more information about linking and embedding files.

Create a Link to Another File

1. Open the source file and any files containing information you want to link.
2. Select the information in the source file, and then click the Copy button on the Standard toolbar.
3. Click the insertion point in the file containing the link.
4. Click the Edit menu, and then click Paste Special.
5. Click Paste Link.

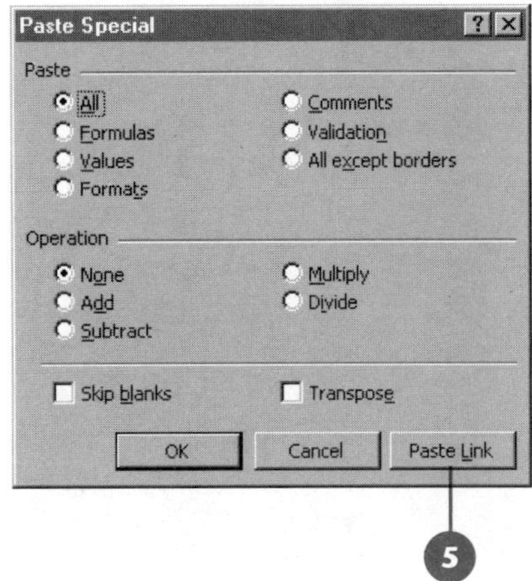

Modify a Link

1. Open the file that contains links.
2. Click the Edit menu, and then click Links.
3. Click the link you want to change. (You can select multiple links by holding down the Ctrl key while you click each link.)
4. Click Change Source.
5. Select a file from the Change Links dialog box, and then click OK.
6. Click OK.

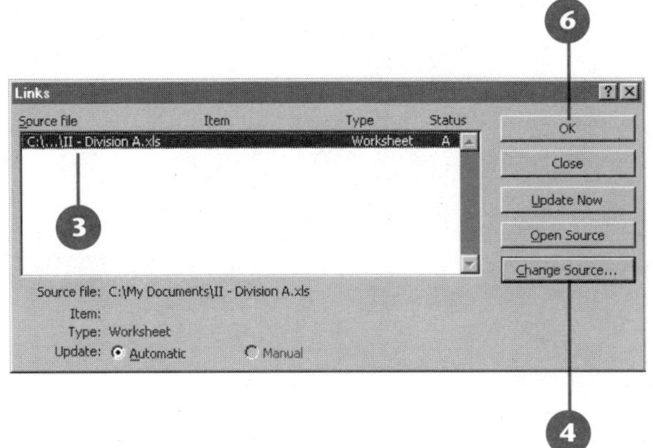

TIP

An embedded object can be edited in the worksheet by double-clicking the object. *When double-clicked, the program that created the object opens, and changes can be made using the tools that created it. Editing an embedded object* does not *alter the source document.*

Embed a New Object

1. Click the Insert menu, and then click Object.
2. Click the Create New tab.
3. Click the object type you want to insert.
4. Click OK.
5. Follow the necessary steps to insert the object.

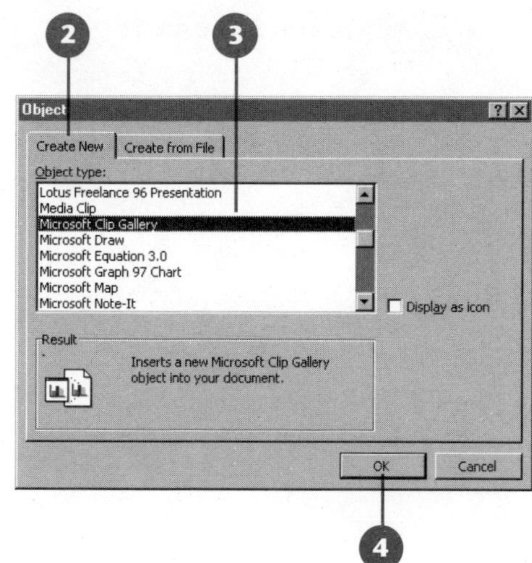

TIP

Each time you open a linked document, you must decide whether to update the links. *When you open a workbook that contains links, a warning dialog box opens asking you if you want to update all linked information (click Yes) or keep the existing information (click No).*

Embed an Existing Object

1. Click the Insert menu, and then click Object.
2. Click the Create From File tab.
3. Click Browse and locate the file that you want to link.
4. Click the Link To File check box.
5. Click OK.

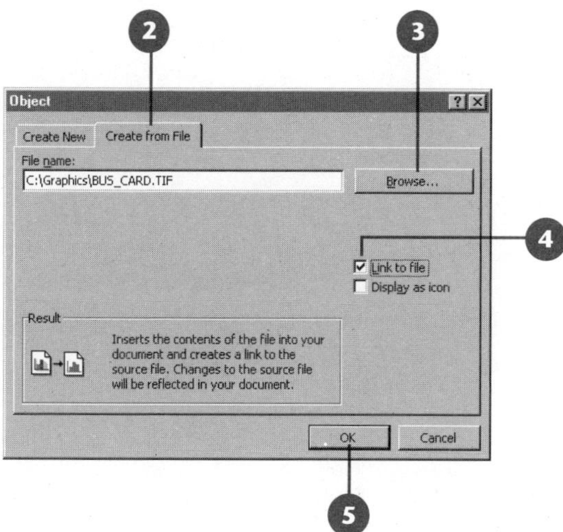

Creating Scenarios

Since some worksheet data is constantly evolving, the ability to create multiple scenarios lets you speculate on a variety of outcomes. For example, the marketing department might want to see how their budget would be affected if sales decreased by 25%. The ability to create, save, and modify scenarios means a business will be better prepared for different outcomes to avoid economic surprises.

Create a Scenario

1. Click the Tools menu, and then click Scenarios.
2. Click Add.
3. Type a name in the Scenario Name box.
4. Type the cells included in the scenario, or click the Collapse Dialog button, use your mouse to select the cells, and then click the Expand Dialog button again.
5. Type optional comments in the Comment box.
6. Click OK.
7. Type values for each of the displayed changing cells.
8. Click OK.
9. Click Close.

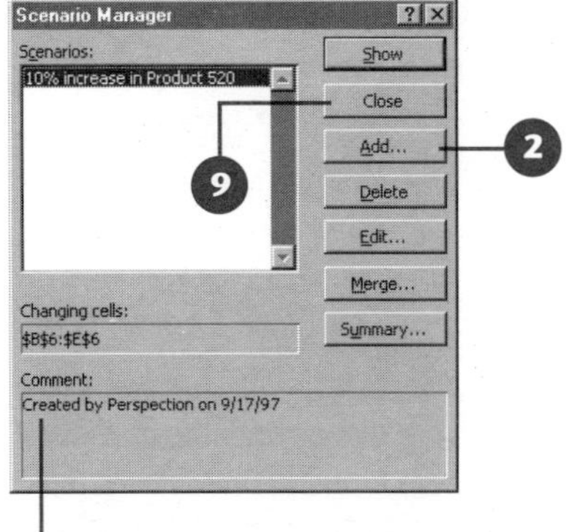

Each time a scenario is edited, Excel automatically adds a comment with the new modification date.

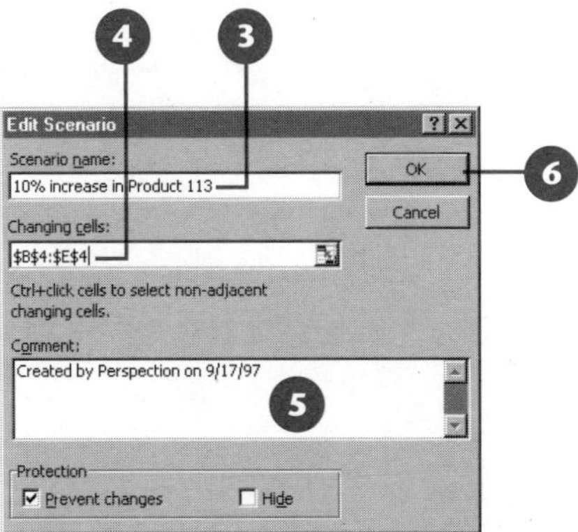

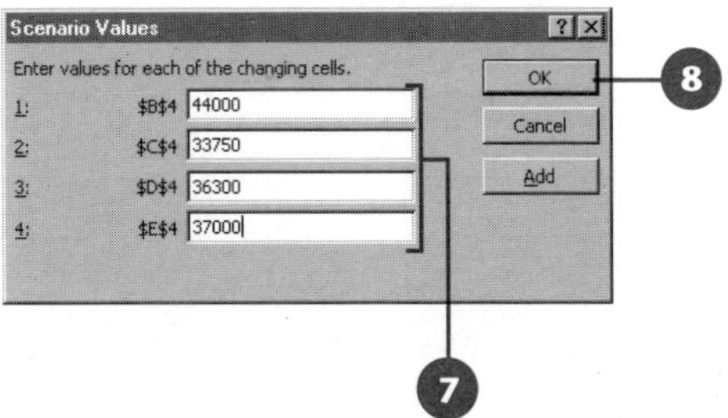

TIP

Don't forget to save your original scenario. *Creating a scenario that contains unchanged values means you'll always be able to return to your original values.*

Show a Scenario

1. Click the Tools menu, and then click Scenarios.
2. Select the scenario you want to see.
3. Click Show.
4. Click Close.

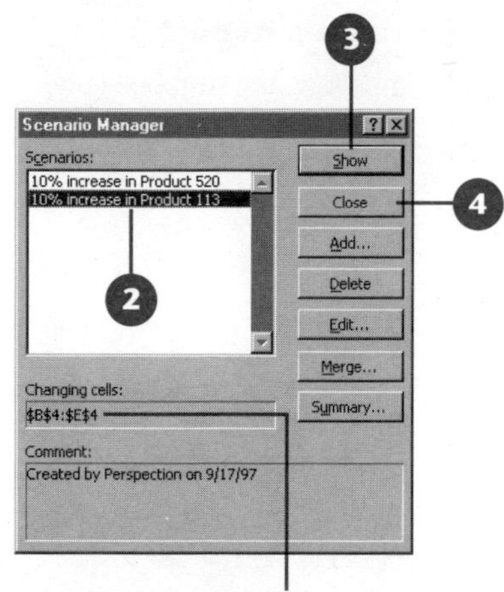

Cells that will change appear here

Cells B4 and E4 change to reflect the scenario selected in the Scenario Manager dialog box.

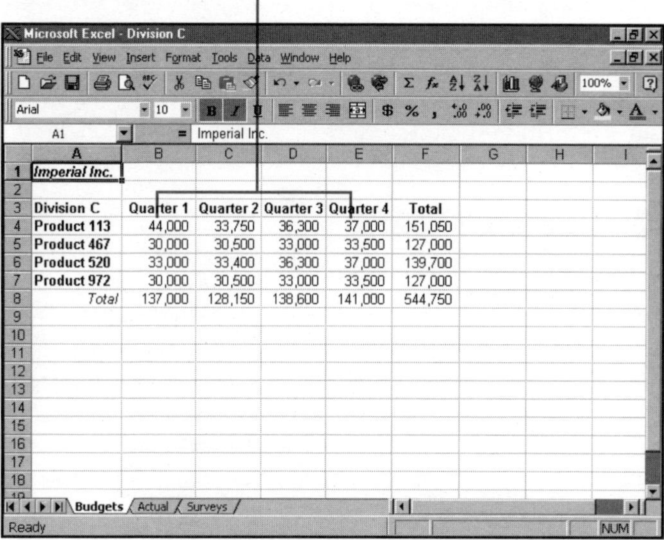

Generating Multiple Page Reports

The sheets, custom views, and scenarios that you create within a workbook combine to produce powerful individual worksheets. Since a workbook contains sheets with related data, you might want to generate reports that contain any combination of the data from your worksheets. Using Excel's Report Manager, you can create reports that contain workbook sheets, as well as custom views and scenarios. You can save and name your reports so you can use them in the future.

SEE ALSO

See "Saving Print Settings" on page 72 for information on creating custom views.

Create a Report

1. Open the workbook you want to use to create the report.
2. Create the custom views you want.
3. Create the scenarios you want.
4. Click the View menu, and then click Report Manager.
5. Click Add.
6. Type a name for the report.
7. Click the Sheet drop-down arrow, and then select a sheet to add to the report.
8. If necessary, select a view and scenario you want to add by clicking the View and Scenario drop-down arrows.
9. Click Add.
10. Repeat steps 7 through 9 until all the necessary sheets have been added.
11. Click the Use Continuous Page Numbers check box to add consecutive numbering to the report.
12. Click OK.

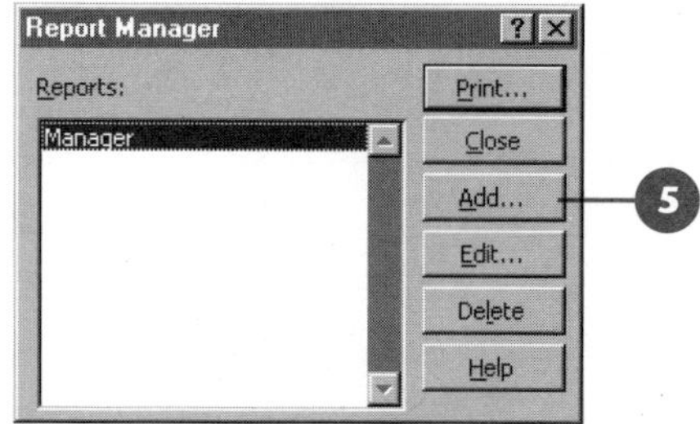

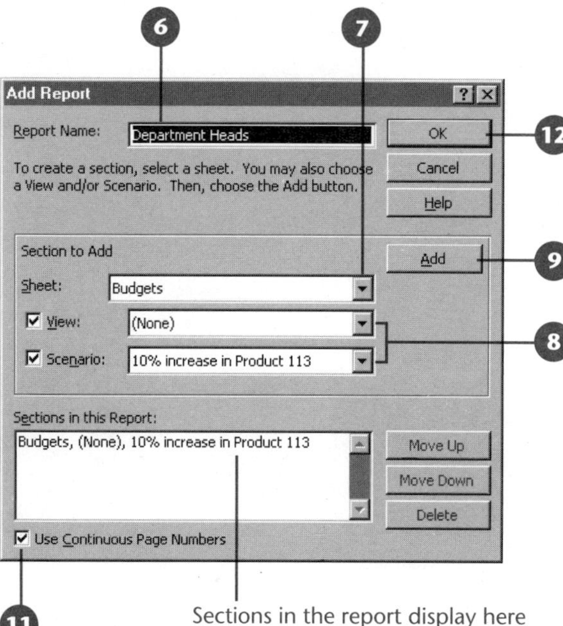

SEE ALSO

See "Creating Scenarios" on page 218 for information on creating scenarios.

Change the Order of Report Sections

1. Click the View menu, and then click Report Manager.
2. Select the scenario you want to see, and then click Edit.
3. Click the section you want to move.
4. Click the Move Up or Move Down button to change the order of the section.
5. Click Delete to remove the selected section if you want to remove it from the report.
6. Click OK.
7. Click Close.

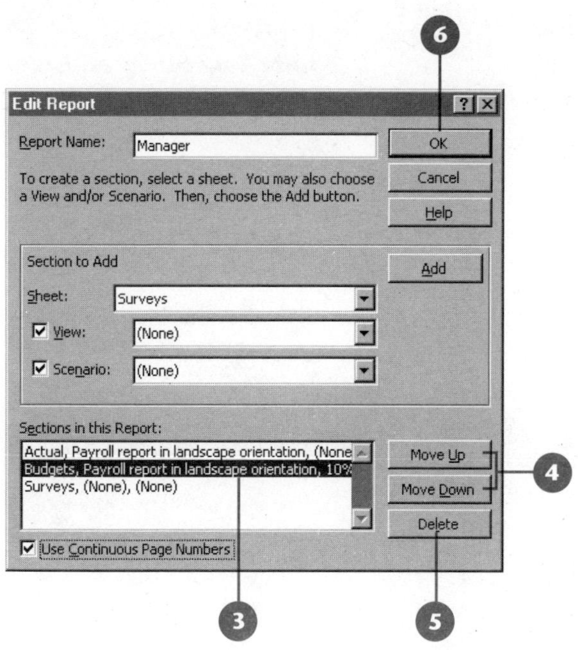

Getting Data from Another Program

Information you want to analyze may not always exist in an Excel workbook; you might have to retrieve it from another Office program, such as Access. Access table data can be easily converted into Excel worksheet data. Once the data is in Excel, you can use all of Excel's analysis tools (such as PivotTable and AutoFilter) on this data.

SEE ALSO

See "Analyzing Data Using the PivotTable" on page 173 for information on creating a PivotTable.

SEE ALSO

See "Displaying Parts of a List with AutoFilter" on page 170 for information on using the AutoFilter feature.

Export an Access Database Table into an Excel Workbook

1. In the Access Database window, click the Tables tab.
2. Click the table you want to analyze.
3. Click the OfficeLinks drop-down arrow on the Database toolbar.
4. Click Analyze It With MS Excel to save the table as an Excel file, start Excel, and open the workbook.
5. Use the usual Excel commands to edit and analyze the data.

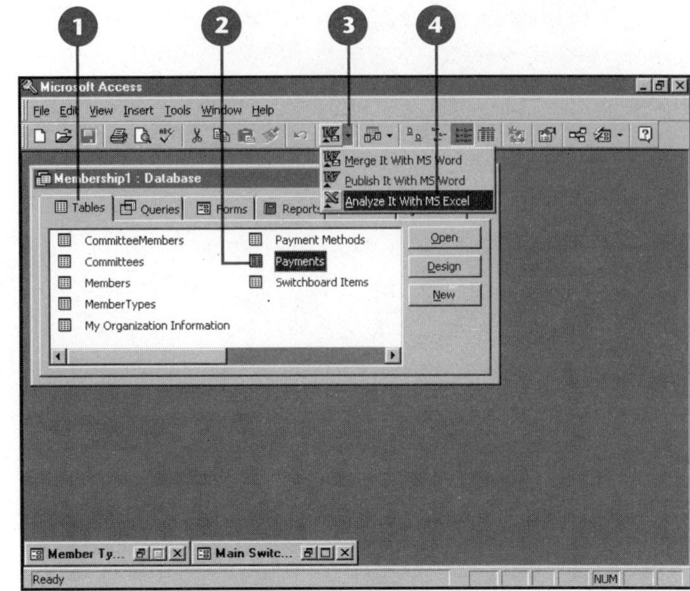

TIP

You might need to install Microsoft Query to create a PivotTable. This program allows you to move information from Access or other database programs to Excel. It is not installed during a Typical Setup. For information about installing Microsoft Query, look up "Installing Microsoft Query" in online Help.

SEE ALSO

See "Working with Dialog Boxes and Wizards" on page 16 for more information about using Wizards.

Create an Excel Workbook PivotTable from an Access Database

1. In Excel, click the Data menu, and then click PivotTable Report.
2. In the first PivotTable Wizard dialog box, click the External Data Source option button.
3. Click Next.
4. In the second PivotTable Wizard dialog box, click Get Data, and then follow the Wizard instructions.

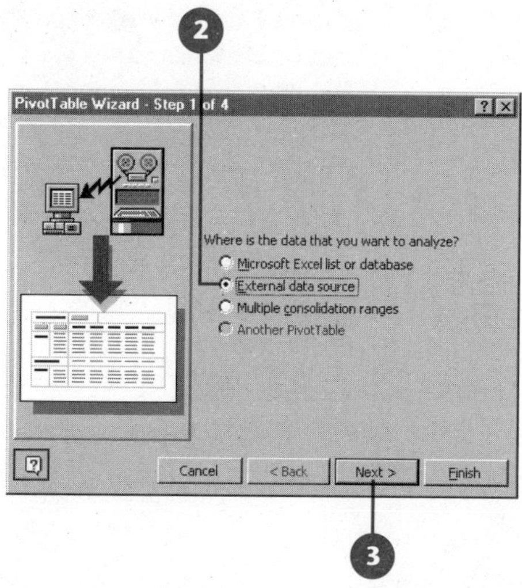

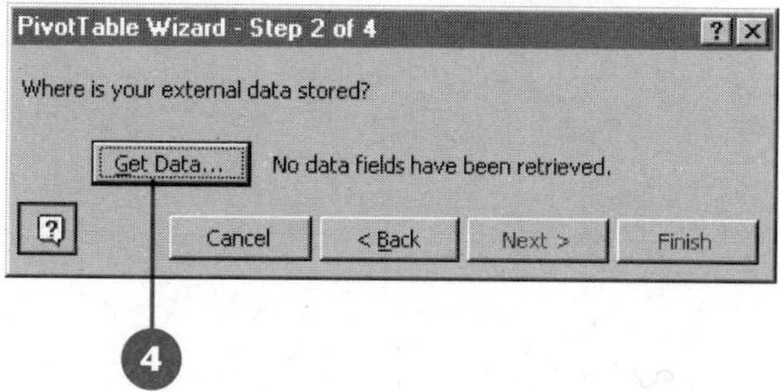

Converting Excel Data into Access Data

You can convert your Excel worksheet data into an Access table data using the File Conversion Wizard. This allows you the flexibility of using data created in Excel in Microsoft Access, where you can take advantage of additional data manipulation features.

TIP

The AccessLinks Add-in may not be installed. *If you don't see the Convert To MS Access command on the Data menu, you may have to install the AccessLinks Add-In program on the Microsoft Office 97 CD.*

TRY THIS

You can also bring Access data into Excel. *Convert an Access table to an Excel worksheet, and then create a PivotTable using the newly converted data.*

Convert Excel Data to Access Data

1. Select the Excel worksheet data you want to convert.
2. Click the Data menu, and then click Convert to MS Access.
3. Choose to create a new database, or open an existing one.
4. Click OK. Access starts and creates a new table based on the Excel data in a new database or an existing one.

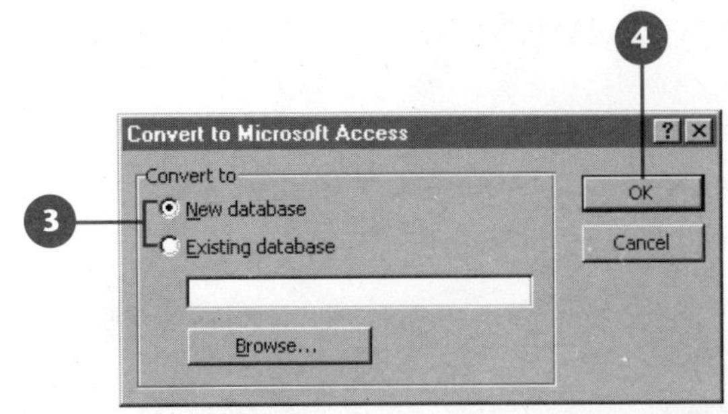

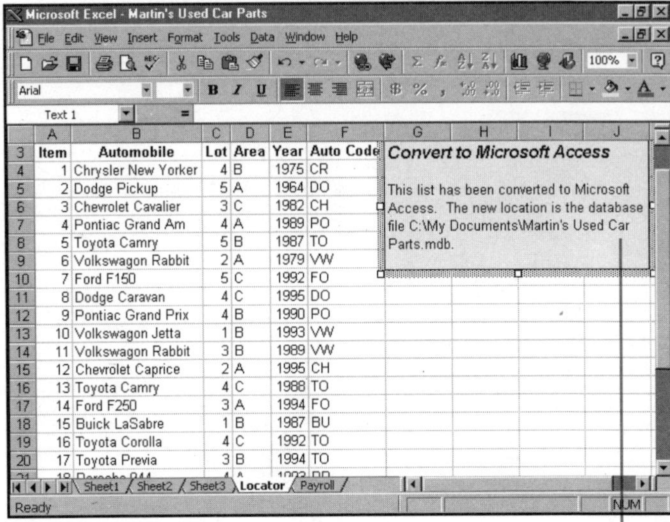

On completion of the conversion, a Note is embedded into Excel.

Inserting an Internet Link

Often supplementary information gets circulated around an office so that everyone gets to read an article of general interest. With instant access to the Internet, your worksheet can contain links to specific sites so you, and anyone else using your worksheet, can access Web information. The Internet link that is embedded in a worksheet is called a *hyperlink*—because when clicked, you are instantly connected to the link's defined address on the Web. If your worksheet contains a hyperlink, the link appears in the worksheet as blue text. To connect to the Web site, just click the hyperlink.

SEE ALSO

See "Linking and Embedding Files" on page 216 for information on embedding.

Create a Hyperlink

1. Select a cell where you want the hyperlink to appear.
2. Click the Insert Hyperlink button on the Standard toolbar.
3. Click Browse to locate the file to be linked, or type the correct Web path.
4. Type an optional location if you want.
5. Click OK.

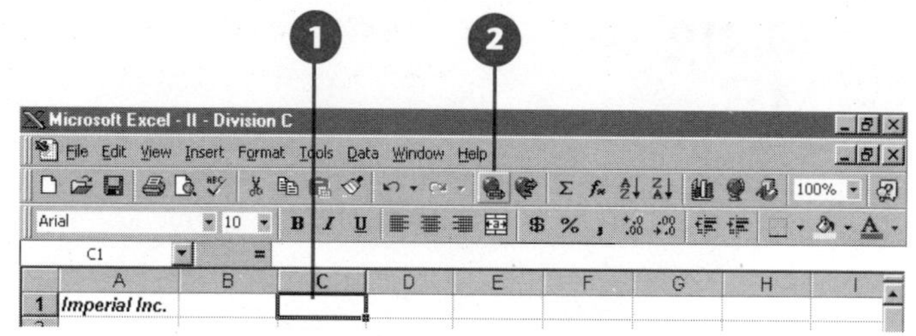

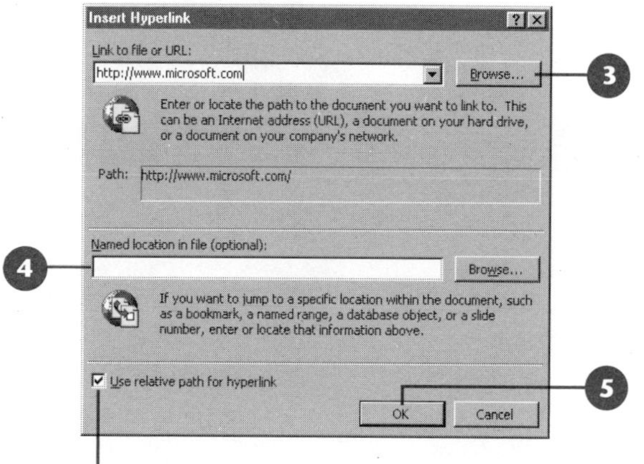

Click to make sure this URL is used, even if the file containing the link is moved.

Connect to an Internet Link

1. Click the hyperlink in your worksheet.

The mouse pointer turns into a hand when placed over a hyperlink

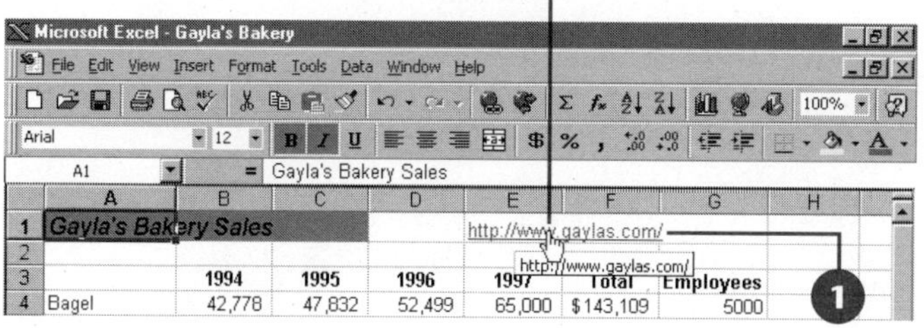

Creating HTML Internet Output

You can take an existing Excel worksheet and place it on the Internet. In order for a document to be placed on the World Wide Web, it must be in *HTML* format—*HyperText Markup Language*. This format enables you to easily post Excel data on a Web site so it can be shared by others. The Internet Assistant Wizard leads you through the steps required to create a Web page using your Excel data, so you don't have to know anything about HTML.

Create HTML Output

1. Select the cell(s) you want converted into a Web page.
2. Click the File menu, and then click Save As HTML.
3. If necessary, click Add to add more cells to be converted.
4. Type additional cell(s) to be converted, and then click OK to return to the first Wizard dialog box.
5. Click Next.
6. Click the option buttons you want, and then click Next.
7. If necessary, supply additional header information in the Description Below Header box, and then click Next.

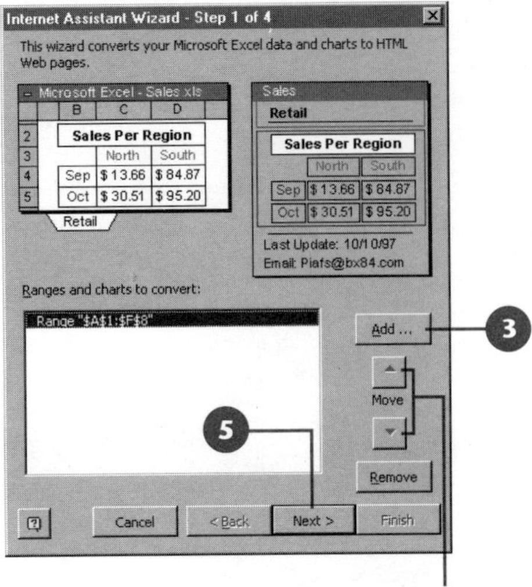

Click to the change the order of selected cells

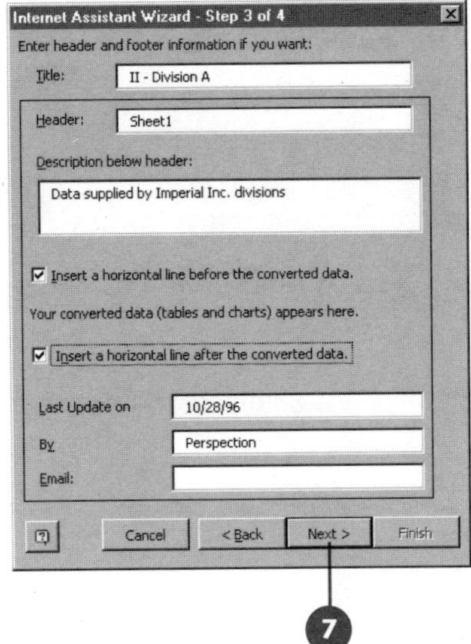

> **TIP**
>
> **You can share workbook files using Internet.** *Rather than mailing or faxing non-sensitive worksheets to co-workers, convert them to HTML output and post them on the Internet.*

> **TIP**
>
> **Make sure you have Internet access.** *In order to get HTML output, you need an Internet account and a Web browser.*

8. Determine the format for the page and assign a name and location for the HTML file, and then click Finish.

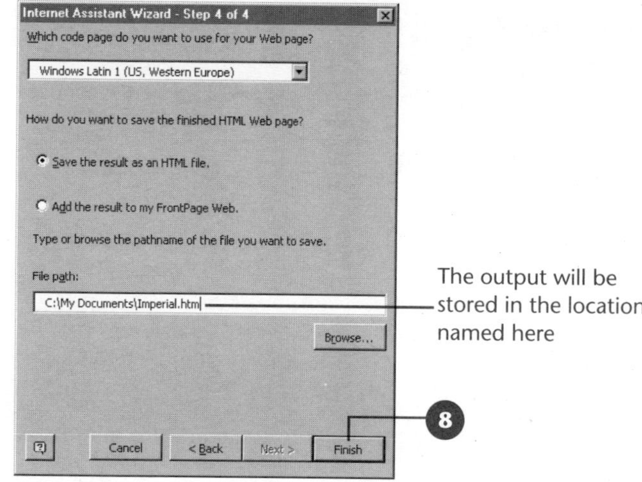

View HTML Output

1. Open your favorite browser.
2. Click the File menu, and then click Open File (if using Netscape Navigator 2.0). If you are using another browser, these commands might be different.
3. Locate the file you want to open, then click Open.

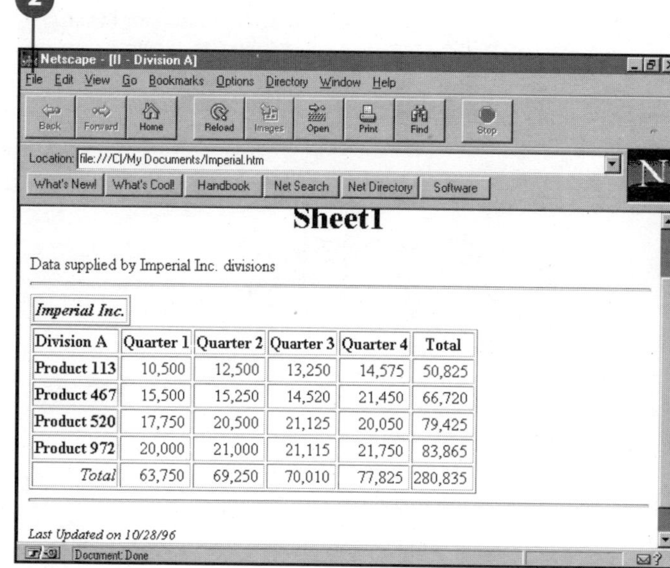

Division A	Quarter 1	Quarter 2	Quarter 3	Quarter 4	Total
Product 113	10,500	12,500	13,250	14,575	50,825
Product 467	15,500	15,250	14,520	21,450	66,720
Product 520	17,750	20,500	21,125	20,050	79,425
Product 972	20,000	21,000	21,115	21,750	83,865
Total	63,750	69,250	70,010	77,825	280,835

Getting Data from the Web

You can look up data on the Web and insert it into Excel using the Web toolbar. Using favorite sites—that you define—you can jump from Web site to site, gathering data to include in your own worksheets.

Web Toolbar button

SEE ALSO

See "Inserting an Internet Link" on page 225 for information on inserting a link to the World Wide Web.

Get Data from the Web Using an Internet Link

1. Insert a link to the World Wide Web.
2. Click the Web Toolbar button on the Standard toolbar.
3. Click the link in your worksheet. Excel opens your Web browser (such as Microsoft Internet Explorer).
4. Connect to the Internet through your Internet Service Provider (ISP) or network.
5. Click the Search hyperlink to find data, and then follow the instructions on the Web site to download data.
6. When you are finished, click the File menu, and then click Close.
7. If necessary, click Yes to disconnect from the Internet.
8. Click the Web Toolbar button on the Standard toolbar.

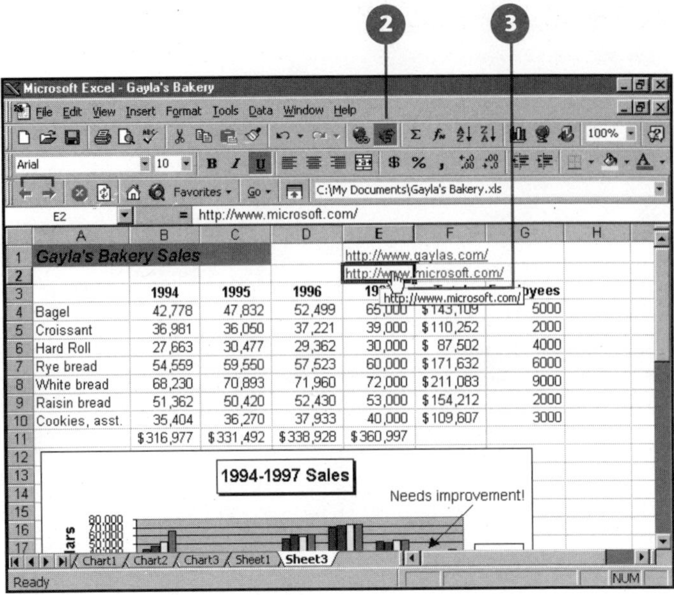

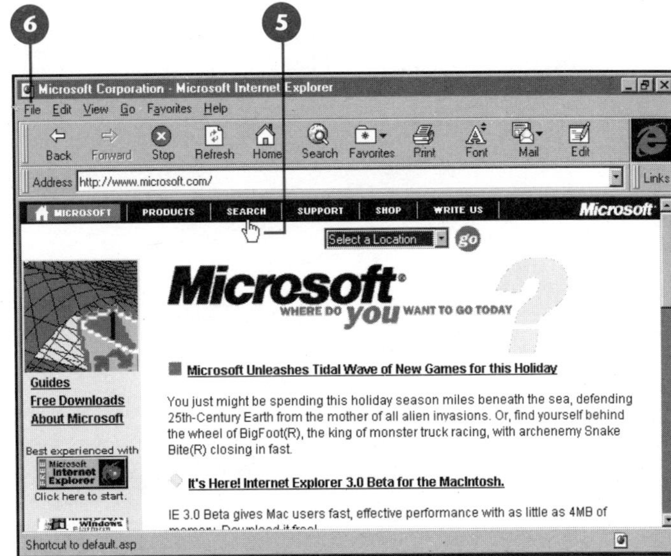

SEE ALSO

See "Inserting Pictures" on page 96 for more information about working with the Clip Gallery.

Connect To Web For Additional Clips

Get Additional Clips from the Web

1. Click the Insert menu, point to Picture, and then click Clip Art.
2. Click the Connect To Web For Additional Clips button. Excel opens your Web browser (such as Microsoft Internet Explorer).
3. Connect to the Internet through your Internet Service Provider (ISP) or network.
4. Click the appropriate hyperlinks as instructed on the Clip Gallery Live Web site to access and download clip art.
5. When you are finished, click the File menu, and then click Close.
6. If necessary, click Yes to disconnect from the Internet.

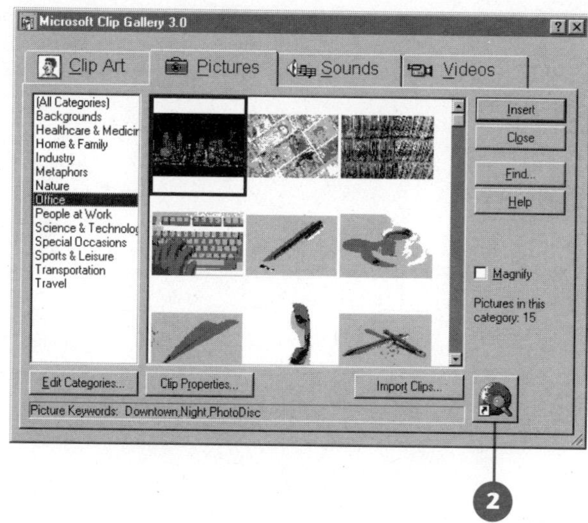

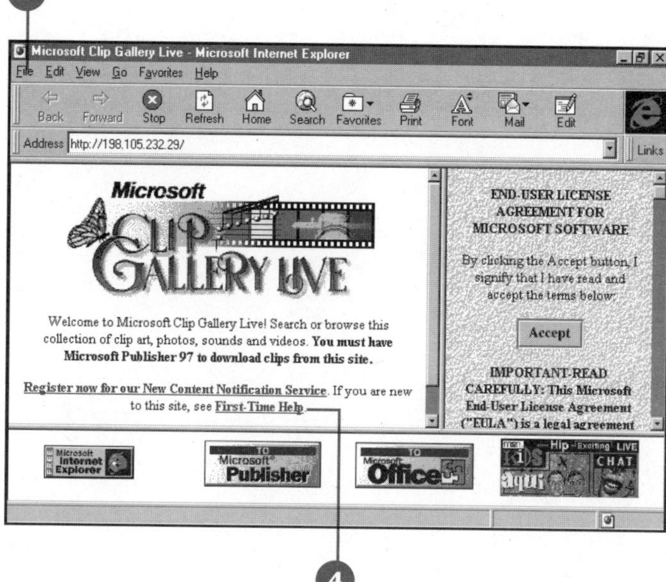

Index

SPECIAL CHARACTERS

' (apostrophe)
  macro comment prefix, 206
  numeric label prefix, 28
▸ (arrowhead), menu symbol, 14
* (asterisk)
  multiplication operator, 46
  wildcard character, 167
✔ (checkmark), menu symbol, 12, 15
$ (dollar sign), absolute cell reference prefix, 51
… (ellipsis), menu symbol, 14
= (equal sign)
  formula prefix, 46
  logical operator, 171
> (greater than sign), logical operator, 171
>= (greater than or equal to sign), logical operator, 171
< (less than sign), logical operator, 171
<= (less than or equal to sign), logical operator, 171
– (minus sign), subtraction operator, 46
<> (not equal sign), logical operator, 171
() (parentheses), changing precedence of operations, 47
+ (plus sign)
  addition operator, 46
  by the mouse pointer, 37, 39, 41
  changing the mouse pointer from, 39, 41
  mouse pointer, 7
? (question mark), wildcard character, 167
" " (quotation marks), macro text delimiters, 203
/ (slash), division operator, 46
NUMBERS
3-D charts, 141
3-D effects, 132, 133
  versus drop shadows, 133
3-D objects
  creating, 132
  setting depth, 133
  setting lighting, 133
  spinning, 132

Absolute cell references, 51
Accept or Reject Changes dialog box, 193
Access databases
  converting Excel data into, 224
  creating PivotTables from, 223
  importing, 222
AccessLinks, installing, 224
actions, undoing and redoing, 27
active cell, 7
  navigating worksheets without changing, 10
Add Data dialog box, 150
add-in programs, 207
  activating, 207
  displaying, 207
Add-Ins dialog box, 207
Add Report dialog box, 220
Add View dialog box, 72
addition operator (+), 46
addresses. *See* cell references
adjusting AutoShapes, 119
adjustment handles, 118, 119
aligning
  cell contents, 80
  objects, 134-35
  WordArt, 105
Alignment tab (Format Cells dialog box), 80
Analysis Toolpak, 207
analyzing worksheet data, 161-75

See also filtering; lists; PivotTables; sorting
AND condition, complex searches with, 171
apostrophe (')
  macro comment prefix, 206
  numeric label prefix, 28
applications. *See* programs
area charts, 141
arguments (in formulas), 46
arithmetic operators, 46
  order of precedence, 47
Arrange Windows dialog box, 13, 178
arranging workbook windows, 13, 178, 197
arrow keys, navigating worksheets, 11
Arrow tool (Drawing toolbar), 116
arrowhead (▶), menu symbol, 14
arrowhead pointer, changing the mouse pointer to, 39, 41
arrows
  drawing, 117, 157
  editing, 117
  modifying, 128, 157
asterisk (*)
  multiplication operator, 46
  wildcard character, 167
AutoCalculate feature, 53
AutoComplete feature, 28, 172
  entering labels, 29
  entering records, 172
AutoCorrect feature, 95, 110
  adding entries to, 110
  changing exceptions, 111
  deleting entries, 111
  editing entries, 110
AutoFilter feature, filtering lists, 161, 170, 171
AutoFit feature, adjusting column width/row height, 66
AutoFormat dialog box, 88, 89
AutoFormats
  formatting cell contents with, 88
  modifying, 89
AutoSave, 207
AutoShape command (Format menu)
  moving objects, 124
  resizing objects, 124, 125
AutoShapes, 115
  adjusting, 119
  drawing, 118
  replacing, 119
  reshaping, 118
  resizing, 118
AVERAGE function, 54

Back button in wizards, 17
Bold button (Formatting toolbar), 74
bold typeface, applying, 74
Bookshelf (Microsoft), looking up references in, 114
borders. *See* cell borders

calculating
  automatically, 53
  with functions, 54
Calculation options, changing, 180
Calculation tab (Options dialog box), 180
calculations, order of precedence, 47
canceling commands, 16
cascading workbook windows, 13, 178
cell borders
  applying, 86-87
  blue, 192
  formatting, 87
cell comments, 95, 112
  adding, 112
  deleting, 113
  display of, 179
  editing, 113
  formatting, 113
  showing, 112
cell contents
  aligning, 80
  clearing, 36, 43
  coloring, 83
  copying, 25, 26, 38-39
    with the Clipboard, 38
    with drag-and-drop, 38, 39
    versus linking, 196
  editing, 32-33, 181
  formatting, 30, 31, 73-85
    with AutoFormats, 88
    with styles, 90-91
  hiding, 65
  moving, 25, 40-41
    with the Clipboard, 38, 40
    with drag-and-drop, 38, 41
  orienting, 80
  overwrite alert, 181
  pasting, 37, 38
  types, 26
  See also entering data
cell entries. *See* cell contents; entering data
cell formats. *See* formatting (of cells)
cell notes. *See* cell comments
cell pointer, redirecting, 181
cell references, 45
  absolute, 51
  entering in formulas, 46
  relative, 50
cell selection after data entry, redirecting, 181
cells, 7
  active cell, 7
  adding, 25
  borders, 86-87, 192
  clearing, 36, 43
  coloring, 84-85
  deleting, 25, 36, 42, 43
  destination cells, 196
  editing cell contents in, 32-33, 181
  entering data into. *See*entering data
  filling with colors/patterns, 84-85
  formulas in, 26
  inserting, 42
  navigating, 10-11
    going to named ranges, 35
  overwrite alert, 181
  pasting, 37
  selecting multiple, 34-35
  See also cell comments; cell contents; cell references; ranges
characters
  printed, reducing/enlarging, 71
  WordArt
    adjusting spacing, 105
    making same height, 104
chart boxes (in org charts), 106, 108

chart boxes, *continued*
adding, 108
entering text into, 107
rearranging, 109
Chart dialog box, changing chart types, 146
Chart Object drop-down arrow
displaying selected chart objects, 145
selecting chart objects, 144, 145
chart objects
adding, 154-55
deselecting, 145
displaying selected, 145
formatting, 152
identifying, 145, 149
selecting, 144, 145
chart text, 158
adding shadows to, 156
changing fonts, 158
text annotations, 154, 155, 156
See also chart titles
chart titles, 140, 154
adding, 154, 155
adding shadows to, 156
chart types, 141
changing, 146
choosing, 141
Chart Wizard, 142
changing, 143
changing chart types, 146
creating charts, 142-43
Chart Wizard button (Standard toolbar), 142
charts, 139
3-D charts, 141
adding/deleting legends, 154
adding gridlines to, 154, 155
adding text annotations to, 154, 155
area charts, 141
combination charts, 141
creating, 142-43
drawing objects on, 156, 157
editing, 144
as embedded objects, 143
moving, 147
pie charts, 141, 148, 149
from PivotTables, 175
resizing, 147
selecting, 144, 145
terminology, 140
types, 141, 146
updating, 144
See also maps; organization charts
checkmark (▸), menu symbol, 12, 15
circles, drawing, 118
clearing cells, 36
versus deleting cells, 43
clip art
inserting, 96, 99
from the Web, 99, 229
Clip Gallery, inserting clip art/pictures/sounds/videos from, 96-97, 99
Clipboard, 38, 40
copying cell contents with, 38
copying formulas with, 48
moving cell contents with, 38, 40
Close button
Data Form dialog box, 164
Excel window, 24
toolbars, 184
closing workbooks, 24
Collapse Dialog button, 55, 70
collating copies, 23
coloring
cell contents, 83
cells, 84-85
data series, 152
fonts, 83
objects, 128
shadows, 130, 131
WordArt text, 103
colors
specifying, 128
See also coloring; fill colors
column headers (indicator buttons), 62, 63, 179
printing, 70, 71
column letters, printing, 71
column titles, printing, 70
columns
adjusting column width, 66-67
deleting, 64
freezing/unfreezing, 182
hiding, 65
inserting, 62-63
See also column headers
combination charts, 141
Comma Style button (Formatting toolbar), 74
commands
canceling, 16
choosing, 14-15
Commands tab (Customize dialog box), 185, 186, 187
comments. *See* cell comments; macro comments
complex searches, 171
conditional formatting, establishing, 76
Conditional Formatting dialog box, 76
Conditional Sum Wizard, 207
Confirm Password dialog box, 194
Consolidate dialog box, 198
consolidated data, displaying, 199
consolidating data from other worksheets/workbooks, 198-99, 212-13
Convert To MS Access command (Data menu), 224
Convert To MS Access dialog box, 224
copies
collating, 23
printing more than one, 23
printing quick copies, 22
copying
cell contents, 25, 26, 38-39
with the Clipboard, 38
with drag-and-drop, 38, 39
cell formats, 77, 84
formulas, 48-49
versus linking, 196
worksheets, 61
COUNT function, 54
Create A Copy check box (Move or Copy dialog box), 61
criteria (for finding records), 166
logical operators/conditions, 171
wildcards, 167
Criteria button (Data Form dialog box), 164
Ctrl+Home keys, navigating worksheets, 11
currency formats, applying, 75
Currency Style button (Formatting toolbar), 74
curves
drawing irregular curves, 120-21
switching between open and closed, 121
Custom AutoFilter dialog box, 171
custom views
creating, 72
creating reports with, 220
displaying, 72
Custom Views dialog box, 72

Customize dialog box
  customizing toolbar buttons, 186, 187
  customizing toolbars, 184, 185

D

Dash Style tool (Drawing toolbar), 116
data
  adding to the Template Wizard database, 213
  consolidating data from other worksheets/ workbooks, 198-99, 212-13
  converting Excel data into Access data, 224
  exporting
    to other programs, 215
    to Web sites, 226-27
  formatting for Web sites, 226-27
  importing
    from other programs, 222
    from the Web, 228-29
  mapping geographic data, 159
  See also cell contents; data analysis; entering data; records; values
data analysis, 161-75
  See also filtering; lists; PivotTables; sorting
Data Form dialog box, 164
Data Forms, 161, 164, 165
  buttons, 164
  entering records in, 165
  managing records with, 166-67
data markers, 140
  See also data series
data points, 150
  deleting, 151
data series, 140, 150
  adding, 150
  adding fill effects to, 152-53
  adding pictures to, 153
  coloring, 152
  deleting, 150, 151
  selecting, 144, 148
databases. *See* Access databases; lists
dates
  adding to worksheets, 69
  entering, 30-31
  formatting in cells, 31
debugging macros, 200, 204
decimal format, applying, 75
Decrease Decimal button (Formatting toolbar), 74
defaults
  cell comments display, 179
  column width/row height, 67
  fill color, 128
  line style, 128
  template, 191
definition boxes, 18
Delete button (Data Form dialog box), 164
Delete Conditional Format dialog box, 76
Delete dialog box, 43
deleting
  AutoCorrect entries, 111
  buttons from toolbars, 184
  cell comments, 113
  cells, 25, 36, 42, 43
    versus clearing cells, 43
  columns/rows, 64
  data points, 151
  data series, 150, 151
  font attributes, 75
  legends, 154
  numeric formats, 75
  pictures, 97
  records, 167
  reversing deletions, 151
  styles, 93
  vertices (in freeforms), 122, 123
  worksheets, 59
depth, of 3-D objects, 133
deselecting chart objects, 145
destination cells/ranges, 196
destination files, 214, 216
destination programs, 214
dialog boxes, 16-17
  Help button, 18
  selecting options in, 16
disk space, saving, 59
distributing objects, 134, 135
division operator (/), 46
documents
  sharing information among, 214-17
  types, 5
Documents menu, opening files from, 8
dollar sign ($), absolute cell reference prefix, 51
double-headed arrow, 67
double-sided arrow, 66
Down arrow key, navigating worksheets, 11
drag-and-drop
  copying cell contents with, 38, 39
  moving cell contents with, 38, 41
drawing objects, 115-21, 128
  arrows, 117, 157
  AutoShapes, 118
  circles, 118
  formatting, 115
  freeforms, 120-21
  lines, 115, 116, 157
  moving through, 137
  ovals, 118
  rectangles, 118
  squares, 118
  types, 115
  See also objects
Drawing toolbar
  buttons, 116
  displaying, 116, 156
  hiding, 156
  shared tools, 117
drawings, ungrouping, 137
drop-down arrows, in dialog boxes, 16
drop shadows. *See* shadows

Edit mode, changing to, 32
Edit options, changing, 180, 181
Edit Report dialog box, 221
Edit Scenario dialog box, 218
Edit tab (Options dialog box), 180, 181
Edit Text button (WordArt toolbar), 101
editing
  arrows, 117
  AutoCorrect entries, 110
  cell comments, 113
  cell contents, 32-33, 181
  charts, 144
  data ranges, 144
  embedded objects, 217
  formulas, 48-49
  freeform objects, 122-23
  lines, 116
  macros, 205
  records, 166
  WordArt text, 102-3
ellipsis (...), menu symbol, 14

embedded objects
charts as, 143
editing, 217
embedding, 214, 216
existing objects, 217
new objects, 217
End+arrow keys, navigating worksheets, 11
Enter button (formula bar), entering labels, 28
Enter key
entering data, 181
entering labels, 28
navigating worksheets, 11
entering
cell references, 46
formulas, 46
functions, 54-55
records, 163, 164
with AutoComplete, 172
in Data Forms, 165
with the PickList, 172
text
into cells, 28-29
into org chart boxes, 107
with keyword strings, 110
See also entering data; inserting
entering data, 25, 26
applying styles before, 91
dates, 30-31
labels, 28-29
numbers, 28, 30
redirecting cell selection following, 181
times, 30-31
equal sign (=)
formula prefix, 46
logical operator, 171
Esc key
canceling selections, 37
deselecting objects, 145
Excel, 5
add-in programs, 207
exiting, 24
saving workbooks to a previous version, 21
starting, 6
Excel window, 12-13
customizing, 177-87
elements, 7
displaying/hiding, 179
opening files from, 8
See also workbook windows
exiting Excel, 24
Expense Statement template, 188
exploding
pie charts, 149
pie slices, 148
exporting data/files, 215

F

F1 key, getting Help, 18
F2 key, changing to Edit mode, 32
F3 key, displaying named ranges, 52
F4 key, making cell references absolute, 51
field names
in Data Forms, 164
in lists, 162, 163
fields
in lists, 162
sorting on, 168-69
File Conversion Wizard, 207
File menu, opening files from, 8
filenames, 20
files
destination files, 214
exporting, 215
filenames, 20
finding, 9
inserting pictures from, 97
linking, 216
opening, 8-9
files created in other spreadsheet programs, 9
recently opened files, 9
routing order, 209
source files, 214
See also workbooks
fill colors
coloring cells, 84-85
coloring objects, 128
setting the default color, 128
fill effects, adding, 128, 152-53
fill handle, copying formulas with, 48
filling
cells, 84-85
data series, 152-53
objects, 128
filtering lists, 161, 170
Find Next button (Data Form dialog box), 164
Find Prev button (Data Form dialog box), 164
finding
files, 9
records. *See* filtering lists
Finish button in wizards, 17
flipping objects, 126
floating toolbars, reshaping, 15
folders
creating new, 21
opening files from, 8
font attributes
applying, 74, 158
deleting, 75
font size, specifying, 78, 158
Font tab (Format Cells dialog box), 78
fonts
adding, 98
coloring, 83
specifying, 78, 158
footers, adding, 69
Format AutoShape dialog box, 125, 127
specifying color and line options, 128
Format Cells dialog box
aligning cell contents, 80
applying borders, 86
coloring cell contents, 83
filling cells with colors/patterns, 84
formatting borders, 87
formatting dates/times, 31
formatting numbers, 75
modifying styles, 90, 92
opening quickly, 75
specifying fonts/font sizes, 78
text flow control, 82
versus Formatting toolbar, 81
format painting, 77, 84
Format WordArt button (WordArt toolbar), 101
formatting
cell borders, 87
cell comments, 113
cell contents, 30, 31, 73-85
with AutoFormats, 88
with styles, 90-91
chart objects, 152
data for Web sites, 226-27
dates/times, 31
drawing objects, 115
labels, 74
numeric data, 74, 75
ranges, 89
WordArt text, 104
worksheets, 73-93
for posting on the Internet, 226-27
See also formatting (of cells)

formatting (of cells)
  AutoFormats, 88-89
  clearing, 36
  conditional, 76
  copying, 77, 84
Formatting toolbar
  adding borders to cells, 87
  buttons, 74
  coloring cell contents, 83
  filling cells with colors/ patterns, 85
  specifying fonts/font sizes, 79
  versus Format Cells dialog box, 81
forms. *See* Data Forms
formula bar, 7, 26, 179
  editing cell contents, 32
  editing formulas in, 48
  Enter button, 28
formula prefix (=), 46
formulas, 26, 45-55
  aligning, 80
  arguments, 46
  cell insertion and, 42
  copying, 48-49
  creating, 46-47
  displaying, 46, 47
  editing, 48-49
  entering, 46
  including links in, 197
  order of precedence of operations, 47
  using ranges and range names in, 52
Free Rotate button (WordArt toolbar), 101
freeform objects, 115, 120
  drawing, 120-21
  editing, 122-23
Freeform tools, 120
freehand drawing, 121
freezing columns/rows, 182
functions, 45, 54
  common, 54
  creating, 55
  entering, 54-55

General options, changing, 180
General tab (Options dialog box), 180
geographic data, mapping, 159
global sharing on the Internet, 209
going to particular cells. *See* navigating workbooks/ worksheets
gradients
  filling data series with, 152
  filling objects with, 128
graphics
  inserting, 95-109
  See also objects
graphs. *See* charts
greater than sign (>), logical operator, 171
greater than or equal to sign (>=), logical operator, 171
gridlines
  on charts, 154, 155
  on worksheets, 140
    improving on, 86-87
    printing, 71, 86
grouping objects, 136

hand pointer, 225
handles
  adjustment handles, 118, 119
  fill handle, 48
  selection handles, 96, 140
Header/Footer tab (Page Setup dialog box), 69
headers, adding, 69
Help, 18-19
  definition boxes, 18
  getting online Help, 18
Help button, in dialog boxes, 18
Help topics, searching, 18
Help Topics dialog box, 18
Hide/Display Assistant button in wizards, 17
hiding
  columns/rows, 65
  Drawing toolbar, 156
  Office Assistant, 19
  toolbars, 15
Highlight Changes dialog box, 192
Home key, navigating worksheets, 11
HTML output
  creating, 226-27
  viewing, 227
hyperlinks
  connecting to, 225
  inserting, 225
  worksheet appearance, 225

importing data
  from other programs, 222
  from the Web, 228-29
Increase Decimal button (Formatting toolbar), 74
index fields, protecting lists with, 169
Index tab (Help Topics dialog box), 18
Insert dialog box, 42
Insert Hyperlink dialog box, 225
Insert menu commands, selections and, 63
Insert Picture dialog box, 97
inserting
  cells, 42
  columns/rows, 62-63
  graphics, 95-109
    clip art/pictures/sounds/ videos, 96-99
    organization charts, 106
    WordArt text, 100-101
  hyperlinks, 225
  reference titles, 114
  vertices (in freeforms), 122
  worksheets, 59
  See also entering
Internet
  access to, 227
  creating HTML output for, 226-27
  global sharing on, 209
  hyperlinks to, 225
  inserting clip art from the Web, 99, 229
Internet Assistant Wizard, 226-27
Internet links. *See* hyperlinks
Invoice template, 188
irregular curves, drawing, 120-21
irregular polygons, drawing, 120
Italic button (Formatting toolbar), 74
italics, applying, 74

keyboard, navigating with, 11
keyboard shortcuts. *See* shortcut keys
keyword strings, entering text with, 110

label prefix ('), 28
labels, 26, 28
  aligning, 80
  copying, 39
  entering, 28-29
  entering numbers as, 28
  formatting, 74
  long, 29
  text flow control, 82
  See also cell comments; cell contents; text annotations
Left arrow key, navigating worksheets, 11
legends, 140, 154
  adding/deleting, 154
less than sign (<), logical operator, 171
less than or equal to sign (<=), logical operator, 171
light bulb, in the Office Assistant, 19
lighting, of 3-D objects, 133
line patterns, creating, 129
Line Style tool (Drawing toolbar), 116
line styles, setting the default style, 128
Line tool, 116
lines, 115
  drawing, 116, 157
  editing, 116
  specifying options, 128
linking, 214, 216
  files, 216
  versus copying, 196
  workbooks, 197
  worksheets, 195, 196
  See also links
links, 196
  breaking, 196
  hyperlinks, 225
  including in formulas, 197
  modifying, 216
  updating, 217
  See also linking
Links dialog box, 216
list ranges, 162, 163
  Data Forms and, 165
lists, 161
  creating, 163
  displaying the top/bottom ten items, 170
  filtering, 161, 170
  protecting with index fields, 169
  sorting, 161, 168-69
  terminology, 162
Locator dialog box, 165
logical conditions, complex searches with, 171
logical operators, complex searches with, 171
logos, creating, 100-101
long labels, 29

macro code, 203
  adding comments to, 206
  debugging, 200, 204
  editing, 205
  resources on, 203
macro comment prefix ('), 206
macro comments, 203
  adding, 206
Macro dialog box, 200
  adding comments to macros, 206
  debugging macros, 204
  editing macros, 205
  running macros with, 202
macros, 200
  adding comments to, 206
  assigning to buttons, 186
  debugging, 200, 204
  editing, 205
  recording, 200, 201
  running, 200, 202
  storing, 200, 202
  versus templates, 189
maps, 139, 159
  creating, 159
  modifying, 160
  refreshing, 160
margins, setting, 68
Margins tab (Page Setup dialog box), 68
marquee, removing, 37, 38, 40
MAX function, 54
menu bar, 7
menus, 14-15
  choosing commands with, 14
  menu symbols, 14, 15
merging styles, 93
merging workbooks, 212-13
Microsoft Access. *See* Access databases
Microsoft Bookshelf, looking up references in, 114
Microsoft Excel 97. *See* Excel
Microsoft Excel 97 At a Glance, 1-3
Microsoft Mouse, navigating with, 10
Microsoft Office 97 CD-ROM, accessing, 98
Microsoft Office, starting Excel from, 6
Microsoft Organization Chart, 106
Microsoft Query, creating PivotTables with, 223
MIN function, 54
Minimize button, 12
minimizing workbook windows, 12
minus sign (–), subtraction operator, 46
Module sheets
  debugging macros with, 204
  editing macro code, 205
  macro code example, 203
mouse
  adjusting column width/row height, 67
  deselecting chart objects, 145
  formatting chart objects, 152
  navigating with, 10
  resizing objects, 125
mouse pointer, 7
  changing from plus sign to arrowhead, 39, 41
  for copying data, 37, 39
  double-headed arrow, 67
  double-sided arrow, 66
  hand, 225
  for moving data, 41
  plus sign by, 37, 39, 41
  wheel button, 10
Move or Copy dialog box, 61
moving
  cell contents, 25, 40-41
    with the Clipboard, 38, 40
    with drag-and-drop, 38, 41
  charts, 147
  from object to object, 137
  objects, 124
  toolbars, 15
  vertices (in freeforms), 122
  workbook windows, 12
  worksheets, 60
  See also navigating workbooks/worksheets
multi-page reports, generating, 220-21

multiple cells, selecting, 34-35
multiple columns/rows, inserting, 62-63
multiple windows, arranging, 13, 178
multiple workbooks, viewing, 178
multiplication operator (*), 46

name box, 7
named ranges
  displaying, 52
  going to, 35
  selecting, 35
names
  adding to worksheets, 69
  range names, 34, 35, 52
naming
  ranges, 34, 35
  worksheets, 58, 69
naming workbooks, 20
navigating keys, 11
navigating workbooks/ worksheets, 10-11, 13
  going to named ranges, 35
networks, sharing workbooks on, 209, 210-11
New button (Data Form dialog box), 164
New dialog box, creating workbooks, 188
New Workbook button (Standard toolbar), 191
Next button in wizards, 17
not equal sign (<>), logical operator, 171
notes. *See* cell comments
Nudge command, 124
nudging objects, 124
Number tab (Format Cells dialog box), 31, 75
numbers
  adding page numbers, 69
  entering as labels, 28
  printing row numbers, 71
  See also values
numeric formats
  applying, 31, 74, 75
  deleting, 75
numeric keypad, entering numbers with, 31
numeric label prefix ('), 28

Object dialog box, 98, 217
objects
  adding shadows to, 130-31
  aligning, 134-35
  arranging in the stack, 136
  coloring, 128
  creating 3-D objects from, 132
  displaying, 179
  distributing, 134, 135
  drawing, 115-21
  embedding, 214, 216, 217
  flipping, 126
  grouping, 136
  moving, 124
  nudging, 124
  resizing, 96, 124
    precisely, 124, 125
    retaining original proportions, 124
  rotating, 126-27
    around fixed points, 127
    in increments, 126, 127
    precisely, 127
  selecting, 96
  See also 3-D objects; drawing objects
Office 97 CD-ROM, accessing, 98
Office Art, 117
Office Assistant, 7
  getting help from, 19, 173
  turning off/on, 19
Office Assistant button (Standard toolbar), 18, 19
Office Documents, opening, 9
Office Shortcut Bar, starting Excel with, 6
Open dialog box
  changing templates, 190-91
  finding files, 9
  opening files, 8-9
  opening templates, 190
opening
  files, 8-9
    files created in other spreadsheet programs, 9
    recently opened files, 9
  organization charts, 108
  templates, 190
operations, order of precedence, 47
option buttons, in dialog boxes, 16
Options dialog box
  customizing the work environment, 180
  displaying worksheet window elements, 179
OR condition, complex searches with, 171
order of precedence of operations, 47
Organization Chart (Microsoft), 106
organization charts
  adding text to, 107
  customizing, 108
  inserting, 106
  opening, 108
  restyling, 108
  See also chart boxes (in org charts)
orienting
  cell contents, 80
  pages, 68
  workbook window panes, 13
ovals, drawing, 118

page numbers, adding to worksheets, 69
page orientation, specifying, 68
Page Setup dialog box
  adding headers/footers, 69
  fitting worksheets on a specific number of pages, 71
  setting margins, 68
  specifying page orientation, 68
  specifying worksheet features, 70, 71
  viewing changes made in, 68
Page tab (Page Setup dialog box), 68, 71
pages
  fitting worksheets on a specific number of, 71
  printing row and column titles, 70
  setting up for printing, 68-71
  specifying number for printing, 23
painting cell formats, 77, 84
panes, splitting the screen into and freezing, 182
paper size, specifying, 68

parentheses (), changing
precedence of operations
with, 47
passwords, protecting, 194
Paste Function button, 55
Paste Function feature, 45
entering functions, 55
Paste Special dialog box
breaking links, 196
linking files, 216
pasting
cell contents, 37, 38
sharing information by, 214
Patterned Lines dialog box, 129
patterns
filling cells with, 84-85
filling data series with, 152
filling objects with, 128
line patterns, 129
Percent Style button (Formatting toolbar), 74
percentage format, applying, 75
Personal Macro workbook,
storing macros in,
200, 202
PgDn key, navigating
worksheets, 11
PgUp key, navigating
worksheets, 11
PickList feature, 28, 172
entering labels, 29
entering records, 172
pictures
adding to data series,
152, 153
deleting, 97
inserting, 96-97
pie charts, 141, 148
exploding single slices, 148
exploding/unexploding, 149
PivotTable toolbar, 174
PivotTable Wizard, 173, 223
PivotTables, 161, 173
accessing functions, 174
charting, 175
creating, 173
from Access databases,
223
with Microsoft Query,
223
updating, 174
placeholders, displaying, 179
plus sign (+)
addition operator, 46
by the mouse pointer, 37,
39, 41
changing the mouse pointer
from, 39, 41
mouse pointer, 7
PMT function, 54
pointer. *See* mouse pointer
points, specifying types, 123
polygons, drawing irregular
polygons, 120
precedence of operations, 47
Preview button (Standard
toolbar), 85
previewing worksheets, 22,
23, 85
print area
changing, 23
including column/row data
in, 71
Print dialog box, specifying
print options, 22, 23
print previews, 22
print scaling, specifying, 68
print settings, 57
customizing, 68-71
saving, 72
printed characters, reducing/
enlarging, 71
printers
selecting, 23
specifying properties, 23
printing worksheets, 22-23
centering worksheet titles, 81
changing print area, 23
with gridlines, 71, 86
more than one copy, 23
page setup, 68-71
quick copies, 22
specifying number of
pages, 23
programs
add-in programs, 207
destination programs, 214
exporting files to other
programs, 215
source programs, 214
Protect Sheet dialog box, 194
protecting worksheets/passwords, 194
Purchase Order template, 188

question mark (?), wildcard
character, 167
quick copies, printing, 22
quotation marks (" "), macro
text delimiters, 203

range names, 34, 35
in formulas, 52
range references, 34
ranges, 34-35
calculating automatically, 53
destination ranges, 196
editing data ranges, 144
formatting, 89
in formulas, 52
list range, 162
naming, 34, 35
pasting, 37
selecting, 34-35
Record Macro dialog box, 201
recording macros, 200, 201
records, 162
deleting, 167
displaying all, 166
displaying selected, 166,
170-71
editing, 166
entering, 163, 164
with AutoComplete, 172
in Data Forms, 165
with the PickList, 172
sorting, 161, 168-69
rectangles, drawing, 118
Redo button (Standard
toolbar), 27
redoing actions, 27
reference material, looking
up, 114
reference titles, inserting, 114
refreshing. *See* updating
regrouping objects, 137
relative addressing, 50
relative cell references, 50
replacing AutoShapes, 119
Report Manager, 207, 220
reports
creating, 220
reordering sections, 221
reshaping
AutoShapes, 118
toolbars, 15
WordArt text, 102
resizing
AutoShapes, 118
charts, 147
objects, 96, 124
precisely, 124, 125
retaining original
proportions, 124
workbook windows, 12

Restore button
Data Form dialog box, 164
Excel window, 12
restoring workbook windows, 12
Reviewing toolbar, adding/editing cell comments with, 112
Right arrow key, navigating worksheets, 11
rotating
objects, 126-27
around fixed points, 127
in increments, 126, 127
precisely, 127
WordArt text, 102
routing order, 209
row headers (indicator buttons), 63, 179
printing, 70, 71
row numbers, printing, 71
row titles, printing, 70
rows
adjusting row height, 66-67
deleting, 64
freezing/unfreezing, 182
hiding, 65
inserting, 62-63
in lists, 163
sorting lists in, 169
See also row headers
running macros, 200, 202

S

Save As dialog box
creating new folders in, 21
creating templates, 189
exporting files, 215
saving workbooks
in a different file format, 21, 215
for the first time, 20
to a previous version of Excel, 21
as templates, 189
saving
disk space, 59
print settings, 72
scenarios, 219
shared workbook changes, 210-11
workbooks, 20-21
in a different file format, 21, 215
before editing macros, 204
on exiting, 24
for the first time, 20
to a previous version of Excel, 21
before printing, 22
as templates, 189
scaling worksheets, 71
Scenario Manager, 218, 219
Scenario Values dialog box, 218
scenarios
creating, 218
creating reports with, 220
saving, 219
showing, 219
screen, splitting, 182
ScreenTips, displaying, 14, 145, 149
Scribble tool, 121
scroll bars, 179
search criteria. *See* criteria (for finding records)
Select Changes to Accept or Reject dialog box, 193
selecting
chart objects, 144, 145
charts, 144, 145
data series, 144, 148
objects, 96
ranges, 34-35
selection handles, 96, 140
selections, canceling, 37, 38, 40
Setup Wizard, 2
shadows
adding to chart text, 156
adding to objects, 130-31
coloring, 130, 131
relocating, 130
versus 3-D effects, 133
shaping. *See* reshaping
Share Workbook dialog box, 210-11
sharing information among documents, 214-17
sharing workbooks (on networks), 209, 210-11
enabling, 210
save options, 210-11
shared workbook alert, 211
Sheet tab (Page Setup dialog box), 70, 71
sheet tabs, 7, 58, 179
displaying, 10
sheets
creating reports with, 220
See also worksheets
Shift key
drawing circles/squares, 118
drawing lines, 157
resizing objects retaining original proportions, 124
rotating objects in increments, 127
Shift+Tab keys, navigating worksheets, 11
shortcut keys, 14, 15
choosing commands with, 14-15, 15
for navigation, 11
running macros with, 202
slash (/), division operator, 46
social security numbers, entering, 28
Solver, 207
Sort dialog box, 169
sorting lists, 161, 168-69
in rows, 169
sounds, inserting, 96-97
source data, 196
source files, 214, 216
source programs, 214
spelling
correcting, 110-11
with keyword strings, 110
spin boxes, in dialog boxes, 16
squares, drawing, 118
stack, arranging objects in, 136
Standard toolbar
Chart Wizard button, 142
Office Assistant button, 18, 19
Preview button, 85
Redo button, 27
Undo button, 27
Start menu
opening Office Documents from, 9
opening recently opened files from, 9
starting Excel from, 6
starting Excel, 6
status bar, 7, 179
step mode, debugging macros in, 204
Style dialog box, 90-93
styles
applying, 91
creating, 90, 92
deleting, 93
merging, 93
modifying, 92
submenus, displaying, 14

subroutines (in macros), beginning and ending, 203
subtraction operator (–), 46
SUM function, 54

Tab key
moving through drawing objects, 137
navigating worksheets, 11
tabs, in dialog boxes/wizards, 16, 17
telephone numbers, entering, 28
Template Utilities, 207
Template Wizard
adding data to the Template Wizard database, 213
installing, 213
merging workbooks with, 212-13
templates, 188
built-in, 188
changing, 190-91
creating, 189
creating workbooks with, 188
customizing, 191
default, 190, 191
folder for, 191
opening, 190
testing, 189
versus macros, 189
text
correcting with AutoCorrect, 110-11
entering
into cells, 28-29
into org chart boxes, 107
with keyword strings, 110
See also cell comments; labels; text annotations; titles; WordArt text
text annotations
adding shadows to, 156
adding to charts, 154, 155
text attributes. *See* font attributes
text boxes
in Data Forms, 164
in dialog boxes, 16
textures, filling data series with, 152
tiling workbook windows, 13, 178
times
adding to worksheets, 69
entering, 30-31
formatting in cells, 31
tips
from the Office Assistant, 19
ScreenTips, 14
title bar, 7, 12
shared status alert, 193
titles
adding to charts, 140, 154, 155
adding to org charts, 107
centering worksheet titles, 81
printing row and column titles, 70
toolbar buttons, 7
adding to toolbars, 185
assigning macros to, 186
changing images on, 187
choosing commands with, 14
deleting from toolbars, 184
Drawing toolbar, 116
Formatting toolbar, 74
restoring originals, 185
running macros with, 202
WordArt toolbar, 101
toolbar icons, on menus, 14
toolbars, 7, 14
adding buttons to, 185
creating, 183
customizing, 184
deleting buttons from, 184
displaying, 15, 184
hiding, 15, 184
moving, 15
PivotTable toolbar, 174
reshaping, 15
Reviewing toolbar, 112
WordArt toolbar, 101
See also Drawing toolbar; Formatting toolbar; Standard toolbar; toolbar buttons
Toolbars tab (Customize dialog box), 184, 185
tools
drawing tools, 117, 120
power tools, 195-208
for teamwork, 209-29
for working efficiently, 177-94
See also toolbar buttons
Top 10 command (AutoFilter feature), 170
Track Changes feature, turning on, 192
tracked changes
accepting or rejecting, 193
viewing, 192
TrueType fonts, 78, 158
typefaces, specifying, 78

Underline button (Formatting toolbar), 74
underlining, applying, 74
Undo button (Standard toolbar), 27, 151
undoing actions, 27
ungrouping drawings, 137
Up arrow key, navigating worksheets, 11
updating
charts, 144
links, 217
maps, 160
PivotTables, 174

values, 26
aligning, 80
entering, 30
formatting, 74, 75
See also cell contents
ValuPack objects (Office 97 CD-ROM), inserting, 98
vertices (in freeforms), 122
deleting, 122, 123
inserting, 122
modifying vertex angles, 123
moving, 122
specifying point types, 123
videos, inserting, 96-97
View tab (Options dialog box), 179
viewing
HTML output, 227
multiple workbooks, 178
previewing worksheets, 22, 23, 85
tracked changes, 192
views
changing worksheet views, 177, 179-87
creating custom views, 72
Village Software template, 188

Web
connecting to, 228
inserting clip art from, 99, 229
Web Form Wizard, 207
Web pages, creating, 226-27
Web sites, formatting data for, 226-27
wheel button (Microsoft Mouse/ mouse pointer), 10
wildcards, as search characters, 167
windows. *See* Excel window; workbook windows
wizards, 16-17, 207
Internet Assistant Wizard, 226-27
PivotTable Wizard, 173, 223
selecting options in, 16, 17
Setup Wizard, 2
Template Wizard, 212-13
See also Chart Wizard
WordArt (Microsoft), 100
WordArt Alignment button (WordArt toolbar), 101
WordArt button (WordArt toolbar), 101
WordArt Character Spacing button (WordArt toolbar), 101
WordArt Gallery button (WordArt toolbar), 101
WordArt Same Letter Heights button (WordArt toolbar), 101
WordArt Shape button (WordArt toolbar), 101
WordArt text
coloring, 103
editing, 102-3
inserting, 100-101
text effects, 104-5
WordArt toolbar buttons, 101
WordArt Vertical Text button (WordArt toolbar), 101
work environment, customizing, 180
workbook windows, 12-13
activating, 13
arranging, 13, 178, 197
moving, 12
resizing, 12
switching between, 12
See also Excel window
workbooks, 5, 25-43
adding data to the Template Wizard database, 213
closing, 24
consolidating data from, 198-99, 212-13
creating, 25
with templates, 188
linking, 197
merging, 212-13
naming, 20
navigating, 10-11
reorganizing, 57-61
saving, 20-21
in a different file format, 21, 215
before editing macros, 204
on exiting, 24
for the first time, 20
to a previous version of Excel, 21
before printing, 22
as templates, 189
sharing, 210
storing macros in, 200, 202
viewing multiple, 178
viewing multiple views of one workbook, 178
See also files; workbook windows; worksheets
worksheet windows. *See* workbook windows
worksheets
activating, 58
adding graphics to, 95-109
adding headers/footers to, 69
consolidating data from, 198-99
copying, 61
creating reports with, 220
deleting, 59
entering data in. *See* entering
fitting on a specific number of pages, 71
formatting, 73-93
for posting on the Internet, 226-27
hyperlink appearance, 225
inserting, 59
linking, 195, 196
modifying, 57-72
moving, 60
naming, 58, 69
navigating, 10-11, 13
previewing, 22, 23, 85
printing. *See* printing worksheets
protecting/unprotecting, 194
scaling, 71
selecting, 58
switching, 10
titles, centering, 81
tracking changes, 192-93
See also workbook windows; workbooks
World Wide Web. *See* Web

x-axis, 140
adding a title to, 154

y-axis, 140
adding a title to, 154

Elizabeth Eisner Reding has authored a variety of computer books, including Microsoft Excel, Microsoft PowerPoint, (several versions of) Quattro Pro, and Lotus 1-2-3 since 1992. In addition, she has worked for many publishers in the capacities of author, technical editor, and development editor. When she's not pressured by unreasonable deadlines—which isn't often—she enjoys mountain biking, four-wheeling, and being a couch potato.

Acknowledgments

The task of creating any book requires the talents of many hard-working people pulling together to meet impossible deadlines and untold stresses. Having said that, I'd like to thank the outstanding team responsible for making this book possible: my editor, MT Cozzola, the copyeditor, Jane Pedicini, and Steve Johnson and David Beskeen at Perspection. What a great team!

I'd also like to thank my wonderful husband, Michael, for putting up with me when I was at my worst. What a sweetheart—and to think I was lucky enough to meet you on the 'T'!

The manuscript for this book was prepared and submitted to Microsoft Press in electronic form. Text files were prepared using Microsoft Word for Windows 95. Pages were composed by Steven Payne and Patricia Young using PageMaker for Windows, with text in Stone Sans and display type in Stone Serif and Stone Serif Semibold. Composed pages were delivered to the printer as electronic prepress files.

Cover Designer

Tim Girvin Design

Interior Graphic Designer

designlab

Kim Eggleston

Graphic Layout

Steven Payne

Principal Compositor

Patrica Young

Compositor

Gary Bedard

Indexer

Michael Brackney

BUSINESS REPLY MAIL
FIRST-CLASS MAIL PERMIT NO. 53 BOTHELL, WA

POSTAGE WILL BE PAID BY ADDRESSEE

MICROSOFT PRESS REGISTRATION
MICROSOFT® EXCEL 97 AT A GLANCE
PO BOX 3019
BOTHELL WA 98041-9946

Register Today!

Return this
Microsoft® Excel 97 At a Glance
registration card for
a Microsoft Press® catalog

U.S. and Canada addresses only. Fill in information below and mail postage-free. Please mail only the bottom half of this page.

1-57231-367-6A ***MICROSOFT® EXCEL 97 AT A GLANCE*** ***Owner Registration Card***

NAME

INSTITUTION OR COMPANY NAME

ADDRESS

CITY STATE ZIP